Robert Hayden in Verse

Robert Hayden in Verse

*New Histories of African American Poetry
and the Black Arts Era*

Derik Smith

University of Michigan Press
Ann Arbor

Published in the United States of America by the
University of Michigan Press
Manufactured in the United States of America
Printed on acid-free paper
First published August 2018

A CIP catalog record for this book is available from the British Library.

Library of Congress Cataloging-in-Publication Data

Names: Smith, Derik, author.
Title: Robert Hayden in verse : new histories of African American poetry and the
    black arts era / Derik Smith.
Description: Ann Arbor : University of Michigan Press, 2018. | Includes
    bibliographical references and index. |
Identifiers: LCCN 2018014316 (print) | LCCN 2018018849 (ebook) | ISBN 9780472124091
    (e-book) | ISBN 9780472073931 (hardcover : acid-free paper) | ISBN 9780472053933
    (pbk. : acid-free paper)
Subjects: LCSH: Hayden, Robert, 1913–1980—Criticism and interpretation.
Classification: LCC PS3515.A9363 (ebook) | LCC PS3515.A9363 Z93   2018
    (print) | DDC 813/.52—dc23
LC record available at https://lccn.loc.gov/2018014316

Cover image of Robert Hayden courtesy Barcroft Media, on behalf of the *Ann Arbor News*.

Preface and Acknowledgments

As in all things, first thanks and praise is to the Most High.

The kindling sparks of this book are gifts from my parents, Alan and Magda Smith, whose commitment to the Bahá'í Faith brought them into close contact with Robert Hayden. Early in life they set me on a quest for spiritual and cultural perception that I've tried to find in many places and in many people, and through writing this book, which is dedicated to my parents. (Hayden dedicated his poem "The Islands" to my folks.) I'm forever thankful to them for all that they have done for me and for putting me in "touch" with Hayden, whose poetry has been a special curriculum in my spiritual and cultural education. Gratitude and humility are my main responses to the art that Hayden created during his life, and—perhaps it goes without saying—my work on this book, however inadequate it may be, attempts to honor the man and his art.

I feel similarly about the many poets whose work I address—people like Gwendolyn Brooks, Margaret Walker, Michael Harper, Amiri Baraka, June Jordan, and Etheridge Knight have fascinated and inspired me. Those living poets whom I have never been able to converse with, but who are important to my understanding of Hayden and who continue to use language in transformative ways, have also helped me over the years: respect and thanks to Haki Madhubuti, Rita Dove, Yusef Komunyakaa, Sonia Sanchez, Nikki Giovanni, Elizabeth Alexander, Natasha Trethewey, Douglas Kearney, and Terrance Hayes. I would not have been able to write this book without reference to their art. Likewise, the book builds from an indispensable foundation provided by a few scholars, John Hatcher chief among them. Simply put, his work on Hayden made this project possible. I'm also thankful for the scholarship of Pontheolla Williams, Robert Chrisman, Phillip Richards, James Hall, Ed Pavlić, and Keith Leonard, whose serious engagement with Hayden and his poetry enhanced my work considerably. I feel that these scholars have been my collaborators; their work has spoken to me, and I only hope that I've properly understood what they have said. Kenneth Warren, Madhu Dubey, Amy Ongiri, Meta Jones, Lorenzo Thomas, James Smethurst, Bernard Bell, Phillip Brian Harper, Eugene Redmond, Houston Baker, Adolph Reed, Ta-Nehisi Coates, Richard Iton, Mark McGurl, and Loïc Wacquant have significantly shaped my understanding of the book's contextualizing material.

I give special thanks to Evie Shockley and Howard Rambsy, whose scholarship has informed me and spurred on my thinking and who offered kind words of support after coming to know me as they facilitated the excellent 2015 NEH Summer Seminar "Black Poetry after the Black Arts Movement." All those who participated in that seminar helped me to refine the ideas that I've worked with in the book—Kevin Quashie, Tara Betts, Joycelyn Moody, and Sequoia Minor were especially generous. The organizing genius behind the seminar, Maryemma Graham, deserves admiration and emulation. Scholarship and community are, too often, antithetical terms, but Dr. Graham's ability to create and nurture community while promoting literary studies is, to my mind, the most advanced form of scholarship. Dana Williams is a similar scholarly leader, whose intellectual project is not separable from her effort to foster opportunities for colleagues. I deeply appreciate her willingness to include me in a number of scholarly activities in recent years.

A small part of this book was published in *Callaloo* as an essay titled "Quarrelling in the Movement: Robert Hayden's Black Arts Era." I thank Charles Rowell for his tireless work at *Callaloo* and for playing an important role in sustaining Hayden's legacy. Nathan Grant, in his capacity as editor of *African American Review*, has done much to cultivate black literary studies for almost a decade now and has been supportive of my work. Before I was able to write anything worth publishing, I was patiently mentored by the members of my dissertation committee in the English Department at Northwestern University: Reginald Gibbons, Paul Breslin, and Kevin Bell helped me to put together my initial thoughts about Robert Hayden. They were gracious and forgiving as I stumbled my way through the PhD program, and they helped me get employed at several universities—specifically, Arcadia University, Zayed University, and Sultan Qaboos University. At each of these institutions I was welcomed by generous colleagues, whose kind words and collegiality made work worthwhile. I especially appreciate the support given to me by Dick Wertime, Lisa Holderman, Jo Ann Weiner, Pradyumna Chauhan, Ana Garcia, Doreen Loury, and Tom Hemeter at Arcadia University; by Peter Stromberg, Abdel-Latif Selami, Mohammad Massad, Angela

Skuba, and my chief homie, Zia Saunders, at Zayed University in Dubai; and by Khalid Al-Belushi, Jamal En-nehas, Nada Al-Ajami, Sandhya Mehta, Christopher Denman (and family!), William Schreck, Diane Buck, and Tyagaraja Balasubramanian at Sultan Qaboos University in Muscat, Oman. The students I encountered at these universities taught me lesson after lesson, and broadened my understanding of life and literature; particular thanks goes out to Murshed Al-Hakmani, who is a deeply generous and enduring friend.

My most meaningful classes have taken place inside the New York State prison system. The Bard Prison Initiative and the Hudson Link Project for Higher Education in Prison have afforded me the opportunity to work with students whose insights, vitality, and wisdom have given me an invaluable education. Time after time these students buoyed my spirits, made me feel worthy and hopeful, and opened my mind to transformational ideas and understanding. I am continually thankful for the brothers and sisters who put so much of their hearts and minds into the work of my classes, despite their often impossible circumstances. This one is for all those midnight readers, the organic intellectuals, the comrades who will bring on the change that is still coming.

My students at the University at Albany have been similarly wonderful and inspiring. I count as a significant blessing the great diversity of striving students who come to my classes each semester. In its best moments the University at Albany is a quintessential example of what a public university should be—providing serious, nurturing, and community-oriented education to anyone willing to make commitments to learning. The opportunity to work with students in the university's English Department has been a professional bounty; I've come to know my own field of study—and the scholarly ground on which this book is situated—by trying to share it with undergraduates each semester. The several dozen graduate students whom I have worked with independently and in seminars have pushed me to deepen my understanding of the material in this book and have taught me much about poetry, pedagogy, and intellectual inquiry for everyday life. A special shout-out goes to Victorio Reyes, keeping it always poetic and real.

University at Albany colleagues have been exceptionally gracious and supportive. Very few laborers enjoy the goodwill that I have routinely felt from my coworkers, and I know that in the world of work, this is no small fortune. Mike Hill let me and my family stay in his apartment when we first arrived, without a clue, in Albany. Bret Benjamin and Laura Wilder found us in a park and then helped us find a place to live—they've been continual, generous friends ever since. Lisa Thompson showed me the lay of the land

and has encouraged me with real talk and (whenever I see her) infectious smiling since I've come to know her. Pat Chu taught me a lot and made me feel like an interesting conversationalist during our many lunch meetings— respect and thanks. I joined Pat, Thomás Urayoán Noel, Tamika Carey, and Glyne Griffith in the short lived but meaningful No Stress Crew, which read an early (and very bad) draft of a chapter in this book. Special thanks to Glyne, who never flagged in his backing of me, my book project, and my ten-ure quest (before and) during his time as chair of the English Department. The same thanks goes to Randy Craig for his continual, wise support and his welcoming spirit. I feel deep gratitude for the many hours that Paul Stasi and Bret Benjamin invested in my project by reading and talking to me about sections of the book, for working on my tenure committee, and for watching basketball with me. Ineke Murakami also did yeowoman's work as one of the members of my tenure committee. Michael Leong gave me important feedback on the final chapter of the book; Ed Schwarzschild lent me his ear and his support on numerous occasions; Wendy Roberts and Charles Shep-herdson helped me along the way. University at Albany colleague-friends like Fardin Sanai, Robert Miller, Tamra Minor, Maritza Martinez, Patrick Ro-main, Debernee Privot, Clarence McNiell, Ekow King, Patrick Jean-Pierre, and Dafney Amilcar-Rodriguez brightened my life. Liz Lauenstein and Lynn Bearup held my hand through the hoops—thanks for your patience.

It took me a long time to write this book, and many people have given me strength and guidance during the process. But the encouragement and goodwill of a few was invaluable: Kevin Meehan had great faith in me and tried to help even when I made it difficult. That won't be forgotten. Charles "Val" Carnegie took me seriously, led me toward light, and offered a model of intellectual and spiritual rigor that I aspire to. Herman Beavers was self-less in his efforts to help me—he demonstrated a rare form of generosity by thoughtfully reading, and advocating for, this book when he might have justifiably gone about his business. Profound thanks.

LeAnn Fields at the University of Michigan Press had faith in me and in this book and ushered me on with gentle, patient direction. I'm not sure what I would have done without her consistent and expert ability working on my behalf. All those at the University of Michigan Press have my gratitude, as do the anonymous reviewers and the readers of my tenure file who offered sup-portive and thoughtful responses to the manuscript. Key financial assistance for the book's publication was provided by Claremont McKenna College and the Gould Center for Humanistic Studies. Much appreciation goes to the

Center's director, Bob Faggen. Special thanks goes to Maia Hayden for allowing me permission to use Robert Hayden's poetry in the text.

Finally, I must give due to the contextual matrix that inspirits my work. The Bahá'í communities in the Virgin Islands, in Chicago and Evanston, Illinois, in Dubai and Muscat, and in Albany, New York, have shown me unwavering love and have always encouraged my scholarship. Scores of individuals in these communities have offered me kind, buoying words and unhesitating assistance. The Bahá'í Black Men's Gathering was a particular source of strength for me as I built up the wherewithal to write—I've been inspired by brothers like Anthony Outler, my uncle Pat Smith, George Canon, Richard Thomas, Charles Lynch, Anis Mojgani, Bruce Reynolds, Pierre Pickens, Artemis Shahid Stover, Xavier Nichols, Frederick Landry, Lloyd Lawrence and Kenneth Ray (mighty UJJ), Raleigh Woods, Renan Woods, Robert Henderson, Glenford Mitchell, and Patrick Patillo, Robert Hayden's son-in-law. The brilliant spirit of William "Billy" Roberts permeates The Gathering, is woven into my life, and is felt in all the good parts of this book.

I will never be able to adequately acknowledge the people who have loved me to action, have prodded and teased me, and have always kept me their concern: true brothers, Shawn and Ian; foundational friends, Gregg, Robert, and Jan; brethren in struggle, Lion and Deuce; grad school compatriot, Glen Sucich; steadfast supporters, Misha, Maurice, Syda, Marina, Hala and Jackson, and the Jackson Five; and all my Smiths, Guennewigs, and Esfahanis. Cliff: Morpheus, making the world capacious for me. KT in the place to be: always in my corner, always in my heart. Sanga: my day one, ride or die—the blessing is mine. Badi, Shiraz, and Bahiyyih, you are the stars in my firmament; you are the best. No one sacrificed more for this book than Narmin, my eternal companion and deepest love, thank you.

Contents

PART I

Meetings and Quarrels

Introduction

Upon Meeting Haki Madhubuti in a Gymnasium

... 'Those years are gone—
What is there now?'

—Rita Dove, "Upon Meeting Don L. Lee, In a Dream"

The gymnasium was filled with black students from Philadelphia. They were waiting to hear from Sonia Sanchez, who was the featured speaker at the symposium put on at the small university where I was teaching just after graduate school. Haki Madhubuti was getting ready to introduce her, and I was preparing to introduce Madhubuti. I remember Sanchez looking like a Jedi wizard, or Chielo, the priestess of Agbala in Chinua Achebe's *Things Fall Apart*. I thought that, if she wanted to, she might raise her fist and cause the gymnasium to fall apart. Madhubuti looked like a man who hadn't eaten meat in decades—he was slim and tall, and his skin was bright. I was a little nervous because in my just-completed dissertation on Robert Hayden I had portrayed Madhubuti as a literary villain, a chief antagonist of the heroic Hayden. In 1968 a younger version of the tall, bright-skinned man towering before me had written, "What we do not need, Mr. Hayden, is people like you telling us what we need" (Lee, "On *Kaleidoscope*" 51). After some small talk, Madhubuti asked me about my research. I gathered my wits and explained that I had recently finished a study of Hayden. As I spoke these words I was preparing for him to glare back at me and say something like, "What we do

3

not need, Mr. Smith, is people like you telling us about Robert Hayden." Instead, he beamed, leaned closer to me, and said, "Hayden is one of my heroes."

That small exchange with Madhubuti significantly altered my thoughts about Hayden, the Black Arts Movement (BAM), and critical narratives about African American poetry since the 1960s. In my dissertation I had followed the lead of many of Hayden's scholarly admirers, offering an appraisal of his poetry that was overdetermined by the idea that during the 1960s and 1970s Hayden was, as one critic put it, "attacked as the scapegoat of choice for a new generation of African American poets" (Conniff 487). My interpretation of Hayden's corpus was tethered to a conventional reading of the events of the Fisk writers' conference of 1966, in which the poet was the subject of "vehement attacks by Melvin Tolson and proponents of the 'Black Aesthetic'" (Kutzinski 173). Critical depictions of these "attacks," well known to scholars of African American literature, often established an antagonistic binary in which Hayden stood beneath the banner of "universalism" and aesthetic freedom while champions of the black aesthetic—like Madhubuti—demanded strident art committed to "race consciousness" (Allison 129). In the standard depiction of the 1966 Fisk episode, Hayden was frozen in a few quotations reported in *Negro Digest*, such as: "Let's quit saying we're black writers writing to black folks—it has been given importance it should not have" (Llorens, "Writers Converge" 62). Critics sympathetic to Hayden portrayed those who disagreed with him as "advocates of Black Cultural Nationalism [who] reacted as though they had come face to face with the Enemy" (Conniff 487).

Until my face-to-face encounter with Madhubuti, I too was invested in a kind of Manichean analytical framework used to demonstrate the efficacy of Hayden's political aesthetic while showing how politically short-sighted, philosophically provincial, and aesthetically limiting it was when the black aestheticians decided that Hayden was to be "vilified," as Elizabeth Alexander once put it ("New Ideas" 598). But, after speaking with Madhubuti, I recognized the need for a different approach to Hayden and critical narratives about the Black Arts Movement and African American poetry. *Robert Hayden in Verse* represents the effort to move beyond "folkloric versions" of the poet that often appear in literary history and critical discourse (Hall 34). Rather than fitting Hayden into adversarial templates that pit him against the BAM or hail him as the cynosure of poetic influence in post-movement decades, I have adopted a more relativist mode of inquiry, committed to the belief that our best understanding of Hayden is achieved when a diverse gallery of voices contextualizes his voice. This book inverts some of the folkloric premises that give rise to common critical conceptions of Hayden and asks what new understanding can be gained through the inversion of standard narratives about Hayden's relation to the African American poetic tradition. For example, what happens when Hayden is understood as one of Madhubuti's heroes, rather than his nemesis? What happens when we conceive of Hayden as a participant in the Black Arts Movement, rather than an enemy of the movement? These are the types of questions that animate *Robert Hayden in Verse* as it reevaluates the poet's role in post-movement critical narratives about African American literary history.

In some of these narratives Hayden is an aesthetic genius whose Apollonian poetry is a paragon representation of twentieth-century African American poetics, but in others his work is reducible to a genteel instrument of "social climbing" (Baraka, "Post-Racial")—a banal counterpoint to the more consequential poetry of a black radical tradition. As a deep study of his poems, *Robert Hayden in Verse* is at least implicitly aligned with the former camp. But it is not a recuperation of Hayden's "writerly" poetics up against the performative and oral poetics that have flourished since his heyday in the 1960s. Instead, it illuminates Hayden's particular quest for spiritual transcendence through the Bahá'í Faith, his commitment to aesthetic distance, and his struggle to make meaning out of history, and it places these primary impulses in Hayden's work in symbiotic—rather than antagonistic—relation to dominant midcentury and Black Arts–era trends in African American poetry. In this rendering, materialist, capitalist, and racialist forces of twentieth-century American modernity constitute a common backdrop before which Hayden produced an erudite, elliptical poetry that both challenged and complemented that of his more populist and militant-minded 1960s peers like Madhubuti, Sanchez, and Amiri Baraka. While these BAM intellectuals sought to obliterate some of the aesthetic and philosophical foundations of Western modernity through radically oppositional poetics scornful of literary tradition and rooted in black orality and music, Hayden worked within the plenitude of literary inheritance while cautiously curating black vernacular culture in his poems. But like those BAM poets who are often cast as his rivals, Hayden had no interest in the preservation of what he identified as the suppressive and destructive forces of American modernity's "tottering power structure" (*Collected Prose* 81). My argument accentuates this commonality by muting hierarchies of artistic efficacy that in critical treatments of Hayden often announce difference rather than similarity, and it figures Hayden as a significant player in what has come to be known as the Black Arts era of the late 1960s and early 1970s. This rethinking of Hayden properly situates him at the heart of the Black Arts milieu and contends that, while he may have been a dissenting voice in the era, any accounting of that literary moment is incomplete without recognition of Hayden's powerful contributions to its discourse. This effort to reconcile Hayden's work with that of the BAM is brought on by the poetry of recent celebrated poets like Terrance Hayes, Kevin Young, Nikky Finney, Douglas Kearney, and others, whose twenty-first-century work owes itself to Hayden's twentieth-century project, yet is also influenced by the BAM. If some of the most prominent contemporary black poetry is a dialectical synthesis of the Dionysian, performative, vernacular impulses of the BAM on the one hand and the Apollonian, interiorizing, writerly impulses exemplified in Hayden's work on the other, then our literary history is best served by a study that suggests the origins of the synthesis.

Straightforward chronology encourages an approach to Hayden's work that links it to the BAM: In 1966 he was awarded the Grand Prize for Poetry at the First World Festival of Negro Arts, and he published his *Selected Poems*; in 1972 he published his enduring collection, *Words in the Mourning Time*; and in 1976 he was appointed poetry consultant to the Library of Congress. The crescendo of Hayden's career in the midst of the Black Arts era helps mark the crucial historical moment after which black poetic expression arguably frayed into three overlapping yet distinct registers: rap, spoken-word and "high-status" print poetry. The full implications of this fraying in black poetry have yet to be documented, but my study pivots on the premise that in the last of these class-marked and separately institutionalized categories, Hayden's influence has been incredibly powerful. The echo of his complex interiority and his seminal poetic historiography is heard continually in the work of revered black academic poets of an ongoing American literary period that, since the 1980s, has been shaped by university-based MFA programs. I argue that, in his response to twentieth-century American modernity, Hayden established a paradigmatic approach to the materials of the black American experience. Through formal discipline (and opacity), intense interiority, and a curatorial, judicious relation to the vernacular cultural richness of the black majority, Hayden developed an *artistically enabling aesthetic distance* from the African American folk figures and culture that populate his work. The archetypal anxieties of the ethnic artist-intellectual, beholden to yet distinctly removed from his folk, were not defining for Hayden—as they were for many of his Black Arts contemporaries. While BAM poets, who were often members of a black cultural elite, created black aesthetics that tried to disappear the distance (and imagine an easy contiguity) between themselves and less socially and economically capitalized black folk, Hayden offered a black aesthetic that acknowledged, explored, and tried to bridge the difficult distance be-

tween himself and the black masses. In the contemporary neoliberal era that
has widened the economic and experiential gap between the black academic
class and those at the bottom of the black class structure, Hayden's writerly
aesthetic has proven generative for those poet-professors seeking an art that
both interrogates and honestly reflects black lifework in the ivory tower.

Yet despite his palpable influence on the work of celebrated poets of the
contemporary moment, like Rita Dove, Yusef Komunyakaa, Elizabeth Al-
exander, Natasha Trethewey, and many others, and his leading role in recent
canon-shaping anthologies like *Angles of Ascent: A Norton Anthology of Con-
temporary African American Poetry* (2014) (which takes its title from Hayden's
poetry) and the *Penguin Anthology of Twentieth-Century American Poetry*
(2011), Hayden has been rather marginal to post-BAM critical analyses of
black poetics. This is partly due to the prominence of the 1980s theorizing of
Henry Louis Gates and Houston Baker, who focused on vernacular-based
literary aesthetics. In their similar contentions that African American literary
aesthetics is formally (and uniquely) linked to the vernacular culture of the
black masses, Gates and Baker helped set American criticism on a hunt for a
model of literary work that "receives its authority from creative imitation of
vernacular exemplars," (Benston, *Performing* 249). Because Hayden's poetry
is a prime example of what Harryette Mullen has called "writerly"—rather
than "speakerly"—black literature, his work has often been occluded in criti-
cal discussions of black poetics, even though his oeuvre has exerted a power-
ful influence on recent black poetry. Like the many female-authored texts
that Mullen identifies as "drawing more on the culture of books, writing and
print than . . . on the culture of orality," Hayden's poems have not been easily
assimilated into prominent vernacular theories invested in the establishment
of an identifiably *black* canon (*Cracks* 80).

Hayden's work puts an X through the black half of the "black poetics"
tandem—crossing out but never fully erasing blackness: Through his well-
known refusal of the label "black poet" and his decidedly writerly aesthetic,
Hayden struck through racial limitation in his poetics, and yet his work re-
tains an ineffable blackness—a fact he seemed to acknowledge by including
his own poetry within *Kaleidoscope*, the 1967 anthology of "poems by Ameri-
can Negro poets" that he edited. In his implicit advocacy for a sense of black-
ness that was kaleidoscopic, shifting, and infinitely multifarious, and in his
poetics that sent roots into variegated cultural soils, Hayden prefigured con-
temporary notions of black aesthetics—exemplified in Evie Shockley's criti-
cal work *Renegade Poetics*—that explode the more narrow and prescriptive
rubrics that held sway in the Black Arts era and its aftermath. In this regard,

to say that Hayden was ahead of his time is not sufficient; the adamancy of his belief that literary blackness was not reducible to any static or prescribed set of aesthetic practices or political commitments actually shaped the black poetic future. In his literary politics and comportment, Hayden helped to create the wide-open conceptions of literary blackness that must be associated with the contemporary poetry scene.

Emphasizing Hayden's writerly aesthetic and his kaleidoscopic sense of blackness in the 1960s and 1970s is not to suggest that his proclivities were singular in the era. A good number of poets ensconced in the BAM were invested in a graphocentric poetics and the production of poetry on the page. (This is most obviously recognizable in the banishment—or alternatively, proliferation—of capitalization and the use of inventive lineation by people like Madhubuti, Sanchez, Baraka, and many other experimental poets.) Neither was Hayden alone in his 1960s and 1970s Apollonian style and his writerly reverence for the forms and themes of literary tradition. The poetry of Gwendolyn Brooks—before, during, and after the Black Arts era—presents a writerly model that exercised great power over post-BAM black poetics. However, Hayden's distinctive ensemble of aesthetics, (transcendent-)identity politics, and thematic interests came into relief in the Black Arts era and offered a veritable blueprint for a host of poets working in the decades that followed. Yet Hayden has received only modest scholarly attention. Gwendolyn Brooks and Amiri Baraka are more frequently evoked forebears for many recent poets, and Brooks and Baraka often serve to anchor critical histories of postwar African American poetry. But Robert Hayden is the less-noted lodestar whose unique project and legacy guide a powerful account of more than a half century of African American poetry.

This study begins in an examination and critique of the scholarly assumptions and critical trends that worked to marginalize Hayden in poetry scholarship produced in the decades after the BAM. In chapter 1, "Quarreling in the Movement," I question the limitations of 1990s literary histories that chronicle the Black Arts era without reference to Hayden. Why did leading narratives of African American literary history have little to say about Hayden's contributions to Black Arts–era discourse, even as many poets of the 1990s and 2000s identified Hayden as an aesthetic forebear? The answer to the question lies partly in the theoretical focus on black literature that was the "creative imitation of vernacular exemplars" but also in overly mechanical and Manichean critical depictions of Hayden's relation to the BAM. To restructure these narratives I return to Hayden's public refusal of the "black poet" designation at the 1966 Fisk writers' conference. Problematizing official accounts of the event that mark it as a moment in which he was exiled from the BAM, I show that the conference actually precipitated Hayden's inclusion in the *For Malcolm* (1969) anthology—a key BAM text. Arguing that Hayden should be understood as a dissenting *participant* in the BAM, I read the poet's contribution to *For Malcolm* and his presence in scores of other Black Arts–era anthologies in order to question his marginalization from critical narratives about the era, like the one offered at the 1996 Furious Flower Conference and the critical volume produced in its wake.

Part 2, "Faith and the Folk" (composed of chapters 2, 3, and 4), ties together the religiousness, the aesthetic distance, and the racial politics of Hayden's mature poetics. These subjects have been addressed by others, but I draw the poet's religious, aesthetic, and racial sensibilities through the thick skein of Black Arts–era discourse saturated in a generative mix of spiritualism, cultural nationalism, and class consciousness. Contextualized by Black Arts responses to twentieth-century hyper-rationalism, racism, and integrationism, Hayden's deep investment in the Bahá'í Faith is understood as something more than what Harold Bloom characterized as his "highly eclectic" spiritual practice (*Robert Hayden* 2). The chapters in this section show that Hayden's religiousness was part and parcel of a significant trend among African American artist-intellectuals who developed midcentury political and aesthetic projects that negotiated a way between the Scylla and Charybdis of Western secularism and the Negro Church.

Although part 2 tags the aesthetic fault lines that separate a "Hayden model" of poetics from models advanced by many of Hayden's Black Arts era contemporaries, it begins with the recognition that these fault lines ran across the common ground of mid-twentieth-century American modernity. That is to say, Hayden and his BAM interlocutors offered differing political-aesthetic responses to the integrating, urbanizing, secularizing, and consumerist forces that operated on post-Fordist, post–Great Migration American society. In the social order of the 1960s, artist intellectuals of the BAM, like Larry Neal, saw a spiritually desiccated "white world" and advocated "psychic withdrawal from its values and assumptions" ("And Shine" 648). The separation they prescribed was dependent on the production of a ritual art that was meant to both emerge from and respond to the needs of an unlettered, lower-class black community thought to be the repository of an authentic national culture that was quintessentially oral and musical, rather than literary. Rising out of this pastiche of socio-aesthetic analysis was the BAM poet who functioned as a priest, shepherding the folk flock toward "psychological liberation" through a performative vernacular liturgy. However, as this model of black artistry was built in the BAM era, Hayden was refining a contrasting poetics that honored the world of literacy, eschewed priestly didactics, and was judiciously distanced from the vernacular aesthetics of the black folk world.

But despite its differences from what Stephen Henderson would in 1973 call "The New Black Poetry," at base Hayden's art also grew out of a rejection of those forces of American modernity that, as he put it, sought "to control and suppress, to destroy in order to shore up a tottering power structure" (*Collected Prose* 81). Several decades before the advent of the BAM era, Hayden had already demonstrated a desire to resist both twentieth-century secularism and Western tradition by converting to the Bahá'í Faith, a religious movement with origins in nineteenth-century Persia. The chapters in part 2 argue that the philosophical and ideological implications of Hayden's conversion helped to shape his aesthetic choices—that his religious devotion played a role in his resistance to the BAM poetic paradigm that remains influential in spoken-word and hip-hop poetries but that has had less purchase among contemporary "blackademic" poets. Unlike the priestly, proselytizing BAM poets whose art created a type of scripture for a quasi-religious nationalist movement that dramatically valorized black folk culture and the vernacular voice, Hayden wrote the verse of an orthodox believer in an organized religion that was anticlerical, that esteemed literacy, and that denied pride of place to any racial, cultural, or class group.

Anchored in a reading of Hayden's "Bahá'u'lláh in the Garden of Ridwan," chapter 2 ("The 'Cosmic Hero'") demonstrates that a religious devotion, not quite evangelical but remarkably premodern in its orthodox piety, constitutes a philosophical foundation of Hayden's mature poetics. In rejecting the modern intensification of secularist rationalism, Hayden did not return to the matrix of his Baptist upbringing or turn toward an à la carte spiritualism, as did many twentieth-century American artists; instead he tried to submit to the systematized theology established by Bahá'u'lláh, the prophet-founder of the Bahá'í Faith. This decades-long attempt at obeisance to an organized religion was rather anomalous during literary years defined by the resolute secularism of figures like Richard Wright, Ralph Ellison, and James Baldwin, the self-fashioned spiritualism of figures like Alice Walker, Sun Ra, and many others, and the frenetic transformations of someone like Amiri Baraka. However, while this turn to the Bahá'í Faith was in keeping with Hayden's independent—even maverick—temperament, I draw on and extend arguments by James Hall about black "anti-modernism" to place his conversion and religious devotion within a pattern of twentieth-century black intellectual self-formation that refused materialist modernity on the one hand and the pull of the Negro Church on the other.

Chapter 3, "The Aesthetics of Changing Churches," is premised on the recognition that Hayden was similar to BAM contemporaries in this double rejection; however, unlike many anti-Christian BAM poets who used art to shore up a connection to the black folk community that was committed to the Negro Church, Hayden's elliptical and sometimes baroque poetry maintained an aesthetic distance from the folk. I devote considerable attention to the argument that BAM poetics was often an Oedipal struggle against the symbolic patriarchs of black community—the preachers. I show that BAM poets—as intellectuals who attempted to wrest social and epistemological power from the clerical class—engaged in an archetypal struggle of Western modernity. In their nationalist political project, BAM poets operated as quintessential intellectuals of modernity, systematically deriding the theological and social teachings of the (Negro) church while asserting themselves as rightful stewards of the masses. Turning the water of Christian ideology into the wine of black nationalism, these poets developed a performative, liturgical poetics that imitated the aesthetic idiom of the preachers they sought to displace. Hayden, in contrast to the BAM poet-intellectuals who tried to usurp the role of the black preacher and draw closer to his flock, cultivated a bookish poetic persona through which he explored his *distance* from what James Weldon Johnson once called "priest-governed" lower-class black life. Hayden confidently followed an isolating artistic imperative and, much like the jazz innovators of his era, he documented and drew upon black folk culture but created a rarefied art that did not actively *seek* purchase among the folk masses.

In their BAM-era verse, poets like Baraka and Nikki Giovanni perfected the black nationalist liturgical poetry that borrowed heavily from the performative and oral motifs of black preachers, even as it derided the Christian theology and politics that the preachers espoused. By adopting the aesthetic accouterments of their clerical antagonists, these BAM poets helped pave the way toward the performative, vernacular-heavy spoken-word and hip-hop poetics of the post-movement era. However, they did not open the way to the interiorizing, writerly poetry associated with the recently ascendant, university-backed, black workshops like the Dark Room Collective and Cave Canem. For the genealogy of the page-, rather than stage-, focused poetry that has been cultivated in these workshops (and regularly honored with the awards of the "literary establishment"), we must look to other midcentury and Black Arts–era models, like Hayden. Chapter 4, "Witch Doctors," which is organized around a reading of the poem "Witch Doctor," demonstrates that Hayden also engaged the figure of the black preacher and his distinctive aesthetic medley—but rather than imitating the preacher's vernacular artistry in literary form, Hayden resists the magnetic appeal of sermonic aesthetics. Asserting his fidelity to a writerly poetics, Hayden uses abstruse diction and literary reference to muffle the preacher's call-and-response structures, additive oral formulas, and vernacular expostulations, referred to in the poem as "hypnotic no-words" and "disheveled antiphons" (*Collected Poems* 36, 37).[1] This consciously erudite, interpolative method exemplifies Hayden's effort to alchemize black oral expression into literary from. Here Hayden distinguishes himself from a tradition of literary fascination with the black preacher that— from the nineteenth century onward—has attempted literary *imitations* of the oral stylizations of this leader of the African American folk world. By refusing to make his poetry into a simulation of oral creativity, Hayden establishes his craft's devotion to an Apollonian and graphocentric world of literacy—to a *writerly* poetics. While his Black Arts contemporaries sought social leadership as they honed a priestly black nationalist poetry that valorized orality, Hayden's poetry reflected his discipleship to a Bahá'í religious tradition that abolished the office of the cleric and concomitantly promoted a culture of literacy in which the layman-believer was expected to independently study holy scripture. Thus his religiousness resonated with his manifestly learned poetics, which was egalitarian, though not populist. I end the chapter with a brief reading of "The Prisoners," a late 1970s poem partly about literary reception, which shows that, despite his apparently esoteric religious belief and his high-literary aesthetics, Hayden wanted his art to be "true" enough—as he puts it in "The Prisoners" (159)—to resonate with black folk in the lowest strata of the American social and class structure.

Part 3, "Hayden's Histories," begins by following scholars like Kenneth Warren and Madhu Dubey to suggest that what we call postmodern, "post-soul," or post-civil-rights-era black studies and literature is perplexed by the intensification of division in the black class structure. I argue that the proliferation of history-focused poetry during what I refer to as *post-movement* decades is one response to the growing experiential differences between a black artistic and intellectual elite and the black classes locked in the benthic sectors of the American socioeconomy. In the attempt to strengthen a black corporate identity melting in the heat of neoliberal regimes that liquefy community, academic poets have often turned to the traumas of a black past that unite them with less socially and economically capitalized members of the American "black community." Much of this poetry is tacitly guided by a "temporal accumulation" theory of history in which time is collapsed into an eternal *now*, suggesting we remain haunted by a past that has not passed (Baucom 30). Robert Hayden, "poet-historiographer of the African sojourn in the New World"—as he is called in the *Norton Anthology of African American Literature* (Gates and McKay 1517)—has certainly offered recent poets, like Dove, Alexander, and Trethewey, a prime model of poetic engagement with the materials of black history, and Hayden's history poems can seem invested in the nonlinear conceptions of time that regularly crop up in contemporary black poetics. However, in part 3 I present a historicized account of Hayden's histories, arguing that his four-decade career, rising out of Harlem Renaissance and Old Left influences, responsive to global calamities of the World War II era, and peaking in tension with the BAM, reveals an ever-evolving approach to history that at times gravitates to the order and linearity of teleology and at other times seeks to disrupt traditional concepts of temporality. In his work we discover seemingly competitive conceptions of history, each attached to conflicting aspects of Hayden's poetic consciousness: one in which humanity is "impelled" (*Collected Poems* 100) toward a telos and another wherein the past chaotically and continually returns like "timeless echoes in echoic time" (77). These visions of history arise with differing implications during Hayden's long writing career and need to be situated along the arc of his artistic development and within the African American aesthetic-intellectual contexts of the middle decades of the twentieth century.

I organize "Hayden's Histories" into three rather distinct but rhizomatically connected phases: Chapter 5, "beckoning beckoning," focuses on Hayden's most well-known early works, "Middle Passage," "Frederick Douglass," "The Ballad of Nat Turner," and "Runagate Runagate," all conceived in the beginning of the 1940s. I argue that, as secularized Negro spirituals drawn through the eye of modernist poetics, the early poems on black history emphasize the dogged, telos-driven rise of a race toward inevitable "freedom." These poems offer salvific narratives of history that respond to both the lingering call of the late 1920s New Negro project and the Old Left materialism and social realism of the 1930s. Chapter 6, "Shadow of time. Shadow of blood.," shows that the salvific narrative of history is completely jettisoned as the elliptical, symbolist, and *pastward*-looking poems of the late 1940s and 1950s grapple with the holocaustal events of the era, place the trauma of black history in the context of general human travail, and abandon any sense of futurity while embracing the "temporal accumulation" motif. Chapter 7, "the fire that will save," takes up the final phase of Hayden's histories, which emerge in earnest with the 1962 publication of *A Ballad of Remembrance*. In that volume, and all those that follow in the sixties and seventies, Hayden returns to a progressivist conception of human history that resembles the salvific vision of the early heritage poems. But these later poems are guided by a devoutly religious hermeneutic of history rather than the materialist teleology that shapes the poems of his early maturity in the 1940s. Deeply influenced by the teachings of the Bahá'í Faith, in the final decades of his career Hayden clung—often desperately—to the belief that, despite its violently jagged grain, history was a divinely guided teleology that would end in a "human world where godliness / is possible" (*Collected Poems* 98).

By arranging Robert Hayden's history poems into three notable phases, each marked by distinctive aesthetics and historiographical orientation, the chapters of part 3 implicitly challenge the impulse to imagine Hayden's vision of history as though it was constant or singular. Scholars have long recognized Hayden's attachment to historical themes and his consistent effort to figure the writing present in relation to a past and future. But none have given an adequate accounting of the prevailing conceptions of history and temporality that contextualized his career. By historicizing Hayden's histories this section makes visible important differences, reversals, and contradictions within his corpus and reveals a historical consciousness buffeted and shaped by events, ideologies, and critical milieus of the middle decades of the twentieth century. My accounting accentuates Hayden's evolving effort to both articulate and resolve internal quarrels about the meaning of history. Calling attention to the several recalibrations of Hayden's approach to history seems particularly appropriate when we consider the poet's stickling penchant for revision. Even though adjustment and readjustment were definitive features of his craftsmanship, critics reading across the arc of Hayden's career have often looked for continuums rather than disjunctions.

Arguing that the lasting meaning of Robert Hayden's poetic project is discerned in the work of his literary descendants, the final section of *Robert Hayden in Verse* examines developments in African American poetry in the decades after the Black Arts era and concurs with critics like Charles Rowell who identify Hayden as a major influence for contemporary blackademic poets. But rather than adhering to a Great Man theory of literary history that attributes Hayden's ongoing influence to the sheer force of his artistic genius, I examine the ways in which the institutionalization of black poetry in major American universities and the concomitant emergence of hip-hop worked to elevate Hayden's importance among poet-professors of the post-movement period.

In chapter 8, "Professors and MCs," I contend that as black poetry was assimilated into predominantly white universities during the 1970s and 1980s, Hayden's writerly, Apollonian aesthetic was welcomed, while the vernacular-based, Dionysian BAM aesthetic was not. As growing numbers of black poets entered MFA programs and sought employment in academia, they were institutionally steered toward the production of "well-crafted" poems that were quite unlike those that BAM poets had pioneered in the late 1960s and early 1970s. Thus the echo of tradition that rings through the work of celebrated poets like Michael Harper, Rita Dove, Yusef Komunyakaa, Elizabeth Alexander, and Natasha Trethewey does not easily resonate with the sounds of the Black Arts era as it is often imagined in literary history and criticism. However, I also use this chapter to show that, while prominent poet-professors of the 1980s and early 1990s abandoned BAM aesthetic models, the vernacular saturated, performance poetics pioneered by BAM poets was fully adopted by the rappers whose poetry has transformed the American cultural scene since the Reagan era. While mainstream rappers often jettisoned much of the political ideology associated with their aesthetic forebears, they managed to create a poetic voice that seemed to emerge organically from the lower parts of the black class structure. I contend that because rappers appeared to offer an authentic poetic representation of the life and vernacular of the struggling "black majority," the poet-professors of the 1980s and 1990s—securely employed and often upper middle class—steered clear of deep engagement with the struggles, the beauty, and the language of what I term the *neofolk*—those black people sequestered in spaces, like ghettos and prisons, most negatively impacted by neoliberal economic and social policies.

In chapter 9, "Hayden's Heirs," I argue that literary poets, who ceded the chronicle of contemporary black abjection to the rappers, instead used their art to document and imagine historical black abjection. Developing a rich strand of research-oriented, archive-animating verse, poets like Dove, Alexander, Trethewey, and the many who followed them looked to Hayden's mid-twentieth-century example as they modeled their poetics of the past. Hayden's seminal work with black historical archives represents one of his most enduring bequests to artistic descendants; another is his commitment to aesthetic distance from black folklife. Beset by what he described as a natal "sense of alienation nothing could alter" (*Collected Prose* 22), Hayden's art was often an exploration of the distance between the lyric "I" and all else, including the black world. While culturally—and sometimes materially—capitalized BAM poets of the 1960s often fashioned poetic voices that hid the distance between the artist-intellectual and the black masses, Hayden delved into his paradoxical relation to a black folk world that was "remotely near" to him (*Ballad of Remembrance* 13). Although he loved that world deeply and knew it well, he did not write as though his poetry was the unmediated bloom of the folk experience; the fact that he was "colleged (as they said)" (*Collected Poems* 5) set a distance between the poet and his people. I argue that Hayden's attentiveness to this distance has been paradigmatic for poet-professors of the post-movement era because of the recently widening experiential gap between those at the poles of the black wealth spectrum. With the end of de jure segregation and the fading plausibility of what Michael Dawson and others have called "linked fate" racial solidarity narratives, black poets with extensive education and secure positions in the American university system cannot credibly inhabit the voices or experiences of the neofolk in the lower strata of the class structure. In the attempt to artistically respond to the intensification of the fragmentation of "black community" in the neoliberal era, important literary poets like Terrance Hayes find a sustaining example in the introspection inherent to Hayden's mid-twentieth-century and Black Arts–era examinations of intraracial difference.

Robert Hayden in Verse concludes by suggesting that a growing cadre of poet-professors, weaned on hip-hop culture, are uniting the Apollonian and the Dionysian aspects of contemporary African American poetry, even as they look to Hayden as a guiding light. In the synthesizing work of poets like Patricia Smith, Kyle Dargan, DJ Renegade, and Douglas Kearney, distinctions between the page and the stage, between the literary and the vernacular, between academic poetry and rap are being blurred, and the legacies of Hayden and the Black Arts Movement are entwined.

This book does not amount to a final or total reading of Robert Hayden's poetry. Indeed, many of his poems are not mentioned in this treatment. The arguments herein are meant to deepen our appreciation for Hayden but also to put him in conversation with others. Rather than offer an exhaustive analysis of his corpus, I isolate key elements of Hayden's métier—his religiousness, his devotion to aesthetic distance, his historical hermeneutics—and contextualize them in appropriate creative and critical milieus. This contextualizing method allows for engagement with a wide range of poets and discourses that are central to the history of African American poetics. I proceed with the premise that, if Hayden's true timbre is to be heard, figures like Margaret Walker, Gwendolyn Brooks, Amiri Baraka, and Terrance Hayes must also come to voice from time to time. By listening for Hayden's contribution to a conversation that extends beyond him, the colloquy of African American poetry and its attendant scholarship are also heard with greater clarity.

Foregrounding Hayden's contexts and the critical discourse that frames the study of African American poetry also leads this study away from the genre of literary biography. Rather than delving into the nuances of Hayden's intimate relationships or using his art to strap the poet to the psychoanalyst's couch, I have focused on the poetry's relation to its sociocultural environments. Of course, the elision of biography in the interpretation of African American cultural texts is practically impossible, and in the chapters to follow the poet is never a mere "scriptor." But my evocations of Hayden's life story are primarily meant to illuminate the poetry, and I am mindful of Roland Barthes's contention that the author is "not the subject with the book as predicate" (145). This approach has its consequences. For example, Robert Hayden's wife, Erma, the woman who was his closest companion for forty years, does not figure in my critical arguments. Erma ushered him toward the Bahá'í Faith, which would become an ontological and ethical anchor for Hayden, and her aesthetic sensibility—she was a Julliard-trained pianist with a deep affinity for classical music—surely had some impact on her husband's poetry. But rather than speculate about the ways in which the unique particularities of Hayden's biography may manifest in his art, this study emphasizes the ways in which Hayden's art uniquely responds to paradigmatic dilemmas faced by the African American poet, or artist-intellectual, of the middle decades of the twentieth century. Seminal studies of Hayden by Pontheolla Williams (1987), Fred Fetrow (1984), and John Hatcher (1984) offer biography-oriented appraisals of his artistic project. Rather than rework ground harvested by these earlier scholars who personally interacted with Hayden, I have rooted my arguments in close readings of the poetry informed by reference to interviews, archived personal papers, and the anecdotal recollections of those who knew the poet. Although distanced from the details of Hayden's day-to-day life, this method nevertheless reveals the singular consciousness of an artist who responded to the predicament of American modernity with powerful consequence.

Chapter 1

Quarreling in the Movement

———

Rethinking Hayden and the Black Arts Era

———

The debate, indeed, may be said to *be* the culture, at least on its loftiest levels; for a culture achieves identity not so much through the ascendancy of one particular set of convictions as through the emergence of its peculiar and distinctive dialogue. (Similarly, a culture is on the decline when it submits to intellectual martial law, and fresh understanding is denied in a denial of controversy.) Intellectual history, properly conducted, exposes not only dominant ideas of a period, or of a nation, but more important, the dominant clashes over ideas. Or, to put it more austerely: the historian looks not only for the major terms of discourse, but also for major pairs of opposed terms which, by their very opposition, carry discourse forward.

—R. W. B. Lewis, *The American Adam*

One of the most insightful treatments of Robert Hayden's place in the Black Arts era is found in James Hall's study *Mercy, Mercy Me: African-American Culture and the American Sixties*. Hall opens a path toward understanding the era in terms that disrupt conventional wisdom and scholarly discourse that is "folkloric" (34). He attempts to demonstrate that, in the black cultural community, a trenchant "anti-modernist" critique of mainstream American culture was not the exclusive province of the recognized Black Arts radicals. He investigates Hayden's contribution to the sixties, along with those of Paule Marshall, William Demby, John Coltrane, Romare Bearden, and W. E. B. Du Bois, to suggest that these figures, some of whom are forgotten in the oft-recalled drama of Black Arts radicalism, were engaged in their own artistic campaigns that vigorously responded to a modernity woefully unable to address the exigencies of African America. Hall's very important chapter on Hayden begins with an epigraph from James Clifford: "What is always torn off, as it were, to construct a public, believable discourse? . . . The 'tearing off,' Nietzsche reminds us, is simultaneously an act of censorship and of meaning creation, a suppression of incoherence and contradiction" (39). Hall goes on to argue that, in certain contexts, Hayden's complex voice was subjected to censoring and censuring during the processes of community and consensus building that characterized African American culture during the 1960s.

I want to modulate Hall's work in order to suggest, contrary to many critical reconstructions of the Black Arts era, that Hayden was not an *excluded* figure. Although too many assessments of the period neglect Hayden, he was an integral part of the "peculiar and distinctive dialogue" that created the literary culture of a period that is now primarily associated with the more radical voices of the BAM. The assumption that Hayden was marginalized and expelled from Black Arts–era discourse can be felt in a 2004 interview wherein Terrance Hayes expresses exasperation as he reminds us that a diverse range of black poets were publishing in the late 1960s:

> If we ignore the narrow dictum of what black poems should be, you're able to embrace a wide range of poets writing and publishing in the midst of the movement: Lucille Clifton published *Good Times*, her first book, in 1969; Audre Lorde and Etheridge Knight published their first books a year earlier in 1968; Bob Kaufman was publishing too around that time. But with the exception of Etheridge Knight, the Black Arts Movement as it was prescribed, excluded all these poets. Not to mention Robert Hayden. That exclusion is as whack—more whack—than the white canon's. (Rowell, "The Poet" 1078)

The perception that Hayden was an excluded poet during movement years is in large part a residue of the often-repeated argument that Hayden was an excluded poet during movement years. A more complicated appraisal is available if we note that any inclination to reject Hayden is explicitly quashed in Stephen Henderson's *Understanding the New Black Poetry*—a primary theoretical text of the BAM and the particular form of the black aesthetic that is associated with it. In 1973 Henderson would write, "The fact of the matter is that the Black community does not intend to give up any of its beautiful singers, whether Countee Cullen or Melvin Tolson or Robert Hayden. We may quarrel with them sometimes, but ain't never gonna say good-bye" (*Un-*

derstanding 27).[1] And, while Haki Madhubuti penned some blistering words about Hayden in a 1968 review for *Negro Digest*, in a 1969 interview for *Ebony* he would testify that Hayden had written "one of the *baddest* lines I ever read" (Llorens, "Don Lee" 80). As these items indicate, Hayden was certainly involved in a number of notable "quarrels" with those affiliated with the Black Arts Movement and with its aesthetics and ideologies, but it is too simplistic to declare that he was debarred from the movement in any absolute manner. In fact, Hayden participated—albeit *as a dissenting voice*—in a number of very significant Black Arts forums. Terrance Hayes and a host of others are able to imagine Hayden as a debarred figure not because of his lack of participation in important events and poetic dialogues during the 1960s and 1970s, but because of Hayden's absence in critical versions of the Black Arts era that hold sway in post-movement literary criticism.

In her prose collection *The Black Interior* (2004), Elizabeth Alexander—like Hall—skeptically regards the conventional, excessively coherent narratives that have come to dominate popular and critical conceptions about black writing in the 1960s. Several of her essays try to vitalize discourse in the field by calling into question "glib summaries" that often represent the era and by reading unlikely figures into the Black Arts milieu (88). In a piece that finds "Black Power" in the cerebral, often abstruse poems of Michael Harper, Alexander dreams of a fantastic gathering of "sixties" writers—alive and dead, associated with the movement and not—that might tell a contemporary audience of the now-misunderstood or forgotten alliances, conversations, and common aims of the era. Alexander conjures this gathering because she, like Hall, seeks a fuller history in which voices often torn from contemporary discourse in order to avoid contradiction and incoherence can sound once again; she imagines that, in her fantastic and necessarily discordant assembly, the nuance and complexity of 1960s African American cultural thought might be heard. Of course, the only place that this fantasy can be approximately realized is in the work of the critic; accordingly, Alexander suggests a model for scholarship capable of reimagining the Black Arts era in all of its diversity and intricacy. As she describes it, her method appeals to "the old fashioned means of storytelling, close reading, and literary reconstruction" (88).

In the effort to stitch Hayden into discourse about the Black Arts era and its legacy, I call upon some of the critical tools suggested by Alexander. In this chapter I will first tell the story of Hayden's signification in three conferences—the 1994 Furious Flower Conference at James Madison University and the 1967 and 1966 Black Writers' Conferences at Fisk University. In this narrative Gwendolyn Brooks appears as an exemplary foil; her celebration in the Furious Flower Conference and her account of the 1967 gathering throw into relief Hayden's marginalization in scholarship of the 1990s and illuminate his relationship to the politics and rhetoric associated with the Black Arts Movement. Brooks also serves as a comparative figure as I question Hayden's displacement from discussions of the Black Arts era by reconstructing his participation in *For Malcolm: Poems on the Life and Death of Malcolm X*, a text that was conceived at the Fisk conferences, became one of the movement's significant collections, and helped bring to life its most prolific publishing house. An extended reading of Hayden's contribution to the *For Malcolm* project demonstrates the poet's abiding interest in the self-same issues that animated the art of those aligned with the BAM, even as it reveals Hayden's most explicit poetic critique of the separatist nationalism associated with the Black Arts and Black Power Movements.

Although my argument conceives of Hayden as an integral participant in the cultural-poetic conversation of the Black Arts era, its purpose is not to mitigate the important differences that set him apart from many of his contemporaries. Indeed, the ways in which Hayden differed from many who are conventionally associated with the Black Arts Movement—his universalism, his reverence for the Western canon, his Apollonian, writerly aesthetic—are precisely the elements of Hayden's artistic comportment that make him an influential figure in American poetry today. I insist that Hayden's various quarrels with certain aesthetic and political conventions of the Black Arts era represent a part of that period's richness and should not be the cause for his omission or avoidance in critical conceptions of the period, just as they did not result in his silencing or banishment during the time in which they took place.

Pruning the Furious Flower of African American Poetry

Twenty-first-century studies like Lorenzo Thomas's *Extraordinary Measures: Afrocentric Modernism and Twentieth-Century American Poetry* (2000), Tony Bolden's *Afro-Blue: Improvisation in African American Poetry* (2004), James Smethurst's *The Black Arts Movement: Literary Nationalism in the 1960s and 1970s* (2005), Keith Leonard's *Fettered Genius: The African American Bardic Poet from Slavery to Civil Rights* (2006), Howard Rambsy's *The Black Arts Enterprise and the Production of African American Poetry* (2011), and Meta Jones's *The Muse Is Music: Jazz Poetry from the Harlem Renaissance to Spoken Word* (2011) have significantly deepened scholarly comprehension of twentieth-century black poetics. But in the 1980s and 1990s there was a paucity of scholarship dealing specifically with black poetry. It was during this late twentieth-century period, when very little was written about black poetics, that Hayden was relegated to the margins of accounts of the Black Arts era. In the sparse scholarship of the 1980s and 1990s Hayden is a peripheral, spectral character who is patched in here and there—often appearing momentarily as a cipher holding stock meaning that can be readily deployed by the versed scholar of African American literature. Sometimes he is assigned an "assimilationist position" without much elaboration; elsewhere he is perfunctorily honored though not engaged; often he is simply evoked as a name on a list, a placeholder.[2]

If there is one critical work in late twentieth-century scholarship in which Hayden's fleeting presences and notable absences created the most interesting figuration of the poet, it is the collection of articles and interviews edited by Joanne Gabbin, *The Furious Flowering of African American Poetry* (1999). The volume, which grew out of the similarly titled conference held at James Madison University in 1994, offers a vivid example of Hayden's fate in a "tearing" that helped to produce one influential and coherent, but partial, narrative celebrating a "literature that," as Gabbin puts it, "is both rageful and resolute in its beauty" (1). As Gabbin explains it in her introductory essay, the Furious Flower Conference assembled the largest gathering of scholars and producers of African American poetry since the Black Arts era. Gabbin, who did vital scholarly work as principal organizer, wanted the event to be understood as both a commemoration of the poetic achievements of the past and a harbinger of African American poetry to come—a confluence of generations and ideas not previously witnessed. The conference must certainly be regarded as a considerable moment in post-movement African American literary history. Besides resulting in the publication of a critical collection and the production of a series of video interviews with poets and critics, the conference attracted a group of thinkers whose work is elemental to the discourse on late twentieth-century poetry. Participants included Gwendolyn Brooks, Amiri Baraka, Haki Madhubuti, Sonia Sanchez, Askia Touré, Pinkie Gordon Lane, Nikki Giovanni, Raymond Patterson, Michael Harper, Elizabeth Alexander, Arnold Rampersad, and Rita Dove, to name only a few. Though the collection of essays that emerged in its lee does not fully capture the complexity of the voices arrayed at that gathering, by virtue of the number and diversity of its contributors—twenty-six, representing several generations—the volume does begin to suggest the scholarly terrain upon which the study of African American poetry now takes place. If only for the fact that it represents the lone multiauthored compilation of essays on the subject to appear in the

1980s or 1990s, its fascination with Gwendolyn Brooks and—more important for my purposes—its disenchantment with Hayden suggest a critical pattern worth evaluating.[3]

In Gabbin's introductory essay Hayden's name appears, without particular comment, on two lists of significant poets (3, 5). She follows a pattern of engagement that holds throughout most of the collection: Hayden's contributions are acknowledged as part of the essential bedrock of the African American poetic tradition, but they do not get much treatment. Aside from a decidedly negative portrayal in one essay, Hayden is mostly an absent presence in the volume.[4] His "Middle Passage" is briefly described in a piece by Raymond Patterson (216), and Joyce A. Joyce asserts that Hayden was among a generation of older poets writing during the sixties who were not affiliated with the BAM and "who reveal their success in honing European forms" (111). In this short list Hayden is joined by Gwendolyn Brooks. These two poets—both considered older voices during the sixties—are also mentioned together in an interview with Hayden's friend, Michael Harper. Here it is remembered that, until the appointment of Rita Dove in 1993, Brooks and Hayden were the only two African Americans to have been honored with the position of poetry consultant to the Library of Congress (79).

There is good reason for the pairing of Hayden and Brooks, which also occurs in several other lists in the volume. As Joyce points out on more than one occasion, both poets had become accomplished practitioners of what she calls "models of mainstream poetry" before the emergence of the BAM and its rejection of poetic forms deemed Eurocentric (105). And after the rise—and denouement—of the BAM both Hayden and Brooks were recognized with their prestigious appointments at the Library of Congress. This general similarity of career trajectory is notable, especially as it is contexualized within the frame of the Furious Flower Conference and the critical work affiliated with it. Gabbin, as editor of the volume and steward of the conference, intended her efforts to be a tribute to Brooks. The *Furious Flowering* title, which deftly metaphorizes the insistent beauty of African American poetry, is drawn from Brooks's poem "Second Sermon on the Warpland." In Gabbin's volume, Brooks presides as a ubiquitous maternal figure. Her poetic genius is evoked in both essays and interviews with a frequency that establishes her as the volume's symbolic cynosure—a revered lodestone. Affirming this status is the photograph of Brooks, taken at the conference, that adorns the softcover volume. Beneath prominent glasses and a headwrap holding back gray curls, her brow slightly furrows as the corners of her mouth dip in a defiant smile; an aged fist is clenched at her shoulder. She is beautiful, undeterred, powerful, and syllogistically established as the embodiment of African American poetry. However, if Brooks is the furious flowering, Hayden is left mostly unnoticed in her shadow. His absence from the questions and conversations that animate the volume is pronounced when contrasted with Brooks's ubiquity.

Poets in Conference

If the 1994 Furious Flower Conference and its sequel in 2004 were some of African American poetry's most noteworthy public gatherings in the post-movement era, they should be considered in reference to the historic spring writer's conferences of 1966 and 1967 at Fisk University.[5] During these conferences that took place as the BAM was beginning to gather momentum, the seeds of the later-celebrated furiousness of Brooks's poetics were planted, and Hayden's thorny struggle with the prominent political aesthetic of his heyday became very public. Thus in the matrix of these generative conferences there appears a narrative that does much to account for the differing positions of Brooks and Hayden within the development of the African American literary tradition in the past five decades.

The most well-known description of the 1967 Fisk conference stands at the heart of Brooks's autobiographical prose collection *Report from Part One*. In this often-cited conversion narrative, Brooks documents her first sustained encounter with the "New Black" that had descended upon the Tennessee campus. She describes her own sense of awakening in explicit terms: "Until 1967 my own blackness did not confront me with a shrill spelling of itself" (83). For the poet recounting her sudden racial awareness in the midst of the dawning movement, the sensibility of the emergent African American artist was epitomized in Amiri Baraka. "He arrived in the middle of my own offering," writes Brooks, recalling her reading at the conference, "and when I called attention to his presence there was jubilee in Jubilee Hall" (84). She was the Pulitzer Prize winner, but Baraka was the rising son, the new way. In Brooks's ear the substance of Baraka's poetics—the poetics of the "New Black"—seemed to shout, "Up against the wall, white man!" (85). This fresh strength was enchanting; Brooks would leave behind much of the traditional form that prominently marked her first four collections, take on a black nationalist rhetoric, dedicate her next book of poems—*In the Mecca* (1968)—to a group that included Baraka, and set at its head the epigraph "There comes a time when what has been can never be again" (2).

Hayden left no first-person account of his experience at the writers' conference held at Fisk one year earlier, but the fact that the poet, who was faculty at the university, chose not to attend the 1967 gathering that so affected Brooks perhaps indicates the dissonance he felt in the wake of events that took place at the first conference. While Hayden offered no published account of the 1966 conference, it was chronicled with extensive detail and alacrity in the pages of the June 1966 *Negro Digest*. Many scholars have gestured toward this narrative of the conference in their attempts to imagine the most public flashpoint in Hayden's long quarrel with the movers and shapers of the Black Arts era; almost all fashion the conference as the exemplary moment in Hayden's apparent exclusion from the BAM. Nevertheless, the 1966 Fisk conference can be understood alternatively as a moment in which Hayden raised his dissenting voice to participate richly in a seminal Black Arts event.

The giddy writing of *Negro Digest* chronicler David Llorens manages to approximate the excitement that must have wrapped conference proceedings. He bounces from one exchange to the next, seeking to record the expostulations of the newly born consciousness that Brooks was to encounter a year later. But scholarly recollection of the conference often centers upon Llorens's portrayal of Hayden as a seemingly abandoned yet uncompromising aesthete holding fast to a racial politics that, in the context of the new black nationalism, seemed dangerously archaic. Hayden was to receive the most explicit chastening of his career during a prominent panel discussion that included Arna Bontemps, Margaret Walker, and Melvin Tolson. Though the panel meant to focus on the development of black poetry in the twentieth century, its central issue became Hayden's refusal of the primacy of race in poetic pursuits. In the discussion, as Llorens describes it, Hayden was "visibly disturbed"; his "anticipation of opposition gave way to a slight stutter"; and "his sensibility [was] shaken to the point of anger" ("Writers" 60). Yet the poet's remarks were bold. Knowing the firestorm it would provoke, Hayden declared himself a poet who only by accident of birth was a "Negro" (60). In striking contrast to the racialized epiphany Brooks experienced in 1967, Hayden urged his audience against newly ascendant ideas about black authorship and aesthetic purpose: "Let's quit saying we're black writers writing to black folks—it has been given an importance it should not have" (63).

Several critics have noted irony in the fact that it was Melvin Tolson, a poet of Hayden's generation whose style was heavily indebted to high-culture, modernist poetics, who attacked Hayden most vehemently during the conference. James Hall's analysis of Hayden's confrontations in the spring of 1966 turns on this irony and does much to disrupt many critical narratives that "misremember" the first Fisk conference as a forum in which Hayden was the victim of an attack by faceless, militant supporters of an invigorated poetics of black cultural nationalism. Hall goes so far as to suggest that, in what he sees as their performative altercation, "Tolson and Hayden cooperate to provide the community an opportunity to restate the importance they attach to the investigation of and interrogation of 'selfhood'" (53). However, this interpretation of the exchange seems a bit too sanguine. In the pages of *Negro Digest*, Tolson's sharp-barbed response to Hayden's position can be read as "cooperative" only if the term is understood in heavy academic abstraction. Llorens records Tolson's fighting words with a journalistic gusto that betrays a certain degree of bias:

> Glancing over his shoulder at Hayden, the grin on his face reminiscent of a mischievous lad, once again Tolson's voice was soft, almost reverent, "Hap, hap . . . let me see hap means accident. Is someone going to make M.B. Tolson an accident? You'll never make me an accident," and by this time his voice was blazing to the rafters as he exclaimed: "I'm a black poet, an African-American poet, a Negro poet. I'm no accident—and I don't give a tinker's damn what you think." ("Writers" 63)

This was followed by a later challenge from an unnamed audience member whose self-declared credentials included being a former "movement activist" and "now a sometime writer" (64). Here, Hayden was scorned for failing to address the delusional self-conception that apparently estranged many Fisk graduates from their own blackness. As far as his antagonist was concerned, Hayden was directly responsible for students' racial dissonance: "I am suggesting that you do have responsibility to them, a responsibility to help them understand that they will become black poets, black teachers, or what have you—and whether you like it or not, that is your problem, baby" (64).

Although Hall is opposed to depicting Hayden's experience at the Fisk conference as a martyrdom and to stoking the narratives of intracultural dispute that so often circulate in scholarship around Hayden, he does momentarily evoke scapegoat theory to help explain the rebuffing of the unnamed audience member (51). Other critics have somewhat reductively asserted that in the context of 1966 writers' conference (and throughout the Black Arts era), Hayden was quintessentially a scapegoat—identified as a Negro heretic by the New Black community and symbolically destroyed because of his unwillingness to accept aesthetic and political precepts that were emergent in African American culture of the mid-1960s.[6] However, this interpretation of

Hayden's experience at the Fisk conference elides certain complexities, such as Melvin Tolson's vexed relationship to the populist tenets associated with the BAM and Hayden's decision to play the role of provocateur. And there is also this: on the evening when poets attending the conference were invited to share their work, Hayden's reading was, in the words of David Llorens, "received with a warm appreciation that was a tribute to his artistry" ("Writers" 66). Llorens's account of Hayden's reading is supplemented by Dudley Randall's intimate remembrance of the occasion:

> That night, he read his poems of the black experience. He read "Runagate" and "Middle Passage" and other powerful pieces. Everybody was moved, even those who had attacked him. The whole audience spontaneously gave him a standing ovation. Offstage, he leaned against the wall exhausted. There were tears in his eyes. I said, "They like your poetry." He said, "It was wonderful." (Boyd 128)

Recognizing that the 1966 Fisk conference was simultaneously a site for Hayden's vigorous—even emotionally injurious—quarrel with ideological adversaries and an occasion for communal celebration of his poetry does much to complicate conventional histories that pit Hayden against the BAM in a vague but Manichean agon. Acceptance of this more complex narrative weakens the constructions of many scholars who, in their sympathy for Hayden, figure the poet a scapegoat decisively exiled by the new black nationalists. However, it also presents a challenge to those who portray Hayden as marginal to the discourse of the Black Arts era.[7]

The reductive inclination to place Hayden squarely outside and in diametric opposition to the Black Arts Movement is implicitly influenced by a dichotomizing logic that figured significantly in Black Arts discourse—and that remains discernable today in a certain brand of African American literary criticism. As Phillip Brian Harper has argued, a rhetoric of intracultural division—most recognizable in Black Arts poetry—was a fundamental and perhaps ironic element of black nationalism in the 1960s and 1970s. Harper has shown that dwelling within the era's black separatist expression was an exclusionary rhetoric that sought to purge the imagined New Black community of a "putatively ineffectual bourgeois accommodationism" ("Nationalism" 184). And, given Hayden's gentilities (he smoked a pipe and wore a bowtie), his commitment to an integrationist politics, and his reverence for elements of Western cultural expression, he might very well have been seen as an exemplar of the "bourgie accommodationist" that served as a negative foil in the era's constructions—poetic or otherwise—of a "politically aware, racially conscious, subject" (P. Harper, *Are We* 48). However, if a type that superficially resembled Hayden was regularly degraded in Black Arts rhetoric, it does not follow that Hayden was, in fact, roundly excluded from the community. Indeed, the folly of disregarding Hayden's influential voice is plainly revealed in a thorough and nuanced portrayal of his participation in black literary circles of the late 1960s. The mostly forgotten standing ovation that he received at the Fisk conference is only one indication of Hayden's complex signification in the Black Arts community. There are other complicating details as well. For instance, in 1968 there was no exclusion when Hayden was among those writers interviewed for a feature on the black aesthetic in *Negro Digest*—then under the editorial supervision of Black Arts lynchpin Hoyt Fuller. And perhaps most significant is the prominent and eloquent space occupied by Hayden in the heart of one of the movement's major texts—the 1969 volume *For Malcolm: Poems on the Life and Death of Malcolm X*.

Hayden's Malcolm

Most who have studied Hayden's biography isolate the Fisk conference as a flashpoint and emotional nadir in the poet's career. David Llorens's journalistic portrayal of Hayden as a lonely naysayer dithering in the midst of impassioned nationalists certainly spurs on such representations. Pontheolla Williams, who on several occasions interviewed Hayden for her 1980 book on the poet, goes so far as to declare that it was four years before Hayden was able to confront the events of the conference in poetic form (32). And in his study of the poet's life and work, John Hatcher describes the conference as the beginning of a "devastating" attack on Hayden's poetics (75). Many of Hayden's contemporary sympathizers seem to imagine the 1966 conference as a decisive moment of separation, sealing the poet out of the Black Arts community. For example, in a defense of Hayden's historical poems during her 2011 Hopwood Lecture at the University of Michigan, Elizabeth Alexander would state:

> And the case of Robert Hayden is well known. His work is profoundly respected in many circles. But from within some black literary communities he has been vilified for insisting that, when it came to his poetry, he was a poet first before racial concerns. The lingering wake of this controversy—which brewed as early as the 1950s, boiled over at the 1966 Fisk Writers' Conference and was covered in *Negro Digest*—

has left him as one who is seen by some as a mainstream sellout. ("New Ideas" 598–99)

Although this narrative is accurate in its key features, it also suppresses some of the discordant complexity of African American poetics of the late 1960s. While the conference may have left Hayden with slow-healing emotional scars, it was not a wounding that cowed his art for years to follow or that made him shy away from questions of politics, aesthetics, and race that were fundamental to the Black Arts era. Nor was Hayden's stand widely regarded as an act of unforgivable treachery that required his silencing. In fact, Hayden's most articulate and explicit poetic engagement with black nationalist ideology came in the form of his contribution to the historic *For Malcolm* anthology, which came soon after—and as a direct result of—the 1966 Fisk conference.

Organized and published by Margaret Burroughs and Dudley Randall, the *For Malcolm* compilation took seed in the conference that put Hayden on trial. The volume, which brought together black America's most significant poetic voices in a collective remembrance of the slain leader, also helped to establish Randall's Broadside Press as the prominent publishing house for Black Arts poets during the late 1960s and early 1970s (Rambsy, *Black Arts Enterprise* 54–56). However, in 1966 Randall was not yet the well-known publisher that he would come to be. Indeed, in a letter written to Hayden only a few weeks prior to the conference, Randall complained of not being especially invited to the event (Letter, 13 Apr.). Nonetheless, he made his way to the conference and, while attending, stayed in Hayden's home.

Both Detroit natives, Randall and Hayden were literary acquaintances and at times exchanged a significant correspondence. In several letters written to his friend after the Fisk conference, Randall describes his meeting with Margaret Burroughs and the excitement they shared about the project after hearing Margaret Walker's reading of her poem "For Malcolm X." He also asked Hayden if he had written or would be interested in writing something on Malcolm for the volume (Letter, 29 Apr.). In the wake of the chaotic, burdening experience at the Fisk conference, Randall's invitation gave Hayden the opportunity once more to declare his positions in the company of the major poets of the era. This time his assertion took poetic form, offering a sharp critique of the racial politics that characterized much of the Black Arts Movement (and much of the poetry in the *For Malcolm* volume), even as it gave tribute to the principal hero of sixties black nationalism.

The inclusion of Hayden's "dissenting" poem in the critically neglected *For*

Malcolm collection represents some of the ideological diversity of the Black Arts era that is mostly glossed over in narratives that figure the development of the African American literary tradition in a unified, politically coherent arc.[8] Because Hayden's "El Hajj Malik El-Shabazz" adeptly memorializes the history that Malcolm made while rejecting the hagiography that typifies much of the collection, there is an ambiguity to the poem that stymies any neat summation of this major Black Arts text. One of the volume's strongest pieces is as much a condemnation of the ideology conventionally associated with Malcolm X as it is a celebration of his life.

In his contribution to the anthology, Hayden works in the historiographical mode that by the late 1960s was among his fortes. The poem, which sweeps its way from Malcolm's boyhood through to his assassination, fittingly concludes the first section of the collection, "The Life." It is preceded by Gwendolyn Brooks's piece, "Malcolm X" (3), which opens the same section and the poetry in the book. Here, the works of the two poet laureates intersect in tellingly contrasting engagements with a common subject. While Hayden's poem offers a challenging interpretation of the Malcolm mythology and intends to discomfit its audience in both content and form, Brooks's poem augments the charismatic mystique conventionally associated with Malcolm as it invites its audience to identify with the speaking voice awed by the nationalist leader. The prominent placement of Brooks's poem—which is dedicated to Randall—at the beginning of the book reveals the importance of her voice to the editors and the status of her reputation. It also suggests that Brooks's piece is something of a "flagship poem" meant to confirm the expectations of reader-consumers in the Black Arts poetry market that bourgeoned in the late 1960s. Nevertheless, Brooks offers an interestingly sexualized rendering of Malcolm that fixates on his masculinity and follows well the volume's prefatory essay by Ossie Davis, which features one phrase in boldface: "Malcolm was a man!" (xxiii). In their introduction, Randall and Burroughs call attention to the collection's continual return to the subject of Malcolm's manhood, his defiance "of white America's effort to emasculate the Blackman" (xxi). Brooks's poem is among the volume's more cunning treatments of the significance of Malcolm's manhood.

Unlike many of the pieces in the collection that X out the X and call him only "Malcolm" to produce a familiarity, or other poems that attempt to enhance this intimacy through familial rhetoric ("brother Malcolm"), Brooks maintains a formal distance and infuses it with a sexual tension befitting the tremendous manhood that others evoke less tangibly. For Brooks, Malcolm X is seminal and earthy; he is a definitely *paternal* life giver. Her opening stanza is wrought in terse four-syllable lines: "Original. / Hence ragged-round, / Hence rich-robust" (1–3). The poem's speaker goes on to speak for a seemingly feminized "we" who are left breathlessly attracted to Malcolm's primal power:

> He had the hawk-man's eyes.
> We gasped. We saw the maleness.
> The maleness raking out and making guttural the air
> And pushing us to walls. (4–7)

The poem closes with suggestive imagery as well: "He opened us— / who was a key, / who was a man" (11–13). Brooks deploys this sexualized language to articulate viscerally the quality of the influence that Malcolm had over his followers. The double entendres work toward the suggestion that he was able to push them to and over walls of self-hate and help give birth to self-pride through a vigorously charismatic magnetism epitomized in sexuality. Davis's prose preface to the poetry, like the testaments of so many others inspired by Malcolm, describes his provoking power and the male surplus that Brooks seizes upon for the effect of her piece: "It was impossible to remain defensive and apologetic about being a Negro in his presence. He wouldn't let you. And you always left his presence with the sneaking suspicion that maybe, after all, you were a man!" (xxv).

Although clever in its suggestiveness, Brooks's poem is less concerned with Malcolm the man than with the effect of his maleness. Her piece, along with almost all the others in the collection, is a celebration of Malcolm that draws its energy from his iconicity. Hayden's poem, as immediately evidenced by its defamiliarizing title, is interested in disrupting the iconography understandably employed by other contributors. (Of the nearly sixty in the volume, only one other poem—Carmin Auld Goulbourne's "Letter for El-Hajj Malik El-Shabazz"—makes mention of Malcolm's post-pilgrimage name.) Hayden's choice of title distances him from his co-contributors by suggesting that the figure honored in his poem is not the iconic Malcolm X so significant to almost all of his fellow poets but rather the El-Hajj Malik El-Shabazz whose name was a reflection of a philosophy and politics that "Malcolm X" did not in fact wholly espouse. The Malcolm esteemed in Hayden's poem was killed a month after responding to a question about interracial communion by saying, "I believe in recognizing every human being as a human being—neither white, black, brown, or red; and when you are dealing with humanity as a family, there's no question of integration or intermarriage. It's just one human being marrying another human being, or one human being living around and with another human being" (X and Breitman 197). This final incarnation of Malcolm, named in the poem's title, "fell upon his face before / Allah the raceless" (89) and espoused a philosophy to which Hayden could comfortably pay tribute.

Carrying the narrative from the early childhood remembrances recorded in his autobiography through to his premature death, Hayden's four-section poem relies on Malcolm's several names and transformations for theme and structure. The first part of the poem is anchored in a pair of nicknames that represent the trough from which the hero must rise in the mythic narrative of Malcolm's life. These are the street names to which he "fled" in his initial attempts to escape "the icy evil that struck his father down / and ravished his mother." In the guise of "Home Boy" and "Dee-troit Red," Malcolm ran from the attack of that "evil" that becomes a protean enemy haunting him throughout the poem: "He conked his hair and Lindy-hopped, / zoot-suited jiver, swinging those chicks / in the hot rose and reefer glow." But here he found no respite: "His injured childhood bullied him" (86). The first section posits a logic that holds throughout the poem: Malcolm's life is a continual attempt to come to terms with his experience of a white supremacy that terrorized him from the earliest hour of his life.

In the poem's second movement, Malcolm himself becomes the figuration of evil. "Satan," the nickname apparently given to him by fellow inmates during his prison days, is the appellation that Hayden chooses to foreground in the section of the poem that chronicles Malcolm's first spiritual conversion. The "reefer glow" that emanated from Dee-troit Red has now become a more sinister "cold satanic sheen," and the petty disguises of fashion that once trapped him have given way to the strictures of solitary confinement in "The Hole." It is within this confinement that his own evil patina sparks the "false dawn of vision" that prompts Malcolm's next transformation:

he fell upon his face before
a racist Allah. Pledged to wrest him from
the hellward-dipping hands of Calvin's Christ—

to free him and his kind
from Yakub's white-face treachery. (87)

Before rising from this prostration, he exchanges an inherited European religious mythology for the spiritual system of Elijah Muhammad, which is evoked by reference to Yakub, the mad scientist who in the creation narrative taught by the Nation of Islam was responsible for allowing evil to enter the world in the form of a white race. This false vision—which racializes evil— allows Malcolm to rise, "redeemed from all but prideful anger." The poem makes it clear that this conversion is another false layering, obscuring the reality beneath, like "adulterate attars" that would only disguise, not clean, "the odors of the pit."

The third section of the poem deals with Malcolm during the iconic period of his life when he took the "X," naming himself for the first time. This is the Malcolm X who was inspiring in his courage, the leader who tapped the emotion of the people and drove them from "their servitude." Hayden depicts a figure similar to the character that Brooks conjures in her poem, although the poets judge the characters very differently. Hayden's Malcolm is an exhorter and an admonisher who gives all of himself to "his people": "He X'd his name, became his people's anger, / exhorted them to vengeance for their past; / rebuked admonished them" (88). For Hayden the replacement of the last name Little with the signifier X—meant to displace an inherited slave name and represent unknown Africanness—seems yet another specious covering that muddles true identity. In becoming "his people's anger" Malcolm loses himself yet again.

The final line-pair of the third section is among Hayden's most explicit poetic confrontations with the black nationalists. Redeploying symbols of the poem's subtitle—"O masks and metamorphoses of Ahab, Native Son"— the poet calls upon topoi of a Western tradition that most Black Arts artists shunned and critiqued. Hayden simultaneously evokes the biblical king Ahab, as well as Melville's captain of the American literary imagination, to articulate his view of the Manichean racial ideology that characterized Malcolm's "X" incarnation and much of the Black Arts rhetoric: "Rejecting Ahab, he was of Ahab's tribe. / Strike through the mask!" (88). These lines, dense in allusion, initially recall the idolatrous king of Israel whose descendants were cursed for his impiety (1 Kings 21:21). The first line of the pair suggests that the Baal of race, deified by those white supremacists whom Malcolm X repudiated, was as sacred for him as it was for those he battled against. His prostration "before / a racist Allah" held no salvation for Malcolm and "his people" because, by adopting the category of race as the organizing object of their political project, he and the nationalists who revered him as an icon remained within the ideological tribe of the white fathers they ostensibly rejected. The poem argues that, just as King Ahab's progeny were blighted, Malcolm X and the nationalists had adopted an inherited and cursed ideology passed down from a corrupted source.

The second line of the pair is linked to the first through literary allusion, though rhythmically and grammatically it does not complement its partner. Separated from its companion sentence by a line break, Captain Ahab's famous call stands by itself and can be read as though it is spoken by several figures. If attributed to Malcolm X, who is to "his people" as Ahab is to his crew, the exhortation, in spite of its philosophical efficacy, is uttered in the context of a misguided pursuit. Metamorphosed into an Ahab crazed in his hatred of a white foe, Malcolm preached, on the one hand, a truth that allowed his people to *strike through* their self-loathing and, on the other, a vitriol that inspired an externalized hatred that was a type of veil itself. Like Captain Ahab, who is unable to pierce the mask before him even as he exhorts his crew to "strike through," Malcolm X is, in the poem's estimation, a great leader blinded by a monomania that was hugely empowering, yet ultimately shortsighted.

The line signifies differently, however, if it is read as though it issues from the mouth of the poet, as though Hayden strikes through the masking mechanisms that he customarily used to create aesthetic distance in his poems. Interpreted as his own call to those still holding fast to a Manichean separatism that Malcolm would leave behind, Hayden confronts the nationalists with an implicitly accusatory command, exhorting his adversaries to look beyond a dogma that only transposed racial terms within an inherently oppressive ideological formulation. This call to "strike through the mask" is illuminated by a signature line of Hayden's that appears in "Words in the Mourning Time"—the poem he placed immediately following "El-Hajj" in his 1970 collection also titled *Words in the Mourning Time*. In his poem for Malcolm, Hayden directs toward the black nationalists the general admonition in "Mourning Time": "We must not be frightened nor cajoled / into accepting evil as deliverance from evil" (98).

In his final manifestation, Hayden's Malcolm is no longer chased by the evil that pursued him previously. The exclamation (uttered during the rites of the Muslim pilgrimage to Mecca) "Labbayk! Labbayk!"—meaning "Here am I, Here am I"—punctuates this fourth section of the poem, implying that the journey toward self-identification has come to a close. Hayden explicitly associates no name with Malcolm's "final metamorphoses." After the self-referential shouts, the poem closes with:

He fell upon his face before
Allah the raceless in whose blazing Oneness all
were one. He rose renewed, renamed, became
much more than there was time for him to be. (89)

This section dramatizes the conversion to orthodox Sunni Islam, which prompted Malcolm to forsake the iconic X and the racialist ideology that it came to stand for and to take on the designation that titles Hayden's poem. Because the final movement of the piece does not state Malcolm's name, the reader must return to the very beginning of the work—to the title that precedes the appearance of the determining evil that shows itself in the first line—to recall Malcolm's new and last name. Thus the logic of the poem's arrangement suggests that El-Hajj Malik El-Shabazz is Malcolm's original, perhaps "true," self that exists outside of and before the evil that held sway during the dispensations of Malcolm's other selves. This evil is fully conquered when finally Malcolm rises from his prostration before a mythology that in its vastness leaves no room for privileging the category of race.

The Black Arts Dialogues

Upsetting the iconography of "Malcolm X," Hayden's tribute produces a critique of separatist black nationalism that is structured and implicitly sanctioned by the biography of one of its greatest heroes. This somewhat ironic use of the life of El-Hajj Malik El-Shabazz exemplifies the way in which Hayden's poetics deployed black subject matter in service of a universalist politics. In the frame of his poem, the celebration of black culture—an embedded function of Hayden's participation in the *For Malcolm* collection—coexists with an argument that forcefully refuses racial separatism. The intensity of both his engagement with the materials of black culture and his rejection of the aesthetic and political platform of the nationalists was unique among poets of the Black Arts era. This distinctive ideological complexity is part of what has made Hayden hard to parse. Gwendolyn Brooks, his generational peer, has been more attractive for many. This is evident in the *Furious Flowering* collection, which figures Brooks as a powerful matriarch, an artistic life-giver. Indeed, her creative power seems comparable to the paternal fecundity that she attributes to Malcolm X in her contribution to the *For Malcolm* collection. As I have intimated, the concentration upon Malcolm in his "X" manifestation led the majority of the *For Malcolm* poets to celebrate an icon that necessarily suppressed Malcolm's post-pilgrimage history and politics. Similarly, the iconic representation of Brooks in *The Furious Flowering* precludes some important aspects of the development of African American poetry in the second half of the twentieth century. In *For Malcolm*, Hayden dredges up Malik El-Shabazz to offer a vision that both complements and challenges the representations of his fellow poets, thus complicating and enriching the character elegized in the collection. Just as Malik El-Shabazz was a facet of Malcolm that was easier for most Black Arts writers to put aside than to engage, Hayden is a Black Arts figure who is often marginalized in the quest for coherent critical narratives.

While it would be foolish to devalue the important role that Brooks has played in the development of African American poetics, it is important to note the lacunae that open in the midst of scholarship that values coherence over the appearance of contradiction. Brooks's reformulation in 1967 brought the politics of her poetry into substantial alignment with that of the leading figures of the Black Arts Movement and eventually helped to make her a metonym for the course of African American poetry in the second half of the twentieth century. But in metonymy something is always lost. That is to say, while the political trajectory of Brooks's career may model the general shifts in the politics broadly espoused in African American poetry from the 1940s to the 1970s more faithfully than Hayden's, serious engagement with a figure like Hayden guards against a convenient critical narrative that can suggest that the Black Arts era produced a relatively uniform politics and poetics.

For the handful of scholars who do champion Hayden's work, the poet is often regarded as a hero holding off the Black Arts barbarians at the gate. In Phillip Richards's unforgiving appraisal of late twentieth- and early twenty-first-century African American literature and criticism, Hayden emerges as an artist-savior who sought to situate his work within the plenitude of the Western cultural tradition at a time when most black artists and intellectuals rejected that tradition and turned solely to the resources of black folk culture to construct an alternative creative ground that, for Richards, was incapable of adequately addressing the humanistic concerns of meaningful art. Richards argues that, because of his willingness to illuminate the African American experience by calling upon the symbolic power stored up in the West's artistic and philosophical canon—as he does in his evocation of Ahab in the Malcolm X poem—Hayden produced a black poetics powerful enough to sustain its relevance and viability generations after it was produced. Richards broadly maintains that "years after his death" Hayden "remains our most influential black poet, and his followers the most productive and distinguished school of artist intellectuals" (178). However, establishing Hayden's seminal role in the development of African American poetics in the last half century is, in Richards's critical framework, a function of deep trepidation about the value and legacy of the BAM. For Hayden to rise, those who quarreled with him fall in an almost zero-sum calculation that explicitly contends that Hayden's poetry "has proved more influential than the Black Arts Movement" and that

Gwendolyn Brooks's conversion to nationalism led to "the collapse of [her] poetic career" (178).

Richards's readings are a vigorous and not easily dismissed response to Hayden's inadequate treatment in much criticism; however, tracing the complex web of influence in African American poetics from the late 1960s up to the contemporary moment is thorny, speculative work. Rather than pitting Hayden in stark, agonistic opposition to Brooks and the Black Arts Movement, we might think of Hayden's involvement in debates of the Black Arts era in dialectical terms. The confrontations of Hayden and poets with differing ideological and aesthetic commitments helped to produce the discourse of the era, just as the twin influences of Hayden and the poets associated with the BAM have been productively synthesized in the work of poets writing in recent decades.

In his critical classic, *The American Adam*, R. W. B. Lewis sketches an instructive approach to cultural analysis. His claim is that "a culture achieves identity not so much through the ascendancy of one particular set of convictions as through the emergence of its peculiar and distinctive dialogue" (2). This assertion supports an argument that recognizes figures like Walt Whitman and Nathaniel Hawthorne as dialogical and similarly vital figures of the so-called American Renaissance, despite their disparate projects (2). In keeping with the logic of Lewis's claim, considerations of the Harlem Renaissance do not cast aside either Langston Hughes or Countee Cullen, although they were aesthetically and ideologically incompatible. Who would argue that the American Renaissance is properly understood without Whitman or without Hawthorne? Or that our conception of the Harlem Renaissance is complete if either Hughes or Cullen is ignored? Appraisals of the Black Arts era need to include the rich contributions of Robert Hayden. His dissenting participation in Black Arts dialogues should be thought of as a discordant but constituent element of the era's discourse. In the chapters of the next section I evaluate his dissonant participation in Black Arts–era aesthetic discourse, arguing that his attachment to writerly poetics in an era when many black poets embraced vernacular orality can be linked to the religiousness that was part of Hayden's soulful response to twentieth-century secular modernity.

PART II

Faith and the Folk

Chapter 2

The "Cosmic Hero"

Hayden's Bahá'í Faith

Reconstructing a narrative history of Robert Hayden's querulous participation in the 1966 Fisk writers' conference and the *For Malcolm* collection weaves the poet into the constituent fabric of the Black Arts era and recent African American letters. However, the aim here is not to produce a comprehensive reconciliation of Hayden and the political-aesthetic ethos of that period. Rather, the point is that Hayden's responses to the cultural impulses of the 1960s and 1970s make him an important Black Arts foil and reveal some of the latent, anxious discourses of the era. In a black literary moment defined by revolutions in poetic form that valorized orality, celebrated masculinism, and advocated for black cultural nationalism, Hayden's reverence for the aesthetic ideals of the putatively Western world of literacy, his skeptical regard for prescriptive definitions of a black aesthetic, his explorations of masculine vulnerability, and his commitment to hoary notions of "race unity" were distinctly out of step with some of the essential maneuvers of the BAM. On the one hand, a contextualized account of Hayden's once-contentious political aesthetics illuminates the literary history of the BAM era, and on the other it refines the genealogy of a post-BAM poetics that frequently returns to Hayden. Many recently celebrated black poets—like Rita Dove, Yusef Komanyakaa, Natasha Trethewey, Elizabeth Alexander, Nikky Finney, Terrance Hayes, and so on—write with a poetic sensibility that traces back to Hayden's mid-twentieth-century work. But critical genealogies of contemporary black poetry often tilt toward the BAM. For example, Harryette Mullen contends that "the current conversation" among black poets is characterized by "tolerance of difference, uncertainty, and even confusion"—qualities seldom associated with the BAM. Yet Mullen credits the BAM for tilling ground in preparation for a deeply heterogeneous black poetics. In 2006 she wrote, "Our embrace of diversity seems to me a consequence of the Black Arts Movement's bold and explicit declaration of a black aesthetic, positing as its foundation the beauty and integrity of black people and cultures" (Introduction 9). There is a strong, dialectical logic to Mullen's genealogy, which imagines that the aesthetic adamancy of the BAM was priming for a subsequent form of black poetics that is more ideologically and aesthetically open. However, this chronicle of aesthetic development suggests only half a story. In their move toward exploratory and uncertain engagements with black people and cultures, and away from the bold, explicit, and declarative ethos of the BAM, contemporary poets have had potent models, like Hayden. If the BAM offered a poetic paradigm that has been warily negotiated by university-employed black poets of the early twenty-first century, Hayden offered another that has been rather fully embraced by that cohort of poets.

In this section, I account for the emergence of Hayden's Apollonian model of black poetics and the more Dionysian BAM model by figuring both as responses to political-aesthetic dilemmas confronting mid-twentieth-century African American artist-intellectuals. Dissatisfied with the existential and political possibilities available to them in Western secular ideologies and the Negro Church, African American poets of the era turned to a variety of alternative cosmologies and religiously inflected social movements as they sought solace and salvation. The contours of aesthetic modes that have organized African American verse for more than fifty years now were shaped by the midcentury spiritual-cum-political quests of discontented poets searching for mediums by which they might imagine cosmologies and human societies not produced in mainstream religious or secular discourses.

Robert Hayden's midcentury move away from secularism and the Negro Church sets him apart from most poets of his generation and those that followed. If other important poets of the middle decades of the twentieth century were spiritual experimentalists, skeptical of any organized religious orthodoxy, Hayden's conversion to the Bahá'í Faith had a recognizable and lasting effect on his art. Indeed, it is no revelation to assert that the Bahá'í Faith gave theoretical pattern and "base" to Hayden's mature poetry—he declared as much on numerous occasions (*Collected Prose* i, 25, 66, 82, 84). But more importantly, from the publication of *Figure of Time* in 1955 until his passing in 1980, the imprint of Bahá'í theology and social philosophy is frequently felt in his work. For example, in poems like "Full Moon," "Sub Specie Aeternitatis," and "Two Egyptian Portrait Masks," a transcendent order inspired by the writings of the religion is a prime subject. "Dawnbreaker," "Words in the Mourning Time," and "From the Corpse Woodpiles . . ." key on figures from Bahá'í history and function as poetic bulwarks in which Hayden finds refuge during engagements with the chaos of life and history. And other poems—such as "Ice Storm," "'As My Blood Was Drawn'" and "The Broken Dark"—reveal a faith-aspiring heart battered by a demanding yet silent God. Moreover, Bahá'u'lláh, believed by Bahá'ís to be the most recent "Manifestation of God," is the *only* frequently appearing character in the poet's corpus. Although the six poems that obviously refer to Bahá'u'lláh represent a relatively small portion of Hayden's canon, these appearances should be considered against the fact that no other historical figure surfaces as a noteworthy character in any more than one of Hayden's poems.[1] And those political-aesthetic qualities that build Hayden's literary reputation—his unyielding struggle to maintain transcendent belief, his apparent rejection of black nationalism, his interests in history, and even his formalist inclination—seem guided, girded, or at least deeply resonant with the teachings of the nineteenth-century Persian nobleman whom the poems variously hail as the "Glorious One," "the cosmic hero," the "Blessed Exile," the "Godlike imprisoned / One," and "He, who is man beatified" (*Collected Poems* 7, 99, 90, 159, 46).

Because Hayden's post-1955 work is deeply marked by reference to the Bahá'í Faith, scholarship on Hayden cannot avoid grappling with his relation to the little-known religion. John Hatcher's invaluable study on Hayden argues for the pervasive influence of the Bahá'í Faith on the poetry, calling Hayden's "a Bahá'í art because at heart of it, organizing it, empowering its themes, are Bahá'í concepts" (73). For Hatcher, the Bahá'í Faith furnished Hayden with a generative mythos inseparable from the poet's analytical and aesthetic consciousness, and Hatcher assumes that responsible audiences will wrestle with the ramifications of Bahá'í ideas in the poetry. However, an argument against using religion as an interpretive lens for reading the poetry emerges from time to time in the scholarship; it occurs most prominently in a prefatory essay to the 2013 reprint of Hayden's *Collected Poems*. In what appears to be an implicit response to Hatcher's methodology, poet Dwayne Betts somewhat ironically calls attention to Hayden's religiousness while also lamenting the impulse to read Hayden's work as "an extension, fully and totally, of his commitment to the Bahá'í Faith" (xvii). This is an odd warning because, besides Hatcher, few critics have interpreted Hayden's work as a total emanation of religious feeling. In their books on Hayden, Pontheolla Williams and Fred Fetrow join most other critics who acknowledge the importance of the poet's faith but do not position it as a central prism in their engagements. However, I follow in the direction suggested by Hatcher, according deep significance to Hayden's midcentury embrace of the Bahá'í Faith—not simply because some of the nuance of the poetry is illumined when Hayden's faith is considered but also because a consideration of Hayden's Bahá'í commitments yields insights about the evolving signification of religion in African American poetry. But rather than attempt to prove that Hayden's oeuvre should be regarded as "Bahá'í art," my arguments focus on Hayden's faith as a response to that constellation of archetypal dilemmas felt acutely by twentieth-century black intellectuals who sought achievement in artistic and professional realms organized by secular, middle-class (and putatively "white") values, even as they desired connection to a black folk world shaped by social and economic repression and the compensatory belief systems of the Negro Church.

While Hayden joined many African American artists of the 1940s, 1950s, and especially the 1960s and 1970s in the expression of spiritualist belief broadly conceived, the quality of his religiousness is most comparable to that of significant black poets like Countee Cullen and Owen Dodson, whose work in the middle decades of the twentieth century was laced with conventional forms of Christian devotion. Yet Cullen and Dodson worked within a tradition of Christian art that was rather exploratory—that allowed for imaginative representations of key theological moments and concepts. For example, in his portrayal of God, Jesus, and Mary as sprightly correspondents in *The Confession Stone: Song Cycles*, Dodson inventively inhabits the characters of the Holy Family, and in a poem like "Judas Iscariot" Cullen would venture far from orthodox Christian theology by portraying Judas as a sacrificial figure who "Loved Christ, and loved him much"—so much that he was willing to bear the burden of becoming the arch villain "In Heaven's holy plan" (335). Hayden's religious poetry is linked to this creative rendering of Christian theology in its novel, yet still faithful, interpretations of a divine plan involving Christ. But Hayden situates Bahá'u'lláh, rather than Christ, at the center of the heavenly order evoked in his mature poems, and the contours of that order are decisively determined by the scriptures of the Bahá'í Faith, rather than biblical sources. While Dodson, Cullen, and a few other poets represented in midcentury anthologies of black poetry used innovative license as they worked within pious Christian theological frameworks—often "blackening" them (Redmond 188)—Hayden's relation to and representation of Bahá'í theology was quite different. Rather than offering creative interpretations of a well-established religious tradition, Hayden attempted to faithfully represent the relatively unknown conceptions of theology and theodicy laid out in the writings of Bahá'u'lláh.

Hayden's "Bahá'u'lláh in the Garden of Ridwan" offers an instructive introduction to the anomalous qualities of his midcentury religiousness. The poem's mysticism—its unabashed portrayal of a transcendent spiritual reality—is not what sets it outside major currents in twentieth-century African American poetry. Rather, the poem is noteworthy because of the assiduously hagiographic tenor of its commemoration of a religious exemplar and its orthodox presentation of Bahá'í subject matter. (Hayden's representation of Bahá'u'lláh finds its closest corollary in the effusion of black nationalist hagiography written by poets memorializing Malcolm X in the late 1960s.) The veneration was originally titled "The Prophet" and appeared in his pivotal 1955 collection, *Figure of Time*. Hayden changed the title to include it in his *Selected Poems* (1966) as "Bahá'u'lláh in the Garden of Ridwan." The revision seems to have been a clarifying gesture because, although alluding to him several times, Hayden does not use the Prophet's formal title elsewhere in the poetry. This alteration speaks to the obscurity of the religious narrative that anchored a belief Harold Bloom once referred to as Hayden's "highly eclectic Bahá'í persuasion" (*Robert Hayden* 2). The subject considered in the poem, the most significant event in Bahá'í history—Bahá'u'lláh's first public claim to the station of Divine Messenger—would not have been recognized by an audience unfamiliar with Hayden's faith. His alteration offers the uninitiated but inquisitive reader footing in a poem that might otherwise be inaccessible. It is worth noting that two of the three book-length studies of Hayden—those written by Williams and Fetrow—make no mention of "Bahá'u'lláh in the Garden of Ridwan," while the third, by Bahá'í critic John Hatcher, devotes considerable attention to the poem and bases its title, *From the Auroral Darkness*, on phrasing in the poem. This contrast indicates that the importance attributed to the poem and, thus, to Hayden's Bahá'í beliefs, has varied significantly, even among the poet's most attentive readers.

The first, and arguably most overtly, Bahá'í poem of Hayden's career positions Bahá'u'lláh as the lodestar of the transcendental universe that the poet began building in the 1950s. In his poetry of the 1940s, Hayden displays deep—and expected—admiration for the audacious, history-shaping lives of figures like Frederick Douglass, Harriett Tubman, and Joseph Cinquez; however, his veneration of Bahá'u'lláh is of a different order. Hayden's later poetry casts the Prophet as something more than an important character; instead he is held to be a force, a first cause, an omniscient overseer, and a goal. His words are final gospel in this poetry. As "architect / of our hope of peace" (*Collected Poems* 99), Bahá'u'lláh and the design of his doctrine shaped Hayden's politics, gave the poet language to articulate his universalism, and as we will see in later chapters, organized his understanding of the trajectory of human history.

"Bahá'u'lláh in the Garden of Ridwan" is composed of seven tercet stanzas and begins by establishing the metaphysical centrality of the protagonist. Hayden slightly revised the poem's first sentence, along with its title, between its appearances in *A Ballad of Remembrance* (1962) and *Selected Poems* (1966). The original rendering of the lines reads, "Agonies confirm His hour / and swords like compass-needles turn / toward His vast heart." In the later iteration of the poem Hayden creates a more focused assertion by excising the adjective that gives description to the moral, emotional "heart" of Bahá'u'lláh. With the elimination of the descriptor "vast," the Prophet's heart is no longer partly a metaphor for his character; it is strictly the locus of his being—his life power. This concentrates the poem by doing away with any attempt to describe the personality of Bahá'u'lláh, for this is not the work's primary concern. Rather, the poem argues for and contemplates the messianic historical *station* of the Prophet.

The initial lines of the poem attempt to supply proof for its later claims that Bahá'u'lláh is in fact the "eternal exile whose return / epiphanies repeatedly / foretell" (47), "the word made flesh again," a human manifestation of God. The opening assertion that "Agonies confirm His hour" is most effectively understood within the context of Bahá'u'lláh's own writing on the subject of his station, and it exemplifies the orthodoxy of the poem, showing that Hayden primarily sought to reiterate the doctrinal teachings of his faith. In one sense, the line refers to Bahá'u'lláh's various declarations that the appearance of a divine revelation in the world of creation has painfully shaken the fundamental ordering of human society.[2] Thus the general agonies of the historical moment are, like the biblical and Qur'anic apocalypses that are to accompany the return of the Messiah, a confirmation of Bahá'u'lláh's lofty station. However, taking the three lines of the stanza in concert invites an interpretation in which the agonies of the first line are borne by Bahá'u'lláh alone, and his persecution signals the veracity of his claim to prophethood ("Agonies confirm His hour, / and swords like compass-needles turn / toward His heart" [47]).

Tortured, imprisoned, and exiled by mid-nineteenth-century Persian and Arab authorities who feared the influence of his teachings, Bahá'u'lláh aligned his own suffering with that of prophets before him. In *The Kitáb-Í-*

Iqán (*Book of Certitude*), a central theological text of the Bahá'í Faith that is primarily an explication of the mediating role played by "Messengers of God" in the interaction between divinity and humanity, Bahá'u'lláh explains that throughout the course of human history these Messengers have been received with similar brutality. In another text he states, "Consider the former generations. Witness how every time the Day Star of Divine bounty hath shed the light of His revelation upon the world, the people of His Day have risen against Him and repudiated His truth" (*Gleanings* 56). Elsewhere he mentions the "agonies" that these rare Luminaries have endured: "At no time, in no Dispensation, have the Prophets of God escaped the blasphemy of their enemies, the cruelty of their oppressors, the denunciation of the learned of their age who appeared in the guise of uprightness and piety. Day and night they passed through such *agonies* as none can ever measure" (*Gleanings* 58, emphasis added). Read in the shadow of these and other pronouncements of Bahá'u'lláh, the opening line of the poem appears to argue that the truth of Bahá'u'lláh's revelation is "confirmed" by the inevitable "agonies" that he, like all other Prophets of God, endured. This reading is augmented by the next two lines of the stanza: the "swords like compass-needles" point toward Bahá'u'lláh precisely because he is a Prophet of God. Hayden's poem suggests that one can identify—or, following Hayden's metaphor, locate—the true Prophet by the inescapable agonies of persecution that will be directed his way. The swords of affliction have no choice; like compass needles that invariably find north, they must "turn / toward His heart."

Of course, the narrative of the prophet rejected inevitably and violently by the misguided is consistent across many cultural traditions and is deeply resonant with the secular Western figure presented in Plato's "Allegory of the Cave." Whether he is a divine messenger or a philosopher-seer, the archetypal prophet is persecuted because he brings word of another reality, a realm that is at once immaterial and *truer* than the lightless cave experienced by the denizens of humanity. Part of Hayden's devout fascination with Bahá'u'lláh arises from his attraction to the mediating role of the prophet who stands between the world of ideal forms and the relatively benighted world of sensory-perceived reality that—as Santayana puts it—"misses and suggests" the ideal (qtd. in Keith 4). The suggestively titled "Travelling through Fog," captures Hayden's frustration with the limits of materiality and best underscores Wilburn William's assessment that Hayden is a poet "whose symbolist imagination is intent upon divining the shape of a transcendent order" barely discernable in the darkness of material reality (66):

Between obscuring cloud
And cloud, the cloudy dark
Ensphering us seems all we can
Be certain of. Is Plato's cave. (*Collected Poems* 122)

In "Bahá'u'lláh in the Garden of Ridwan" materiality alludes to the ideal order beyond the clouds and outside the cave—the prophet's "cosmic" heroism is the function of his unique capacity to straddle these linked realms. The tension between the seen and unseen worlds becomes the central theme of Hayden's hagiography as it turns to a description of the event that took place "in a borrowed garden" just outside Baghdad in the spring of 1863. Having lived in the Ottoman metropolis for nearly ten years after being exiled from his native Persia, Bahá'u'lláh was again banished by authorities fearful of his influence but not prepared simply to bring about his death. In the days leading up to his departure from the city, Bahá'u'lláh, his family, and several hundred followers gathered on the outskirts of Baghdad. It was there that Bahá'u'lláh is said to have announced that he was a Prophet of God.

Aside from the title, only two lines give clear indication that it is the Prophet's public declaration that is under consideration. The second stanza of the poem begins with one of those points of reference but immediately moves into the more mystical register that describes the metaphysical significance of Bahá'u'lláh's material proclamation:

The midnight air is forested
    with presences that shelter Him
        and sheltering praise
The auroral darkness which is God
    and sing the word made flesh again
        in Him,
Eternal exile whose return
    epiphanies repeatedly
        foretell. (47)

The presences foresting the night air exist in an invisible realm that is the compliment of the visible, material world but that is alive with recognition of divinity's nearness. These numinous forms that shelter and praise Bahá'u'lláh from their unseen world are the ideal and almost antithetical counterparts of the debased material beings that persecute rather than celebrate the spirit of God returned in human form.

While Hayden seems syntactically clever by playing upon Bahá'u'lláh's several banishments and making him into an "Eternal exile whose return" is continually prophesied, the poet also gestures toward a fundamental tenet of Bahá'í theology, which holds that not only was Bahá'u'lláh the return of Christ—which Hayden intimates by evoking the Gospel of John and calling him "the word made flesh again"—but also that all the Prophets of God are essentially one and the same. Bahá'u'lláh is an eternal exile because his suffering is only the latest to be visited upon those Prophets who are periodically sent to humanity and whose advents are always awaited and "repeatedly foretold." For the reader familiar with the writings of Bahá'u'lláh, this recalls another passage from the *Kitáb-Í-Iqán* that articulates foundational theology of the Bahá'í Faith:

> It is clear and evident to thee that all the Prophets are the Temples of the Cause of God, Who have appeared clothed in divers attire. If thou wilt observe with discriminating eyes, thou wilt behold Them all abiding in the same tabernacle, soaring in the same heaven, seated upon the same throne, uttering the same speech, and proclaiming the same Faith. Such is the unity of those Essences of Being, those Luminaries of infinite and immeasurable splendor! Wherefore, should one of those Manifestation of Holiness proclaim saying: "I am the return of all the Prophets," He, verily, speaketh the truth. In like manner, in every subsequent Revelation, the return of the former Revelation is a fact, the truth of which is firmly established. (141–42)

Compressing Bahá'u'lláh's theological schema into verse, Hayden's poem affirms that the Prophet is the manifestation of an eternal being who, though continually anticipated and heralded, has appeared throughout history only to be subjected to agonies of persecution and rejection.

The second reference to the event around which the poem is organized places Bahá'u'lláh in the Garden of Ridwan—meaning "paradise" in Persian. Here, the description of the scene is sustained for a stanza and a half as Hayden's verse dramatizes accounts of that night in which the Prophet is said to have chanted prayers while most of his companions slept:

> He watches in a borrowed garden,
>   prays. And sleepers toss upon
>   their armored beds,
> Half-roused by golden knocking at
>   the doors of consciousness. (47)

Hayden's Bahá'u'lláh watches more than the restless sleepers in his immediate vicinity. With slumber the symbol of spiritual heedlessness, the disturbed sleep that Bahá'u'lláh observes while praying metaphorizes the agitation of a humanity that, though desirous of salvation, persists in its negligence, asleep to the appearance of a new Prophet of God.[3] The "golden knocking"—which the sleepers discern only as faint disruptions outside the ironically armoring shell of their dreams—is produced by the "presences" that animate that parallel world of ideal forms that is unseen though completely awake to the momentous occasion of Bahá'u'lláh's declaration. Indeed, Hayden closes the poem with the midnight torpor of a heedless humanity set against the frantic excitement that prevails in a spiritual, idealized reality:

> Energies
>   like angels dance
> Glorias of recognition.
>   Within the rock the undiscovered suns
>   Release their light.[4]

Hayden's hymn to Bahá'u'lláh demonstrates a remarkable fidelity not only to the theological tenets of his faith but also to thematic and metaphorical structures that are found throughout Bahá'í writings. For example, the poem appears as though it could be Hayden's versification of the following prose passage written by 'Abdu'l-Bahá, the son of Bahá'u'lláh and the chief promulgator of the Bahá'í Faith in the early twentieth century:

> The Call of God, when raised, breathed new life into the body of mankind, and infused a new spirit into the whole creation. It is for this reason that the world hath been moved to its depths, and the hearts and consciences of man been quickened. Erelong the evidences of this regeneration will be revealed, and the fast asleep will be awakened. (qtd. in Effendi, *World Order* 169)

In "Bahá'u'lláh and the Garden of Ridwan" Hayden's interpolation of key Bahá'í ideas demonstrates a type of orthodox religious fidelity that is deeply consequential to the hermeneutic of history that dominates the final twenty-five years of his career—a fidelity that sets him apart from just about every other significant black poet since the 1940s. These points merit reiteration in order to distinguish Hayden's religiousness from that of a poet like Sonia Sanchez, who—for a few years in the early 1970s—wrote as a disciple of the

Nation of Islam. During that period, Sanchez produced religiously devout poems, but as her feminism clashed with some of its tenets, Sanchez discarded the Nation of Islam and its theology (see Tate 138–39). Hayden's contrastively long commitment to the Bahá'í Faith was characterized by an enduring devotion that persisted through personal crises of faith. He expressed religious and theological doubts in later poems like "Ice Storm" that seem to question the possibility of divine will and benevolence, but he would never reject his religion or attempt to fashion a self-satisfying spiritualism. Unlike a spiritually inclined poet such as Jay Wright, a "cherished friend" of Hayden and one of his literary descendants (see Rowell, "Unraveling of the Egg" 8; Hayden, letter to Wright), Hayden never expressed a desire for religious license or asserted interest in a self-conceived spiritual framework like that of Carolyn Rodgers, who in 1969 claimed belief in "the power of NOMMO, JUJU and the collective force of the positive spirits, moving in time with the universe" (10). While Wright could produce lines such as, "Arrogant like this / I have begun to design / my own god" (151), in his artistic maturity Hayden's explorations of spirituality—whether celebratory or resistant—were continually constructed in relation to sanctioned interpretations of Bahá'í teachings. Hayden wrote as a disciple (albeit a sometimes questioning disciple) bound to his faith in a Prophet who spoke of a transcendent and ideal world that Hayden called the "reality behind appearances" (*Collected Prose* 121).

The poet described the search for this reality as one of his "favorite themes" (*Collected Prose* 121). And in some senses the effort to make out a reality beyond the appearances of the material world is an archetypal theme in African American cultural life. Indeed, as Mullen and others have pointed out, the African American literary tradition finds part of its origin in spiritual autobiographies in which narrators "often forsake a 'bourgeois perception' of reality for 'things unseen' or 'signs in the heavens'" (*Cracks* 84). The transcendent cosmology that emerged in the Negro Church of the nineteenth century gave organization and meaning to the experience of black folk who, "losing the joy of this world, eagerly seized upon the offered conceptions of the next," as W. E. B. Du Bois put it (*Souls* 192). Hayden was raised squarely within the cultural and epistemological tradition of the Negro Church, and his interest in the call of another world, his response to "golden knocking at the doors of consciousness," is in one respect the expected inclination of the folk believer. But it can only be called a vestige inclination, because like that of the great majority of twentieth-century black intellectuals, Hayden's encounter with a larger kingdom of culture estranged him from the folk matrix closely linked to the Negro Church.

Chapter 3

The Aesthetics of Changing Churches

———

Religiousness in Black Arts–Era Poetry

———

James Hall profitably describes Hayden's conversion and serious devotion to the Bahá'í Faith as an instance of African American "anti-modernism"—a sign of implicit grievance with an American modernity that failed to sustain the black artist-intellectual. By figuring his conversion as a response to the "dis-ease" brought on by midcentury American life, Hall is able to put Hayden in a diverse group that includes icons like W. E. B. Du Bois, Bob Kaufman, John Coltrane, and Malcolm X, all of whom underwent significant ideological conversions in the middle decades of the twentieth century. As Hall explains it,

> These alterations of faith are certainly indicative of the ways in which previously held cosmologies cease to produce comfort. Collectively, however, they are emblematic of a more general dis-ease or disappointment with American culture and the resources, both material and spiritual, that that culture provides to the black artist. Conversion is a rich means of organizing the self in which a sense of alienation from modernity often resides. (16)

In labeling these icons and their conversions "anti-modern," Hall emphasizes their general rejection of rationalist, consumerist, and racist logics of American modernity. However, implicit in Hall's reading of midcentury black intellectual history is the understanding that the Negro Church was the primary locus of those "previously held cosmologies" also rejected by the

52

black creative elite. Thus, although Hayden's intense and orthodox expression of religious belief was anomalous among black intellectuals, in turning to the Bahá'í Faith he joined the great majority of twentieth-century black artist-intellectuals who sought philosophical and spiritual sustenance from sources outside of Christianity. While the critique and refusal of key elements of Western modernity is a crucial and often-explored aspect of black intellectual and cultural production in the twentieth century, the black artist-intellectual's rejection of the Negro Church is an equally important narrative in American social and cultural history. In abandoning the cosmology of the Negro Church, black intellectuals necessarily migrated out of the institutional structures that were at the heart of the black folk community and to varying degrees found themselves estranged from the beliefs and social practices of the black majority—even as they often wanted to represent, celebrate, and commune with that majority.

Perhaps more than any other influential black poet of the twentieth century, Hayden used verse to consciously consider his *distance* from forms of community and culture associated with the black folk masses. In poems written in the 1950s, 1960s, and 1970s, Hayden frequently contemplated his vexed relation to the denizens of the Detroit ghetto in which he was raised. He also used these poems to question his youthful desire to move beyond the ghetto—his desire "to get out of Detroit in order to survive," as he once put it in a private letter (Letter to Dorothy Lee). His poetic remembrances of the black folk world which he escaped but never left behind are consistently marked by ambivalent reference to the cosmology and culture of the Negro Church.

In his "Electrical Storm," for example, Hayden charts his own uneasy, conflicted response to the social processes that separated him from the "true believers" of his Baptist childhood. The downed electric wires of the poem's storm spare the speaker but kill some, creating a "sill" between this world and another. For the "grey neglected ones" who populate the speaker's remembered childhood, the storm would be heaven's open window through which Jehovah shouts in thunderous "oldtime wrath," calling over some but leaving others. Hayden's sophisticated adult narrator must rebut the superstitions of his people and his youth. But unwilling to attribute his survival of the storm to either "heavenly design / or chance," Hayden's speaker cannot easily abide by the meteorological explanations of a learned materialism:

I huddled too, when a boy,
mindful of things they'd told me

God was bound to make me answer for.
But later I was colleged (as they said)
and learned it was not celestial ire
(Beware the infidels, my son)
but pressure systems,
colliding massive energies
that make a storm.
Well for us. . . . (5)

Here and throughout the poem, the discourse of science will not silence those folk voices shaped by the lessons of the church. And so it is Hayden's speaker who straddles worlds in tension. The poem is not strictly an affirmation of faith, as Hatcher (149) characterizes it, or an example of his devotion to black vernacular tradition, as other critics have noted (Turner 97); rather, it is also the staging of an archetypal dilemma in African American literary history. Hayden's poem considers what can be termed *the anxiety of rootedness*. Planted in the soil of black folklife but "colleged" and growing beyond it, Hayden's speaker experiences "a storm" that has continually rocked African American intellectual life. The "pressure systems, colliding massive energies" that Hayden places in the poem are competing epistemologies that press upon the black artist-intellectual who will not abandon the premodern black folk matrix from which he emerges, despite being schooled in the ways of a Western modernity that implicitly urge him away from the folk. Thus the poem's central existential question—is our stormy journey through life determined by "heavenly design / or chance"?—braids into a value judgment about the efficacy of folk philosophy and, by extension, black folklife. As one perceptive critic notes, Hayden is content to leave the existential question "dangling like the electrical wires" that the storm makes deadly (Post 199). But in refusing to commit fully to the empiricism of secular Western thought, Hayden also asserts a lingering allegiance to his roots in the Baptist Church of his childhood and youth. While it was the metaphysics of Bahá'u'lláh, rather than that of the Negro Church, that illuminated his mature poetry, Hayden never relinquished his deep attachment to theories of "heavenly design" that he learned from the "true believers" of his folk childhood.[1] Hayden's Bahá'í Faith extended a mystical and transcendent sensibility that was contiguous with the religious philosophy of the folk.

In his postconversion maturity Hayden appreciated the church and its people, but from a distance that readily is felt in "Those Winter Sundays," the anthology fixture that one aggressively comparative critic calls "one of the best published sonnets ever written" (Schneider). As in "Electrical Storm," Hayden's speaker is the grown, "colleged" man reflecting on his folk roots. The autobiographical persona of "Those Winter Sundays" shows belated appreciation for a father who could articulate paternal compassion only through his manual labor. The formal artistry of the poem is well documented, as is the poignant admixture of gratitude and remorse that wracks the speaker when he comes to his final declarative question—"What did I know, what did I know / of love's lonely and austere offices?" (41). While the poem evokes the father's "labor in the weekday weather," it is his Sunday work in the home that sparks the speaker's recognition. There are only two symbolically charged tasks that the father performs on what should be his day of rest: before the speaker wakes, his father has "driven out the cold / and polished my good shoes as well." With the poem's early alliterative attention to the "blue black cold" that is subdued as the father makes "banked fire blaze," it is the creation of physical warmth that prominently represents the emotional care that the hard-laboring father cannot put into words. This deeply symbolic work overshadows the seemingly secondary and minor task that the father performs in polishing the speaker's "good shoes." But these are his Sunday church shoes, and the polishing is something more than the paternal preparation of a sheltering physical space. Here Hayden's adult speaker expresses decades-delayed appreciation for his father's efforts at spiritual guidance through the church.[2] First published in *Ballad of Remembrance* (1962), in the wake of James Baldwin's deeply critical and influential treatment of the Negro Church in *Go Tell It on the Mountain* (1953), not long before the BAM would produce its own powerful critique of Christian ideology, and several decades after Hayden's turn to the Bahá'í Faith, the poem's positive allusion to the influence of the church is somewhat unexpected. But the resonances between the spiritual teachings of the Bahá'í Faith and the Negro Church meant that Hayden felt a religious connection to the black folk world even though he, like most black artist intellectuals, was estranged from it as he accumulated intellectual, cultural, and material capital—or by what Phillip Brian Harper has called "inexorable social processes" (*Are We* 51).[3]

Hayden used his poems to explore the *cleaved* relation between the artist-intellectual and the folk—at once strangers and family. This acknowledgment of the experiential cleavage created by the inexorable social processes of education and employment in academia, and so on, set him apart from many black writers of the 1960s and 1970s who sought to eliminate rather than contemplate the distance between themselves and their folk subjects. (As I'll argue in chapter 7, Hayden's acceptance and poetic study of the vexed relation between the black folk and the black artist-intellectual is part of what makes him so attractive to "postsoul" poets who came of age in a post–civil rights, neoliberal era characterized by intensifying fissures in the black class structure.) In "Those Winter Sundays" the stark distance between Hayden's speaker and his conjured father figure is felt even as the poem manages to create a momentary connection between the "colleged" intellectual whose mastery of language is on display in the text and the older man who can communicate only through the labor of his body. Indeed, much of the poem's power is generated through Hayden's effort to simultaneously *create and bridge* the gulf of separation between its two characters, one emblematic of the black artist-intellectual and the other emblematic of the folk masses. This somewhat paradoxical relation, wherein the speaker is at once near and far from his people, is characteristic of Hayden's representations of folklife in the northern ghetto. It was also reified in Hayden's devout belief in a Bahá'í Faith that, with its emphasis on transcendence and a teleologically organized cosmos, allowed him to maintain a connection to the mystical folkways institutionalized in the Negro Church, even as it pulled him from Baptist roots and positioned him in an integrated, Eastern-oriented American religious community that was quite foreign to the black masses.

Written in the late 1950s, E. Franklin Frazier's venerable sociohistorical analysis *The Negro Church in America* (1964) suspiciously regards the small number of black converts to the Bahá'í Faith. Frazier attributes their attraction to the faith to middle-class race shame and a desire to evade association with poorer black brethren. He writes, "Some middle-class Negroes in their seeking to find escape from the Negro identification have gone from the Catholic church to the Christian Science church and then to the Bahaist church [*sic*]" (84). Locating the Bahá'í Faith at the far reaches of a religious continuum that stretches away from the Baptist heart of black community, Frazier's assessment helps explain why some scholars with black nationalist inclinations have looked skeptically on the Bahá'í inflection of Hayden's spiritualism. And considered in the light of Frazier's study of political economy and religion, Hayden's embrace of the Bahá'í Faith can appear as though it is the complement of a poetics characterized by a certain aesthetic distance from black folklife. That is to say, coupling Hayden's move away from the Baptist heart of the black folk community and his unwillingness to aesthetically assert a simple commonality with the folk masses, some unsympathetic observers have concluded that Hayden harbored Western modernity's general disdain for black life. Indeed, one 1970s critic first notes Hayden's use of "standard academic English with no black flavor" and then goes on to contrast the poet's reverence for Bahá'í subject matter with his apparent degradation of "Afro-American religions, religious leaders and believers." The critic concludes that "since religion is a controlling element in any culture, one can only infer that [Hayden's] overall attitude to his own Afro-American culture is correspondingly negative" (Jemie 166).

While this type of crude inference has rarely been articulated in more recent assessments of Hayden's work, a similar—but class-inflected—critique appears in Amiri Baraka's scathing review of the Charles Rowell–edited and Hayden-centric *Angles of Ascent: A Norton Anthology of Contemporary African American Poetry* (2013). Showing that Hayden's political and aesthetic commitments remained a flashpoint in critical discourse about African American poetry almost fifty years after his well-known encounters at the Fisk conference, Baraka produces a *false* memory in which he confronts Hayden at the 1966 conference and implies that Hayden's effort to write the graphocentric, transcendent poetry that put him at odds with some common tenets of the BAM was motivated by a desire for upward class mobility.[4] At one point Baraka—once a student of E. Franklin Frazier—keys on the Hayden line that gives title to the anthology and asks sarcastically, "Ascent to where? A tenured faculty position?" He goes on to contrast Hayden's work, and that of his literary descendants, with BAM poetry that putatively could "function in the ghettos where we lived" ("Post-Racial" n.p.).

Baraka's ivory tower/ebony ghetto dialectic activates a familiar discourse that ties together race and class to impugn Rowell and Hayden's attenuated relation to the black folk community and, in turn, question the political-aesthetic judgment of black poets like Hayden who have placed high value on what Rowell calls "the interior world" and who take only limited guidance from black vernacular aesthetics (*Angles* xxix). But while the consideration of class dynamics is essential to the assessment of literary production of the Black Arts era, Baraka's strategic application of this framework does little to illuminate Hayden's political-aesthetic motivations. It implicitly chalks up Hayden's distanced aesthetic to racially irresponsible material aspiration and occludes the possibility that Hayden's Apollonian, writerly poetics represented a form of cultural production that was most authentic for artist-intellectuals who were inevitably distanced from the folkways of the black "ghettos" by the inexorable social processes that customarily spawn literary life. It also hides the class complexities and anxieties that produced the strong folk sympathies of Baraka and other poets associated with the BAM.

In defending against the accusation that his poetry could not "function" in the world of poor black folk and was thus racially inauthentic, Hayden and his critical advocates often evoked his impoverished childhood and youth. A veritable orphan, adopted and raised with love but also abuse in the often-destitute home of an uneducated "coal-wagon driver" (Fetrow, *Robert Hayden* 5), Hayden knew the ghetto well and was intimately familiar with both its privations and its rich folk culture. The implication that this biography served to authenticate the blackness of his poetry surfaces on several occasions in Hayden's interviews and prose of the 1970s. Feeling a need to underscore obscured origins, from time to time the poet would testify on his own behalf: "My family was poor, hardworking, with no education. . . . My roots are really very deep in what I like to call Afro-American folk life" (*Collected Prose* 79). As if to remind interlocutors that his adolescent formation was not like that of Baraka and other BAM poets who came from middle-class contexts, Hayden was wont to point out that "some of us know what real poverty is" (*Collected Prose* 15). Clarifications such as "Remember, I grew up in the ghetto" (*Collected Prose* 25) crescendo in sections of his late-in-life essay "The Life: Some Remembrances," which employs the distancing properties of third-person narration while evoking the poet's visceral familiarity with "slum life": "How well he knew this part of town, having spent twenty-seven years of his life there, moving always, as he liked to say, from one dilapidated house to another" (*Collected Prose* 20–21). These reminders attempt to give credence to Hayden's defensive, yet confident, boast that "I could have been the blackest of the blacks if I had wanted to do it" ("Interview with Gendron" 20).

A similar parry operates in the work of Hayden's scholarly defenders. Michael Harper's obituary remembrance of his friend, which seems to leverage Hayden's biography in order to authenticate the blackness—or the gritty depth—of his poetry, exemplifies a tenor characteristic of critics compelled to substantiate his place in an African American literary cannon. Harper's eulogy returns Hayden to a proverbial bosom of blackness, offering the reminder that Hayden had "done time, as a youth, in the red-light district; he'd done time in the Baptist church, where so many folk people lived" ("Every Shut Eye" 110). The pregnant phrasing—"he'd done time"—is multivalent. While it begins a form of credentialing that would seem to imbue Hayden's voice with black legitimacy, it also suggests that the poet was once imprisoned within a folk community from which he had been released—or escaped. Harper explicitly associates his friend with the profane and sacred spaces where so many folk people lived because Hayden's aesthetic practice, like his spiritual practice, seemed like willful moves away from those spaces. In the wake of the BAM, the distance between Hayden and folk people could appear particularly pronounced. As I will elaborate later in this section, although many BAM poets were very much like Hayden in their affiliations with academic institutions—as opposed to red-light districts—and in their flight from the Baptist Church, in poetry they bonded themselves to economically and socially marginalized black folk by combining vernacular aesthetics with a quasi-religious black nationalism. In the socioliterary atmosphere of the Black Arts era and subsequent decades, Hayden's contrasting adherence to a writerly aesthetic and to the religious frameworks of the Bahá'í Faith produced an appearance of racial disconnection that he and his supporters addressed through the type of exculpatory, extrapoetic testimony noted above.

Eugene Redmond's sweeping treatment of the African American poetic tradition, *Drumvoices: The Mission of Afro-American Poetry: A Critical History* (1976), alludes to the *historically unique* forms of literary judgment that coalesced in the Black Arts era and prompted Hayden and his advocates to marshal biographical defenses of his poetry. Somewhat wary of the stifling propensities in the new forms of black literary criticism, Redmond notes that "over the past few years of social change and unrest, the black poet whose aesthetic or religious position was not aligned with that of vested interest groups came up before many a *strange* court" (421, emphasis in original). Although Hayden is not singled out as one of these prosecuted poets, it is likely that Redmond—whose study returns to Hayden with fair frequency—had him in mind when evoking the unaligned "aesthetic or religious position" of some poets. Elsewhere in his indispensable book, Redmond seems to conflate Hayden's religious and aesthetic positions, attributing to the poet a "Bahá'í aesthetic" that exists in opposition to a "black aesthetic" advanced by other Black Arts–era poets (415). But it is confusing to assert that Hayden worked with a Bahá'í aesthetic, as opposed to a black aesthetic. Some of his poems engage Bahá'í subject matter, and many are thematically and even formally impacted by Bahá'í theology and social philosophy, but Hayden's aesthetic position is actually grounded in the African American literary tradition chronicled in Redmond's work. The principle of "aesthetic distance," which is a defining element of Hayden's philosophy of art, was a guiding ideal in most African American literature up until the radical revolutions and *strange* courts of the Black Arts era. As I will examine at greater length at the end of this section, certain elements of the anticlerical, highly literate Bahá'í culture and doctrine seemed to endorse Hayden's Apollonian and graphocentric poetics, but his penchant for aesthetic distance grew out of a long tradition in African American literature.

Aesthetic Distance and the Circle of Blackness

In a Black Arts literary context that put a premium on poetic magic that disappeared the space between the artist-intellectual and the black urban masses, Hayden was both odd and consistent in his use of an aesthetic technique that called attention to the distance separating his poetic personae from the folk. For example, in his highly regarded renderings of black life in the urban North, such as "Elegies for Paradise Valley," Hayden constructed necessarily distanced *remembrances* of an ennobled folk world that is judged beautiful, derelict, and painful. Retreating into third-person narration, Hayden most brilliantly captures his paradoxically cleaved relation to the folk ghetto in the opening octave-stanza of "'Summertime and the Living . . .'":

> Nobody planted roses, he recalls,
> but sunflowers gangled there sometimes,
> tough-stalked and bold
> and like the vivid children there unplanned.
> There circus-poster horses curveted
> in trees of heaven
> above the quarrels and shattered glass,
> and he was bareback rider of them all. (39)

Hayden's speaker remembers his own "unplanned" childhood and is both near and far from the sharp, cutting life of the ghetto folk world. "He" floats above it as a Pegasus-mounted observer—yet, as "bareback *rider*," *writer* Hayden is viscerally attuned to the hurt of that ghetto world. First published in the mid-1950s, "'Summertime'" establishes the distanced perspectival design that Hayden would use to great effect in his later intimate-yet-detached remembrances of the black folk world in poems like "Those Winter Sundays," "The Whipping," "Electrical Storm," and "Elegies for Paradise Valley." These poems and others play in an erudite diction and emphasize temporal separation to create a lens that removes the poet-speaker from the folk milieu and affords him a space for an analysis of black life. When an interviewer asked Hayden about the "impersonal tone in almost all" his poems, he justified his method in expected terms: "Let me say that perhaps the detachment you mention is a matter of aesthetic or psychic distance. By standing back a little from the experience, by objectifying to a degree, I'm able to gain a perspective not otherwise possible" (*Collected Prose* 121). Phillip Richards has identified this distance from the folk world as a chief virtue of Hayden's poetry. For

Richards it is a function of Hayden's "cosmopolitan" perspective that favorably contrasts with the parochialism and under-distancing of the Black Arts ethos that very often pushed poets into uncomplicated identification with the black community (174, 178). In African American literary criticism of the (vernacular valorizing) post-movement era, finding *positive value* in any artist's distance from the folk is a contrarian move that few besides Richards have explored. Prevailing forms of recent criticism have shared the evaluative premises of a black aesthetic that most valued art as a form of ritual springing from and immediately usable by the folk community.[5] Richards's esteem for Hayden is based largely on principles derived from an aesthetic tradition that was rejected by Black Arts advocates and that is often eschewed in recent African American letters.

When Richards avers that "Hayden, years after his death remains our most influential black poet, and his followers the most productive and distinguished school of artist-intellectuals" (178), his framework of assessment implicitly esteems the aesthetic principle of "psychical distance" first explicitly theorized by Edward Bullough in 1912. Among Hayden and "his followers" Richards values a deliberate form of artistic detachment or distance, a modicum of which Bullough thought necessary for the production of worthwhile art. Hayden, like many poets who have learned from him, was indebted to and spiritually near the black folk community, but his mature poetry never masqueraded as an unreformed folk art. Instead it issued from the involved distance Bullough described: "Distance does not imply an impersonal, purely intellectually interested relation of such a kind. On the contrary, it describes a *personal* relation, often highly emotionally coloured, but *of a peculiar character*. Its peculiarity lies in that the personal character of the relation has been, so to speak, filtered" (461, emphasis in the original).

Hayden's general affinity for the filtering distance of an observational perspective is felt strongly in his late poem "American Journal." Narrated by a "humanoid" alien anthropologically documenting American society, the poem is transmitted from a conscience that is removed distinctly from the social milieu it traverses. Like other critics, Yusef Komunyakaa has admiringly compared Hayden himself to the narrator of "American Journal," who identifies with his object of study yet is also alien to it—who, as Komunyakaa puts it, is "an insider/outsider, a freak in an elastic limbo" (334). The quandary of liminality evoked in Hayden's "American Journal" has been apparent to the black artist in America since before Du Bois made his endlessly influential effort to concretize the dilemma as the condition of double consciousness. As Houston Baker notes, the literary works of the earliest African

Americans "reveal a vista of searching men and women caught between two worlds" (*Journey Back* 3). In the black intellectual tradition, the "peculiar sensation" of double consciousness—which, in one respect, simply amounts to an alienation from mainstream society—is often linked to a "second sight" that gives special clarity to black observation of American society.[6] However, in Hayden's poetry a generative sense of alienation is felt not only in the poet's relation to mainstream America but also in his relation to the black folk community. By the time he began writing his mature verse, it seems that Hayden had stepped outside of a "circle of blackness." In Richards's anomalous but formidable assessment, it is this liminal relation to the folk that significantly contributes to Hayden's lasting achievement as a poet-documentarian of black folklife. Having "done time . . . in the place where so many folk people lived" but also having consciously escaped that place, Hayden was positioned to be like Bullough's ideal filtering artist: "He will prove artistically most effective in the formulation of an intensely *personal* experience, but he can formulate it artistically only on condition of a detachment from the experience *qua personal*" (463, emphasis in original).

Bullough's artist was to be, like Hayden, only slightly removed from his object—striving for "the *utmost decrease of Distance without its disappearance*" (463, emphasis in original). This call for intimate distance resonates with early theory at the nexus of literary aesthetics and the interpretation of black folk culture. In his famous reflection on the "sorrow songs" in *Narrative of the Life of Frederick Douglass, an American Slave* (1845), Douglass archetypally evokes a literal and aesthetic *distance* that would characterize the interpretive work of those who, like Hayden, emerged from the bosom of black folk culture to become literary artists. Douglass writes, "I did not, when a slave, understand the deep meaning of those rude and apparently incoherent songs. I was myself within the circle; so that I neither saw nor heard as those without might see and hear" (24). The sorrow songs—quintessential folk texts—were functional for those who produced them but, according to Douglass, not fully comprehensible until the singer was "without" the circle. He counsels one who desires an understanding of the black songs to "place himself in the deep pine woods, and there let him, in silence, analyze the sounds that shall pass through the chambers of his soul" (24).

This nineteenth-century call for interpretive distance endorses Hayden's artistic relation to black culture; he was like Douglass's passionate analyst who stood just beyond the circle, lonely perhaps, but attentive to the sounds of blackness and personally familiar with their folk origins. For Hayden, the black writer was not rightly a *producer* of folk culture but rather its interpreter, tasked to render its insights in the medium of literature. This type of literary ethic went mostly unchallenged from the antebellum period until the advent of the Black Arts era. Although James Smethurst's work calls attention to the fact that African American poets of the 1920s and 1930s displayed "a relative identification with the black folk subject" (*New Red* 24), aesthetic distance remained the order of the day, even at the height of the Old Left social realist moment. Indeed, only a year before Hayden produced his first collection of verse in 1940, the influential black critic J. Saunders Redding published his assessment of the African American literary tradition, *To Make a Poet Black* (1939). Redding's prescriptive effort in canon formation—one of the first studies to make such an attempt—advises black writers to seek inspiration in the "enigmatic soul of the simple negro" (48), but Redding hoped that the literary artist would effect an elevation of folk material or carry "the folk-gift to the altitude of art," as Alain Locke had endorsed during the Harlem Renaissance ("Negro Youth" 48). Redding enthusiastically quotes James Weldon Johnson, who finds the proper relation to folk culture captured in the poetry of Sterling Brown's *Southern Road* (1932). In reference to Brown, Johnson would write, "He has made more than mere transcription of folk poetry, and he has done more than bring it to mere artistry; he has deepened its meaning and multiplied its implication" (qtd. in Redding 122). Like Brown, Johnson, Locke, Redding, and Douglass before him, Hayden believed that the infinite, enigmatic experience of the folk contained a meaning that was to be *transubstantiated* into a valuable literary art.[7]

But, by the middle of the 1960s, guiding lights of the BAM began to attack long-held aesthetic ideals as they characterized the African American literary tradition as a failure, addressed to whites and inconsequential to the black folk (Neal, "Shine Swam" 650). The thin layer of interpretive distance prescribed by Douglass, Bullough, and Redding became suspect in black aesthetic theories that argued for what was essentially a premodern art that was both social activity and folk ritual and taught that the separation of the artist from his social milieu was an ideal of the dying West. As James Stewart asserts in the opening essay of the *Black Fire* anthology, "white Western aesthetics is predicated on the idea of separating one from the other—a man's art from his actions. It is this duality that is the most distinguishable feature of Western values" (9). While influential BAM figures attempted to destroy this value system, they necessarily questioned the validity of the literary enterprise itself. Compelled toward "relevance," BAM writers could adopt somewhat paradoxical, seemingly contra-literary positions. Despite attending a New England preparatory school before matriculating into Barnard College, June Jordan could write,

> Fuck you and your
> damned verbs
> let me tell it like
> it is
> nasty and funkey (qtd. in Redmond 382)

Amiri Baraka could charge that, "words are not immediate change. Crackers killed in revolutionary sentences are walking around killing us in the real streets" (Baraka and Abernathy, *In Our Terribleness* n.p.). And Don L. Lee/Haki Madhubuti, donning the folk language of the "real streets," wrote poems about the impotence of poetry: "i ain't seen no poems stop a .38 / i ain't seen no stanzas break a honkie's head" (qtd. in Henderson, *Understanding* 332). Frustrated by having to work with the enemy's language and aesthetic standards, purveyors of the new black literature sought to break the white man's tradition—if not his head—with a poetry in which the class and social position of the black artist-intellectual often disappeared in an undistanced poetics wholly guided by the idiom and exigencies of the northern urban folk masses.

Although the work of Smethurst and others has shown that the Black Arts Movement was composed of a great diversity of cultural production that emanated from a variety of regional loci, much of the production was informed by new guidelines that emphasized black particularity rather than universality—that emphasized the creation of art that appealed to an imagined black community rather than an abstract universal subject. In the BAM context, Hayden's attachment to a poetry of transcendence, achieved through distancing "angles of ascent" and linked to his universalist religious beliefs, seemed to align him with the, by then outmoded, integrationist stance of the civil rights movement. In 1970, when Hayden published "Words in the Mourning Time," his universalism could appear to be the poetic leftovers of high-minded speeches that Martin Luther King delivered in the mid-1960s. The poet's hope for a world where

> man
> is neither gook nigger honkey wop nor kike
> but man
> permitted to be man (98)

mirrored the millennial visions that King delineated in 1965 when it was not uncommon for the leader to conjure an integrated utopian future: "That will be the day not of the white man, not of the black man. That will be the day of man as man" (qtd. in Dance 324). Like King, Hayden hewed to a religiously inspired, teleological conception of history and also echoed the consensus of a postwar American and European intellectual elite that theoretically repudiated the language and logic of racial difference. But in the years leading up to King's assassination in 1968, primary voices of the Black Arts Movement maligned notions of aesthetic inclusivity and reverence for the universal "man" evoked by King—the universal "man as man" that Hayden's poetry was meant to touch with its aesthetic distance.[8] While Hayden testified, "As a Bahá'í I am committed to belief in the fundamental oneness of all races, the essential oneness of mankind, to the vision of world unity" (*Collected Prose* i), many poets of the Black Arts era sought a voice that was defiantly particular and—arguably setting the stage for some of the drawbacks of postmodern identitarianism—thoroughly skeptical of pluralist ideals. Because the particularity of this voice was enhanced if it appeared to spring from the very heart of the community to which it was meant to appeal, many influential BAM poets eliminated signs of aesthetic distance from the black world.

Finding hypocrisy at the heart of Western humanism and its apparent attachment to universal man, BAM poets wrote in the spirit of thinkers like Frantz Fanon, who counseled revolutionaries to "leave this Europe where they are never done talking of Man, yet murder men everywhere they find them, at the corner of every one of their own streets, in all corners of the globe" (235). As Etheridge Knight would phrase it in his poem "On Universalism,"

> I see no single thread
> That binds me one to all . . .
> . . .
> No universal laws
> Of human misery
> Create a common cause (qtd. in Henderson, *Understanding* 330)

BAM poets who were most concerned with strengthening the thread that bound the black artist to the black folk often tried to eliminate all traces of the distance that lay between the artist and "the people" as they mocked calls for interracial unity that were integral to Hayden's Bahá'í Faith and to that element of the civil rights movement strongly associated with King. Concisely capturing the evolution of political and aesthetic sensibility that marked the emergence of the Black Arts era, Madhubuti's 1968 poem "The New Integrationist" would become a touchstone for poets moving toward the "new black consciousness":[9]

> i
> seek
> integration
> of
> negroes
> with
> black
> people. (qtd. in Brooks, *Treasury* 13)

This was all at once a manifesto for racial unification, a repudiation of integrationist politics, a charting of the shift in the language of self-identification, and a subtle play on intraracial class dynamics. Its urge toward consolidation of disparate elements of an imagined African American community also points the way toward a BAM aesthetic that dispensed with the distance separating the culturally capitalized artist-intellectual and the folk subject-audience.

It is evident that the elimination of this aesthetic distance went hand in hand with a refusal of the integrationist agenda that guided the "the first stage of the black freedom movement in the 60s" (West 49), but it should also be noted that this repudiation of integrationism was bound up with a concomitant rejection of the doctrines of the Negro Church, which, through organizations like the Southern Christian Leadership Council, gave much institutional structure to the southern civil rights movement. The desire to bond closely with the black masses while also renouncing key doctrines of black Christianity presented some dilemmas for BAM poets. In the next chapter I argue that the remarkably influential model of performance and aesthetics honed by BAM poets emerged from their efforts to work though these dilemmas. If Robert Hayden tried to maintain a connection to the folk through honoring his Baptist roots and the theories of spiritual transcendence that linked the Bahá'í Faith of his maturity to the Negro Church of his youth, BAM poets who were deeply and vocally opposed to the theology and ideology of the Negro Church tried to connect themselves to its many followers in other ways. While rejecting the ideological and theological content of black Christianity, they reflexively honored its vernacular aesthetic by becoming black nationalist priests modeled after the church leaders so familiar to the folk masses.

Religious Black Nationalism, Preacherly Aesthetics, and the Office of the BAM Poet

As I have argued, the quality and degree of Hayden's religious orthodoxy was anomalous among postwar African American creative intellectuals, most of whom were moderns practicing the agnosticism of the Left or sporadic spiritual experimentalists. Very few of Hayden's peers took on a similarly rigorous commitment to organized religion or tried to filter their art through a consistently sacred eschatological skein. For BAM intellectuals like Addison Gayle, the political mandates of the black aesthetic grew from the basic materialist-humanist view "that in a universe devoid of gods, man is the central and most important entity" (Gayle 47). In the godless universe Madhubuti would testify, "I didn't pray—kept both eyes open" (qtd. in Henderson, *Understanding* 333), while in his "Keeping the Faith Blues" Henry Dumas summed up a prominent sentiment among nationalist artist-intellectuals that gave context to the later part of Hayden's career: "I'm keeping my own faith, people / Can't let religion / bust open my head" (qtd. in Henderson, *Understanding* 376). And as Amiri Baraka would put it, the proper black art "must kill any God anyone names except common sense" (qtd. in Baker, *Journey Back* 90).

In particular, it made good sense for major voices of the Black Arts Movement to proclaim the death of the Christian God of the West. Attacking the center of the white man's cosmology, nationalists were able to undermine Western value systems and distance themselves from the integrationist Christian rhetoric of the southern civil rights movement. This double move is exemplified in Charles Anderson's "Prayer to the White Man's God," the second poem printed in the *Black Fire* anthology:

> I've been prayin' for centuries
> To some God up in the sky.
> Lord, what's the delay?
> Help me live today.
> God said, Go 'way, boy
> I don't want to hear you cry,
> But I know Jesus heard me
> Cause he spit right in my eye. (Baraka and Neal 191)

Anderson's God is as good as dead, and his spitting Jesus is a perverse inversion of the nurturing protector evoked in gospel classics like "Jesus Gave

Me Water." The poem is a frank expression of the widely held nationalist opinion that throughout African American history, Christianity and the Negro Church mostly served as folk opium—a "great pacifier and palliative," as Baraka would characterize it in *Blues People* (38). The impulse was not new to African American letters—in the 1930s Langston Hughes, Richard Wright, and others had prominently and powerfully critiqued the Negro Church. However, the BAM critique was more than a repackaging of the Marxian and Communist Party thinking that underlay writers' attacks during the 1930s and 1940s; the strong criticism of the Negro Church that circulated in the BAM was an approximation of strategy that Malcolm X used to discredit the mainstream of the civil rights movement and its Bible-based theories of perpetual nonviolence rooted in faith that "unearned suffering is redemptive" (M. King 41). For Malcolm, the integrationist pacifism of the civil rights movement and the Negro Church from which it emerged were insidious tools of white oppression that had been in operation since the slavery era: "To Keep you from fighting back, he gets these old religious Uncle Toms to teach you and me, just like novocaine, to suffer peacefully. Don't stop suffering— just suffer peacefully. . . . This is a shame" (X and Breitman 12).

As BAM poets followed Malcolm into a powerful critique of the Negro Church, they both responded to and hastened the dissolution (or significant reorientation) of a spiritual practice that Du Bois had termed the "Faith of our Fathers" (*Souls* 183) and the institution that E. Franklin Frazier would call "the major form of social life among Negroes" (*Negro Church* 87). This attack on the principal belief system and institution of the Negro community is a key and rarely remarked upon complex of the BAM.[10] For, while its major theorist-explicators declared the movement "opposed to any concept of the artist that alienates him from his community" (L. Neal, "Black Arts Movement" 55), a significant mode of Black Arts poetry operated as a philosophical and political rebuke to the institution that stood at the very center of the black community. While aiming to create an art that addressed the exigencies of the folk, BAM poets had to negotiate the fact that the mass of black people were spiritually invested in the Negro Church, which was a prominent target of nationalist ideology and rhetoric.

Because primary agents of the BAM were cultural elites, artist-intellectuals, and—as in the case of Baraka—members of a midcentury black middle-class that had been drifting away from the church for decades (Frazier, *Negro Church* 84), their critique of the Christian tradition threatened to further distance them from the underclass that the Black Power movement "idolized"—to use terminology employed by Cornel West in his retrospective appraisal, "The Paradox of the Afro-American Rebellion" (53). Written in the mid-1980s, West's essay examines the Black Power era by way of political economy to highlight the intraracial class tensions at its heart. He characterizes the nationalist movement of that time as the project of a black petit bourgeois that harnessed for its own ends the culture and predicament of an oppressed, angry black proletariat. (When he writes, "Dashikis and Afros made non-bourgeoisie black folks of us all," Houston Baker's self-mocking lament over the denouement of the Black Power era similarly hints of the instrumentalist cultural strategies used by the middle-class black intelligentsia of the 1960s and 1970s [*Afro-American Poetics* 112].) While West's account tends to undervalue the movement's impact on cultural aesthetics and self-conception at all levels of the black class structure, his emphasis on the disconnection between the black petit bourgeois and proletariat draws attention to the potentially contradictory position of BAM artists who aggressively turned on the Negro Church even as they sought to "speak to the spiritual and cultural needs of Black people" (L. Neal, "Black Arts Movement" 55). West writes that, throughout the tumult of the era, "the black underclass continued to hustle, rebel when appropriate, get high and listen to romantic proletarian love songs produced by Detroit's Motown; they remained perplexed at their idolization by the 'new' black middleclass which they sometimes envied. *The black working poor persisted in its weekly church attendance*, struggled to make ends meet and waited to see what the beneficial results would be after all the 'hoopla' was over" (53, emphasis added).

Framed by West's schemata, Black Arts disdain for the Negro Church of the working poor calls to mind the Black Arts doublespeak pointed out by Phillip Brian Harper. Juxtaposing the BAM's general call for "nationalistic unity among people of African descent" and specific Black Arts poems that direct rhetorical violence at "negroes" who failed to exhibit the qualities of a conscientious "black nationalist subject," Harper shows that the poetry paradoxically proclaimed the virtues of black community while inciting and instantiating intraracial division (*Are We* 40). As the practitioners of the 1960s aesthetic attempted to carve out a viable nationalist ideology, many of them cut away at "counterrevolutionary" villains who were black—but misguided. Many of these misguided villains were upwardly mobile middle-class aspirants affecting whiteness. Harper calls attention to figures like Baraka's "imitation greyboy" trying to make an "ultrasophisticated point" and June Jordan's "Negroes" characterized by

clean fingernails crossed legs a smile
shined shoes
a crucifix around your neck
good manners. (qtd. in P. Harper, *Are We* 193, 201)[11]

These imagined characters were sullied by material success that brought them near a whiteness that perverted blackness. The straightforward title of Reginald Lockett's *Black Fire* poem, "Die Black Pervert" (Baraka and Neal, 354), epitomizes this strand of BAM poetry as it conflates economic achievement, Europhilia, and homosexuality in a single black straw man who can do nothing for the revolution except die. Although this type of aggressive rhetoric sacrificed a thoroughgoing racial solidarity, excising such strivers from the revolutionary community was a logical maneuver that exploited class tension. The educated poets of the BAM drew nearer to the "idolized" black underclass by castigating a bourgeoisie that, according to the influential social science of E. Franklin Frazier, had "rejected identification with the masses" in its attempts to integrate into the white mainstream (*Black Bourgeoisie* 168).

Degrading black middle-class culture was strategic counterpart to the BAM celebration of folkways preserved in an underclass that had neither the means nor (apparently) the desire to escape racial identity. To be accurate, not all poets associated with the BAM adopted the stridently anti-middle-class rhetoric of Lockett's "Die Black Pervert." Still, signs of bourgeois gentility, high-culture erudition, or even cerebral peculiarity were scrubbed from the work of many poets as they attempted to unify themselves with the working poor and stave off the appearance of effete intellectualism. These political-aesthetic strategies are apparent in any sampling of poetry from the era's many anthologies, which—as print culture scholar Howard Rambsy points out—collectively "solidified the formation of a distinct discourse and a canon of black poetry . . . that promoted black consciousness and made direct appeals to African American audiences" (*Black Arts Enterprise* 52). Once again, I am particularly interested in the *For Malcolm* collection, which became "one of the most well-known anthologies published by an African-American press" (Rambsy, *Black Arts Enterprise* 54). A gloss of this text, to which Hayden contributed, suggests that the "distinct discourse" that it helped establish was characterized by the efforts of poets not only to pay homage to Malcolm X, as Rambsy and others have pointed out, but also to graft themselves to those lower strata of the black class structure that Malcolm so inspired. Many of the poets included in this key BAM collection place themselves squarely in the folk milieu by liberally using collective pronouns of solidarity and by specializing their address to folk brothers and sisters through the use of what Stephen Henderson termed "Soul Talk" or "the living speech of the Black Community" (*Understanding* 33, 32).

This strategic employment of "living" black speech is striking in the two poems that Ted Joans contributed to the *For Malcolm* project. Although he was a surrealist poet with roots in the Beat movement and an accomplished painter and jazz musician who had close relations with luminous artist-intellectuals of the mid-twentieth century, like Aimé Césaire, André Breton, and Salvador Dalí, Joans drew near to the urban folk through an accentuation of vernacular language in the tellingly titled "True Blues for a Dues Payer" and "My Ace of Spades." He sent his contributions to Broadside Press from Morocco (where he lived in the late 1960s) and located a speaker "under quiet Maghreb bright night sky" (Burroughs and Randall 25), but Joans closes one poem with a rap couplet from the street corner ("I said goodbye to my soothsayer His Hipness Malcolm X / a true dues payer!" [25]) and punctuates the other by declaring that "Malcolm X tol' it lak it DAMN SHO' IS!!" (5). Venerated poets of an older generation, like Gwendolyn Brooks and Margaret Walker, also linked themselves to the folk community through the language they used in memorializing Malcolm. For example, Walker's poem evokes both racial and class discourses as her narrator addresses the folk as "you gambling sons and hooked children and bowery / bums / Hating White Devils and black bourgeoisie" (32); she then unites with the folk in the politicized camaraderie of collective pronouns that seem to exclude whites and middle-class blacks. Addressing Malcolm, Walker's speaker declares, "Beautiful were your sandpapering words against *our* skin / *Our* blood and water pour from your flowing wounds" (33, emphasis added). In her poem for the anthology, Brooks makes pointed use of collective pronouns that seem to be marked by race and gender, though not by class. Her speaker declares that, in response to Malcolm, "We gasped. We saw the maleness" (3).

That Joans, Walker, and Brooks make efforts to weld themselves into the black collectives impacted by Malcolm seems unremarkable—until it is contrasted with Robert Hayden's effort to narrate his "El Haj Malik El Shabazz" from a position outside the folk community that is embraced by just about all the other black contributors to the *For Malcolm* anthology. The aesthetic distance that Hayden so studiously and so anomalously applied to his engagements with black folklife is announced when his speaker asserts that Malcolm "became *his* people's anger" (15, emphasis added). Hayden's refusal to seamlessly melt into Malcolm's people is further underscored as he distances his poem from the world of vernacular orality through overt appeal to a Western and American high literary tradition. Rather than figure Malcolm as a familial and political saint—as the brother and savior who appears in so many of the *For Malcolm* poems—Hayden compares him to the complicated biblical king Ahab and to Melville's obsessive Captain Ahab. The poem ends up elegizing Malcolm without entering into total communion with the black folk world that poets so frequently identified with during the BAM era, and without being hagiographic. Indeed, Hayden subtly troubles the impulse to worship Malcolm as he ends the poem with an image of the leader's humbled genuflections as "He fell on his face before / Allah the raceless" (15). Here it must be recalled that it was Bahá'u'lláh who was the prophetic exemplar that Hayden turned to as he moved away from both Baptist roots and mainstream American modernity. Although Hayden's religious commitment is not evident in "El Hajj Malik El Shabazz," when he included the poem in his 1970 volume, *Words in the Mourning Time*, it was paired in a section with the volume's title poem, which pivots around Bahá'u'lláh and identifies him as "Logos, poet, cosmic hero, surgeon, architect of our hope of peace" (*Words* 50). This arrangement suggests that, although Hayden admired Malcolm's power and search for truth, his singular devotion to the teachings of Bahá'u'lláh precluded a type of poetic "Malcolmism" that BAM poets harnessed in their efforts to unify with the folk masses.

The quasi-religious form of black nationalism that animated the BAM era gave life to poetry that was a kind of vernacular or plain-spoken liturgy through which artist-intellectuals transformed themselves into priests who strongly identified with the black masses but also led them into "new consciousness" and away from both "Western Syphilization" and the Negro Church (Redmond 410). A potent example of this poetry-as-liturgy is witnessed in one of Etheridge Knight's three poems in the *For Malcolm* collection. Knight's remembrance, "It Was a Funky Deal," exemplifies the BAM aesthetic and political ideal that centered the language and sensibility of the streetwise black man-in-the-mass. Its tribute registers implicitly through what the editors of the *For Malcolm* anthology called the "hip dialect" that appears throughout the volume and that is manifest in the refrain-title of Knight's poem (Burroughs and Randall xxi). Its raucous syntax, a hallmark of Black Arts poetry, expresses strategic irreverence for tradition. The simple move of describing Malcolm's death as a "funky deal" represents a frank refusal of the solemnity and lofty rhetoric associated with the elegiac mode and a poetic embrace of black street savoir faire. Thus the poem enacts the break from Western cultural tradition (and from putatively adulterated, outdated forms of blackness) that Malcolm advocated and performed in his life. But

Knight, who discovered poetry and black nationalism while incarcerated, also alludes to his own Malcolm-inspired prison transformation in the closing lines of the poem and suggests that the Western tradition and cosmology shucked off in the poem can be replaced by the Afrocentric ideal that Malcolm preached. Rhyming *guys* with the earlier *jive*, Knight writes,

> You reached the Wild guys
> Like me. You and Bird. (And that
> Lil LeRoi cat.)
> It was a funky deal. (Burroughs and Randall 21)

The lumpen, male heart of the imagined community—its "Wild guys"—is called implicitly to a higher consciousness as Knight's poetic persona recalls his own conversion and elevation from delusion to a condition of clear-sighted self-knowledge epitomized by Malcolm, who earlier in the poem is explicitly likened to a Jesus who "Saw through the jive" (21). As the poem emphasizes its seemingly imprecise but purposeful black slang, it becomes a praise song valorizing a black folk community and honoring a trinity (Malcolm, Charlie "Bird" Parker, and LeRoi Jones) who inspired the revolution in self-conception that was a principal aim of much cultural work of the Black Arts era. All at once, the poem seems to spring from the bosom of street blackness as it operates as a deformed elegy and an instructive conversion narrative identifying masculine prophets of a black nationalism that cloaked itself in religious forms while drawing the folk masses away from the apparently outdated epistemologies of the Negro Church.

In some respects, Etheridge Knight was the ideal deliverer of this liturgical strand of BAM poetry. He came to his art and his intellectual black nationalism through trials of poverty, addiction, and incarceration that conferred a biography of *authenticity* that could not be claimed by some of the middle-class and university-educated poets who perfected the liturgical poetics. Like Malcolm, Knight had a life experience that was much like that of the imagined "Wild guys" who were meant to be a key audience of the new black poetry. As Phillip Brian Harper points out, many artist-intellectuals of the BAM were exceptional figures whose university training and literary milieu necessarily estranged them from the folk they wanted to write to and for (*Are We* 52). These figures gravitated to Malcolm not simply because of his nationalist message but also because his street pedigree and unorthodox education made him a quintessential example of the ideal "organic intellectuals" who in the Gramscian model of social transformation "arise directly out of the masses, but remain in contact with them" (Gramsci 340). Malcolm's critique of white supremacy could be easily approximated by BAM poets who—like any black person—bore the burdens of modernity's racist formations. But for BAM figures attempting to cultivate an interclass relation to the black masses, criticism of the Negro Church seemed to contravene their veneration of folk culture.

An additional problem for the serious poet-activists of the BAM era was the lack of an institutional structure that could actually create the social change they wanted to bring about. If the masses were to follow this avant-garde away from the Negro Church, where would they go? While Malcolm consistently presented the Nation of Islam (and finally orthodox Sunni Islam) as an alternative to the church, the black avant-garde had no ready cosmology, community, or institutional framework to offer the unlettered. Despite its energizing power and its attractive potential, the political philosophy of black nationalism was a farrago of social, economic, and political ideas that foundered when it was not supported by organizational structure. Even with all his charisma and intellectual ability, Malcolm himself had trouble articulating and practically advancing a nationalist agenda once he moved beyond the Nation of Islam. Indeed, recognizing the need for institutional allies, he began to rein in his critique of the Negro Church in later speeches. For example, in his 1964 speeches organized around "The Ballot or the Bullet" theme, Malcolm obviously (and not always successfully) repressed his instinct to attack the church, spoke of keeping one's religion "in the closet," and prescribed interfaith nationalist coalitions (X and Breitman 25). However, his late-in-life conciliatory gestures toward Martin Luther King Jr. and other Christian leaders never grew into a programmatic effort to make use of the Negro Church as a platform for nationalist action. Instead, after his death the BAM intellectuals who cast themselves as Malcolm's ideological successors extended the critique of his Nation of Islam phase and set about creating literary scripture for quasi-religious philosophies and organizations that were meant to be nationalist substitutes for the Negro Church of the folk.

Deifying Folk Blackness

In an unpublished essay written late in his career Hayden laments the aggressive rationalism of secular modernity. He speculates that poetry itself is a casualty of a historical moment that is obsessed with detached analysis that drains spirit from the world. "Our age," he writes, harmonizing himself with a "universal" audience unmarked by race, "has thought it wanted objective, measurable truth; it has wanted to cancel out those factors making for error and the irrational. We have been busy denying the importance of the subjective. We have rather been embarrassed by such words as 'soul,' 'spiritual,' 'moral,' and so on. We have come pretty largely, I think, to prefer statistical tables and documentary writing to poetry." Of course, in this essay Hayden locates himself in opposition to the statistic-gathering impulse of the age. But, somewhat ironically, in his own effort to objectively analyze the zeitgeist, Hayden leaves aside the particular attraction that moral certainty, spiritual vitality, and the concept of "soul" held in the counterpublic of black American culture. Indeed, Hayden's poetics of faith—his own investment in those subjective categories jettisoned in "our age"—draw him quite near to the BAM poets who were similarly at odds with the hyper-rationalism and spiritual desiccation of American modernity. What is remarkable, then, is that Hayden advanced a writerly, Apollonian poetics of the page at the same moment that so many like-minded black poets pursued a dramatically different aesthetic course. In the balance of this chapter, I offer a detailed assessment of the logics of that powerful strand of BAM liturgical poetry that embraced spirituality, soul, and the accouterments of religion as it waged a two-front attack on American modernity and the Negro Church. Robert Hayden waits in the wings during my accounting of the rise of a BAM liturgical poetics deeply invested in vernacular orality. But this accounting sets the stage for a contrastive illumination of Hayden's efforts to maintain a writerly poetics while so many African American poets worked in a speakerly performative mode.

If Bahá'u'lláh was the "cosmic hero" that Hayden turned to as he moved away from Baptist roots and into his writerly poetics, then Malcolm X was the prophet of a religious black nationalism that many BAM poets embraced as they battled the "white world" and the epistemologies of black Christendom. And if Hayden offered one of the most humbled representations of Malcolm in the *For Malcolm* collection, then Amiri Baraka probably offers the anthology's most exalting image of Malcolm when his poem, "For Black Hearts," describes the spiritual father of modern black nationalism as the "black god of our time" (Burroughs and Randall 61). Perhaps more than any of his BAM peers, it was Baraka who felt that the new black consciousness epitomized in Malcolm needed to take on religious rhetoric and social form if it was going to gain serious traction in the folk community. But in the effort to promote the new consciousness, Baraka did not simply elevate Malcolm as a figure of worship. As his political and aesthetic influence peaked in the late 1960s, Baraka promoted a deification of blackness itself while aligning himself with Ron Maulana Karenga and the spiritualized cultural nationalism of Karenga's Kawaida sect. Although he would recant his faith in Karenga and Kawaida after he moved away from black nationalist politics in 1972, the poet's attraction to Karenga's group was intense and clearly grew out of his belief that the nationalist movement needed to be animated by organization and the comprehensive systemic qualities of a religion. Recalling his connection to Karenga, Baraka would write, "I was . . . impressed by the images presented by this well-disciplined organization. By the seeming depth and profundity of his Kawaida doctrine. I felt undisciplined and relatively backward. Here was organization" (*Autobiography* 357). In his Kawaida period Baraka paid respect to Karenga by calling the scholar of African languages by his self-given title of Maulana, meaning "master-teacher." And, though it is understated in his *Autobiography*, Baraka's faith in Kawaida and in Karenga's leadership is manifest in the poet's writing from that period—particularly in the collections *Spirit Reach* (1972) and *In Our Terribleness: Some Elements and Meaning in Black Style* (1970). In an explication of the seven principles of Kawaida—the Nguzo Saba—he declares, "The Nguzo Saba is the key to the new Nationalism. It is the key to the new learning. And that learning is the complete doctrine of Maulana Karenga" (*Raise, Race* 146).

With Kiswahili-laced lexicon and African garb, the Kawaida system ornamentalized the Maulana's teachings on black pride, solidarity, and self-determination, and with its hierarchy and ritual, Kawaida attempted to routinize life around black nationalist philosophy. But despite its creative, innovative energy and its emphatic disavowal of transcendent, "pie in the sky" cosmology, the Kawaida faith remained within the proverbial orbit of the Negro Church. Karenga himself was the product of a deeply religious household, and though he harbored significant "hostility toward Christianity" as he built his cultural nationalist society, the formal attributes of the Negro Church were discernible in its ceremonies (Scot Brown 33). Scot Brown's study of Karenga's U.S. organization describes the church's influence on Kawaida practices:

> The US chairman's heterodox religion and anti-Christian rhetoric would have offended the sensibilities of the Black community that raised him in the 1940s and 1950s. Yet, US's cultural nationalist alternative, as presented in its weekly gatherings called "Soul Sessions" at the organization's headquarters, took on the tenor and feeling of the African American church that Karenga once knew. As one former US member recalled, the Sunday afternoon meetings nourished hard-

core members and sympathizers just as "Christians going to church on Sunday, [were] getting their message that was going to carry them through the week." Karenga's own oratorical style captured the cadence of Baptist ministry and beckoned the call-and-response participation of his audience. (35–36)

During his important dalliance with Kawaida, Amiri Baraka—like Karenga—expressed his own disdain for Christian ideology even as he borrowed from the aesthetics and belief structures of the Negro Church to shape his black nationalist politics and poetry. In 1970 Baraka wrote, "Simple faith, like church people say, that's what we want—hard rock emotional faith in what we are doing. The same way your grandmama used to weep and wring her hands believing in Jeez-us, that deep deep connection with the purest energy, that is what the Nationalist must have" (*Raise, Race* 143). Baraka viewed his work within Kawaida as a means of inspiring commitment to the nationalist cause that he hoped would replace the feminized "Jeez-us" faith of an older generation. In the poetic scripture of the new religious nationalism, Baraka disseminated a theology that displaced Jesus, maligned otherworldly conceptions of divinity, and took cues from the Nation of Islam and Moorish Science Temple mythology that located God *within* the black man. Baraka's Kawaida poetry called for a "Faith in Blackness" that was imbued with godliness: "By Race and by Culture, by color and hopefully by consciousness, we can move with the deep old feeling of our ancient communion with unmanifest being, which is the final reality. And that was, and is blackness, god" (Baraka and Abernathy n.p.). This was the poetic reflection of theology made plain in Kawaida's instructional literature, which established that "we are Gods ourselves. . . . Each Black man is God of his own house" (Scot Brown 35). As this relocation of divinity undercut the foundations of the Negro Church, it sought to exalt the black man-in-the-mass and make sacred a community linked in black godliness.

While few BAM artists followed Baraka into Kawaida, he was not alone in his attraction to the Afrocentric cosmology that was systematized in Karenga's sect. The deification of black humanity performed diverse ideological work as it emerged as a recurring motif in BAM texts. The trope was a seemingly empowering inversion of Western hierarchies in which blackness was the mark of deficit, sin, and Satan. It concentrated spiritual energy in material reality rather than in a "hereafter," and it became a philosophical mechanism that helped fuse the artist-intellectual to the black folk community. Through the trope, BAM poets became rhetorical priests and priestesses of the nationalist religion, but their purpose was not hierarchical separation from the folk. If blackness was godly, then ostensibly all black people were holy ones. For example, riffing on a hodgepodge theology of black holiness, the priestly speaker of Askia Touré's "Extension" unites with a congregation of "brothers" who initially are addressed in the second person—"You are men of the spirit—earth-gods; reclaim your thrones!"—but ultimately are linked to the poet-speaker in the collective *we* that triumphs in an envisioned Armageddon that will occur "When we release the Black Spiritual Oil within our Minds" and "ten thousand Muslim Angels shall / light our way through the burning, bloody Night" (qtd. in Henderson, *Understanding* 305). But, while it may have been an empowering form of rhetoric, the unifying potential of the black godliness trope was limited. When Nikki Giovanni plays on the idea in her well-known "Ego Trippin," her speaker makes use of a communal *I* that seems to include all black women. However, the devout churchwoman would have trouble identifying with Giovanni's heretical black goddess-speaker who declares,

> I turned myself into myself and was
>> jesus
>> men intone my loving name
>> All praises All praises
> I am the one who would save

The decidedly unchristian logic of the trope restricted the imagined community of black gods. Allegiance to the Negro Church would seem to preclude membership in the black pantheon of the nationalist theology. Indeed, the quasi-religious mien of many BAM texts necessarily offended as it aimed to "idolize" and attract youthful street brothers—the "Wild guys"—who might have been drawn to the aggressively vernacular style exemplified in this priestly assurance by Baraka: "We are in our most holy selves niggers / god is a nigger really . . . a nigger is holy" (Baraka and Abernathy n.p.).

Taken together, Baraka's hard turn into street language, his deification of the urban folk, and his use of the solidarity-inspiring *we* demonstrate the peculiar role of the BAM's priestly poets who wanted to fully identify with the folk while also guiding them into the promised land of black nationalist consciousness. The somewhat paradoxical compulsion to follow the urban folk in aesthetic matters while leading them ideologically is an example of what Amy Ongiri has identified as the contradictory disposition of BAM intellectuals who "imagined themselves as both leaders . . . and the incarnations of the 'various selves' of the masses of African American people." Building from Phillip Brian Harper's attention to the "anxious identities and divisional logic" of the BAM, Ongiri finds "tension over intragroup class division" in much Black Arts writing (119). She also notes that

> the Vanguardist, yet insistently populist, demand of the Black Arts Movement created a dynamic in which Black Arts poets stood not for what the average African American man of woman *could* strive to be, as in the earlier Du Boisian "Talented Tenth" model, or what they *should* want to be, as in even earlier "uplift" paradigms, but rather what African American people would naturally and essentially be if it weren't for their lack of spiritual enlightenment and political consciousness. (116–17)

As the BAM artist became, in the words of Larry Neal, "a kind of priest, a black magician" of the new nationalist religion, he taught the masses about the spirituality and politics they lacked ("Shine Swam" 655). In Kenneth Warren's estimation, these tutors mistakenly saw themselves as "capably trained or properly positioned activists and intellectuals acting on behalf of those too damaged to know what was best for them" (*So Black* 71–72). And in assuming this pastoral position the BAM poet-cum-activist-intellectual attempted to usurp the most hallowed position in African American society.

Usurping the Porkchop Pulpit

In their attempt to formulate a quasi-religious nationalist creed that deified the blackness of the folk and denigrated the spiritual and political ideologies of the Negro Church, BAM artists engaged in an oedipal battle against mighty fathers of the black community—against the preachers. In 1927 James Weldon Johnson could say that the "Negro today is, perhaps, the most priest-governed group in the country" (3), and at the outset of the century, Du Bois called the preacher "the most unique personality developed by the Negro on American soil. A leader, a politician, an orator, a 'boss,' an intriguer, an idealist,—all these he is, and ever, too, the centre of a group of men, now twenty, now a thousand in number" (*Souls* 184). Although black clerical power perceptibly diminished as the twentieth century progressed, the artist-intellectuals of the Black Power era sought a radical transformation of culture and politics that would require nothing less than the overthrow of these versatile patriarchs. But just as religious black nationalism both rejected and emulated the Negro Church, the poet-priests of the BAM owed much of their self-conception and aesthetic ideal to the preachers they sought to dethrone.

In a 1968 poem published in *Negro Digest*, S.E. Anderson paired exasperated rhetorical questions—"But why do porkchop preachers collect welfare checks on Sunday? / But why hasn't the white empire crumbled?" (62)—to imply that the black revolution, both cultural and political, had been stymied by "porkchop preachers" wielding outsized power in black America. This implicit indictment and open insult directed at the preachers evokes a historied conundrum of would-be race leaders hailing from the intellectual—rather than the clerical—class and exemplifies one aspect of the BAM response to it.[12] Anderson's poetic persona is dismayed by the preachers' powerful connection to the black masses, evidenced by their material patronage, and responds by turning to the folk language regularly deployed by the BAM intelligentsia. The strategic epithet "porkchop preachers" uses vernacular to position the poet-speaker close to the street as it pulls the preacher from his pulpit into a swinish kind of unholiness. Anderson's insult coupled with Baraka's proclamation that "a nigger is holy" exemplify tandem tactics of the artist-intellectuals who villainized the preachers they aimed to unseat and idolized the folk they sought to lead.

This double-action Black Arts strategy is most clearly on display in Ben Caldwell's 1969 play "Prayer Meeting; or, The First Militant Minister." The one-act play, which appears in *Black Fire*, involves the folk, the preacher, and the nationalist intellectual in a triangular contest of influence and ideology. It opens on a petty thief burglarizing an apartment that turns out to be the home of a black minister. The minister enters the apartment, unaware of the burglar's presence, and begins a prayer in which he tells God of the difficulty he has encountered while trying to console his congregation following the death of a black man at the hands of white police officers. While the congregation hoped for a violent response, the minister counseled pacifism and even "tried to show them where it was really brother Jackson's fault fo' provokin' that officer" (Baraka and Neal 590). Seeing an opportunity, the burglar assumes the voice of God, berates the minister—"YOU STOP PREACHING AND TEACHING MY PEOPLE THAT SHIT!" (591)—and commands him to establish a ministry of militancy that rejects Christian forgiveness in favor of Old Testament retributive justice. Obeying the voice of the burglar/God, the minister finds his pistol, places it near the Bible, and presumably prepares to lead his people into militant action.

In his positive assessment of the play, Larry Neal says that Caldwell "twists the rhythms of the Uncle Tom preacher into the language of the new militancy" ("Black Arts Movement" 65). This synoptic description actually, I think, encapsulates the political-aesthetic twisting that characterizes much of the artistic output of the Black Arts era. In the play's confluence of elemental BAM discourses, the ideology of the Negro Church is degraded as it is bonded to the nonviolent strategies of the southern civil rights movement; the urban folk figure is not simply the hero of the play, he virtually is deified in his role as divine ventriloquist; and though the artist-intellectual is the invisible vertex in the triangle that joins him to the folk and the preacher, it is his political vision—elevated to quasi-religious status—that guides the text. As the burglar speaks in the voice of God, he actually articulates the social philosophy and political program of the artist-intellectual; thus the street "Wild guy" and the intellectual are united in a single dramatic persona, exemplifying how BAM artists simultaneously "imagined themselves as both leaders . . . and the incarnations of the 'various selves' of the masses of African American people" (Ongiri 119). By eliminating the aesthetic distance that traditionally separated the artist from the folk and incarnating themselves in "Wild guy" and Stagolee avatars, BAM artists attempted to occupy two poles of the social spectrum. They were among the most educated and socially capitalized figures in black America and, at the same time, they wanted to be fully aligned with the most materially deprived. Leveraging the discursive power of an intelligentsia and the aesthetic genius and moral authority of a folk class that had been multiply disenfranchised by the failures of American democracy, nationalist artists and intellectuals of the 1960s and 1970s were able to wage a powerful intraracial fight against "the petty tyrants" (Frazier *Negro Church* 90) of the black clergy.

Almost without exception, the preachers who appeared in BAM texts were like the nefarious shepherd introduced in Caldwell's play: avariciously self-interested, dull-minded, and hypocritical pied pipers. However, the tradition of leadership developed within the office of the black preacher was not simply moral and political, it was also aesthetic. And while the social power of the preacher attracted the folk and their "welfare checks," the preacher-leader's unique combination of black statecraft and showmanship had long mesmerized American cultural producers of all stripes. It is no exaggeration to say that black writers have enviously admired the preacher's art for some time. In *The Folk Roots of Contemporary Afro-American Poetry*—an underutilized critical study that emerged from the Black Arts milieu—Bernard Bell tracks the formal influence of the black sermon through key texts of Paul Laurence Dunbar, James Weldon Johnson, Langston Hughes, Richard

Wright, Gwendolyn Brooks, Ralph Ellison, and others. But Bell, who primarily is interested in the appearance of call-and-response structures, which he distills as "a favorite device of the slave exhorters and folk preachers" (54), does little to follow the trace of the black sermon into the Black Arts era. Fahamisha Brown devotes more space than Bell to readings of the "poetry of preachment" in the 1960s and 1970s (45–61). However, arguing that "African American poets, like the evangelists of the traditional church, have been called to proclaim the good news (and the bad)," Brown's purpose is to find the likening imprint of vernacular sermonizing in African American poetry of every era (61). The interplay between preacherly aesthetics and BAM-inspired poetry is also important to Tony Bolden's strong analysis of Jayne Cortez's poetry that "riff[s] on the black sermon form," allowing the poet to enter into a "secular priesthood" (*Afro-Blue* 122). But Bolden, Brown, and Bell are not invested in an examination of the ironic tension in Black Arts poetry that commandeers the form and themes of the Negro sermon to advance explicit and de facto attacks on the church and what Baraka calls "the ruthless preacher and his pitiful tastes," (*Autobiography* 461).[13] For example, when Bell offers criticism of Nikki Giovanni's gospel-backed poetry album *Truth Is on Its Way* (1971), he does not note that, in performing her poetry with the New York Community Choir singing backgrounds, Giovanni obviously *supplants* the preacher-patriarch and his message of Christian transcendence. Instead he writes, "The themes moods rhythms, idioms and images in marriages like 'This Little Light of Mine' with 'Second Rapp Poem' are, at best, amusingly incompatible. The image of the fiery Rapp Brown as a little light just does not come across for me" (60). Yet it is the seeming incompatibility of militant nationalism and Negro agape that is discovered in the contested heart of the Black Power era. Giovanni's showy effort to disseminate an ideology of black nationalism while appropriating all the aesthetic trappings of the black preacher's office—including his faithful choir—simply clarifies the major project of BAM artist-intellectuals who sought to steal away the preacher's working-class flock.[14]

Although Bell has little to say about the incongruity of the Christian folk ethos and the militant ideologies of the BAM, his study of the folk origins of African American poetry is significant because it is the earliest critical study to firmly situate literary black nationalism of the 1960s and 1970s in the context of Western modernity. Bell roots the valorization of folk culture that is found throughout much of the African American literary tradition—and that reaches crescendo in the Black Arts era—in the late eighteenth-century aesthetic nationalism of the German philosopher and critic Johann Gottfried von Herder, who sounds very much like the strident essayists of the BAM in arguing that, "unless our literature is founded on our *Volk*, we shall write eternally for closet sages and disgusting critics out of whose mouths and stomachs we shall get back what we have given" (qtd. in Bell 17). Bell's critical genealogy makes a persuasive case for recognizing that black literary nationalism finds its seminal precedent in Herder's disdain for the French critical establishment that dominated the eighteenth-century German scene and in his advocacy for an "inward"-looking nationalist art (also see Smethurst, *Black Arts* 59). Linking the underlying aesthetic project of the BAM to the European paradigm is counterintuitive in a superficial sense because of the militancy of the movement's anti-Western rhetoric and its announced effort to destroy the Western strand of African American double consciousness (Neal, "Shine Swam" 655). The surface-level, emotional discordance of Bell's crucial finding may be part of the reason that his study has been neglected, particularly by critics interested in underscoring the innovative and inventive elements of literary production in the BAM. But Bell's work is an important Black Arts–era contribution to a critical discourse that explores the hybridity of African American cultural production—a discourse epitomized in Paul Gilroy's more recent theorization of the "black Atlantic" elements of Western modernity.

Gilroy's foundational claim that "the intellectual and cultural achievements of the black Atlantic populations exist partly inside and not always against the grand narrative of Enlightenment and its operational principles" should frame any assessment of the folk-focused literary nationalism of the BAM (48). This is not simply because the black aesthetic of the 1960s and 1970s partly is anticipated in the pattern of nationalist ideals and philosophical principles propounded in eighteenth- and nineteenth-century Europe. Gilroy's frame also helps explain the conflict between Black Power intellectuals and the preachers of the Negro Church as a reflection of "the rift between secular and sacred spheres of action" triggered by the modern "Death of God" (Gilroy 50) and as a relatively late-arriving variation of the struggle that has characterized Western modernity as the secular intelligentsia have vied with clerical authority over the moral stewardship of society. Indeed, both inter- and intraracial dynamics of the political and intellectual contests of the Black Power era are illuminated by Julia Kristeva's seemingly axiomatic assertion that "in the wake of the priest, it is the Marxist and the Freudian who today have become these manufacturers of an all-embracing rationality" (294). Like the Marxists and the Freudians, the BAM artist-intellectuals offered their own absolute mythology in substitution of the church's. George Steiner's articulation of the essential secularizing process of modernity maps neatly onto the BAM artist-intellectuals who became the anamorphic reflections of the black priests they opposed and sought to replace:

> The major mythologies constructed in the West since the early nine- teenth century are not only attempts to fill the emptiness left by the decay of Christian theology and Christian Dogma. They are them- selves a kind of substitute theology. They are systems of belief and argument that may be savagely anti-religious, which may postulate a world without God and may deny an afterlife, but whose struc- ture, whose aspiration, whose claims on the believer are profoundly religious in strategy and in effect. . . . Those great movements, those great gestures of imagination, which have tried to replace religion in the West, and Christianity in particular, are very much like the churches, like the theology, they want to replace. And perhaps we should say that in any great struggle one begins to become like one's opponent. (4)

While the artist-intellectuals of the BAM were working to unseat the Negro priests, they were "partly inside" the grand narrative of Western modernity— offering a "gesture of imagination" very much like that of their clerical oppo- nents. But they were simultaneously scornful of their white secular analogues, their Marxist and Freudian brothers-in-arms. Although conscious of this Western inheritance, they could not fashion themselves after any Western model. (Baraka notes as much when, looking back upon Kawaida doctrine, he writes, "Karenga hid the bits he had taken from white revolutionaries" [*Autobiography* 357].) The tenor, the aesthetic of the revolution would have to appear new and black—as Askia Touré put it,

> The planet is ours for the taking—Now.
> But not on his terms, with his methods; no not
> carbon-copy devils: Capitalists, Marxists, Christians,
> Materialists, etc.
> But a New Thing that's the Oldest Wisdom in the Universe.
> A New Thing bursting out of Black saxophones (qtd. in Henderson,
>   *Understanding* 305)

Touré's poetic disavowal—indeed, his *repression*—of white Western social theories and his celebratory evocation of the free-jazz model—the "New

Thing bursting out of Black Saxophones"—is characteristic of BAM poets who merged sociopolitical and aesthetic terms to fashion themselves as literary approximations of the avant-garde black jazz men. If BAM writers often reincarnated themselves as priestly ghetto rogues with nationalist consciences, they also aspired to be like the free-jazz outsiders who tested the limits of art.

All That Jazz: Hayden as Avant-Garde Jazz Man

Fully unpacking the relation between BAM advocates and the musicians they idolized—to reassign Cornel West's term—is beyond the scope of my argument. Much has been written about the kinship felt between literary artists of the 1960s and 1970s and the male horn players of the era.[15] Suffice it to say that many associated with the BAM, and many critics writing in its lee, took jazz to be the artistic practice that best embodied those essential elements of black cultural expression—the antiphonalism, improvisation, montage, and dramaturgy that Gilroy calls the "hermeneutic keys to the full medley of black artistic practices" (79). Of these artistic practices, many—following a lead established by Baraka in the early sixties—considered music to be the purest, the form of black expression that was most readily linked to an African past through a cultural continuum that Baraka would figure as "the changing same" (Smethurst, *Black Arts* 62). While BAM writers like Baraka and Neal rejected their African American literary inheritance because they viewed it as the polluted and inauthentic work of the Negro middle-class—only a means of "gaining prestige in the white world" (Baraka, *Home* 127; Neal, "Shine Swam" 654)—they embraced the formal, stylistic materials of folk expression found in black music and particularly in the free-jazz movement (Ongiri 133). As BAM poet and jazzman A. B. Spellman averred, "We are too poor a people to have a culture of literacy, but music is rescue and release, and the slaves proved it was possible to dance in chains" (Baraka and Neal 165).

For many, the apotheosis of black musical expressivity was witnessed in the 1960s playing of John Coltrane, who was celebrated as frequently as Malcolm X in BAM poetry and whose artistic integrity was seen as a "sort of objective correlative for the integrity of radical nationalist leaders, specifically Malcolm X," according to James Smethurst (*Black Arts* 75). However, the BAM intellectuals were not the first literary cohort to embrace a blues and jazz ideal—although they may have been the most resolute and exclusive in that embrace. Langston Hughes is most often credited as the seminal contributor to a literary tradition that attempts to bridge the aesthetic distance between black music and poetry. And Ralph Ellison's devotion to a jazz aesthetic is well documented in many of his essays and in critical analyses of *Invisible Man*. Indeed, establishing a musical standard for his literary project, Ellison opens his landmark novel with its protagonist journeying into the exploration of invisibility via the "beam of lyrical sound" produced by the blues jazz of Louis Armstrong's horn. However, descending through that beam dream, the consciousness of the writer-protagonist finally lands on another aesthetic model in the surrealist sermon of a preacher whose vernacular performance is the improvisational, antiphonal, and staccato compliment of a jazz solo:

> and below that I found a lower level and a more rapid tempo and I heard someone shout:
> "Brothers and sisters, my text this morning is the 'Blackness of Blackness.'"
> And a congregation of voices answered: "That blackness is most black, brother, most black . . ."
> "In the beginning . . ."
> "At the very start," they cried.
> ". . . there was blackness . . ."
> "Preach it . . ." . . .
>
> "Now black is . . ." the preacher shouted.
> "Bloody . . ."
> "I said black is . . ."
> "Preach it, brother . . ."
> ". . . an' black ain't . . ." (9)

By using his prologue to nest the existential and archetypal sermon on the "The Blackness of Blackness" within the sonic "beam" of Armstrong's instrument, Ellison constructs a triple-helix tradition that binds his literary achievement to both the aural art of the jazzman and the oratorical art of the preacher. Ellison's tacit acknowledgment of participation in a creative practice that finds its quintessential realization not only in jazz music but also in the communal, dialogic performance of the preacher contrasts with the more vexed relation that BAM artists had with their priestly forebears. Seeking not simply to emulate but actually to usurp the role of the black preachers and turn the water of their Christian ideology into the wine of black nationalism, it was difficult for writers of the BAM to *positively* identify with the political performers who were their closest aesthetic kin.

Prefacing an analysis of Baraka's extensive engagement with the musical origins of his black aesthetic, Kimberly Benston insists, "Afro-American writers have generally asserted that the musician affects black people more immediately than any preacher, politician or ideologue" (*Baraka* 69–70). Although Ellison's prologue and several other key texts complicate Benston's hedged claim, its primary substance rings true, particularly for the host of BAM writers who in poetry and prose "asserted" their strong belief in the black magic of the musician. However, the free-jazz innovators who were BAM favorites had a very limited effect on the mass of black people. The midcentury jazz innovators, like Charlie Parker and John Coltrane, who were most celebrated in the movement pursued an aesthetic imperative that alienated them from the black folk community. As Amy Ongiri has compelling shown (128–42), BAM theorists struggled to reconcile their own difficult demands for art that was both popular and avant-garde with the estranging individualism of their jazz heroes, who worked in a genre that was not particularly populist. While jazz may offer a preeminent model of antiphonalism and improvisation among *experts*, the technical ability required to participate in—or even recognize—its democratic rituals sharply delimits the communitarian experience that jazz makes available. This is particularly true of the work of the free jazz of innovators like Ornette Coleman, Sun Ra, and Albert Ayler. The BAM's theoretical elevation of "public collective performance over more individual modes of cultural production and reception" (Smethurst, *Black Arts* 89) would seem to lead away from esoteric experimentalist modes of jazz and toward an appreciation of the black preacher's oral craft, so fully enmeshed in, and dependent on, the participation of a lay congregation. But because the artist-intellectuals of the BAM were locked in an archetypically modern and oedipal struggle against black America's powerful priests, they surely suffered from an anxiety of influence. It was not possible for them to acknowledge the many tacit debts they owed to their preacher-fathers. In spite of all the poetry written about Bird, Trane, and the masculine passion bursting through "Black Saxophones," for critics seeking the aesthetic genealogy of the BAM, the jazzman may be something of a red herring. Or, to put it differently, it may be necessary for critics charting BAM aesthetic affinities to consider the jazzman alongside the often-reviled black preacher, who, in his nearness to the folk, his versatile political leadership, his advocacy of an all-embracing ideology, and his performative, communal, improvisational aesthetic, represents the unacknowledged hero of the BAM.

In his artistic manifesto poem "Black Boogaloo"—with sections directed at "Black Poets," "Black Painters," and "Black Musicians"—Larry Neal seems intent on urging the musicians away from individualized aesthetic expression as he bids them, "Stop bitching. Take care of business. All get together all over America / and play at the same time. Combine energy. Combine energy. Play to- / gether" (*Black Boogaloo* 43). Neal's directives seem to be arrayed in opposition to the modern forces of "alienation" that act upon the black musician as they are theorized by A. B. Spellman in his *Black Fire* essay on the free-jazz aesthetic. Spellman accounts for the social isolation of the midcentury jazz innovators by evoking the romance of the uncompromising artist whose pursuit of an aesthetic ideal leads to isolation. "Alienation," he contends, "is a part of the artist's situation in capitalist industrial society. For the black musician, it meant alienation from his black brothers, since he was born alienated from whites" (Baraka and Neal 167). But Spellman also acknowledges the agency or willfulness of the musicians, remarking that "their distance was cultivated" (166). While this willful distance may have helped to produce the music celebrated in the BAM, it was anathema to the BAM ethos promoted by Neal, Baraka, and others who instructed the artist to "hasten his own dissolution as an individual" in order to become one with the imagined black nation (Knight 38). The aesthetic politics emerging from their yearning for close connection to black brothers made it impossible for BAM artist-intellectuals to follow their bop and free-jazz heroes into alienation from the masses (Thomas 154).[16] Indeed, the populist mandates of the BAM made poets more like the black preachers they despised and less like their jazz heroes, who often followed a Romantic model of artistic production as they cultivated social isolation, producing art beholden to aesthetic ideals.

Somewhat ironically, then, it was Robert Hayden who might be considered the Black Arts era's literary analogue of the individualist jazzman. Nurturing an aesthetic that posited an artful space between himself and the folk he came from and so often wrote about, Hayden worked at the cultivated distance that Spellman rightly attributed to the jazz masters. In personal notes Hayden formalized an artistic creed in which he urged himself to "seek solitude and stand alone" (qtd. in Hatcher 25). He was wary of the collective and understood the artist to be anything but a leader of men. Remarking on his independence in a 1976 interview, he declared, "I'm not a joiner. I don't get involved with groups." But Hayden added a caveat, saying, "The Bahá'í Faith is about the only organized body I can stand. I cherish my individuality and don't want to be a conformist except (paradoxically) on my own terms" (Hayden, "Interview" 82). If Hayden's commitments to a writerly—

rather than a populist, vernacular-based—poetics distanced him from folk audiences courted by the BAM, then his singular attachment to the Bahá'í Faith further enacted the type of double alienation that Spellman found in the avant-garde black musician. Because it effectively detached him from both "black brothers" and the white mainstream, the poet's intense faith was on some level a cultivation of distance indicative of willful independence—a spiritual practice befitting the uncompromising, self-determining Romantic artist Hayden believed himself to be. Accompanying and interactive with his desire for aesthetic independence and freedom, Hayden's esoteric yet universalist religious inclination is profitably linked to the similarly questing and independent spiritual allegiances of twentieth-century jazz innovators. Rather than associating Hayden with E. Franklin Frazier's characterization of midcentury black Bahá'ís as "middle-class Negroes . . . seeking to find escape from the Negro identification" (*Negro Church* 84), it is more instructive to think of Hayden's intense religiousness as a form of the "antimodern," nonconformist beliefs that attracted artists like Dizzy Gillespie,[17] who also converted to the Bahá'í Faith, like Coltrane, who gravitated toward Buddhist spiritualism, like Sun Ra with his sci-fi mysticism, like Albert Ayler, who often spoke of personal aspirations for transcendence, or even like Charlie Parker, whose self-destructive heroin and alcohol jags might be interpreted as a form of isolating spiritual journeying.

Like these midcentury jazz icons who pursued aesthetic originality and independence, Hayden was among that large cohort of black postwar artist-intellectuals whose art and spiritualism reflected an "antimodern" impulse that responded to the perceived inadequacies of both Western modernity and Negro folkways anchored in the church. Although his poetry seems little influenced by the jazz aesthetics that so many midcentury and BAM-era writers drew into their work, Hayden was the "writerly" companion of horn players like Gillespie, Coltrane, and Ayler, who—within their medium—aspired to expert expression of a blues-tinged universalist spirituality. The BAM poets and intellectual leaders whom Hayden is often set against were also negotiating a way between the Scylla and Charybdis of Western secularism and the Negro Church, but the path that they proposed was a quasi-religious black nationalism with populist ambitions. Anxious populism braided into the infectious power of vernacular aesthetics and gave rise to a BAM poetics that hewed closely to the model of performance forged in the church and quintessentially expressed in the spectacular homiletics of its preachers. Hayden's navigation of the straits between modernity and the church led him in a different direction: toward an ideological and aesthetic independence that was amplified by conversion to an Eastern faith little understood in the black folk community, or the American mainstream. Without a populist urge, Hayden developed a poetics that most often regarded black folk culture as object of distanced contemplation and elucidation rather than as an aesthetic paradigm and ideal. Hayden *curated* black vernacular culture in a painstaking print poetry characterized by obviously sober planning and revision, rather than by the appearance of improvisation and ecstatic creation. On the lower frequencies, he joined the avant-garde jazz players and the BAM poets in their quest for ideologies and art that responsively rejected both secular modernity and the Negro Church. But, as I contend in the next chapter, Hayden was led away from vernacular aesthetic paradigms—especially those of the vastly influential black preachers—by his strong devotion to the "culture of books, writing and print," which was augmented by an emphasis on the world of literacy in his adopted Bahá'í Faith.

Chapter 4

Witch Doctors

———

Hayden's Writerly Rejection of Vernacular Poetics

———

Hayden's distanced, curatorial relation to black vernacular culture is felt throughout his mature corpus. The deliberate approach is on full display in the heritage poems conceived near the beginning of his career in the late 1930s and early 1940s. In "Runagate Runagate" and "O Daedalus, Fly Away Home," elliptical modernist technique offers thick context to snatches of vernacular voice; in "Middle Passage" and "Frederick Douglass" vernacular voices and forms are simply held in abeyance. And as I have emphasized earlier in this section, in those mid- and late-career poems that remember the rich world of Hayden's childhood and adolescence in Detroit, black vernacular culture is drawn through the learned psychic skein of an intellectual struggling to make sense of his vexed relation to a folk matrix. Any reader of Hayden realizes that it is literacy, rather than orality, that is the sine qua non of his poetic project. Once it was established in his early maturity, he never relinquished the belief that the poet's relation to vernacular culture is that of transubstantiator or alchemist who lifts the rough beauty of the oral world into the refined, golden strata of literate realms. Or, to distill this belief through the pre-BAM verse of his hyperliterate aesthetic compatriot (and ironic antagonist) Melvin Tolson, "Out of the abysses of illiteracy / . . . We advance!" (qtd. in Walker, "New Poets" 349).

   In this martial declaration from his 1953 poem "Dark Symphony," Tolson suggests the marching orders of his own poetics, led by ideals of literacy, erudition, and esoteric allusion. As Rita Dove once put it, to read Tolson is to "confirm that one is in the presence of a brilliantly eclectic mind determined not to hide its light under a bushel" (Introduction xii). Although Hayden's desire to shine the light of his literate learning was not as intense as that of his generational peer, it is no oversimplification to say that both Hayden and Tolson have been pushed into the shadows of recent African American literary criticism precisely because of their brilliant esteem for literary culture. In the influential post-BAM theorizing of Henry Louis Gates Jr. and Houston Baker, formalist arguments gave shape to a dominant critical discourse focused on developing a cannon of African American literature that is essentially shaped by black vernacular culture. In response to earlier BAM efforts to theorize a racially essentialized black aesthetic, Gates, Baker and others fashioned their scholarship in an academic era that rejected essentialisms on the one hand but allowed for the institutionalization of black studies on the other. As such, they rejected most of the mystical and tautological rhetoric that cropped up in BAM writing that defined the "blackness of black literature" (Warren, *So Black* 19), even as their theories put a premium on identifying elements of aesthetic and formal distinctiveness that set African American texts apart from the national literature of America—and helped justify academic specialization in the category of African American literature. As Evie Shockley and Harryette Mullen have pointed out, although black literary criticism of the poststructuralist era considered itself more sophisticated and less prescriptive than that associated with the BAM, the influential theories of Baker and Gates ensure that "black music and black speech become, once again, the defining rubrics for understanding black literature" (Shockley, *Renegade* 7).

Hayden's marginal status in post-BAM African American literary criticism—as elaborated in chapter 1—is partly due to his strong allegiance to a print culture tradition and his efforts to make a distanced and beautiful ethnography of the speech, songs, and sermons conceived in the "enigmatic soul" of black folk community. This style of approach represents a striking contrast to African American print literature focused on by Gates and Baker—literature that makes efforts to appear as though it is quite close to (and can "function in," to recall Baraka's claim) the bosom of vernacular blackness. Hayden, obviously out of step with patterns of literary expression that held sway during much of the 1960s and 1970s, not surprisingly has been sidelined in major discussions of the notable formal innovations of the era. Neither is it surprising that Hayden, as a stylistic outlier, is not a significant figure in the cannon-building projects of Gates or Baker. However, as the vernacular impulse of the BAM dissipated in the literature of the "postsoul era," and as

African American high literary culture became increasingly distanced from the working-class black majority (whose cup of vernacular poetry overflowed with oceans of hip-hop music), the writerly model of aesthetic engagement offered by Hayden grew prominent. Studying Hayden's model, we find that his conscious disavowal of oral paradigms does not represent a disdain for vernacular culture itself but rather a desire to engage that culture from a perspective of intellectual independence and authenticity. This style of engagement has been particularly attractive to certain types of post-civil-rights-era poets. While it is primarily spoken word and hip-hop artists who have inherited the performative oral aesthetics that BAM poets learned from black preachers, the page-focused—rather than stage-focused—poets of contemporary academia have been deeply influenced by the writerly aesthetic in which Hayden excelled. In this chapter I offer a close reading of Hayden's "Witch Doctor," a poem in which he rather resolutely rejects the vernacular aesthetic paradigm of the black preacher's oral art. First published in the 1950s, the poem is another example of the archetypal exchange between the black intellectual and the black cleric. But instead of paying homage to the style of performance perfected by the black preacher—as many poets did both before and after Hayden—he refuses both the message and the methods of a preacher figure who is at once a fraud and a master of vernacular aesthetics. While a diverse cohort of African American intellectuals—like James Weldon Johnson, Zora Neale Hurston, Ralph Ellison, James Baldwin, and Amiri Baraka—obviously admired the oral artistry of the black preachers, in "Witch Doctor" Hayden offers a critique of ecstatic preachment itself and calls attention to the way in which vernacular performances that seem to create community may actually enable perfidy.

Hayden's distanced relation to performance poetics in vernacular modes can be assessed against the critical backdrop afforded by Kimberly Benston's study of the "performative ethos" that marks cultural expression of the Black Arts period and after. Benston's important appraisal of recent African American literary culture follows that of his significant peers, Gates and Baker, and builds from the premise that the primary ambition of recent black literature is the "construction of a powerful cultural voice that receives its authority from creative imitation of vernacular exemplars" (*Performing* 249). Because Hayden mostly refused this model, the poet is not prominent in Benston's work. However, I will further explicate Hayden's skeptical view of black modernism's vernacular pattern as it is found in what Benston calls the "chant-sermon" of the black preacher. Benston's study is particularly attractive here because, unlike Gates, Baker, and others, he gives special attention to the Black Arts–era nexus of poetry, theater, and the paradigmatic artistry of preachment found in the heart of the black church—an artistry that interested Hayden as much as it influenced the office of the BAM poet.

In the churchly performance of chant-sermons Benston finds a "reflexive modernism every bit as politically charged and aesthetically resourceful as that envisioned by practitioners of genres habitually associated with the Black Arts Movement" (*Performing* 263). Procedurally unpacking the rhetorical machinery of several civil rights–era sermons, Benston complicates Manichean formulations that might simplistically segregate the quiescent religious (Christian) from the militantly secular in black cultural performances. He ultimately attributes a meaningful form of nationalism—"eschewing doctrines of apolitical transcendence" (281)—to the performative practice associated with some black churches of the urban North. However, in constructing what amounts to a recuperative reading that highlights the ameliorative, political potency of the preacher's art, Benston occludes the possibility that it is precisely the performative prowess witnessed in the chant-sermon that gives cover to, and thus enables, the "pork choppiness" of those preachers regularly reviled by black artist-intellectuals. That is to say, Benston's method—so keenly focused on the text-event of the performed sermon—unlinks the preacher's vernacular performance from some of the polluted sociopolitical economies in which it participates.

This unlinking becomes particularly noteworthy as Benston celebrates C. L. Franklin's signature performance, "The Eagle Stirreth Her Nest," as a representative model of the potent chant-sermons of the civil-rights-movement-era urban North. Franklin's performance is undoubtedly a work of vernacular genius that can be deeply appreciated for its communal, improvisational, melodic, exegetical, ecstatic, or admonitory force. But because the rhetorical achievement of the preacher is often the index of his social power, a fully elaborated assessment might place Franklin's performance in a chiasmic relation not only to his accomplishments as a political activist but also to the elements of his biography that suggest he exploited his power with unsavory egoism and self-interest. Touched by a weakness for opulent living and a "powerful sexual appetite" (Salvatore 205) that gave rise to numerous liaisons with his congregants—one a thirteen-year-old who gave birth to his child—Franklin was in some respects the embodiment of the clichéd porkchop preacher often castigated in BAM poetry. Benston's limited mode of assessment severs Franklin's public and private personas, attributing political significance only to his impressive leadership in the public sphere. Using a nearly New Critical analysis of Franklin's sermon, Benston leaves aside some of the complexities that emerge when the preacher's biography is considered in relation to his performance. But one of Franklin's chief biographers draws attention to the crucial relation of performance and personal perfidy when he points out that it was during the period when the preacher's behavior was most scandalous that Franklin became "ever more aware of his magnetic appeal and preaching prowess" (Salvatore 62). This is worth noting because it is the *facilitating* relation between vernacular performance and egoistic black clerical leadership—and its symbiotic partner, black folk worship—that Hayden takes up in his most direct engagement with the primary institution of black community.

While prominent BAM poets insinuated themselves into the black folk matrix through a political aesthetic that was the "creative imitation" of the model provided by clerics like C. L. Franklin, Hayden's distanced assessment of the black pastoral congregation is especially striking because of its obvious efforts to *avoid* imitation of the preacher's vernacular art. Although the spectacular sermon of an imagined urban preacher is climax and center of Hayden's "Witch Doctor," unmetered free verse, baroque syntax, and writing-culture symbolism ensure that the "hypnotic" power of vernacular performance is observed from a distance rather than felt viscerally.

The poem opens with clear symbolic enunciation of its primary point:

> He dines alone surrounded by reflections
> of himself. Then after sleep and benzedrine
> descends the Cinquecento stair his magic
> wrought from hypochondria of the well-
> to-do and nagging deathwish of the poor;
> swirls on smiling genuflections of
> his liveried chauffeur into a crested
> lilac limousine, the cynosure
> of mousey neighbors tittering behind
> Venetian blinds and half afraid of him
> and half admiring his outrageous flair. (35)

Hayden's preacher is damned with narcissism—a lavish, encircling self-concern that parasitically feeds on the spiritual needs of his congregation. His "magic" is conjured by calibrating a life that is itself performance art to the gaze of a longing audience that observes only an act. Interposing "blinds" between performer and audience, the poem begins its challenge to romanticized renderings of the reciprocity and communalism associated with the antiphonal patterns conducted by the paternal leaders of black church worship. While Benston treats C. L. Franklin's sermon as an act of collective creation orchestrated by a preacher who is an "active, aware, trenchant and emotively committed exemplar of collective consciousness" (*Performing* 266), "Witch Doctor" emphasizes the *illusion* of community whipped up by the preacher's performance and the possibility that such a theatrical community may in fact give life to forms of avaricious individualism.

The elaborate rituals of the Witch Doctor's church take place in a "quondam theater" primed by the rousing folk speech of the preacher's queen mother, who "prepares the way for mystery / and lucre. Shouts in blues-contralto" (35). Pointedly, the poem's only moment of vernacular transcription is offered in the voice of the church mother, who casts her leader as blessed pugilist, eager to join in entertaining battle with the collective malaise of the congregation; her words are the stylized approximation of black folk language:

> 'Oh he's the holyweight champeen who's come
> to give the knockout lick to your bad luck;
> say he's the holyweight champeen
> who's here to deal a knockout punch to your hard luck.' (35)

Hayden's decision to curate the poem's one unfiltered vernacular performance in the preparatory speech of a secondary female character is significant for several reasons. On the one hand, it evokes the gendered distribution of labor in the patriarchal black church, and on the other it offers a tantalizing moment of folk oratory thrown into relief by the poem's abstruse contextualizing diction. However, even as the poem highlights the appeal of the vernacular voice, it refuses the allure of the performance that is the poem's main event. The Witch Doctor's sermon is not captured in quotation or approximated in poetic form, rather it is described in the deliberate free verse and the rarified phraseology that is part of the poem's distancing method. The preacher is set in "chatoyant" (36) robes and "sinuously trembles" (37) as his sermon builds "theophatic tension" (36) and elicits paradoxical "cries of eudaemonic pain" (36). And in pointed departure from a venerable African American poetic tradition extending back to the nineteenth-century verse of Paul Laurence Dunbar and others, Hayden frankly rejects the aesthetic and formal magnetism of the preacher-performer's art. Rather than reproduce and harness the power of the black sermon's call-and-response structure or ride the familiar rhythms of its black chant, the poet turns clinically descriptive and nearly condemnatory: Theatrical exchange between the preacher and congregation occurs through "disheveled antiphons" (37) and the entrancing vernacular homily appears maligned as "wildering vocables, / hypnotic no-words planned (and never failing) / to enmesh" (36).

Hayden's apparent diminishment of both the form and content of the sermonic performance, his rejection of the preacher as "vernacular exemplar," is deeply felt through contrast with the specific damning cast on the preacher figure in Baraka's "Dope," a poem that is the shadowing doppelgänger of "Witch Doctor." By contrasting these poems we can see that although Hayden joined his BAM contemporaries in African America's modern contest between the intellectual and clerical classes, the aesthetic weaponry of Hayden's engagement dramatically differed from that of the BAM poets who sought to usurp the preacher's mantle while *mimicking* his vernacular style.

Emerging in the context of the Third World Marxist phase in Baraka's career, "Dope" collides scientific socialism into the folk bosom of the black church to create a frenzied, humorously signifying voice in which the materialist critique of the intellectual is heard *within* the tongues of the "opium"-peddling preacher.[1] Like any good sermon—but quite unlike Hayden's poetry—Baraka's text is much diminished by its representation on the page:

> owowoo! Just gotta die
>> just gotta die, this ol world aint nuthin, must be
>>> the devil got you
>> thinkin so, it cain be rockefeller, it cain be mor-
>>> gan, it caint be capitalism
>> it caint be national oppression owow! No Way!
>>> Now go back to work and cool
>> it, go back to work and lay back, just a little
>>> while longer till you pass
>> its all gonna be alright once you gone. gimme
>>> that last bitta silver you got
>> stashed there sister, gimme that dust now broth-
>>> er man, itll be ok on the
>> other side, yo soul be clean be washed pure
>>> white, yes. yes. yes. owow. (*Baraka Reader* 266)

Described by Tony Bolden as "the full maturation of Baraka's approach to a sound-based poetics" ("Cultural Resistance" 538), the poem gave rise to dramatic recitations that should be considered signal achievements in the "spoken word" genre crystalized in the Black Arts era.[2] Through performances that revel in the tension between the intellectual's critique and the hijacked moans, repetitions, elongated vowels, antiphonal cadences, and additive oral formulas of the sanctified preacher, Baraka inhabits the preacher's aesthetic robes as he extends the BAM struggle against the clerics for leadership of the black masses. And thus, even as the poem exacts an eviscerating attack on principles of Christian transcendence sold by the mocked folk leader, it is also a form of homage in which the poet's achievement is measured by his approximation of a performance that "sister" and "brother man" reward with "that last bitta silver." Here the hope is that the symbolic silver of folk allegiance will shift from the intoxicating preacher to the creeds of the approximating poet.

In its attempt to expose the mendacity of the generic black clergyman while inhabiting the sermonic language that Hayden had neutered as "wildering vocables, / hypnotic no-words," "Dope" can be read as an oral-culture rendition of Hayden's writerly poem; indeed, it may even be read as a response to "Witch Doctor."

When Hayden's poem first appeared in *A Ballad of Remembrance* (1962), Baraka was apparently unimpressed by the "fancy-pants big words" deployed in the poem that Hayden would defend as purposefully "baroque" ("Interview with Gendron" 21).[3] As variation on a theme, Baraka's performances of "Dope"—initially given a decade after "Witch Doctor" first appeared— reform Hayden's poem by not only eliminating its "fancy-pants big words" but also "raising it off the still Apollonian, alabaster page" and apparently giving it to the masses—thus carrying out some of the essential aesthetic labor that Baraka attributed to the BAM (Oyewole et al. xiii).

Of course, Hayden's poetics esteemed the word confined to the page that Baraka would stigmatize. While the BAM imbued poetry with the vernacular artistry epitomized in the performative practice of the black preacher, Hayden committed himself to the printed page and to an individuating, Apollonian writing culture that Walter Ong describes as hinging on "the reduction of dynamic sound to quiescent space, the separation of the word from the living present" (80). In the abundant theorizing of poets like Baraka, Neal, Madhubuti, Spellman, and James Stewart, this severance of word and action was a chief symptom of the spiritual anemia afflicting Western writing culture. Moreover, as Baraka's denigration of the "alabaster page" intimates, BAM artist-intellectuals (and the literary-critical schools that they inspired) deeply felt the links between white supremacy and graphocentrism. But, steeped in the practices of the very writing culture they eschewed, the literary workers of the BAM must have endured an acute form of the "agony" that

Ong attributes to those aware of the versatile power of writing while emotionally invested in vernacular culture. According to Ong, "This awareness is agony for persons rooted in primary orality, who want literacy passionately but who also know very well that moving into the exciting world of literacy means leaving behind much that is exciting and deeply loved in the earlier oral world. We have to die to continue living" (14). Certainly, BAM literary artists joined reflective writers emerging from a host of oral cultures to produce a strong challenge of the zero-sum inclination of Ong's mortal analogy; nevertheless, the "performative ethos" of black literary modernism exemplified in "Dope" might very well be interpreted as the ecstatic death rattle of a body between worlds.

In "Witch Doctor" Hayden's contrastingly quiet allegiance to the Apollonian powers of the world of literacy is asserted through the bookish language that transubstantiates the preacher's vernacular artistry into literary form. This adamant transubstantiation attempts to demonstrate that the flamboyance and histrionics of the preacher's vernacular show can be matched by a literary show—that the world of literacy might refract rather than imitate the oral world. It equally is a conspicuous demonstration of Hayden's belief in the analytical and communicative powers of the written word. The esoteric phrasings of the poem, which Hayden acknowledged as intentionally "highfalutin and inflated" ("Interview with Gendron" 21), is part of a purposeful denaturalizing apparatus that pulls the Witch Doctor from his oral world in order to study him by literate light. Hayden's examination, sober yet "chatoyant," suggests that the homiletician's performance stirs irrational passions that obfuscate the patriarchal, economically exploitative, homophobic, and antidemocratic conditions attributed to the black church by its critics.[4] But however germane Hayden's critique may be, by drawing his title from the discredited lexicon of colonial-era anthropology, he casts the poem in a curiously judgmental and observatory mode that seems to naturalize and exalt the learned literacy of the speaker and his audience while invasively examining black vernacular culture's folk milieu. Wrought in the exacting language of the distanced observer, this seemingly reproving analysis of the tumult of inferior folk religion carries in it more than a hint of the West's obsession with the Manichean struggle of reason and passion—which is so easily and often projected into parallel binaries of civilization and savagery, literacy and orality, whiteness and blackness, and so on. However, Hayden's poem complicates its critique of the preacher and his vernacular performance by playing upon another requisite pairing in discourse on culture and society: that of individual and community.

As suggested at the outset of the poem, "Witch Doctor" is organized around tensions between the isolated preacher and the undifferentiated folk community that takes in his performance. Although the poem reaches climax in the performative fever that seems to join the preacher to his audience in a type of Dionysian communion (sought after in the spoken word aesthetic of the BAM), the poem is proportionately focused on the solitude of its preacher-performer who not only "dines alone" when he is introduced but remains so even near the peak of his interaction with the congregation: "Disheveled antiphons proclaim the moment / his followers all day have hungered for / but which is his alone" (37). Through the perfect internal rhyme of *antiphons* and *alone* Hayden both ironizes and emphasizes the preacher's seclusion, prying apart the call-and-response pattern of African American worship to reveal an exemplary vernacular artist who is quite similar to the solitary romantic artist esteemed in the world of Western literacy and literature. Indeed, the Witch Doctor is not so different from the type of distanced artist Hayden esteems—not so different from Hayden himself. He is a troubled craftsman whose art emerges from isolation and who, despite his familiarity and mastery of its folkways, is distanced from the black community that gives life to his performance.

Readers have generally understood the poem to be a pejorative assessment of the preacher and his theatrics. In an early review of *Selected Poems* one critic calls the character simply "an extravagant charlatan" (Emanuel 63); elsewhere the Witch Doctor's interior complexity is flattened as he is described as "clearly a conman" (Shaw 179), and the Hayden entry in the *Dictionary of Midwestern Literature* loses some credibility by reductively noting "the jive black man religious leader" (Greasley 252). The character—whom Hayden based on the midcentury Detroit preacher Prophet Jones ("Interview with Gendron" 15)—has far more depth than any of these summations allow. In fact, unmistakable complexity, and even pathos, is woven into the preacher-antihero. Before the pandemonium of the climactic sermon, the Witch Doctor is chauffeured along a lonely, circuitous route from mansion to church. Through this journey sympathetic texture is added to the character: the preacher is queered as he rests on "cushions of black leopard-skin" while watching for "sailors"; the ironically calculated nature of his improvisation— his *sprezzatura*—is emphasized as "he rehearses in his mind / a new device that he must use tonight" (36); and he is layered in literary typology as he "peers questingly / into the green fountainous twilight, sighs" (35). All of these details work to nuance the quality of the preacher's loneliness. His gaze into the green light is an allusion to *The Great Gatsby*, which casts the preacher in a familiar mold and gives literary ambience to the character's isolation. As a Gatsby from the gilded section of the mid-twentieth-century black ghetto, the Witch Doctor's performative lifework registers as a tragic, misguided navigation of the funhouse of American possibility. He is half feared and half admired but ultimately unknown and alone, hidden within a sequestering disguise fashioned for the purposes of a quest that proceeds through "artistry."

As the sheltering limousine nears his theater-church, the Witch Doctor hides himself behind the mask that ensures solitude even as it enables communal performance:

> Approaching Israel Temple, mask in place,
> he hears ragtime allegros of a 'Song
> of Zion' that becomes when he appears
> a hallelujah wave for him to walk. (36)

Hayden's preacher is not just the transparent folk subject of a poetic-ethnographic inquest. The Witch Doctor is also a recognized artist—one who, like Hayden himself and like Paul Laurence Dunbar's archetypal black poet-singer, creates only with "mask in place." For Hayden, the mask is a principal term in the symbolic glossary of poetic craft. It appears at key moments in his oeuvre, and he often acknowledged his attraction to its varied powers as a distancing mechanism: "Frequently, I'm writing about myself but speaking through a mask, a persona" (*Collected Prose* 120). In his symbolist *ars poetica* "The Diver"—the poem he set at the beginning of his *Selected Poems*—Hayden figures the artist's mask as indispensable equipment, which allows him to confront reality's miasma through art. Recalling his descent into the Eros and Thanatos–pressurized depths of the symbolic ocean, Hayden's speaker says,

> I yearned to
> find those hidden
> ones, to fling aside
> the mask and call to them,
> yield to rapturous
> whisperings, have
> done with self and
> every dinning
> vain complexity. (3)

Here the poet figures the distancing mask as a paradoxical device, both pain-
ful and protective. Taking it off would bring on desired communion, yet to do
so would invite death by drowning, an overwhelming of "self." While Ether-
idge Knight explains that it is the bounden duty of the black artist to "hasten
his own dissolution as an individual" (38), Hayden portrays the abdication
of selfhood as reckless but powerful temptation. The artist's responsibility
involves not abandoning but rather confronting the self through the medi-
ating apparatus of the mask. As a prophylactic barrier protecting him from
dangerous exposure or as a respirator giving him room to breathe, the mask
enables the artist's expression. But it is also an instrument that enjoins isola-
tion. Hayden seemed to believe zealously in the creative benefits of isolation
and masking. Late in life he would write to Michael Harper, informing him
that "it's clear to me now that my best and only maneuver is to withdraw,
retreat, isolate myself" (Hayden and Harper 993). In personal notes, his am-
bition to "seek solitude, stand alone" was joined to a set of comprehensive
disciplines that the poet, almost schizophrenically, urged on himself. Among
them were commands like, "No longer share what is most personal with
anyone—neither wife, friend, nor child. Express it only in poetry, and in an
indirect and objective way. . . . Read and think more and talk less. Or not
at all, unless in a fairly objective and impersonal way" (qtd. in Hatcher 25).[5]
These directives imply that self-revelation, the removal of the mask, in art or
life might be emotionally compromising, perhaps dangerously so. But it is
crucial to recognize that, for Hayden, the seclusion and opacity he sought was
also a form of sacrificial asceticism meant to bring forth worthy art. In the
poet's imagination, creation (and compassion alike) flowed through "austere
and lonely offices" (41).

His personal and aesthetic commitment to distance, isolation, and mask-
ing suggests a reading of "Witch Doctor" in which the oral-culture preacher
is understood as an ironic projection of Hayden himself, the print-culture
poet. When the Witch Doctor has stirred his congregational nest to frenzy,
"Behind the mask he smiles" (36). And behind the preacher who smiles be-
hind the mask, we imagine the smiling poet, pleased by his own artistic per-
formance. But Hayden's Witch Doctor is obviously not a pleasing artist. His
narcissism is shown to be absolute as he spins "aloof" amid his hungering flock
and finally conceives "himself as God" (37). In the Witch Doctor Hayden has
conjured—and perhaps attempted to exorcise—an aspect of himself. Amid
the black magic of his poem he has also produced an acknowledgment of the
dangers of isolation—a recognition that the inward orientation of his own
artist-creator aspect invites the risk of a descent into total self-absorption.

But by attributing unchecked egoism to the Witch Doctor and tying it to the preacher's performative prowess, the poem also counters a political-aesthetic logic that has guided much African American literature and criticism since the Black Arts era. In the wake of the BAM, African American literary culture has been worried by the assumption that the print-culture artist devoted to the Apollonian demands of the "alabaster page," rather than the communal-minded vernacular orator, would be most likely to fall into the narcissistic abyss, or to fall away from community. This is an understandable concern; indeed, contrasting the rich social context that attends the words of a spoken performance with the desiccated surroundings of the word on the page, Ong points out that written "words are alone in a text. Moreover, in composing a text, in 'writing' something, the one producing the written utterance is also alone. Writing is a solipsistic operation" (99). Considering the isolating requirements of the written word—so troubling for BAM artists who pioneered new forms of theatrical spoken word poetry modeled on the preaching of church fathers—subtle irony accompanies Hayden's decision to embody artistic solipsism in a paragon figure of oral performance.

"Witch Doctor" is then a defense of print-culture literacy built on an unromanticized evaluation of one significant strand of black oral aesthetics. In the exposure of his Witch Doctor avatar, Hayden writes a self-exorcism that pointedly rejects an alluring oral-culture paradigm. There is no suggestion that orality *necessarily* leads into solipsism, but Hayden's poem makes clear that vernacular artistry as witnessed in the archetypal black preacher provides no guarantee against divisive egoism. While the BAM's attraction to vernacular orality rested heavily on the premise that the spoken word creates immediate community, Hayden's poem suggests that the seemingly organic connection between vernacular interlocutors may be illusory, particularly when it takes place in a highly performative context. In itself, the sermonic text, collaboratively produced in the antiphonal exchange between artist-preacher and audience-congregation is not a spell that wards off the dangers of community-fracturing individualism. Indeed, while the call-and-response patterns of sermonic performance give the appearance of organic communalism, they may in fact be effective covers of invidious demagoguery. During his sermonic performance, a preacher like C. L. Franklin may seem to be, in Benston's words, an "active, aware, trenchant and emotively committed exemplar of collective consciousness" (*Performing* 266), but once the ritual smoke lifts we find the child congregant impregnated by the preacher and expelled from her community, even as the potent performer continues his social ascent. Hayden's unromantic appraisal of vernacular performance bears some resemblance to the opinions of materialist intellectuals—like E. Franklin Frazier and, more recently, Adolph Reed—who argue that the black church model of authority, so dependent on ministerial charisma, is "fundamentally antiparticipatory and antidemocratic" (Reed 56). In this view, the antiphonalism, improvisation, montage, and dramaturgy at the heart of black vernacular performance breed a convivial but easily compromised form of community.

However, Hayden's critique of the charismatic vernacular performances of the black church does not emerge from the perspective of a secular materialist. While "Witch Doctor" evokes an array of now-familiar criticisms of the black church, the poem does not participate in one of intellectual modernity's customary suits against Christian folk belief: it does not slur—as Baraka does in "Dope"—the theistic spiritual impulse that animates church community. Indeed, the Witch Doctor's primary sin is that his spectacle-performance, with its chatoyant exteriority, outshines, obscures, and ultimately replaces what Hayden—in his poem about Bahá'u'lláh—describes as the "auroral darkness which is God" (47). For Hayden, the gaudy church leader obstructs the glimmerings of divine light.[6]

The Bahá'í Faith, Literacy, and the Folk

As shown in chapters 2 and 3, Hayden's connection to the black folk world was sustained by the orthodoxy of his Bahá'í religiousness, by his commitment to the ideal of mystical transcendence made possible through the teachings of a "cosmic hero" who mediates connection between humanity and divinity—between "appearances" and "reality." In his "Full Moon," Hayden similarly sacralizes Christ and Bahá'u'lláh ("The Glorious One"), the mediating prophets at the respective hearts of the black church and the Bahá'í Faith. These figures are homologized through their similar, sanctifying relation to the moon that

> burned in the garden of Gethsemane,
> its light made holy by the dazzling tears
> with which it mingled.

> And spread its radiance on the exile's path
> of Him who was The Glorious One,
> its light made holy by His holiness. (7)

Unlike the great majority of modern black intellectuals, and particularly those of the BAM, Hayden's quarrel with the clerical leaders of the black church was primarily methodological and existential, and secondarily ideological. He did not want to seize the preacher's role so that he might lead the folk to a "superior" and categorically different ideology. Like the church folk of his childhood and youth, Hayden believed in divinity, prophethood, worship, prayer, and transcendence. However, as is suggested by "Witch Doctor" and the lamentations of "The Rabbi" ("I used to see / the rabbi, dour and pale" [9]), Hayden's skepticism is directed at the rites, duties, and performances of the clerical class—at the very office of the cleric, an oral-culture remnant lingering in the modern era of ever-widening literacy.

The spiritual-cum-religious sensibility that permeates almost all of Hayden's post-1955 work is conceived through an intellectual medley that brings together religious orthodoxy with an apparently modern attack on the efficacy of professional religious authority. This somewhat incongruous mixture was the compliment of Bahá'í teachings that admonished and abolished clerical power while vesting the individual believer with a high degree of self-direction in matters of the spirit. The Bahá'í Faith, which was rabidly opposed by the monarchical regime and Shi'i Muslim mullahs of mid-nineteenth-century Persia, developed an organizational order that eschewed concentration of authority in any expert caste of administrators or theologians. Bahá'u'lláh declared that "from two ranks among men power hath been seized: kings and ecclesiastics" (Effendi, *Promised Day* 71). From this pronouncement (and many others like it) Hayden's "Glorious One" drew the outlines of a religious practice quite resonant with the democratic, anticlerical impulses of Western modernity. The Bahá'í Faith correlates its divestment of ecclesiastical authority with the directive that believers independently examine sciences, arts, and scripture. Note this representative instruction from the Bahá'í writings suggesting the intellectual seriousness expected from all adherents:

> They must study for themselves, conscientiously and painstakingly, the literature of their Faith, delve into its teachings, assimilate its laws and principles, ponder its admonitions, tenets and purposes, commit to memory certain of its exhortations and prayers, master the essentials of its administration, and keep abreast of its current affairs and latest developments. (Effendi, *Advent* 41)

This emphasis on the lay believer as independent investigator and apprehender of theological and social matters, coupled with the Bahá'í Faith's rather unprecedented eradication of clergy, meant that the religious culture of Hayden's adopted faith contrasted sharply with that of the Negro Church. In migrating away from the Baptist congregationalism of his youth, Hayden could, in the fashion of the folk, maintain his stated belief "that there is transcendence, that there is a spiritual dimension and there is God, and that we do have obligations to God and there is a divine plan for the world" ("Interview with Gendron" 16). However, in the modern, literate, and democratic religious culture of the Bahá'í Faith, the poet settled on a spiritual practice much at odds with the preacher-centered, oral communalism of the Negro Church.

While it is difficult to determine the intensity of the causal forces connecting Hayden's religiousness and the development of his writerly, curatorial method of engaging the black folk community and vernacular culture, it is worth noting that the relatively unmediated folk voice is a prominent element in Hayden's first volume of poetry, *Heart-Shape in the Dust* (1940), published three years before his 1943 conversion to the Bahá'í Faith. Although only three of *Heart-Shape*'s fifty poems are cast exclusively as dialect monologues ("Shine, Mister?," "Bacchanale," and "Ole Jim Crow"), there is more vernacular language in *Heart-Shape* than in the entire body of work that Hayden published thereafter. As his career and ability blossomed, the poet developed a pronounced disdain for *Heart-Shape*, calling its poems "'prentice pieces" and even wishing that all extant copies of the book might be burned ("Interview with Gendron" 22). Taking their cue from the poet himself, critics like Hatcher have offered a dim view of the collection, describing it as derivative, somewhat banal protest verse that weakly imitates the work of Harlem Renaissance luminaries (15). But some scholars have recently taken a less dismissive approach to Hayden's early work. James Smethurst's brief but cogent reading of *Heart-Shape* is particularly insightful because he carefully measures the tensions in Hayden's use of "low" folk and "high" literary forms in an effort to situate the poet in the Old Left–influenced aesthetic milieu of the 1930s and 1940s. Taking stock of the competitive interplay between the folk and literary voices in the volume, Smethurst concludes that the volume's divided formal allegiances signal deep ambivalence about the relation between the artist-intellectual and the black community at large. Particularly insightful is Smethurst's contention that, even as *Heart-Shape* experimented with blues forms and a faithful rendering of the black voice from the bottom of the class structure, the young Hayden's continual return to high literary forms offered subtle critique of the folk-oriented, populist poetics pioneered by Langston Hughes. Smethurst contends that Hayden's volume does not simply imitate the style of the older poet, as some have suggested, but consciously "critiques Hughes's work with its implicit insistence that Hughes's location of the narratorial consciousness–poet as an insider (or potential insider) is simplistic and in fact is a capitulation to an oppressive race identity imposed on African Americans" (*New Red* 193). As Smethurst indicates, this reading of the implications of Hayden's early formal choices can be extended into his mature work.

Hayden's judicious, perhaps trepidatious, regard for vernacular aesthetics represents a powerful form of *authentic* expression for the black artist-intellectual who, no matter his or her wishes or background, cannot easily claim to be a folk community "insider." As Hayden entered his maturity, the distance between himself and the black folk represented by the Witch Doctor's flock as well as the churchgoing, manual-laboring father of "Those Winter Sundays" was increased not only by the "inexorable social processes" that customarily trouble the relation between the intellectual and the masses but also by the spiritual intuition that led him into the highly literate and interiorizing world of his Bahá'í Faith. While the Black Arts era birthed a populist poetics modeled after the aesthetic example of the folk preacher—the figure at the symbolic heart of black community—Hayden resolutely abided by an observational artistic vision that located him outside the proverbial circle of folk blackness. The poet's selective resistance to the magnetism of black vernacular aesthetic forms was a function of his effort to forge an independent voice expressive of the multiple insights and burdens of the black artist-intellectual; in short, it was a form of intellectual authenticity. This resistance to relatively unmediated imitations of vernacular aesthetics organic to the lower sections of the black class structure may be viewed as a type of heroic subduing of the class-laced anxiety that registers in poetics emerging from the BAM. However, as I suggested earlier in this section, Hayden's aesthetic commitment was not without its own "anxiety of rootedness." While the BAM poetry is, I think, anxiously marked by strong, perhaps dubious, identification with folk "Wild guys," Hayden used extrapoetic forums like interviews and prose to authenticate his life through appeal to the authorizing power of blackness conceived as an essential property of poor colored folk. However, Hayden never assumed that his poetry ought to spring directly from the "slum life" and "real poverty" that he knew in his formational years. Instead, he crafted a high literary, writerly art that filtered his self-described "predilection for the folk idiom" (*Collected Prose* 22) through years of academic study, an engagement with aesthetic traditions sustained in universities, and a dogged commitment to revision, lexical precision, and psychic distance.

This poetics is evident in extant sections of his never-finished autobiography, "The Life," in which Hayden mostly offers remembrances of his childhood in Detroit's Paradise Valley. One highly allusive sequence recalls the procession of costumed children who roamed the streets for Halloween, transforming the neighborhood so that it "took on something of the color and spirit of Mardi Gras" (*Collected Prose* 19). Not surprisingly, the symbol of the mask does crucial work in this remembered scene. While the cheap facial coverings worn by the other children allowed them to become "unknown beings," Hayden remained identifiable behind his dime store disguise. This was "the poet's" burden: "The poet always hoped nobody knew who he was, but the thick glasses made it hard for him to wear the mask so that his face was completely hidden" (20). The young child—who is already "the poet"—joins in the folk masquerade but cannot hide himself as he would like because he is already concealed behind thick glasses. These glasses become a paradoxical mask that all at once obscures, reveals, and stigmatizes the identity of the bookish boy who cannot play as the other children do. Hayden imagines himself forced into an uncomforting authenticity, unable to wear the disguises of his peers, unable to melt into the Dionysian folk scene that surrounds him.

As "the poet" matured, his long experience with the kind of forced authenticity he metaphorizes in the Halloween sequence made it difficult for him to join poetic peers who worked in "imitation of vernacular exemplars" of the black folk world. (Indeed, his "Witch Doctor" suggests that these vernacular exemplars are themselves complex characters who wear their own masks, which the poet might pry away rather than appropriate.) Unable to join any throng because his visual impairment, his intellectualism, and eventually his faith alienated him from the black folk community that would seem his safest refuge in mid-twentieth-century America, Hayden grew organically into the role of the Romantic exile-poet. But his high-literary print-culture poetry was not an attempt to assert elitist distance from his natal vernacular world—he did not take pride in the idea that "poetry is something which few people enjoy, and which fewer people understand," as his poetic ancestor Countee Cullen once declared (603). Instead, Hayden seemed to believe that if poetry was "true" it might strike through masks of subjective separation and authentically communicate with anyone, including those folk figures of the vernacular world that he escaped but would not leave behind.

As this section of *Robert Hayden in Verse* has focused on the connections between Hayden's faith, his writerly penchants, and his aesthetic relation to the socially and economically marginalized black majority, it is fitting to draw

it to a close with a brief reading of his late poem "The Prisoners." First pub-
lished in *American Journal* (1978), it is a minor but remarkable piece about
aesthetic reception that is as forthrightly autobiographical and realist as any
in his corpus. In it Hayden's speaker-poet recalls a volunteer visit to an Amer-
ican prison and thus dramatizes an archetypal scene in African American
literary production by bringing together the black artist-intellectual and the
suffering black folk figure. In Hayden's sanguine rendering of the encounter,
the oft-estranged brothers meet behind the prison's "guillotine gates"—so
evocative of social severance and class conflict—to bridge their differences
first through touch, then through prayer, and finally through poetry:

> Hands intimate with knife and pistol,
> hands that had cruelly grasped and throttled
>
> clasped ours in welcome. I sensed the plea
> of men denied: Believe us human
> like yourselves, who but for Grace . . .
>
> We shared reprieving Hidden Words
> revealed by the Godlike imprisoned
> One, whose crime was truth.
>
> And I read poems I hoped were true.
> It's like you been there, brother, been there,
> the scarred young lifer said. (159)

Curating a splinter of the era's vernacular voice, and comingling it with the
intellectual's literary language, Hayden represents a version of his ideal black
community. It is vivified by the ethereal stewardship of Bahá'u'lláh ("the
Godlike imprisoned / One"), it transcends generational and class differences,
and it coheres around "true" poetry. But most fascinating is the depiction
of the aesthetic sensibility of the scar-hardened, masculine folk figure with
whom Hayden's speaker communes. The final stanza's internal rhyme, linking
the poet's hope to be "true" to the young lifer's utterance of "you," accentuates
the vernacular speaker's station as an aesthetic arbiter who confirms the truth
and value of the poet's print-culture art and, transitively, of the poet himself.

Here, in Hayden's most literal poem about poetic reception, the lumpen
"Wild guy" courted in the oral-culture aesthetics of the BAM uses vernacular
language to proclaim the efficacy of Hayden's writerly poetry. It is a rather

bold declaration of aesthetic confidence and a challenge to the girding logic of political-aesthetic positions that, perhaps condescendingly, assumed that writerly poetry like Hayden's could not be comprehended or appreciated by the black majority. In a 2014 critique, Amiri Baraka appeals to this presumptive logic as he contrasts Black Arts poetry with that of Hayden and his aesthetic descendants. Speaking of the poetry of a BAM collective, Baraka writes, "We wanted it to be a mass art, not hidden away on university campuses. We wanted an art that could function in the ghettos where we lived" ("Post-Racial"). But in "The Prisoners" Hayden takes his poems inside the ghetto's carceral extension, obviously asserting a similar desire to produce art that is not "hidden away" in academic space. Moreover, with his vernacular-voiced "brother" declaring the truth of Hayden's poetry, the poet insists that his art could "function" for even the most oppressed segments of the black folk world, for the people who had been distanced from Hayden by social processes that inevitably estranged the successful poet-professor and the black sufferers in the lower reaches of America's social and economic hierarchy.

As "The Prisoners" and many other poems make clear, Hayden never turned away from those brothers and sisters who constituted the folk matrix that gave him life. But neither did he pretend that there was no separation between himself and the black vernacular world. Instead, Hayden's poetics drew on the plenitude of writing culture as it represented—rather than imitated—black orality with an aesthetic distance that, for Hayden, was a sign of cultural authenticity. Because he was content to speak to the people, rather than lead the people, he eschewed the ecstatic performativity that infused the preacherly poetics of the BAM and the spoken word and hip-hop movements that have descended from it. But in his reverent—rather than begrudging—acceptance of a writing culture inheritance, and in his attempt to explore and bridge the distance between the black artist-intellectual and the black folk world, Hayden left a potent model to writerly poets of the post-movement era. The most successful of these poets work in an academic world that, in recent neoliberal decades, has become increasingly accepting of black scholars and literary artists, even as it has remained distanced from the black masses more impacted by America's prisons than its universities. For those academic poets consciously and unconsciously attempting to plumb and bridge the space between themselves and less socially and economically capitalized African Americans, Hayden's poetry presents guideposts in aesthetic matters, even as its thematic concerns—particularly its attention to the literate and oral archives of black Atlantic history—have also proven paradigmatic for recent black poets.

I begin the next section with the almost self-evident proposition that Hayden is a chief progenitor of the recent efflorescence of history-exploring poetry produced by African Americans in the academy. However, the chapters of part 3 primarily work to complicate the vision of history that emerges in the corpus, showing that Hayden's poetry does not operate in accordance with a single version of history and temporality. The next section's historicized appraisal of Hayden's forty-year writing career demonstrates that he worked with three distinctly identifiable hermeneutics of history—each linked to the others but also independently reflective of Hayden's responses to the intellectual-historical contexts of the middle decades of the twentieth century. As the poet's sensitive powers of perception reacted to New Deal–era racial politics, the holocaustal events of World War II, and the rise of the civil rights and Black Power movements, his poetic expression revealed shifting attachments to secular teleology, existential despair, and religious theodicy. If Hayden's aesthetics often balanced identification with the orality of the black folk world and an attraction to the modern power of literacy, his philosophies of history were also a type of balancing act wherein the poet walked a line between belief in an ordered cosmos bending toward justice and the haunting idea that chaos and evil were the dominant forces of the universe.

PART III

Hayden's Histories

Chapter 5

"beckoning beckoning"

───────

Salvific History in the Early Heritage Poems

───────

In "The Prisoners" Robert Hayden stages the archetypal encounter between the black artist-intellectual and the folk figure within the American institution that, near the end of his life, was quickly emerging as the nation-state's primary apparatus of race- and class-inflected social control and oppression. Hayden's poem registers the dehumanizing functions of an American system of incarceration on the verge of a historically unprecedented metastasization. With his lumpen, scarred prisoner seeming to plead, "Believe us human / like yourselves" (25), Hayden takes his place among African American cultural producers sensing the beginnings of state-orchestrated *hyper*incarceration in an era when leading-edge Western intellectuals were (perhaps ironically) prophesying the retreat of violent state power. As Michel Foucault offered theories of "genealogy," rather than history, to describe and predict the rise of capillary and diffuse forms of power and to caution against an "overvaluing of the problem of the state" (109), black cultural production of the era was regularly confronting the problem of an American state that expressed itself with increasing aggressiveness through penal technology. Eloquent in their arguments against American prison policy, the widely read autobiographical narratives of Malcolm X, Huey Newton, Eldridge Cleaver, George Jackson, and Angela Davis were prose correlatives to the prison poetry of Etheridge Knight and a host of lesser BAM poets. Notably, the period in which the black prison-centric text achieved its greatest literary prominence (1965–75) coincided with an explosion of black popular literature similarly focused on the American prison. The street-life, picaresque novels of Robert Beck (Iceberg Slim) and Donald Goines—more widely read than any black literary texts theretofore (or since)—were effectively moored to the oppressive weight of the prison system and steadfastly disparaged an American legal code stewarded by "black-robed men who sat up high on the benches dispensing their so-called 'justice'" (Goines 26). The genuinely populist novels of Beck and Goines, much like the overtly politicized texts produced by Black Power poets and intellectuals, often figured the injustice of American penal policy as an evolved extension of a long-historied mass black oppression sanctioned by the state. Almost all of these black artists and intellectuals sought to underscore what Huey Newton described as "the similarity between the prison experience and the slave experience of Black people" (278).

In contrast, Hayden's prison poem avoids the stridently politicized historicization of his contemporaries. Rather than situating it in relation to a history of interracial strife, Hayden uses the prison to sanguinely stage the rapprochement of the middle-class intellectual and the lumpen folk figure and thus keys on the class-marked severing of black community that has so worried African American letters of the late twentieth and early twenty-first centuries. As I've suggested by calling the scene of interclass reconciliation and identification "archetypal," Hayden's poem is not at all original in concept. For example, Langston Hughes's "The Weary Blues," published a half century before Hayden's poem, is a more intriguing representation of communion between the artist-intellectual and the folk figure. But "The Prisoners" is remarkable because it showcases the subtlety of Hayden's historical perception. While his contemporaries—along with many recent observers—attempt to understand the prison by looking backward into the slavery era, Hayden discerns the class-stratifying functions that the American prison has carried out in the post–civil rights era. He recognizes the prison not simply as a state institution that oppressively places the humanity of the inmate in doubt. By giving the prison its allusive "guillotine gates," Hayden also intimates the catalytic role that the prison—and thus the state—would come to play in exacerbating the bifurcation of the "black community" into a dehumanized lower class and a supposedly healthy middle and upper class. Hayden's sensitivity to the state's facilitating participation in processes of intraracial class division set him apart from many black critics of prison policy—like Huey Newton—who conflated incarceration and slavery without noting that American penal policy began devastating the bottom of the black class structure at the moment when middle-class blacks began reaping the benefits of the legal and policy advances of the civil rights and Black

Power movements. The notable point here is that Hayden's appraisal of the prison anticipates an American future, while most of his contemporaries understood the prison in terms of an American past.

Literary scholars like Madhu Dubey and Kenneth Warren have offered persuasive readings of post-civil-rights-era cultural discourse that are especially attentive to the feeling of crisis that marks the work of African American artist-intellectuals grappling with—or evading—the reality of class difference in late twentieth- and early twenty-first-century black America. Following political scientists Adolph Reed and Michael Dawson, they argue that, in this era, the very idea of "corporate racial identity" or of a singular "black community" is almost impossible to sustain, given the divergent political interests of black Americans. As Dubey puts it, "The racial politics forged in the era of segregation as well as the nationalist politics of the 1960s, presuming a cohesive community of racial interests, begin to appear increasingly obsolete in the post–Civil Rights period." She goes on to contend that "the question of how to build an antiracist politics that gives due weight to intraracial differences forms the central challenge of the post modern period in African American studies" (228). As I suggest in chapter 4 (and as I'll elaborate on in chapter 8), part of what makes Hayden particularly resonant for poets produced by MFA programs in the postmodern period is the manner in which his print-culture aesthetic and distanced, curatorial relation to black oral culture reflect a resolute effort to *consider*—rather than erase—the intraracial differences complicating connections between the "colleged" artist-intellectual and black folk in the class structure's benthic region. However, in the post-movement period Hayden has also garnered attention and admiration, even among those skeptical of his print-culture modernist poetics, because of his poems on "black history." This was true even in the midst of the Black Arts era, when preeminent advocates of the black aesthetic, like Larry Neal, were eager to teach his "Middle Passage" and Haki Madhubuti offered singular praise for "Runagate Runagate" (see M. Harper, "Every Shut Eye" 107; Llorens, "Don Lee" 80). More recent fascination with Hayden's work on the slavery era can be analyzed in relation to a historical turn in African American critical and high cultural production. In an era defined by the widening of economic and experiential gaps between the folk and the middle-class, artists and scholars firmly situated in the academy have frequently turned to Jim Crow and slavery-era narratives in conscious and unconscious bids to establish bases for transclass racial solidarity. Wanting to hold onto a "cohesive community of racial interests" but unable to fully identify with folk deprivations of the post-movement era, these artists' and scholars' explorations of the traumas of black history worked to create racial ontology based on collective memory (i.e., holding that, as African Americans, our life experiences and class-interests may make us different, but our shared memory of history makes us the same). Ironically, this focus on the past meant that many high-culture black critics and literary artists only obliquely confronted the traumas faced by lower-class folk enduring the rise of the prison state, the rollback of the welfare state, and employment scarcity in the 1980s, 1990s and early 2000s. These literary decades will be remembered by the ascendancy of Toni Morrison, a writer whose genius is expressed primarily through imaginative representation of black folk history.

The "Morrisonian" vision of history that has been most influential in recent African American letters is one that, at first blush, appears to be quite similar to that of Hayden. In this vision, doubt is cast upon the inclination to divide the past from the present; rather than looking at history as a linear, sequential narrative, these models compress history into an eternal now. Kenneth Warren, who believes that disregard for historical sequentialism often breeds suspect analysis, finds this theory of history exemplified in critical works like Ian Baucom's *Specters of the Atlantic: Finance Capital, Slavery, and the Philosophy of History*, the title of which intimates its basic argument that the present is haunted by the past (Warren, *What Was* 82–84). Baucom suggests that history is best understood as a "temporal accumulation" wherein there is "no such thing as a fully discrete or isolated 'present' or 'past,' . . . only a nonsynchronous contemporaneity" (30). This understanding of history is the abstracted and elaborated echo of Huey Newton's assertion of "the similarity between the prison experience and the slave experience of Black people" (278). Like many interested in the idea that American modernity is forever haunted by the specter of slavery, Baucom thinks of Toni Morrison's 1987 novel *Beloved* as a literary exemplification of his theory. Specifically, he evokes the memorable words of Morrison's title character—a ghost figure who contains within her a number of selves that seem to have existed at disparate moments in a transatlantic, antebellum past. Morrison's character Beloved condenses the theory of history as "temporal accumulation" by saying, "All of it is now, it is always now" (Baucom 30).

In an early 1970s assessment of the implications of his own penchant for the poetic present tense, Hayden describes a personal view of history that anticipates the theories of temporal accumulation that have enjoyed recent prominence in a wide range of scholarly and creative disciplines:

I've made a superficial—very superficial—analysis of the recurrence of the present tense in my poems, and I think I may be using it to achieve dramatic immediacy and because in a sense there is no past, only the present. The past is also the present. The experiences I've had in the past are now part of my mind, my subconscious, and they are forever. They have determined the present for me; they exist in it. (*Collected Prose* 123–24)

Hayden's shift from abstract axiom—"the past is also the present"—to the very personal psychology of "my mind, my subconscious" suggests that the poet was, in modernist fashion, interested in the relation of time and self-hood. The personalization of his commentary on the present's palimpsest relation to the past calls to mind poems like "Those Winter Sundays," "Electrical Storm," "'Summertime and the Living . . . ,'" "The Whipping," and still others in which the sensitive perspective of Hayden's professorial persona boomerangs into and out of a folk world left behind but ever present. In these poems both the vibrancy and the trauma of that world thunder through time so that, like the deep-sea storms that haunt the shore-walking speaker of "On the Coast of Maine," they are "remotely near" (*Ballad of Remembrance* 13). As demonstrated in chapter 4, Hayden's desire for aesthetic distance and intellectual authenticity often compelled him to assert a remote observational relation to black folk culture that placed him "above the quarrels and shattered glass" of his inescapable youth. Hayden's autobiographical poems enact the spatial-temporal paradox that makes the ghetto "remotely near" to the college professor, but they are careful not to assert an overly simplistic continuity between his temporally separated selves.

However, in many of his engagements with history more broadly conceived—black history, American history—Hayden is moved to emphasize the nearness, rather than the remoteness, of what has gone before. One critic notes the "presentness of the past" as a major theme in his work (Howard 135), another finds that his "best poems are preoccupied with processes of displacement, both in historical and literary terms. . . . He displaces traditional concepts of order (unity) and of time (linearity) as they manifest themselves in the form of certain literary and historical (or historiographical) conventions" (Kutzinski 173). For these readers Hayden's poems might appear to be prototypes of the postmodern approach to history as "temporal accumulation" in which there is only "nonsynchronous contemporaneity." Indeed, Hayden's assertion that "there is no past, only the present" and his construction of an oeuvre that continually returns to the inspiration of the historical record suggest his status as a significant precursor for historiography-oriented postmodern critics, artists, and (especially) black poets committed to comingling past and present.

But it is impossible to unify all of Hayden's history poems beneath the banner of a singular historical vision. The historicized readings that are presented in this section begin to demonstrate that the hermeneutic of history evident in the relatively well-known poems he conceived in the early 1940s—what I refer to as his "early heritage poems"—contrasts considerably with the visions of history that guided Hayden later in his career. In the paradigm-forging archival history poems like "Middle Passage" and "Runagate Runagate" we find him committed to a teleological version of historical progress—a version of history that is significantly modulated in poems that he published later, in the shadow of World War II and in the 1960s and 1970s. Respectively, chapters 6 and 7 consider poems from these phases of Hayden's career in order to reveal significant reorientations in the historiographical and philosophical frameworks that gave rise to the poetry. The trio of chapters in this section lays bare disjunctions in Hayden's oeuvre that have not been recognized in previous scholarship. These disjunctions have been overlooked in extant assessments of Hayden partly because of justifiable limitations in the critical approach adopted by foundational Hayden scholars. In their books on the poet, Pontheolla Williams (1987), Fred Fetrow (1984), and John Hatcher (1984) sought to make him legible and iconic for a broad academic audience only vaguely familiar with his work. As such, their efforts tend to unify the poet's motivations and give stability to his mature poetics. Hatcher's work, which is the most comprehensive early treatment of Hayden, is particularly important in its tabulation of the poetry's consistencies. In his book the urge to find unities is evident in the introduction to the section tellingly titled "The Continuity of Hayden's Poetry." Here Hatcher points to a remarkable accord among all of Hayden's books and articulates a desire to survey "the progress of Hayden's themes throughout the entirety of these ten volumes to understand the underlying progress and unity which renders these separate works part of one *magnum opus* whose structure and meaning takes its overall significance from Hayden's belief as a Bahá'í" (94). In an effort to listen for harmonies, this methodology necessarily downplays discordances and adjustments within the opus. Although Hatcher acknowledges Hayden's thinking was "not precisely linear in its development," like all others who have written on the poet, Hatcher does not account for the considerable variation in Hayden's historical visions. By keying on these variations and organizing his histories into three phases, this section of the book dramatizes Hayden's "re-constructive imagination" in which the past is, in the words of Jan Assmann, "'processed' and mediated" in a way that is responsive to "the semantic frames and needs of a given individual or society within a given present" (10).

Modernism and Teleology in Hayden's Black Histories

Postmodern interests in black history have underwritten a number of in-sightful appraisals of Hayden's early poems about antebellum events and figures. The most engaging of these studies focus on "Middle Passage" and figure Hayden as a master innovator who couples high-modernist patterning and black insight in a revisionist, intertextual, fragmentary, heteroglossic and mythic poetry that does not simply imitate "white" modernist technique, but powerfully responds to it by implicitly exposing its myopias. Significant read-ings by a number of scholars, particularly Brian Conniff, construe Hayden's poetic reconstructions of slave history as a censuring, "conscious and stra-tegic" engagement with Eliotic modernism's tendency to search the past in hopes of discovering the broken remains of a moral civilization capable of reviving a spiritually collapsed West (492). By rendering the brutal history of slavery through a modernist poetics, poems like "Middle Passage" critique any form of nostalgia that would easily valorize a passed Western culture and its texts while also questioning the shallow anxieties that animate some strands of literary modernism. To take just one example, the modernist wor-ries about sexual repression or boredom that mark some of Eliot's poetry pale as Hayden recalls the endemic sexual violence that New World slavery wove into the fabric of Western modernity (see *Collected Poems* 50).

"Middle Passage," along with the other early heritage poems that I will address—"Frederick Douglass," "The Ballad of Nat Turner," and "Runagate Runagate"—had been evolving in Hayden's notebooks for a number of years before its initial publication in 1945, and even before his study under W. H. Auden and his conversion to the Bahá'í Faith in 1941–43.[1] The period during which the poems incubated coincides with what Hatcher, and just about every other interested scholar, recognizes as a "vast change" in Hayden's poetry (17). It was during this time that Hayden internalized a mathematical metaphor offered to him by Auden—that the best poetry was like "solving for X" (*Collected Prose* 99). For Hatcher, the work gathered in 1940's *Heart-Shape in the Dust* is elementary arithmetic against the algebraic poetics of Hayden's matu-rity. In this chronology, "Middle Passage" and the other prominent black his-tory poems emerge in the earliest phase of what Arnold Rampersad describes as Hayden's "modernist poetry of technical meditative complexity, in which judicious erudition and imagination, rather than pseudo-folk simplicity or didacticism were vital elements" (Introduction xviii). Although the best readings of these 1940s heritage poems focus on the modernist complexity that Hayden seminally applied to the "African sojourn in the New World" (Gates and McKay 1517), these poems also derive power from the "folk simplicity and didacticism" that they subtly retain. Indeed, despite its almost emblematic prominence as Hayden's signature history poem, "Middle Passage" is a transitional piece—one that carries in it vestiges of ideas that the poet would shed in his later poetry. Much more than his later work, the early heritage poems use black history to produce confident narratives of moral and political ascent laced with strong black nationalist sentiments. Reflecting on the period during which his well-known history poems were written, Hayden would say, "My outlook, my style, my technique were changing" (*Collected Prose* 187). It is important to recognize that the wide appeal of these early heritage poems may be at least partly a function of their "didactic" and "simple" core—their appeal to a linear, heroic, and hopeful conception of black history.

It is fitting that Hayden's modernist-cast poem on the middle passage was first printed by *Phylon* magazine in 1945. W. E. B. Du Bois had handed over the reins of the magazine to his protégé, Ira B. Reid, a year earlier, but even after his departure the sociologically oriented quarterly out of Atlanta University mostly published poetry that squared with Du Bois's midlife convictions that art ought to be nationalist propaganda and that black folk experience and expression ought to be alchemized into the most advanced forms of the "kingdom of culture." In keeping with prevailing black literati sentiment of the late 1930s and early 1940s, the modernist uplift of "Middle Passage" is marked by a strong racial consciousness and is built upon an ultimately optimistic, progressivist conception of history that is the secular echo of the Negro spiritual. These elements of the poem are best understood as the expression of an African American intellectual tradition that in the period of Hayden's transition was worked upon by Communist aesthetics but was also still strongly influenced by the residual New Negro thinking of figures like Du Bois, Alain Locke, and Arthur Schomburg. For these senior race men, history was a field to be leveraged for the creation of a racialized collective memory that might help propel the social advancement of a Negro nation within a nation. As Du Bois put it in *Dusk of Dawn* (1940), the autobiographical text published only a few years before "Middle Passage" appeared in *Phylon*, "Among American Negroes, there are sources of strength in common memories of suffering in the past" (110). In the early 1940s Du Bois was intently promoting camaraderie and (quasi-self-segregating) group coherence among the geographically, culturally, and economically heterogeneous American Negroes. This intragroup disparateness forced Du Bois to find the theoretical grounding of group "essence" in history—he felt that "the real essence of this kinship" was to be found in the "social heritage of slavery" (59). It is likely that Du Bois appreciated "Middle Passage" as the type of cultural text that could help bring about needed solidarity because of its aestheticized remembrance of racial "suffering in the past." In Du Bois's political mind, strong group identity, necessary for the advancement of the race, could be fostered through instrumental—and thus subtly didactic—"modern" art rooted in the Negro experience. Contrasting the idealized organic identity of the African clan with that of the fragmented Negro American group, Du Bois indicated his hopes for an instrumental African American art:

> Here in subtle but real ways the communalism of the African clan can be transferred to the Negro American group, implemented by higher ideals of human accomplishment through the education and culture which have arisen and may further arise through contact of black folk with the modern world. The emotional wealth of the American Negro, the nascent art in song, dance, and drama can all be applied, not to amuse the white audience, but to inspire and direct the acting Negro group itself. (110)

Hayden's early heritage poems rise out of institutional frameworks established by Du Bois and others for the promotion of Negro group interests. However, most discussions of Hayden's early histories underplay or ignore this matrix and begin with the poet's purported effort to create a "black skinned epic" that would respond to the specific call issued in Stephen Vincent Benét's Pulitzer-winning Civil War epic *John Brown's Body* (1928). Declaring that his speaker had "too white a heart," Benét hoped that an appropriately "black skinned epic, epic with the black spear" would someday be sung by a black poet (qtd. in Davis 254).[2] As it is often figured, Hayden's desire to be that poet apparently formed the catalytic impulse for "The Black Spear," a historical sequence he plotted during his time as a graduate student at the University of Michigan and that was the germ of the early history poems. In recalling an encounter with Benét, Hayden himself frames the origins of these poems in a narrative of friendly racial competition: "And when I met Mr. Benét several years after reading his book I told him I also intended to write a poem of slavery and the Civil War, but this time from the black man's point of view. He was enthusiastic and encouraged me to do so" (*How I Write* 169–70). This myth of origin, with its focus on Benét's challenge, both obscures and calls attention to the larger and more significant contextual influences that shaped Hayden's acclaimed early heritage poems. While it exaggerates Benét's inspirational part, it also underscores the strong sense of racial identity that the poet brought to his explorations of slavery in the 1940s. Contrasted with his position during the 1966 Fisk conference, Hayden's explicit desire to write from the "black man's point of view" seems to issue from an altogether different artistic consciousness. In 1966 Hayden was adamant: "Let's quit saying we're black writers writing to black folks—it has been give an importance it should not have" (Llorens, "Writers" 63). But the younger poet of "The Black Spear" seems to have felt that his rendering of slavery and the Civil War would differ from Benét's *precisely* because of the importance of his black identity. The desire to write history from a pointedly black perspective would fade out of Hayden as his commitments to a mystical universalism grew in the 1950s and 1960s. But calling attention to the latent black nationalism in the celebrated early histories loosens a coupling that often links Hayden's poetic achievement to the universalism—or the sublimation of blackness—that is associated with his mature work. That is to say, some of Hayden's most widely appreciated work emerges from a political-aesthetic impulse rarely connected to his ideological reputation.

Although Benét hoped for a "black skinned epic" sung by a black poet, he could scarcely have imagined a black poem like "Middle Passage." Seemingly blind to the developments in black literature of the 1920s, the white liberal poet envisioned a "black skinned epic" crooned in romantic plantation melodies of

> truth and mellowness,
> —Deep mellow of the husky, golden voice
> Crying dark heaven through the spirituals,
> Soft mellow of the levee roustabouts,
> Singing at night against the banjo-moon— (348)

Hayden's "Middle Passage" is in one sense the sharp refutation of black history understood through plantation fantasy conventions like the "levee roustabout." If Hayden's modernist poem sings, it sings while smashing Benét's banjo against the slavery-era documents gathered by Arthur Schomburg— collector, archivist, and "preeminent black bibliophile" of the early twentieth century (Meehan 18). In 1941 Hayden spent considerable time researching in the Schomburg Collection in Harlem, deepening his understanding of material that he would poetically assemble in a self-described effort to "correct the misconceptions and to destroy some of the stereotypes and clichés which surrounded Negro history" (*Collected Prose* 162). Hayden's "Middle Passage," which is largely an arrangement of fragmentary voices culled from documentary material of the Atlantic slave trade, participates in a tradition of reconstructive history that traces back to Schomburg's Harlem Renaissance–era efforts to promote "the true story of race vicissitudes, struggle and accomplishment" (236). Like his contemporaries Du Bois and Locke, Schomburg declared a "racial motive" for this recuperative work. As he put it at the outset of his major essay "The Negro Digs Up His Past," "The American Negro must remake his past in order to make his future" (231).

In "Middle Passage," Hayden set about this motivated remaking via an experiment in modernist craftwork. Appearing to piece together transcribed excerpts of the historical record, the poem opens with a double descent into the apparently truth-telling archive and the "charnel stench" of the Atlantic slave trade. The opening 120 lines are mainly an arrangement of archival fragments that form a documentary tableau unsentimentally evoking the horror and hypocrisy of the economy that brought "black gold, black ivory, black seed" across the Atlantic. In its final fifty lines the poem shifts to a description of the famous maritime uprising aboard the *Amistad*. Led by Sengbe Pieh, who would come to be known as Cinquez, a group of Mende prisoners captured from the western coast of Sierra Leone commandeered *La Amistad* during the final leg of its journey to the New World. Eventually the African insurgents were detained in Connecticut and their status—whether property or not—was determined by the U.S. Supreme Court. Hayden's poetic description of the 1839 uprising comes through approximation of court testimony of the Spanish slave handler Pedro Montez, who made claim to the Mende group before the court. The long introductory movement of the poem, a prelude to its rendering of the *Amistad* uprising, gathers together the tremulous and falsely pious journal entries of a slaver's crewman, the testimony of a "deponent" who recounts the depravities that occurred on his ship with relative detachment ("stowed spoon-fashion there; / . . . some went mad of thirst and tore their flesh / and sucked the blood" [249])[3] and the remorseless anecdotes of a retired slave catcher ("I'd be trading still / but for the fevers melting down my bones" [251]). These European voices—which Hayden imagined via the documents in the Schomburg Collection[4]—are interrupted by an evocation and revision of Shakespeare's *The Tempest* and by the disembodied presence of an interested narrator who guides an interpretive path through the collected fragments.

In this panoramic yet particular descent into the Atlantic slave trade, Hayden seems to hold the black voice in notable abeyance. The absence of black speakers in the poem is, on the one hand, a stark refusal of the "husky, golden voice" of black poetics expected by Benét and other racial romantics. It is also an enactment of Schomburg's belief that the black historian needed to take on a "truly scientific attitude" (236)—that it was accuracy rather than compensatory mythology that would most effectively address racist distortions of the black past. In his seemingly forensic reconstruction of slavery's crime scene(s) through verisimilitudinous testimonial documents, Hayden performs as archivist and prosecutor, holding to an ethic of scientific objectivity that would satisfy influential black scholars of the era like Schomburg and John Hope Franklin, who believed that history ought to be "less a matter of argument, and more a matter of record" (Schomburg 231) and that the historian ought to use the "indispensible tools of his art—dispassion, impartiality and cautious judgment" (Franklin 256). But Hayden also operates as creative historian, the poet-mythmaker producing a racially motivated interpretation of the past that indicts and wrests power from a white Western tradition. The black voice of the poet filters into the text in a ghostly manner, as the ventriloquist speaking through and beneath the European citations that fill the poem. Aldon Nielsen figures this as a rhetorical seizing of power, "a scriptural revolution that mirrors the revolt of the *Amistad* Africans. Hayden, in rewriting the words of the slave owners and captains, in ironically voiding them and redeploying them within his historical discourse, effects a metaphorical repetition of the *Amistad* rebellion, a rebellion in which the cargo, the tenor, seizes the vehicle and redirects it homeward" (*Writing Between* 122).

While redirection of the words of those who carried out the slave trade constitutes a literary rebellion reflective of Hayden's desire to "write a poem that would give the lie to the bigots" (*Collected Prose* 173), another aggressive insurgency is recognized in the poem's revisionist deformation of Ariel's song from *The Tempest*. Here, in the depths of "Middle Passage," the words of Ariel, emissary of Prospero's established and oppressive power, undergo a sea change. The revision gives some credence to W. H. Auden's belief that "*The Tempest* inspired people to go on for themselves . . . to make up episodes" (297). But while Auden calls attention to the play's invitation to "extension"—and to the fact that he wrote such an extension himself ("The Sea and the Mirror")—in "Middle Passage" Auden's student produced an *alteration*. Hayden's revision puts him in league with a host of colonial and postcolonial writers who refashioned *The Tempest* for their own, often dissident, purposes. While Auden referenced European writers drawn to *The Tempest* in the effort to fill in what Shakespeare "forgot to tell us" (297), Hayden joins a darker contingent most interested in revising what the Bard seems to tell us. In "Middle Passage" part of Ariel's famous song—

> Full fathom five thy father lies,
> Of his bones are coral made,
> Those are pearls that were his eyes,
> Nothing of him that doth fade
> But doth suffer a sea-change
> Into something rich and strange (1.2.397–402)

—is twice recast as:

> Deep in the festering hold thy father lies,
> of his bones New England pews are made,
> those are altar lights that were his eyes. (248)

And,

> Deep in the festering hold thy father lies,
> the corpse of mercy rots with him,
> rats eat love's rotten gelid eyes. (251)

In these revising manipulations, Hayden mutinies against both Shakespeare and Prospero in order to ventriloquize through Ariel. He also spars with T. S. Eliot, who studded "The Waste Land" with continual allusion to *The Tempest*, and Ariel's song in particular. Hayden's intertextual foray is an obvious case of what Henry Louis Gates calls "motivated signifying," wherein the black author critically parodies literary ancestors in a rhetorical effort "to redress an imbalance of power, to clear a space" (*Signifying* 134). The decision to signify upon Eliot, the proverbial father of poetic modernism, and Shakespeare, the presiding father figure of the Western cultural tradition—or the very father of "the human," according to people like Harold Bloom—is an incursion on the power vested in those paternal figures who wrote the cultural history that young Hayden set out to "correct." In Hayden's revision it is the black father who lies "deep in the festering hold" of the dark ships that weave their way across the Atlantic. But in telling the horror story of black ancestors, "Middle

Passage" is an indictment of the white fathers, whose "lies" have shaped the festering hold of Western consciousness. While Ariel's song in *The Tempest* is itself a lie—a deceiving text meant to convince Ferdinand that his living father has died in Prospero's storm—in Hayden's revision the song "doth suffer a sea-change" that transforms it into "truth." The religious hypocrisy and human exploitation integral to the slave trade are laid bare in these revised, punctuating fragments. If the European "fathers" have produced a lying narrative of history that helped to keep the Negro below the proverbial decks of modernity, Hayden's early heritage poem embodies the revolutionary spirit that refuses those lies in a mythic inversion that celebrates the will to freedom demonstrated in Cinquez's uprising aboard the *Amistad*.

Hayden's disembodied narrator, the spectral curator whose presence is felt in the textual splinters that are gathered in the poem, interprets the meaning of the *Amistad* rebellion—and black history—in a final coda:

> The deep immortal human wish,
> the timeless will:
> > Cinquez its superb Homeric image,
> > life that transfigures many lives,
> > life that defines our history upon these shores.
> Borne from that land—
> > our gods false to us, our kings betraying us—
> like seeds the storm winds carry
> to flower stubbornly upon these shores. (253)

The affirmation of a transcendent human reality, "immortal," "timeless," and "deathless," is consonant with the poet's career-long mystical belief. But these staggered closing lines also anchor the poem in an ideological milieu that Hayden would move away from in the 1950s. The coda celebrates the violent slave revolt within a liberal humanist philosophical paradigm, it concentrates the will to freedom in a single symbolic hero, and it figures the "death" of the black past as preparatory prelude to future life. To be sure, these are markers of Hayden's early maturity.[5] For example, the poem's commemoration of the will to power exercised in Cinquez's revolt represents an acceptance of violence as a necessary engine of historical progression. Hayden would not be able to maintain such certainty later in life. The evolution of his thinking on the efficacy of liberatory violence can be felt in a brief reading of "John Brown," published thirty years after "Middle Passage." While "machete and marlinspike" are the weapons that make good on the "deep immortal human wish" celebrated in the slave revolt of the early poem, an older Hayden regards John Brown's violence at Harper's Ferry with the deep ambivalence registering in the poem's unresolved question about Brown's symbolic identity: "Axe in Jehovah's loving wrathful hand?" (*Collect Poems* 149). For the older poet, the violence of the white freedom fighter is not easily assimilated. Brown's famous attack must be presented as paradoxical interrogative: "angelic evil / demonic good?" (151). By contrast, "Middle Passage" is free of the almost paralyzing moral questioning that marks "John Brown." Cinquez's heroism is offered with a comparative "simplicity"—to recall Rampersad's description of Hayden's juvenilia.

Hayden uses the coda to single out Cinquez as a repository of transformative power and thus riffs on a Great Man theory of black history that allows Schomburg's "true story of race vicissitudes, struggle and accomplishment" to neatly and optimistically coalesce in an ascendant black hero. Concluding with "accomplishment," this is a black modernist poetics that reassuringly teaches hope. "Middle Passage" crescendos with freedom-loving Cinquez willing his way through "the rocking loom of history," emerging from the poem's wasteland of documented death in an image of flowering renewal that both responds to the pessimism of white modernism and proves true Schomburg's assurance that, through the opened archive of the black past, "the ambition of Negro youth can be nourished on its own milk" (236). Cinquez's heroism transfigures a death-poisoned slave history into a nourishing ideological milk, usable in life "upon these shores."

This poetic rendering of Schomburg and Du Bois's belief that "memories of suffering in the past" could become "sources of strength" for the new Negro hinges on a progressivist historical model that posits a dark, cold past, identifies a will-induced spring, and anticipates the bloom of future life. Although this utopian model resonates with the Marxist teleology that would have been influential in circles that Hayden traversed in the 1930s, it has a more extensive history in the black Christian mythology of Hayden's formational adolescence. Eddie Glaude has called this typically African American teleology "salvific history" and notes its emergence from an "extraordinary religious imagination" that allowed African Americans to endure various abjections by locating spiritual, and also political, salvation in a divinely promised future (94). This is, of course, the eschatological model that shaped the Negro spiritual—the vernacular mode that Du Bois called the "Sorrow Songs," despite his recognition that these songs inevitably turned to promise. In *The Souls of Black Folk* Du Bois would write, "Through all the sorrow of the Sorrow Songs there breathes a hope—a faith in the ultimate justice of things.

The minor cadences of despair change often to triumph and calm confidence. Sometimes it is faith in life, sometimes a faith in death, sometimes assurance of boundless justice in some fair world beyond" (251). Concluding with the seeming promise "to flower stubbornly upon these shores," "Middle Passage" approximates the linear, salvific history modeled in the Sorrow Songs. But in "Middle Passage," and its 1940s companion pieces "Runagate Runagate" and "Frederick Douglass," Hayden follows the secularizing impulse of the New Negro era and 1930s Communist-influenced black intellectuals like Langston Hughes who, in poems like "Goodbye Christ" and "Christ in Alabama," essentially argued that the freedom dream sustained in the religious singing of the folk would be assured through heroic material struggle, rather than godly ordinance. Hayden's poems elegize a black past but then elevate figures of triumph—Cinquez, Douglass, and Harriet Tubman—whose heroic will serves as guidance to a readership that is directed toward a prophetic future.

The anticipatory, progressive narrative of salvific history is readily felt in Hayden's sonnet-seeming "Frederick Douglass":

> When it is finally ours, this freedom, this liberty, this beautiful
> and terrible thing, needful to man as air,
> usable as earth; when it belongs at last to our children,
> when it is truly instinct, brain matter, diastole, systole,
> reflex action; when it is finally won; when it is more
> than the gaudy mumbo jumbo of politicians:
> this man, this Douglass, this former slave, this Negro
> beaten to his knees, exiled, visioning a world
> where none is lonely, none hunted, alien,
> this man, superb in love and logic, this man
> shall be remembered—oh, not with statues' rhetoric,
> not with legends and poems and wreaths of bronze alone,
> but with the lives grown out of his life, the lives
> fleshing his dream of the needful, beautiful thing.[6]

The initial, subordinating "When" immediately imbues the history poem with a sense of both urgency and futurity that is extended and reinforced as the word is repeated in the heartbeat pacing, the "diastole, systole," of the opening adverbial sestet. Oriented toward a halcyon day that seems assured, the heroic elegy is emphatic about the catalytic role that "this man, this Douglass, this former slave, this Negro *will have played*" in a historical narrative that must end in "freedom." Hayden gives the poem a sonnet's dialectical logic by describing a future condition made possible by transformative black life in the past. While "Middle Passage" uses Cinquez's heroism to give hopeful meaning to a black past that sprawls darkly and perhaps inertly in the poem's documentary fragments, "Frederick Douglass" does not linger long in history. Here the past is legacy that clearly bears on the future; Douglass's suffering is made visceral through a single remembrance of racialized corporal abuse—"this Negro / beaten to his knees"—but the slave past is primarily recalled in the fleeting abstraction of "exiled," "lonely," "hunted," and "alien." Using exemplary "love and logic," Douglass rises from his knees, through the abstract abjections of the slave past into the triumphant future anticipated in the poem's first word. As in "Middle Passage," here Hayden works with a Janus-faced approach to a linearly imagined history that promises redemption in future "lives."

These poems breathe with the "faith in the ultimate justice of things" that Du Bois attributed to the Sorrow Songs. However, as Du Bois would have recommended, Hayden's early histories place their faith in the dogged will of Promethean black heroes, rather than in divine will.[7] Indeed, in "The Ballad of Nat Turner"—also designed to be part of the "Black Spear" project and reflective of Hayden's research in the Schomburg Collection—divine will is tragically impenetrable. While heroic Cinquez and Douglass are forward-moving figures set in a linear history never linked to Christian eschatology, Hayden portrays Turner—the Virginia slave-preacher who led one of the bloodiest slave revolts in American history—as a failed visionary, locked in the historical past, overwhelmed by scriptural typology that he cannot properly map onto his own experience. Begging his God for interpretive guidance, the night-wandering Turner imagines the "belltongue bodies" of lynched Africans—"Ibo Warriors"—as symbols, but symbols not easily deciphered in his insistent search for spiritual meaning. His frustrated questioning— "Is this the sign, / the sign forepromised me?"—becomes a demand that is answered not by God but by the encompassing night: "Speak to me now or let me die. / Die, whispered the blackness" (*Ballad* 68).[8] As in all of the early heritage poems, here divinity is silent—God has no agency in history. Turner's delusion is recognized not so much in his desire for emancipatory violence but rather in his desire to understand his revolutionary inclination through biblical paradigm. The incompatibility of Turner's revolutionary will and the religious template that he tries to fit it in is evoked in the formal construction of the poem. Although Hayden totally eschews rhyme in some of his quatrains, he scatters slanted consonant and assonant rhymes in many, and in a few he hints strongly at conventional ballad rhyme, as when Turner's visions produce an angelic battle in the night:

> And there were angels, their faces hidden
> from me, angels at war
> with one another, angels in dazzling
> battle. And oh the splendor (69)

By offering the enticing possibility of perfect ballad rhyme, but more frequently disturbing it, Hayden suggests Turner's unrealized desire for an "absolute"—divinely sanctioned—interpretation of his slave condition.[9] The deformed ballad evokes an ideal form but does not follow through to deliver the easy, perfect rhymes of the traditional ballad. The noncompliant rhymes of "The Ballad of Nat Turner" evoke the preacher's problematic millennialism, but they also disrupt and slow down a poem that, quite unlike "Frederick Douglass," is not ever-advancing. While Hayden's treatment of Cinquez and Douglass directs us into futurity, Turner's biblical hermeneutics do not provide a way forward. Although we know the famous consequences of Turner's eschatological thinking, Hayden ends his history before the revolt. It is to the point that, in the final stanza of the poem, time is all but stalled as Turner uses the past tense employed throughout to describe the period between his visions and his rebellion:

> And purified, I rose and prayed
> and returned after a time
> to the blazing fields, to the humbleness
> And bided my time. (70)

The temporal caesura that Hayden imposes at the close of the ballad stands in contrast to the onward-thrusting conclusions of the other hero poems in the "Black Spear" sequence. Indeed, if the suspension of time sets the Nat Turner poem at odds with "Middle Passage" and "Frederick Douglass," the poem's delay is the blasphemous antithetical of the sense of temporal, spatial, and spiritual advancement imprinted on "Runagate Runagate." Considered Hayden's "masterwork" by many—particularly by those with 1960s black aesthetic sympathies (see F. Brown 73)—"Runagate" is a poem of the Underground Railroad rendered through a modernist amalgam of fragmentary voices, songs, documents, and guiding narration that recalls the form of "Middle Passage." But the poem also returns to a conceptual template that offers salvific history through remembrance of a singular hero—Harriet Tubman—who teaches by way of secularized transformational will operating within a progressivist stream of history that moves from a desperate, dark past into a bright, freedom-promising future.

In its appearances in *Selected Poems* and *Angle of Ascent*, Hayden follows "The Ballad of Nat Turner" with "Runagate." This contrastive arrangement accentuates both the stoppage at the end of the Turner poem and the description of headlong advancement in the opening strophe of "Runagate":[10]

> Runs falls rises stumbles on from darkness into darkness
> and the darkness thicketed with shapes of terror
> and the hunters pursuing and the hounds pursuing
> and the night cold and the night long and the river
> to cross and the jack-muh-lanterns beckoning beckoning
> and blackness ahead and when shall I reach that somewhere
> morning and keep on going and never turn back and keep on going

The sequence plunges into the slave past via margin-to-margin long lines that recall Whitman's antebellum American verse and, perhaps specifically, the "runaway slave" section of *Song of Myself*:

> The runaway slave came to my house and stopt outside,
> I heard his motions crackling the twigs of the woodpile,
> Through the swung half-door of the kitchen I saw him limpsy and
>   weak, . . . (8)

But Hayden desires more than the sympathetic observation of Whitman's speaker. The poem seeks to create the racialized embodiment that Baraka evoked in his 1964 "Numbers, Letters," wherein the speaker associates poetic breath and blackness, declaring himself "a black nigger in the universe, a long breath singer" (*Baraka Reader* 215). In early iterations of "Runagate," Hayden follows the opening sequence with the words "Runagate nigger Runagate," a pacing refrain that employs the visceral charge of the word *nigger* to tightly couple ascriptive blackness and the gasping flight of the anonymous slave ("Runagate" 46). The flight onward, toward the beckoning light of the lantern, signaling safe harbor for the fugitive, and toward the light of "that somewhere / morning" foregrounds the desperate black body through a somatic poetics that dispenses with punctuation and uses stringing conjunctions to reproduce the breathlessness of the runagate in the poem's reciter. Although the strophe begins in third-person descriptive observation, Hayden eases the narration into first person by inserting the archaic colloquial "jack-muh-lantern"—a term understood well by the runagate but unfamiliar to most readers of modernist poetry—and then by fully entering the uncertain consciousness of the runaway, who asks himself and the reader, "when shall I reach that somewhere"? The brilliance of the sequence shines most in its final line, which responds to the question of the self-doubting runner with focused encouragement: "keep on going and never turn back and keep on going." These words braid together reader, narrator, and character in a single consciousness willed toward freedom; they are uttered simultaneously by the sympathetic reader urging on the hunted, by the supportive narrator dispensing with objective distance, and by the escapee pushing himself on through doubt. This triple urging, in which character, narrator, and reader are joined together in a single adamant voice, is also employed at the very end of the poem as it closes with the injunction "mean mean mean to be free." In this unabashedly didactic conclusion the reader is oriented toward a future freedom to be achieved through the hard-willed spirit exemplified in the courageous renegade slave whose voice is heard, along with that of Hayden's narrator, in the final instruction internalized by the reader.

Although Alain Locke's introduction to *The New Negro* anthology was written about fifteen years before Hayden's early histories take shape, its anticipatory energy generates some of the pulse beating in the opening of "Runagate." Locke characterizes the early twentieth-century cityward migration of blacks as the manifestation of desire for democratic advancement and the expression of spiritual determination. As Hayden's runagate flies impulsively North for freedom, so too do Locke's "migrant masses," who will themselves through space that they might travel from a "medieval" to a "modern" moment in history:

> The migrant masses, shifting from countryside to city, hurdle several generations of experience at a leap, but more important, the same thing happens spiritually in the life-attitudes and self-expression of the Young Negro. . . .

We have tomorrow
Bright before us
Like a flame.

Yesterday, a night-gone thing
A sun-down name.

And dawn today
Broad arch above the road we came.
We march! ("New Negro" 4–5)

Locke continues the theme further in the essay:

> The wash and rush of this human tide on the beach line of the north-
> ern city centers is to be explained primarily in terms of a new vision of
> opportunity, of social and economic freedom, of a spirit to seize, even
> in the face of an extortionate and heavy toll, a chance for the improve-
> ment of conditions. With each successive wave of it, the movement
> of the Negro becomes more and more a mass movement toward the
> larger and the more democratic chance—in the Negro's case a de-
> liberate flight not only from countryside to city, but from medieval
> America to modern. (6)

Hayden's early heritage poems, with their future-oriented salvific versions
of history, recapitulate the sustaining but simple and perhaps naïve optimism
of both the Negro spirituals and the New Negro sensibility exemplified in
the Hughes poem "Youth," which Locke takes as a touchstone for his essay.
In "Runagate," Hayden—who was in his heady youth during the years im-
mediately following the peak of the New Negro movement—works with the
self-same metaphors of teleological history that organize Hughes's poem.
For the runagate, who is allegory for a Negro nation in Hayden's writing past
and present, the jack-muh-lantern flame and the "somewhere / morning" are
beckoning lights of hope situated at a distance that is both spatial and tem-
poral. The opening strophe is a dramatic concretization of Hughes's rather
abstract poem, but its conceit of illumination follows the same progression
as Hughes's—first metaphorizing future freedom as summoning flame, then
as certain dawn. While the actual escape of a runaway slave may have been
hindered by the arrival of dawn's light, Hayden's poetic runaway anticipates
morning as symbolic liberation. Hayden, like Hughes, employs the symbol of
inevitable daylight to endow the poem with inspiration and with the assur-
ance that black history moves toward freedom, just as morning follows night.
    However, Hayden's progressive teleology is not propelled by the divine

force that animates the Negro spiritual, and, while a young Hughes and many of his New Negro contemporaries emphasized the glory of the coming "tomorrow," Hayden is more interested in the frictions of progress. The lesson taught by the ancestors—by the runagates, the poem's "many thousands done crossed over"—is the same lesson of hope, will, and dogged strength learned from the lives of Cinquez and Douglass. And in "Runagate," as in "Middle Passage" and "Frederick Douglass," Hayden concentrates the instructive meaning of black history into a single transformative hero. By the time we read "mean mean mean to be free" as the final phrase of the poem, Harriet Tubman has been so lionized that it is her voice that sounds above the others.

Like Cinquez in "Middle Passage," Tubman enters the poem following a tableau that evokes the slave experience of the Underground Railroad by way of the research archive. However, in "Runagate" Hayden opens the ambit of documentation; rather than interpolating the historical record of the slavers to illuminate the brutality and hypocrisy of their trade, here he primarily samples from the oral tradition—the "mythic tablets" (Redmond 16)—of the enslaved to illuminate their sustained hope and determined will for freedom. The slave spiritual "No More Auction Block," standardized by the Fisk Jubilee Singers during their nineteenth-century concert tour, appears in anthemic fragments at several points, as do imagined transcriptions of the black folk voice.[11] An inchoate black nation, united in its embattled yet advancing, freedom-loving culture, is constructed through poetic collage. A champion then materializes as the logical expression of this indefatigable nation—

> Rises from their anguish and their power,
>> Harriet Tubman,
>>> woman of earth, whipscarred,
>>> a summoning, a shining

As though willed into being by the folk community, Tubman is the human "shining" of the beckoning lantern and the figurative morning that gives hope through the night darkness of the poem's opening stanza. The famed "Stealer of Slaves" had fascinated Hayden for some time before "Runagate's" initial publication in 1949. In the late 1930s, he had written a play about her—a play that in his unforgiving self-judgment "was just as bad as it could be" (*Collected Prose* 183). Tubman had also inspired Margaret Walker, a poet who is often recognized as Hayden's generational peer but whose career bloomed before his and influenced Hayden's early artistic vision. (Her nationalist classic of the late 1930s, "For My People," is the superior model for Hayden's *Heart-Shape* poem "These Are My People." In private correspondence to Walker in the mid-1970s, Hayden would describe their relationship as one of "comrades-in-arms" [letter to Walker].) Walker's "Harriet Tubman," published in *Phylon* in 1944, bears significant resemblance to "Runagate" in its focus on Tubman and its effort to create a charged symbolic relation between the poem's primary hero and the folk culture that gives her context:

I'm bound to git to Canada
Before another week;
I come through swamps and mountains
I waded many a creek.

Now tell my brothers yonder
That Harriet is free;
Yes, tell brothers yonder
No more auction block for me. (328)

From their similar construction of Tubman as embodiment of the hard-willed black desire for ascent into northern freedom, to their representation of the vernacular voice, to their common citation of the same slave spiritual, Walker's poem and "Runagate" are thematic twins. But while Walker's poem, confined by strict ballad rhyme and meter, angles readers toward history as a somewhat static artifact, Hayden's free verse, wild lineation, wide range of address, and sense of futurity handle the same substance with a dynamism—a modernism—that Walker's poem cannot accommodate.

Recognizing the stark formal differences between the two efforts, so similar in theme and material, both complicates and validates an admiring assessment of Hayden's poem by Calvin Hernton, who claims that "there is nothing new or original in 'Runagate Runagate,' *except* the genius of Robert Hayden and the genius he recognized in the experiences and aesthetic tradition of the African American people" (326, emphasis in the original). The contention that there is "nothing new" in Hayden's poem appears true enough when it is grouped with Walker's take on Tubman and the slave past. But, pace Hernton, there is also nothing new in Hayden's recognition of the genius "in the experience and aesthetic tradition of the African American people." Walker and other major poets of the 1920s and 1930s, like Hughes, Sterling Brown, James Weldon Johnson, or even Stephen Benét, fully recognized the inspirational power of black folk experience and culture. Hayden's originality is most deeply felt in his deliberate effort to render that experience in an experimental poetics that borrows innovations from putatively white modernist sources. Hernton's resistance to this type of reading, his desire to tie Hayden's genius specifically to the recognition of black cultural and experiential "genius" rather than modernist form, reflects black nationalist–inflected approbation of the ideological work carried out in "Runagate." Hernton, a one-time Umbra poet and contributor to the *Black Fire* anthology, deflects attention from Hayden's high modernist technique while highlighting Hayden's politicized engagement with the materials of black history.

In its appreciation of the motivational and monumentalizing nature of the poem's representation of black history, rather than the implications of its formal apparatus, Hernton's 1992 appraisal returns us to the ideological context that gave rise to Hayden's early heritage poems, with their allegiances to both populist social realism and modernist form. These poems, conceived in the 1930s and 1940s, are vivified by the current of cultural nationalism that was characteristic of black artistry of the period. It is this particular current in Hayden's early histories that is so attractive to Hernton and to latter-day cultural nationalists like Haki Madhubuti, who in 1969 declared "Runagate's" closing flourish—"mean mean mean to be free"—"one of the *baddest* lines I ever read" (qtd. in Llorens, "Don Lee" 80; also see F. Brown, *Performing* 73). The emotional, inspirational power of these poems is a function of Hayden's response to a moment in African American letters heavily invested in the belief that art should impact American social and political culture and also gird up an affirming sense of group identity in black readers. These poems are not sketched in exact obedience to Richard Wright's "Blueprint for Negro Writing," but as Hayden asserted, they are "written from the black man's point of view" (*How I Write* 169–70), and they are alive to the provisional forms of black nationalism that Wright advocated when he published his influential 1937 essay in *New Challenge*—the short-lived leftist magazine to which Hayden made editorial contributions. "Runagate," "Frederick Douglass" and "Middle Passage" are not "protest poems" as the term is generally understood, but they strikingly evoke racial hardship, faithfully posit black utopian possibility, and offer up satisfying heroes whose lives didactically model ideal forms of black resistance. They are not perfect examples of the "social realist" mode that ascended in the interwar years, but the stylized documentary representation of the black historical archive in "Middle Passage" and "Runagate" reflects the influence of the social realist impulse. And, in their propulsive futurist orientation, they are products of a period in African American letters energized by the lingering influence of New Negro optimism, the Red-tinged promise of revolution and New Deal social evolution, and the apparent advancements of Negro life–prospects brought on by the buildup for World War II.

Finding the ideological genealogy of Hayden's early heritage poems in historiography and politics emerging from the New Negro movement and modulated by interwar, left-wing black nationalism is particularly compelling in light of Margaret Walker's pronouncement that "the New Negro came of age in the 1930s." Written in 1950, Walker's essay "New Poets" suggests that the potential of New Negro poets was scuttled because they "lacked social perspective and suffered from a kind of literary myopia" (345), but gesturing toward her own 1930s achievement, along with that of Hayden, Gwendolyn Brooks, Owen Dodson, and a few others, Walker finds poets with proper "social perspective, and intellectual maturity" (353). Although she does not make reference to the "Black Spear" history poems, Walker includes a Hayden poem from *Heart-Shape in the Dust* when praising the 1940s poets for their "note of social protest . . . and militant attitude not evidenced in the poets of the Twenties" (349). However, she also points to weakness in *Heart-Shape* as she contrasts it with *The Lion and the Archer*, the volume that Hayden—in collaboration with Myron O'Higgins—would publish in 1948:

> Robert Hayden shows a decided growth and advance in this volume over his first, *Heart-Shape in the Dust*, which was uneven and lacked the grasp of a true Negro idiom which he seemed to be seeking at that time. His sense of choric movement and his understanding and perspective of peoples have increased to a telling degree and he writes now with due maturity and power. (352)

Hayden's early history poems hover in the major transitional moment between the "social protest" and "militant attitude" of *Heart-Shape*, published in 1940, and the full "maturity and power" that Walker recognizes in *The Lion and the Archer*, which appeared later in the decade. Although most of Hayden's twenty-first-century readers overlook the transitional character of the early history poems, in 1955 Sterling Brown isolated the period between the publication of *Heart-Shape* and *The Lion*, calling it Hayden's "second phase," in which he "explored the heroic and the tragic in the history of the Negro" (200). Properly historicized, these "second phase" poems are not only touched by the simmering black nationalist protest of his "first phase," they are also organized by certain kinds of simplicity that Hayden studiously avoided in almost all of his other post-1941 work. In Hayden's poems of the late 1940s and 1950s, the rather straightforward black heroism and life- and hope-affirming teleology of the early histories give way to what Brown calls a "densely symbolic" poetics (200), but also to a more complicated characterization of human psychology and to a conception of history that meditates on the inescapability of the past, the ubiquity of war death, and modernity's radical evil.

Chapter 6

"Shadow of time. Shadow of blood."

Forgetting the Future in the Dark History Poems of the 1940 and 1950s

---

As Hayden moved out of the "second phase" of his career, his work refracted through the major prisms of his algebraic modernist poetics, his migration to the South, and his effort "to write poetry after Auschwitz" (Adorno 34)—which is to say, his engagement with a human history considerably darkened in the aftermath of World War II. These major influences are on full display in *The Lion and the Archer*, which John Hatcher and Keith Leonard both describe as an *ars poetica* collection, serving as "preface to all his subsequent work" (Hatcher 107). While Hatcher insists that "there is little if any racial point of view" in this new poetics (108), Leonard more intricately and accurately describes a method that "juxtaposes . . . two cultural traditions—African American populism and surrealist art—as part of an ideal unity that is central to the hybrid ethnic self that is at the heart of Hayden's verse" (171). While I would quibble that it is over-wedded to the argument that Hayden's mature poetry is marked by "African American populism," Leonard's assessment is sound and it follows the appraisal of *The Lion* poems offered by Robert Chrisman, whose careful study of Hayden's notebooks shows that "from 1946 to 1948 Robert Hayden transformed his poetry from a Left Populist style that favored social commentary to a modernist aesthetic rich in symbolism and surrealist method. The fruition of this effort was *The Lion and the Archer*" (152). Although I believe that Hayden's transformation can be discerned a bit earlier in the 1945 publication of "Middle Passage"—a poem that does some of the ideological work associated with black Left populism, but in high modernist "style"—the poems published in *The Lion* are certainly the aggressive announcement of his new aesthetic. Later in life Hayden would call these poems "baroque" and "rather heavily ornamented" (*Collected Prose* 107). They are also prime examples of the "elliptical poetry" that Robert Penn Warren had associated with modernism and that in 1946 Frederick Pottle descriptively distilled by saying that, for most readers, "the prime characteristic of this kind of poetry is not the nature of its imagery but its obscurity, its urgent suggestion that you add something to the poem without telling what that something is" (qtd. in Hirsch 200). In Hayden's words, this poetry was like "solving for X" (*Collected Prose* 156).

Conceptual ellipses had appeared in some of Hayden's early work, and in his arrangement of fragmentary voices in "Middle Passage" and later in "Runagate," he had insisted that a fair amount of connective logic be produced by readers. But the six poems of *The Lion* are wholly guided by Hayden's new commitment to an elliptical aesthetic and ornate lexical ornamentation. It is this aesthetic that produces the surrealist environment of "A Ballad of Remembrance," the one poem from the 1948 book that Hayden included in his *Selected Poems* in 1966. The opening stanza reads:

> Quadroon mermaids, Afro angels, saints
> blackgilt balanced upon the switchblades of that air
> and sang. Tight streets unfolding to the eye
> like fans of corrosion and elegiac lace
> cackled with their singing: Shadow of time. Shadow
> of blood.[1]

Here, "the racial point of view" has not been abandoned; it has been deeply interiorized by a speaker responding to the hazard of southern space, of New Orleans. There is no easy footing for the reader of this stanza, no sure way of knowing setting or protagonist, only an abiding sense of danger and obviously black presences singing—but certainly not in the melodies of the Negro spirituals that breathed with the hope of "justice in some fair world beyond" (Du Bois, *Souls* 251). Indeed, the presences of this ballad seem to sing their threatening song from a *dark* world beyond. The documentary archives of American history, from which Hayden seemed to transcribe his early heritage poems, have been replaced by the subjective impressionism of the poet-speaker's consciousness. Obliterating the hold of social realism, Hayden now enters a period in which the speaker of "Theme and Variation," first published in 1950, asserts, "I've spied from the corner of my eye / upon the striptease of reality."[2] Through this voyeuristic vision—libidinous, oblique, and perhaps untrustworthy—Hayden offers the black past, not as heroic teleology, but as surreal and crowding trauma. This radically altered approach to black history is condensed in the image of the "Quadroon mermaids" that usher in "A Ballad of Remembrance." The grotesque exaggeration of New World race consciousness is evoked in the pejorative *Quadroon*, the definition of which is provided deadpan in C. L. R. James's description of the 128 strands of blackness defined in eighteenth-century Haiti. Of the "quarteron" James writes, "The true Mulatto was the child of the pure black and the pure white. The child of the white and a Mulatto woman was a quarteron with 96 parts white and 32 parts black. But the quarteron could be produced by the white and the marabou in the proportion of 88 to 40, or by the white and the sacatra, in the proportion of 72 to 56, and so on all through the 128 varieties" (38). Entering Hayden's poem through the antiquated "Quadroon," readers are turned toward history by way of a racial taxonomy that, as James tacitly points out, is both real and absurd. Western modernity's confusing and obsessive effort to read blackness in the human body is multiplied and underscored as Hayden makes these raced figures into "mermaids"—half-human fantasies of a sexualized imagination unwilling or unable to organize history through stable realist narrative. More painter than historiographer, in "A Ballad of Remembrance" Hayden records the dark impression of history preserved in the Mardi Gras streets by the "Quadroon mermaids, Afro angels, saints" and other carnival characters whose "cackled . . . singing" is the synesthetic, encroaching "Shadow of time. Shadow / of blood." Whatever the difficulties or pleasures created by Hayden's new baroque, elliptical method, it is clear that the history that haunts this stanza will not be easily converted to the same type of nourishing milk that flowed from the early heritage poems.

The significant reorientation of Hayden's poetics was in part an attempt to slough off the demanding propagandistic expectations of black art by centering associational symbols rather than narrative and argument—it was the artistic enactment of ideas that Hayden set down in a 1948 manifesto titled "Counterpoise." This terse document was published by a small collective of black male writers who gathered around Hayden in the years after his 1946 move from teaching assistant at the University of Michigan to a post teaching creative writing and literature at Fisk University, the major black school in Nashville, Tennessee. The insistent "Counterpoise" statement, without capitalization or punctuation, announced the contours of a political aesthetic that would guide Hayden through the remainder of his life and that would influence his approach to history. Advocating experimentation but not claiming the artistic "avant-garde in the accepted sense of the term," the manifesto essentially refuses the limitations prescribed by social realism and the black nationalist drum-major impulse:

> we are unalterably opposed to the chauvinistic, the cultish, to special pleading, to all that seeks to limit and restrict creative expression

> we believe experimentation to be an absolute necessity . . .

> as writers who belong to a so-called minority we are violently opposed to having our work viewed, as the custom is, entirely in the light of sociology and politics . . .

> we believe in the oneness of mankind and the importance of the arts in the struggle for peace and unity (*Collected Prose* 41–42)

Although it borrows language and principles—like the "oneness of mankind"—from the midcentury lexicon of the American Bahá'í community that Hayden entered into in the early 1940s, the "Counterpoise" statement also reflects post–World War II intellectual consensus contained in the early documents of the United Nations, such as UNESCO's 1950 "Statement on Race," which opens by declaring, "Scientists have reached general agreement that mankind is one" (qtd. in R. King 2). The positions that Hayden articulated in the "Counterpoise" Statement were equally in keeping with midcentury trends in African American letters. In 1950 Langston Hughes would assert, "The most heartening thing for me . . . is to see Negroes writing works in the general American field, rather than dwelling on Negro themes solely" (311). And Margaret Walker, with the work of Hayden in mind, along with that of Gwendolyn Brooks and Bruce McWright, would encourage the broadening perspective of poets for whom "race is rather used as a point of departure toward a global point of view than as the central theme of one obsessed by race." She would add that "this global perspective is an important new note in poetry" and the "new poetry has universal appeal coupled with another definite mark of neo-classicism, the return to form" ("New Poets" 350). Brooks, the exacting formalist of 1940s Negro poetry, would also endorse the move away from pure protest and overt social realism, declaring that "no real artist is going to be content with offering raw materials. The Negro poet's most urgent duty, at present, is to polish his technique, his way of presenting his truths and his beauties, that these may be more insinuating, and, therefore, more overwhelming" ("Poets Who Are Negroes" 312).

Hayden's move away from transparently "Negro themes" determined by straightforward "sociology and politics" and toward elliptical techniques of insinuation was in many respects the order of the day by the late 1940s. Along with Hughes, Walker, Brooks, and others, Hayden sought to escape the inertia of the realist protest so powerfully epitomized in the earlier fiction of Richard Wright. Of course Hayden, and others of his generation, may have also been awakened to the powers of insinuation and aestheticism by the onset of a Cold War political climate that readily equated black cultural protest with prosecutable dissidence (See Smethurst, *New Red Negro* 51). However, the adamant way in which Hayden used his "Counterpoise" statement and *The Lion* poems to bolt into a symbolist poetics that eschewed any semblance of familiar racial protest was likely his response to a logic employed by Alain Locke in 1947 to explain a problem faced by poets caught in the aesthetic undertow of late 1930s and early 1940s black populist social realism:

> For those who belong to a transitional generation, there is always the inescapable dilemma of being caught between two contrary minded aesthetics; still, one has ultimately to choose, if for no other reason than to achieve proper fusion of style and integration of feeling. Whereas to remain in doubt as whether to be racial or generic, introspective or expressionist, symbolic or realistic, mystic or socially oriented, is to hover rather ineffectually in a poetic void. ("Reason and Race" 22)

Although he would have questioned the efficacy of such hard dichotomies, in *The Lion* Hayden signaled that he was not going to float in the uncertain void that Locke imagines. The poet's aggressively baroque ellipticism represented a decisive break from the old regime and was recognized as such in forums like the *New York Times Book Review*, which conjectured that *The Lion* might come to represent "the entering wedge in the 'emancipation' of Negro poetry in America" (Rodman 27). But, as Hayden attempted to escape aesthetic shackles by widening the interpretive possibility for his poems and by asserting "global perspective," in his work of the late 1940s and 1950s he also moved toward a worldview in which history and violence melded into in an almost inescapable "Shadow of time. Shadow of / blood." In effect, Hayden's turn to symbol and image facilitated narratives of history that were less linear and salvific and more imaginative than those of his earlier phases, more alive to ideas of temporal accumulation in which the past is never dead.

As the speaker of "A Ballad of Remembrance" moves through the streets of Jim Crow New Orleans—which both revolted and fascinated Hayden during his first trip to the Deep South in 1946—he is followed by the returned "dead," "ghosts," and a Mardi Gras spirit that dresses characters in "an undertaker's dream / of disaster." Seemingly disinterred from the past, these haunting characters accost the speaker, but they are not simply static remembrances. They actively furnish Hayden's poetic persona with programs designed to cope with what Hayden in an interview called the "dehumanizing" present of the segregated South:

> Accommodate, muttered the zulu king, throned
> like a copper toad in a glaucous poison jewel.
> Love, chimed the saints and the angels and the mermaids.
> Hate, shrieked the gunmetal priestess
> from her spiked bellcollar curved like a fleur-de-lys:

Some four decades before Octavia Butler, Toni Morrison, and other practitioners of the neoslave narrative helped readers to understand that black ghosts might speak through time, producing a pedagogy for the present based on stories from the past, Hayden's spectral resurrections offer their advice to the harried protagonist of the poem. Here antebellum history is lodged not in interpolated written or oral texts but prominently in the "spiked bellcollar," a stark metonym that shrieks its name through the ghostly figure that Hayden places within the crude surveillance machine of the slavery-era South. Whereas "Middle Passage," "Frederick Douglass," and "Runagate" transmuted slave history into clear messages of encouragement and perseverance, the advice of the gunmetal priestess that animates the slave collar is quite different and represents only one of several social-emotional programs available to the speaker. The priestess advises "Hate," but her collar, "curved like a fleur-de-lys," is both torturous and—in the speaker's eye—ornamental, suggesting surreal contradiction and unstable signification. Speaker and reader cannot fully trust perceptive powers that can turn the collar into ornamental jewelry. Similarly, in Hayden's new poetics history does not reliably translate into pat lessons—the figure within the slave collar urges hate, but the other apparitions direct the speaker to "accommodate" and "love." However, none of these programs, all responses to the dark past that looms behind encircling "metaphorical doors" and "decors of illusion," satisfy the speaker.

In the 1940s, intellectuals as diverse as Richard Wright and Gunnar Myrdal suggested that the history of racism had produced an "American

dilemma" for the white majority—how could ongoing legacies of racial op-
pression be morally squared with the nation's liberal ideals? What political
and social imperatives did history produce? But "A Ballad of Remembrance"
posits a somewhat different dilemma—one more individual and inward:
How could the historically aware (black) American construct a personal race
politics sturdy enough to deal with the realities of a Jim Crow nation? In
New Orleans, "down-South arcane city / with death in its jaws like gold teeth
and archaic / cusswords," Hayden's speaker finds himself unsustained by the
prepackaged options of political discourse. To simply hate, love, or accommo-
date is not to truly escape the shadow of time that Hayden felt so viscerally.
Nevertheless, the poem's speaker finally does find respite from the past and
the "minotaurs of edict" it has produced. Battered about by these minotaur
and mermaid images of a history that is part "true" remembrance and part
aestheticized nightmare-elegy, he finds shelter in the "meditative, ironic, /
richly human" companionship of another poet, "Mark Van Doren," whose full
name—weighted by three stresses falling heavily, successively on its first three
syllables—enters the poem as an anchor in the midst of allusive welter. In this
resolution there is no program, no didactic cartography that leads a people
toward "freedom." Hayden's speaker finds only a provisional, temporary, and
very personal means of escaping the shadow of time. If the poet once trans-
formed the historical archive into nourishing ideological milk usable by a
forward-marching race, the subjective symbolism of Hayden's new interior-
izing poetics renders the past as an impinging, dark chaos that does not eas-
ily inspire new life or lead toward freedom. Once the speaker finds comfort
in interracial companionship (Van Doren was white), his "heart rested"—as
though his escape from the burden of history is only a temporary respite and
preparation for future struggle.

Few of Hayden's readers note the early arrival of this darkened historical
vision in the poet's career. For example, Charles Davis's seminal assessment
of Hayden's "use of history" locates the poet's transformed approach to the
historical record much later, in the 1970 collection *Words in the Mourning
Time*, which I take up later. Skipping Hayden's development in the late 1940s
and 1950s, Davis contrasts the early heritage poems of the "Black Spear" proj-
ect with the *Mourning Time* material that responds to the social tumult of the
1960s. He writes, "Hayden's poems published in 1970, *Words in the Mourning
Time*, reveal a persistence of an interest in historical materials, but they do
not have the focus or the concentration which the ideal of *The Black Spear*
provided. . . . Hayden faces a world not entirely reassuring to the firmness of
his early vision." Referencing the salvific rhetoric of the earlier history poems,

Davis continues, "The consequences of 'middle passage' are not all good, nor all life" (263). In pointing up this significant shift, Davis deepens understanding of Hayden for those who know the poet's historiography only through the persevering, expectant, and somewhat nationalist vision of his widely anthologized "Middle Passage," "Frederick Douglass," and "Runagate." But by passing over the work that Hayden produced in his postwar period and focusing on poems like "El Haj Malik El-Shabazz" and "Words in the Mourning Time," Davis's analysis makes it appear as though it was the turbulence of the civil rights era that shook Hayden's confidence in the teleological optimism of his early histories. Closer reading of Hayden's development finds that it is the immediacy and ubiquity of death in the 1940s that troubles both the promise of life and the realist stability that marked poems coming out of the "Black Spear" project.

If "A Ballad of Remembrance" is a baroque, surreal chronicle of the struggle not for progress but for mere footing in a Jim Crow setting haunted by the memory of death, it must be linked to the equally ornate and nightmarish vision of postwar Europe offered in Hayden's 1948 collection. "Eine Kleine Nachtmusik" expresses the "global point of view" recommended by midcentury black intellectuals who in a variety of ways sought to underscore the links between African American social concerns and a global matrix. But while poets like Countee Cullen (in "Apostrophe to the Land") and Gwendolyn Brooks (in "Negro Hero" and the "Gay Chaps at the Bar" sequence) used World War II poems to consider permutations of the call to a Negro "Double Victory"—against racists at home and abroad—Hayden insinuates the connection between American racial trauma and World War II travail only via the thematic and aesthetic commonality that links "Remembrance" and "Nachtmusik." Read in isolation, "Nachtmusik" appears to abandon blackness and America altogether as Hayden confronts the dark night of European civilization with allusive high-culture references, preciously esoteric syntax, and a lexical range that includes French, German, and Spanish. But while Hayden aggressively stakes out poetic space far from the territory of black folk culture and history, it is the problem of an ever-returning, violent past that Hayden posits in both "Remembrance" and "Nachtmusik," the latter of which begins,

> The siren cries that ran like mad and naked screaming women
> with hair ablaze all over Europe, that like ventriloquists
> made steel and stone speak out in the wild idiom of the
>   damned—

oh now they have ceased but have created a groaning after-
silence.

And the mended ferris wheel turns to a tune again
in nevermore Alt Wien and poltergeists in imperials
and eau de cologne go up and up on the ferris wheel la la
in contagious dark where only the dead are relaxed and
    warm.

Pontheolla Williams reads "Nachtmusik" as an example of Hayden's "human-
istic interests that take him out of the category of the ethnic poet" (60). In
the wake of the Black Arts era, Hayden was from time to time upbraided for
this "humanistic interest," and for the baroque style on display in *The Lion*. A
few critics attacked Hayden's high-culture register because it had "no black
flavor," but they also felt that "the problem of language is less important than
the overall problem of sensibility and viewpoint" (Jemie 166). While this
flavor of analysis builds from the folk-focused, oral culture imperatives of the
1960s and 1970s black aesthetic school of critique, some critics of the 1940s
also resisted Hayden's effort to fashion a poetic identity not easily aligned
with the label "ethnic poet." Although Alain Locke had warned poets to
avoid the ineffectual aesthetic space between "introspective or expressionist,
symbolic or realistic," he felt *The Lion* ventured too far into "esoteric mood"
and "cryptic style and symbol" ("Dawn Patrol" 12). And in a very unsympa-
thetic response to the collection, a reviewer in the *Crisis* derided its poems
by adopting a satirical voice to note its "dazzleclustered trees and jokes of
nacre and ormolu and poltergeists in imperials," its "exploring the navel with
candybar joy." Unwilling to give Hayden's new mode more than the most
superficial appraisal, the reviewer mocks, "Indeed all for a dollar you can join
robert hayden's heart when it escapes from the mended ferris wheel and the
clawfoot sarabande in its dance" (Dover 252). Facetiously deflating Hayden's
symbolism and allusiveness, the review in the *Crisis*—which was no bastion
of earthy folk expressive culture—reveals that derisive opposition to Hayden's
mature aesthetic began as soon as it was codified through the "Counterpoise"
statement and *The Lion* poems. The barb at the end of the review's rhetorical
spear was the same one that would be used against Hayden almost twenty
years later in the pages of *Black World* and at the 1966 Fisk writers' confer-
ence, and more than sixty years later in Amiri Baraka's time-traveling review
of Charles Rowell's *Angles of Ascent* anthology: Hayden's mature poetics was a
self-seeking abdication of black artistry—or, as the reviewer in the *Crisis* put

it, an effort to "get right into selden rodman's anthology instead of the *negro caravan*" (Dover 252).[3]

Of course, the criticisms have some truth to them because the proverbial Negro caravan was headed in a direction that Hayden did not follow. In the postwar moment Hayden viscerally recognized a horrific historical "reality" that could be spied upon only "from the corner of my eye"—however, the limitations that Hayden rejected are not those of the "black man's point of view" per se but of the poetic and rhetorical strategies that had been so closely *associated* with that point of view. Hayden probably had his own verse in mind when, writing of American poetry generally, he pointed out that "during the war years and after, poetry tended to grow more subjective and metaphysical" (*Collected Prose* 49). The tradition of folk romance or lyric realism and the politics of protest would not suffice in the face of the sublime, unspeakable history that Hayden confronted in the aftermath of World War II—nor would teleological models of historical progress. It is no coincidence that in his effort to write "poetry after Auschwitz," Hayden seemed to turn away from teleology while also moving toward deep ellipticism and conspicuously esoteric, estranging, "dazzleclustered" syntax. The horrors of the Holocaust and the war brought on not only a crisis of faith in human (Western) civilization but also a crisis of faith in artistic representation. Hayden's poems register these twin crises. In 1948, just a few years after the cessation of systematized genocide that Hayden would repeatedly evoke in later work, notions of salvific history seemed impossibly simple, even cruel. Hayden's *least* salvific versions of history are found in those poems published in the decade after the end of World War II, and his *most* baroque and elliptical poems were published in the same period. Surely, the arcane, oblique diction of *The Lion*—so easily (maybe too easily) mocked—is part of Hayden's effort to find a language calibrated to the twentieth century's most mind-defying events.

Theodor Adorno's dictum that to write poetry after Auschwitz is barbarism has been understood in myriad ways since it appeared in 1951, but two responses to it are particularly relevant to Hayden's work in *The Lion*. The first comes from Lyn Hejinian, who keys on Adorno's word *barbarism* to suggest that his statement is not a condemnation of poetry after the Holocaust but a "challenge and behest" to produce a new "foreign" poetry. Hejinian writes, "The word 'barbarism,' as it comes to us from the Greek *barbaros*, means 'foreign'—that is, 'not speaking the same language' (*barbaros* being an onomatopoeic imitation of babbling)—and such is precisely the task of poetry: *not to speak in the same language as Auschwitz*. Poetry after Auschwitz must indeed be barbarian; it must be foreign to the cultures that produce atrocities."

She goes on to argue that Adorno wanted a poetry possessed by "the barbarism of strangeness" (326, emphasis in the original). Certainly, the recurrent use of neologism and the polyglossic gaudiness of "Nachtmusik"—its "clawfoot sarabande," "knucklebone passacaglia," and "poltergeists in imperials and eau de cologne"—ought to be considered signs of a serious poet searching for language, for the destabilizing, unfamiliar syntax of a horror that, if represented, must always remain destabilizing and unfamiliar. Ironically, but not surprisingly, the "strangeness" of Hayden's late 1940s poetry—and his major aesthetic transformation of that period—has *never* been figured as a reaction to World War II, despite the fact that his oeuvre shows a deep sensitivity to the historical nightmare emerging from what he would later call "the corpse woodpiles . . . the ashes and staring pits / of Buchenwald, Dachau" (*Ballad of Remembrance* 42). Still later, in the last collection published during his life, the "staring pits" of the European bloodlands would return in "Killing the Calves," a poem that approaches the human cataclysm of Nazi death factories by way of the industrial farm—

> —men women children
> forced like superfluous animals
> into a pit and less than cattle
> in warcrazed eyes like crazed cattle slaughtered.
> (American Journal n.p.)

A second response to Adorno's aphorism, this one from Primo Levi, helps us to think about how the existential shocks of World War II facilitated Hayden's move toward "humanistic interests"—that is, toward subject matter not especially tied to black life. Levi, referring to his own time in the death camp, explains, "In those days I would have reformulated Adorno's remark like this: After Auschwitz, there can be no more poetry, except about Auschwitz" (qtd. in Guyer 4). Whether or not Levi would have all poetry be "about Auschwitz" in a literal sense, or about the human capacities for evil, suffering, or survival metonymically represented in Auschwitz, his reformulation is actually a concurrence with Adorno that deepens the millennial demarcation of the Shoah and makes it a massively magnetic point of reference. For Adorno, the German-Jewish intellectual, and Levi, the Holocaust survivor, this rendering of Auschwitz as a historically exceptional event, capable of defining all art in its wake, was at once eminently reasonable and ethnocentric. National Socialist ideology, combined with modern mechanization and organizational bureaucracy, produced forms of atrocity that were unique in all human history, while especially targeting a particular group of humans. This historically unprecedented form and concentration of violence allowed Jewish intellectuals to speak in universal terms while also ethnocentrically focusing on Jewish abjection. But Hayden's gravitation to the same locus of history obviously represents a rejection of ethnocentric historical vision. Unlike Adorno or Levi, whose responses to Auschwitz are marked by forms of ethnic solidarity, Hayden's impulse to write about "skin and bones Europe [that] hurts all over from the / swastika's / hexentanz" indicates an unrestricted humanism. By foregrounding Europe and the Jewish Holocaust, Hayden pulled the Negro caravan into explicit universalist terrain, laying claim to historical subject matter—and specifically to what he would in another context call "man's cruelty to man" (*Collected Prose* 170)—apparently distanced from Negro exigency.

In "Nachtmusik" Hayden's seeming Eurocentrism arises from this interest in "man's cruelty to man"—from a compulsion to encounter the very darkest elements of human history and subject them to aesthetic power. Simon Gikandi suggests that this compulsion is at the heart of Hayden's work, that his best poems are "about the capacity of the writer to turn to abjection as the source of creative energy and thus to bring some of the excesses—and ugliness—of modern life into a measure of control" (319). Following Gikandi's assessment, it is no surprise that the sublime horror of Auschwitz called to Hayden. In the early heritage poems, he had managed to both record and control the abjections of the African American slave experience by reading them through a narrative of progress stretching from the antebellum period into the early 1940s. But the staggering scale and stark, seemingly irrational evil let loose by World War II tested the "measure of control" that Hayden had exerted over the black strands of history. In "Middle Passage," for example, Hayden uses teleology to give redemptive order to black Atlantic history; he also brings comprehension and analysis to this history by placing an emphasis on the Christian hypocrisy that facilitated the slave trade and by joining it to the economic rationalism of the trade ("bringing home / black gold"), thus laying bare the ideological contradictions and ironies at the heart of New World slavery. But the Nazi totalitarian ideology that produced the Jewish Holocaust was not as manifestly hypocritical as the brand of Christian thinking that justified slavery; neither was it primarily motivated by economic rationalism. Nazi extermination efforts differed qualitatively from the systems of race-based abjections found in New World slavery. Without a primary economic motivation, Auschwitz was for many the sign of a new form of mass abjection, a new form of immorality that Hannah Arendt would call "radical evil" or "absolute evil." For Arendt, writing only months after the publication of *The Lion*, this was an evil that "could no longer be deduced from humanly comprehensible motives" (ix). Hayden's inclination "to turn to abjection as the source of creative energy" meant that the radical evil of World War II presented him with a new challenge or a new "source," kin to the "ugliness" of the slave history he had confronted and controlled in his earlier poetry.

The point here is that Hayden's fascination with evil—or alternatively, his sensitivity to "man's cruelty to man"—drew him into a poetics that subsumed Negro subject matter within a universalist vision that could as readily focus on Europe qua Europe as on the horrors found in black history. Indeed, read in the light of Hayden's compulsion to engage history's darkest episodes, the opening words of "Nachtmusik"—"The siren cries"—represent more than spectral alarms lingering in the poem's postwar setting; they are also acknowledgement of the perverse attractiveness and the inescapability of Europe in the 1940s. The sublime, incomprehensible nature of absolute evil called to Hayden. Induced to bring "the excesses—and ugliness—of modern life into a measure of control" (Gikandi 319) at the outset of his artistic maturity, he turned toward Europe, but not because it represented the cultural or moral ideals that he sought. Quite the opposite. Hayden turned to Europe at midcentury because it was the heart of darkness. The negative review of *The Lion* in the *Crisis* may have detected aspirational pretension in the title of "Eine Kleine Nachtmusik," borrowed from Mozart's late eighteenth-century serenade, which is practically an accompanying soundtrack for the courtly opulence of imperial Europe. But Hayden's appropriation is manifestly ironic and indicting. If rhythms of perseverance and the will to life can be felt in the Negro spirituals of "Runagate" and in the blues lyrics of *The Lion* (offered in "Homage to the Empress of the Blues"), Hayden strikes up Mozart's music so that it may bleed into the sounds of death—the "cries," "screaming," and "groaning" of the poem's opening stanza. The serenade is appropriated as the cultural metonym for a Western civilization that, in the aftermath of World War II, seemed to culminate in radical evil and the material and moral rubble of "skin-and-bones Europe." "Nachtmusik's" evocation of Mozart's iconic text suggests that postwar desolation calls for a skeptical rereading of Western cultural history at the moment when, as Arendt put it, "the subterranean stream of Western history has finally come to the surface and usurped the dignity of our tradition" (ix). Hayden's early heritage poems ("Middle Passage" in particular) showed keen interest in exposing that dark stream as its currents flowed through the black Atlantic. In "Nachtmusik" Hayden joins his poetry to a European tradition in its darkest hour, not because he seeks a normative humanism epitomized in Western art but rather to impute a relation between radical evil and the cultural lifeblood of the West.

In assessing historicity and the failed promises of Western rationalism, scholars from a wide range of disciplines have called on Walter Benjamin's "Theses on the Philosophy of History." Benjamin's aphoristic and therefore somewhat malleable proposals attempted, in 1940, to disrupt the historical teleology embraced by many Marx-inspired materialists—like the social realist writers surrounding Hayden in the 1930s. Recognizing Stalin's travesty of the Communist revolution and unwilling to subscribe to faith in any utopian narrative of progression, Benjamin's theses describe temporality as disjunction and offer a sense of history in which the past continually impinges on the present. In the field of black studies Benjamin's essay has been prominently evoked in the effort to underwrite arguments about the presence of the past in the post–civil rights era and to validate the historical turn in black cultural production of recent decades.[4] But portions of the essay are especially helpful in explaining the sense of history and temporality expressed in the poetry Hayden wrote soon after the publication of "Theses on the Philosophy of History."

Benjamin produced the essay as a hunted Jewish intellectual on the eve of European cataclysm, and though he committed suicide before the most terrible events of World War II took place, "Theses" is written with an understanding of what was to come. Perhaps this premonitory knowledge helped conjure the essay's "angel of history," a figure that will not look into the future—a figure I take as a representation of Hayden's midcentury poetic consciousness:

> This is how one pictures the angel of history. His face is turned toward the past. Where we perceive a chain of events, he sees one single catastrophe which keeps piling wreckage upon wreckage and hurls it in front of his feet. The angel would like to stay, awaken the dead, and make whole what has been smashed. But a storm is blowing from Paradise; it has got caught in his wings with such violence that the angel can no longer close them. This storm irresistibly propels him into the future to which his back is turned, while the pile of debris before him grows skyward. (257–58)

If in 1939 the disasters of the past made Benjamin's angel unable to attend to the future, by the late 1940s the angel of Hayden's poetic consciousness was similarly oriented. In the wake of World War II, his poetry admits no sense of futurity as it fixates on the past's "wreckage upon wreckage." The symbol of Hayden's early heritage poems must be an amalgam of the West's Janus head—looking both forward and backward—and West Africa's *sankofa* bird that reaches back in order to move forward. But at midcentury, Hayden's resolutely pastward-looking poetry is best captured in Benjamin's angel of history, which is itself the interpretation of the Paul Klee painting *Angelus Novus*. The figure produced between Benjamin and Klee stares, disturbingly transfixed as he sails through time into a "future to which his back is turned."

As I have suggested, the historical appearance of radical evil, in seeming defiance of "humanly comprehensible motives," helps to account for the surrealism and the elliptical, baroque method developed in *The Lion* and honed in Hayden's later poetry. It also repelled him from confidently salvific, linear models of history common to Western rationalism, Negro spirituals and the Negro Church, and Marxist teleology. In both "A Ballad of Remembrance" and "Nachtmusik," the postwar moment is the territory of the dead, who are "relaxed and / warm" and exercise a haunting dominion over a present that seems mostly animated by the recycling of the "smashed" past. Rather than fixing on a telos, in these poems and in almost all of his 1950s poetry Hayden occludes what is to come. Benjamin offered the pastward-facing angel of history as a preface to suicide, suggesting that he wanted to escape the storm that "irresistibly" pushes his angel into the future. But Hayden's midcentury pastward poems pretend as though the future does not exist; they respond to the failed utopias of European and American modernity with doses of frenzied but stationary movement in the present. For midcentury Hayden, history moves but it goes nowhere—like "Nachtmusik's" "mended ferris wheel" with its poltergeist passengers. The sense of advancement that was so much a part of the early heritage poems, born of a Negro faith in Enlightenment principles of perfectible society, has been checked in these postwar poems that, like the stationary spinning of the Ferris wheel, are full of movement without progression. Composed of two stanzas, each beginning with the adverb *now*, the final section of "Nachtmusik" is anchored in a present defined by death.

> Now as the ferris wheel revolves to extrovert neomusic
> and soldiers pay with cigarettes and candybars
> for rides with famished girls whose colloquies
> with death taught them how to play at being whores:

Now as skin-and-bones Europe hurts all over from the swastika's
hexantanz

In a geography desiccated by the dance of radical evil, painful memory
teaches and defines. Notice that, for the "famished girls" riding the fixed
wheel, it is past experience with death—rather than immediate hunger—that
most informs their strategies of compromise, their inauthentic "play at being
whores." Trapped in the present by "colloquies / with death" in the past, these
figures have no cause to preserve virtue because they have no future.

At midcentury, after Auschwitz, Hiroshima, and more than a half cen-
tury of Jim Crow, the ubiquity of death—particularly war death—permeates
Hayden's poetry, undermining Enlightenment conceptions of temporality
that imagine the "secular future as dynamic and superior to the past" (Huys-
sen 8). In a rarely noticed poem published in *Phylon* at the height of Ameri-
can involvement in the Korean War, Hayden dispenses with the baroque style
of *The Lion* and with narratorial detachment observes the incomprehensible
scale of modern warfare. The three-quatrain "Dead Soldiers: Pacific Theater"
suggests that to record, represent, or even conceive of modern war casualties
is to engage in theatrical distortion. In the poem's final stanza, Hayden sets
the accumulation of corpses against the possibility of imagination:

> Dead and multi-single and of no further use
> to ambitious death, they lie
> in the burning zero weather of logistics,
> in the fire-path of advance. In the foreground of the mind. (172)

Here, the dead choke off progressive "advance" and crowd the stage of the
"mind," foreclosing any sense of futurity. For Hayden the postwar accumu-
lation of battle corpses leads to the shifting sense of history that Andreas
Huyssen captures in a contrastive formulation: "History as narrative of eman-
cipation and liberation always points to some future. . . . On the other hand,
history as memory and remembrance is always a narrative concerned with a
past" (87). Blocked from the future by "corpse woodpiles," Hayden shifts into
a temporal accumulation model of "history as memory and remembrance"
that exhumes not only the Ferris wheel poltergeists of "Nachtmusik," but
also the postwar Mardi Gras ghosts of "A Ballad of Remembrance."[5] These
poems—both responses to racialized terror—are populated by the returned
and encroaching dead and set the stage for a period of output in the 1950s in
which Hayden repeatedly turns his poetic gaze on American scenes of the

writing present that appear to him as "palimpsests / new-scrawled with old embittered texts" ("Locus" *Ballad* 8).

A series of landscape poems initially published in the 1950s exhibit Hayden's postwar pivot toward the South and its past, which, in his words, loomed in southern consciousness like an "atavistic memory" (*Collected Prose* 157). This negative shading of southern memory—characterized by the aberrant recurrence of a past that refuses to pass away—positions Hayden as a northern, black outsider in the haunted southern space that he reads in "On Lookout Mountain," "Locus," and "Tour 5." (He would eventually gather these poems, initially published in 1952, 1955, and 1958, respectively, sequentially in his 1962 collection, *A Ballad of Remembrance*. All quotations from the poems are taken from *Ballad*.) If Hayden primarily sought the elliptical evocation of overwhelming history in *The Lion*, by the 1950s he returned to some of the interpretive work carried out in his early heritage poems. Although "On Lookout Mountain," "Tour 5," and "Locus" are negations of the progressive historical narrative of his early heritage work, like those poems, these landscape pieces are also correctives that illustrate and challenge the "atavistic memory" of the American "victimizer victimized by truth / he dares not comprehend" ("Locus" 8). Emphasizing the white southerner's selective relation to the past—at once amnesic and nostalgic—Hayden uses his landscape poems to supply his version of "truth" as antidote.

"On Lookout Mountain" is an elegy in which the site of significant Civil War combat in Chattanooga, Tennessee, inspires remembrance of both the nineteenth-century battle and the Korean War that, at the time of the poem's publication, was raging "a world away / yet nearer than our hope or our belief." Hayden begins with an aural conceit whereby sonic echo is used to join past and present:

> I listen for the sounds of cannon, cries
> vibrating still upon the rocky air,
> timeless echoes in echoic time—
> imagine how they circle out and out
> in concentricity with Kilroy's cries
> as now somewhere beyond
> tangent calm of this mid-century morning (*Ballad* 10)

Using paradoxical juxtaposition—a signature maneuver of his later work—Hayden calls attention to the *imperceptible* relation of past and present by claiming that the Civil War sounds are "vibrating still." The poem allows *still* to function as both adverb and adjective: the sonic tumult of the war, and thus some sense of the war itself, can "still" be experienced almost a century after it took place; yet in the placid morning of the speaker's present, the air is "still"—it seems to carry no sound. As the poem concludes, Hayden's speaker will call attention to the historical deafness of his fellow Lookout Mountain sightseers while pointing out that the "alpinists of Sunday / choose souvenirs and views." They are content with "views" and the visual mode of perception, unable to hear the relation between past and present as the speaker does. (Considering his use of auditory imagery, the poet once remarked, "As a compensation for my poor vision, I have extremely good hearing" [*Collected Prose* 159].) The unrecognized relation is one of repetition—as asserted and performed in the line "timeless echoes in echoic time—." Here, repetition itself is doubled, as both *time* and *echo* are repeated (with the dash potentially indicating endless reverberation); in the following line there is the single echo of "out and out"; and in the next, "Kilroy's cries" are the distant echo of the Civil War "cries" of the poem's first line. Although he is the suffering soldier of the middle twentieth century, Kilroy—the generic, everyman-GI evoked in the widespread World War II–era graffiti tag "Kilroy was here"— voices an anguish that has sonic origins in the middle nineteenth century. The deceptive "calm" of the poem's setting is "tangent" partly because of the word's resonance with its near homonym, *plangent*—a word of aural melancholy that Hayden calls upon in other poems (*Collected Poems* 22). But the setting itself is a "tangent" connecting two moments of war: one that occurred a hundred years in the past at Lookout Mountain and the other that occurs in the poem's writing present but ten thousand kilometers away from Lookout Mountain. Collapsing time and space into a single node, the "mid-century morning" evoked by the speaker is as much a reference to the Civil War's middle nineteenth century as it is to the Korean War's middle twentieth century. And as the poem continues, the soldiers who "clambered up the crackling mountainside" in Chattanooga are resurrected in the combatants of the Pacific Theater who "climb endless carrion-blooming hills of war." Like the riders of the spinning but stationary Ferris wheel of "Nachtmusik," the soldiers of "Lookout Mountain" are caught in place and time. They move up endless hills of war without progress.

"Tour 5," first published in *Phylon* in 1958, similarly resists futurity by sketching an American geography that condenses past and present. In southward descent, Hayden's speaker narrates a highway journey along the Natchez Trace—"the route of phantoms, highwaymen, of slaves and armies" (*Ballad of Remembrance* 9) extending from Nashville, Tennessee, to Natchez, Mississippi. As "the road winds down" into deep southern space, once again Hayden sees ghosts of the past, but he also imagines that his black character—referred to in the second person—is phantom-like for the whites "whose eyes revile / You as the enemy." The hamlets traversed in the poem are "static / villages" where the gears of history have seized up; they are "watched over by Confederate sentinels." Evoking mythical Gorgon, a sister of Medusa also invested with petrifying power, the speaker describes one of these sentinels: "Shrill gorgon / silence breathes behind his taut civility / and in the ever-tautening / air." While "Lookout Mountain," "Nachtmusik," and "Ballad of Remembrance" are agitated by the imagery of stationary movement in a present that will not give way to a future, "Tour 5" uses a diction of stasis to suggest that, in parts of America, tautening time has congealed in a Civil War or antebellum moment.

It is this early and pre-American past that controls "Locus," the 1955 *Figure of Time* poem fixated on southern flora charged with memory of "belles / and massas" lingering among "rock-hoisted hills where sachems / counseled or defied, where scouts gazed down / upon the glittering death-march of De Soto" (*Ballad of Remembrance* 8). The poem is paced by the repetition of adverbial phrases beginning with "here," an emphatic anchoring device that positions readers in the "here and now" of mid-twentieth-century southern space even as the temporal locus of the poem seems to float in a long-gone, ever-present historical context:

> Here guilt,
> here agenbite
> and victimizer victimized by truth
> he dares not comprehend.
> Here the past, adored and unforgiven,
> its wrongs, denials, grievous loyalties
> alive in hard averted eyes—
> the very structure of the bones: soul-scape
> terrain
> of warring ghosts whose guns are real.

Hayden's haunted southern landscapes of the 1950s are dangerous and violent, "hard bitten and sore-beset." They flower "with every blossom fanged and deadly." They are sharp, serrated by alliteration: "the landscape lush, / metallic, flayed; its brightness harsh as bloodstained swords." And thus they are another rejoinder against the fantasy imagery of plantation literature suggested in Stephen Benét's hope for a black-skinned poetics harmonized in the "Soft mellow of the levee roustabouts, / Singing at night against the banjo-moon—" (348). Hayden's southern landscapes, imbuing natural ecology with a history of violence, participate in a tradition that Édouard Glissant finds throughout the postcolonial writing world. While planter and colonial classes of European stock willed into being the sensuous literary charm of the plantation landscape (Benét's "banjo-moon" in the soft night), ethnic writers of the twentieth-century Atlantic world stamped that same space with the viciousness that gave life to colonial society. As Glissant puts it, the colonial world developed an aesthetic emphasizing "the gentleness and beauty" of the landscape, meant to "blot out the shudders of life, that is, the turbulent realities of the Plantation, beneath the conventional splendor of scenery" (70). The response was an ethnic literature that "went against the convention of a falsely legitimizing landscape and conceived of landscape as basically implicated in a story, in which it too was a vivid character" (71).

Hayden's "bloodstained" southern landscapes are then in keeping with a resistive paradigm of representation that Glissant thinks of as "creative *marronage*." Likening cultural dissent to the political insurgency of the Maroons (slaves who escaped into the hills of the Caribbean islands to form fugitive communities in opposition to plantation order), Glissant identifies several forms of representational disruption in the work of New World writers. Violent vivification of landscape is only one strategy of interference he recognizes. More central to creative *marronage* is the deformation of a traditional linear concept of time so at odds with a New World reality marked by the continual explosion of linguistic, familial, and ethnic continuities. Within the reality that Glissant metaphorically spatializes as the "Plantation," "the always multilingual and frequently multiracial tangle created inextricable knots within the web of filiations, thereby breaking the clear linear order to which Western thought had imparted such brilliance" (71). Hayden's 1950s poems, stabbing fragments of the past into landscapes of the writing present, cutting through tidy temporal boundaries, seem to be quintessential examples of the creative *marronage* undertaken by New World writers who responded to "Plantation" history by exploring the "coils of time" and asserting that, to quote Glissant once again, "Memory in our works is not a calendar memory; our experience of time does not keep company with the rhythms of month and year alone" (72).

Yet, as I've argued, the temporal manipulation and deformation of Hayden's poetry of the late 1940s and 1950s can also be read as a Western modernist response to the staggering scale of systemic, mechanized, global death fully fathomed at midcentury. Which is to say that, while the comingling of the past and the present in Hayden's southern landscape poems (and "Remembrance") is a species of Glissant's *marronage*, the absence of futurity in these poems—their conception of "history as memory and remembrance" rather than as salvific narrative—is also a sign of Western secular pessimism that bloomed after the war. In *The Lion and the Archer*'s similarly baroque and equally death-obsessed "Ballad of Remembrance" and "Nachtmusik," Hayden uses form and temporal orientation to associate the trauma of black life in America and the suffering of World War II–era Europe. The associative effort signals Hayden's desire to be the Negro poet with the "global point of view," as recommended by Margaret Walker and most other black artist-intellectuals of the 1950s. In his subsequent collection, *Figure of Time*, Hayden continues to build an ambit of engagement simultaneously ethnic and universal, placing black life in America in a postwar global context while looking into an encroaching, violent past. A sense of temporal accumulation is felt in the collection through "Locus," and in the northern landscape poem "On the Maine Coast," where "ghostly thunders are / remotely near," like the past that Hayden's speaker sees in the "Puritan shadow / Indian dark" of his night walking (*Figure 16*). The collection begins with a *remembrance* of a brilliant but hardscrabble ghetto childhood in "'Summertime and the Living . . .'" and achieves its greatest intensity in "Figure," a reimagining of the antilynching genre that was a staple of social realist protest verse of the 1920s and 1930s. Using an emotionally detached, photorealist method, the poem renders the image of a dead man's body:

> We observe how his jeans are
>   torn at the groin:

> How the lower links of the chain cut deeply into
> the small of the back and counter the sag, the downthrust.
>   And the chain, we observe the chain— (*Figure 12*)

By returning to the antilynching genre several decades after its initial prominence and suggesting that "we observe" not an actual lynching but a detail-preserving photographic representation of its result, Hayden's "Figure" alludes to an earlier American era. Although 1955, the year *Figure of Time* was published, witnessed the notorious murder of Emmett Till, there were "only" five other lynchings in the 1950s. Like Hayden's poem, these comparatively rare atrocities recalled the late nineteenth- and early twentieth-century decades during which several thousand black people were lynched. Indeed, part of the reason Till's execution helped spark a major intensification of the civil rights movement was because it was a shrill reminder of a past that had not passed.[6]

In "Figure" Hayden considers this determining past amid conceits of shadow-darkness and light (refrains of his oeuvre) to suggest that the lynched black man is the quintessential symbol of a bloody modernity: "He is a scythe in daylight's clutch. Is gnomon. / Is metaphor of a time, a place. Is our / time geometrized." As the "gnomon"—the central style—of a sundial, the chain-hung black man marks a particular *hour* in Jim Crow space some decades before Hayden's writing present. But *gnomon* is also a term of geometry referring to the part of a parallelogram that remains after a similar parallelogram is taken away from one of its corners. Thus the lynched man is a disfigured figure—what remains after something has been excised.[7] In the eyes of his murderers he is *no man*, a figure robbed of dignity and life by those modernity-compatible ideologies that so readily scythe out the humanity of the dishonored. As the central symbol of "our time," the strange fruit of the "torture tree" becomes, in Hayden's poem, something more than a racially specified American horror. This "time" is possessed not just by blacks or Americans but by humans in every space—the final lines of the poem exemplify what Arnold Rampersad and many others recognize as Hayden's commitment to "linking the particularities of black culture to the universal concerns of the human condition" (Afterword 205).

But more specifically, Hayden's arrangement of the poems in *Figure of Time* again links black travail amid American ethnocidal culture to the Nazi Holocaust. In *The Lion*, Hayden creates aesthetic synergy between "A Ballad of Remembrance" and "Nachtmusik" to suggest an affiliation of black and Jewish trauma; similarly, in *Figure of Time* Hayden immediately follows the American lynch scene in "Figure" with an evocation of European death factories in the poem "In Light Half-Nightmare and Half-Vision," which opens onto the "corpse woodpiles . . . / of Buchenwald, Dachau" (see Chrisman 151). Circumspectly, Hayden makes no play toward comparative victimology with these horrors of modernity's obsession with ethnic hierarchy. Instead, he seems to renovate the African American tradition that often looked typologically to the Exodus narrative and the exilic ordeals of Israel. The affinities of Negro and Jewish abasement are evoked in the attempt to identify and exert aesthetic control over the brutal excesses and wreckage of modern history. Hayden's bid to generate an unbounded sympathy that could radiate from the particularity of Negro experience into the unique circumstances of Jewish suffering was especially noted by Rosey Pool, one of his most en-thusiastic European advocates. For Pool, who was both a significant scholar of African American poetry and a concentration camp survivor, Hayden's alchemic power was felt in his ability to recognize "the suffering of the men and women who died at Dachau and Buchenwald for their specific Negri-tude" (43). Hayden would reciprocate this form of admiration in his eulogy for the Dutch scholar, explaining that "having suffered Nazi persecution, she understood the realities of American race prejudice and identified with its victims" (*Collected Prose* 72). In his 1966 *Selected Poems*, Hayden dedicated a poem to Pool. That poem, "Belsen, Day of Liberation," is yet another of his responses to the Jewish Holocaust.

In the postwar moment, Hayden's effort to comingle black and Jewish histories of ethnocide does the work Paul Gilroy thinks necessary for a full understanding of not only the black Atlantic but modernity at large. Gilroy suggests the rewards of the associational method that Hayden uses to repre-sent the kinship of black and Jewish histories:

> There might be something useful to be gained from setting these his-tories closer to each other not so as to compare them, but as precious resources from which we might learn something valuable about the way that modernity operates, about the scope and status of rational human conduct, about the claims of science and perhaps most im-portantly about the ideologies of humanism with which these brutal histories can be shown to have been complicit. (217)

By drawing together black and Jewish experiences of modernity, Hayden enacts Gilroy's recommendation—some forty years before Gilroy made it. The poet knew that he could not rightly "compare" these experiences, but he brought them together beneath the black light of his art so that the congru-encies of black and Jewish modernity might show fluorescently.[8] These con-gruencies become shockingly bright in Hitler's American-inspired vision of a Nazi empire in central and eastern Europe: As Hitler himself imagined it, "in the East [of Europe] a similar process will repeat itself for a second time as in the conquest of America" (qtd. in Snyder 160). The enabling mechanisms of (realized) American and (thwarted) Nazi expansionism were ethnic exter-mination and slave labor. Intuitively, Hayden recognized that both nation-building projects were reliant on theories of Manifest Destiny that posited future utopias that not only tolerated the suffering of dehumanized peoples but required it.

Chapter 7

"the fire that will save"

————

*History as Theodicy in Poems
of the 1960s and 1970s*

————

If the visions of history that dominated mid-twentieth-century modernity were those that underwrote Nazism, Stalinist Communism, and Jim Crow Americanism, it is no wonder that, like so many others, Hayden turned his back on the future. The almost exclusively pastward historical vision of his poetry published in the immediate postwar period was one version of a midcentury pessimism or spiritual exhaustion that was widespread among black artist-intellectuals of the era. For example, the pointless motion, spiritual emptiness, and living death of LeRoi Jones's mid-1950s work, perfected in "Preface to a Twenty-Volume Suicide Note," is the brilliant correlate of Hayden's past-haunted and futureless poems of the same decade. Taken together, the 1950s poetry of Jones and Hayden powerfully reflects the truth of James Hall's assertion that despite significant civil rights gains of the postwar period, the era was certainly *not* characterized by "the increasing accommodation of black life to modernity and/or the increasing accommodation of modernity to blackness," as some have argued (22). While literary histories of the 1960s have fixated on Jones's radical rejection of Western cultural order and the spiritual malaise it brought to him in the 1950s, Hayden's complicated response to that same order has received comparatively little attention and has most often been thought of in convenient contrast to the Black Arts radicalism embodied by Jones/Baraka. Because the fiery, spectacular style of literary black radicalism of the 1960s so profoundly shapes narratives of African American cultural history, the nuance and intensity of Hayden's own "antimodernism" is boiled away, leaving the idea that his work is usefully understood as an expression of "intellectual calm and pliability" and "integrationist politics," even by his most astute and ardent admirers (Rampersad, "Biography" 204).

Hall is probably the only scholar to adequately challenge a critical formulation that pits Hayden against the Black Arts radicalism in a binary that tends to obscure the poet's dis-ease with modernity. As noted in previous chapters, Hall productively approaches Hayden's work of the 1960s as a prime example of African American "antimodernism"—as a constituent part of a black intellectual mainstream that was thoroughly disaffected by the atomic, self-congratulatory, consumerist moral order of Cold War America. Fittingly, a key dimension of the black antimodernism that Hall finds in the 1960s is skepticism toward Enlightenment narratives of progress founded on rational, secular cults of scientism. The skeptical, black antimodernism was an ethnic species of a general sense of midcentury disquiet that the sociologist C. Wright Mills had diagnosed in 1959—"The very shaping of history now outpaces the ability of men to orient themselves in accordance with cherished values. And which values? Even when they do not panic, men often sense that older ways of feeling and thinking have collapsed and that newer beginnings are ambiguous to the point of moral stasis" (4). If modernity had offered nothing more than spiritual desiccation, the most tenuous forms of black citizenship, and much barbarism rather than civilization, it seemed that by the 1960s a black intellectual consensus had determined that one of the only ways forward was to look to a premodernity. As Hall puts it, "Black anxiousness about the promises of modernity has been articulated most forcefully through an extended evaluation of the possibilities of 'past-ness'" (187). These evaluations of the past were often accouterments of spiritual practices meant to shore up meaning for black intellectuals who had lost faith in both Western modernity and the Negro Church, which had served as bulwark against modernity throughout much of African American history. Many cultural nationalists set about constructing spiritual mythologies that posited halcyonic black pasts assembled out of desirable fragments of premodern—and thus prelapsarian—Africa. Some followed Malcolm X toward the Nation of Islam and its narrative of premodern black purity undermined by the mythic eugenicist Yakub. And others renewed the ethos, and even some of the rituals, of traditional West African ancestor worship.

In 1943, some time before the concretization of Cold War modernity, Hayden had also moved toward a spiritual faith with its own narrative of history. But as my discussion of his midcentury work shows, in the years immediately following his conversion, Hayden's adopted religion, the Bahá'í Faith, seemed to have little to no effect on his poetry, or his sense of history. Late in life he would recall his early days in the faith using somewhat ambiguous terms: "I saw very little influence on my work for the first several years . . . but now I realize that it has given me a base, a focus." John Hatcher leverages the second part of this reflection to imply that Hayden's conversion represents a clean demarcation in the poet's career—a point after which "the Bahá'í Faith shaped his themes and approaches to subjects" (*Collected Prose* 27). But, until the 1955 publication of *Figure of Time*, it is impossible to find clearly marked Bahá'í themes in Hayden's poems, and it was only in the mid-1960s that Hayden started to appeal to a fully developed hermeneutic of history based on Bahá'í teachings. These distinctions are worth making because, as I've argued above, Hayden's early heritage poems are best read via the secular, leftist intellectual and political context of late 1930s and early 1940s African American letters. These poems are deeply invested in salvific narratives of race progress that recall the Negro spirituals but are actually expressions of the Enlightenment's *secular* humanist faith in the perfectibility of society through determined (black) will. In the wake of World War II, Hayden's historical vision remained secular and materialist but abandoned futurity—where he once cast the black past as preparatory darkness birthing future dawn, Hayden's midcentury poetry is overwhelmed by what Richard Rubenstein calls the "night side of Judeo-Christian" civilization (qtd. in Bauman 9)—that is, modernity's facilitation of incomprehensible human suffering. With the future obscured by the accumulation of war horror and the unfulfilled promises of American modernity, for a period the poet was capable only of managing a present haunted by the ghosts of history. In concluding my reading of Hayden's evolving historicity, I want to chart the full emergence and consequence of the Bahá'í hermeneutics that delivered him from the darkest, most past-obsessed period in his career and that reanimated his earlier, Janus-faced approach to history, this time conceived as a salvific, linear, and spiritualist—rather than materialist—teleology.

Although the nuance of this teleology is not discernable until his work of the mid-1960s, for all intents and purposes, Hayden announces his antimodernist spiritualism in the final movement of the carefully arranged *Figure of Time*. With the lynch scene of "Figure" leading into an evocation of Nazi death factories in "In Light Half-Nightmare," Hayden produces the seemingly inescapable darkness of global modernity—of "our time." The first half of "In Light" traps the speaker in an encompassing travail exemplified by, but not limited to, the Jewish Holocaust:

From the corpse woodpiles, from the ashes and staring pits
    of Buchenwald, Dachau they come—
O David, Hirschel, Eva, cops and robbers with
    me once, their faces are like yours—
From Johannesburg, from Seoul. Their struggles are all
    horizons,
    their deaths encircle me. (*Figure 13*)

Sites of suffering in Europe, Africa, and Asia are offered as coordinates in
a circuit of inhumanity that girdles the globe, forming a horizon of hor-
ror. Hemmed in, Hayden's speaker produces a classical apostrophe ("*O Da-*
vid . . ."), and momentarily turns away from the suffering of our time to
address those absent. Of course, the Jewish friends who were his playmates
"once" are apparitions of the past. To make humanizing meaning of the global
travail of the era, it seems the speaker can only turn to the past. Here again
the future is unmentionable, lying in forbiddingly unseen territory some-
where beyond the dark horizon.

Yet, as its title intimates, light and vision are key elements of the poem,
and following a subtle volta—shifting from nightmare to vision—a new,
"transilluminating" figure appears in Hayden's corpus.[1]

    Through ruins,
through target streets I run, fleeing what I cannot
    flee; behold in light half nightmare and
half vision that cold cloacal dripping place
    where he, who is man beatified
and Godly mystery, lies chained in criminal darkness.
    The anguish of those multitudes
is in his eyes, his suffering transilluminates
    an era's suffering.

Considering Hayden's body of work in chronological terms, it is hard to over-
estimate the significance of this inaugural moment. Here, Bahá'u'lláh, "man
beatified / and Godly mystery," fully enters into and significantly reorders
Hayden's imaginative landscape. As I argue in chapter 2, Bahá'u'lláh—the
nineteenth-century Persian nobleman who laid claim to a divine revelation
giving rise to the Bahá'í Faith—occupies a singular position in Hayden's
corpus. He is its most frequently appearing character, referred to as "cosmic
hero" and "Divine Surgeon"; he is the transcendent, mediating figure, bridg-

ing the material and the ideal worlds that operate in the continual tension of Hayden's later maturity; his social teachings provide faith-based girding to Hayden's universalist inclination; and his hermeneutic of history as theodicy shapes the final and most prolific decades of Hayden's career.

In conjuring the "Godly mystery" of *Figure of Time*, Hayden initiates a shift in the tectonics of his art. Bahá'u'lláh makes successive appearances in the 1955 collection—once the Prophet is introduced in "In Light," Hayden immediately expands upon his portrayal, following with "The Prophet," the panegyric explication of Bahá'u'lláh's transcendent station. As expressions of a Bahá'í *weltanschauung*, these poems announce an orthodox relation to the religious system built upon the writings of the figure that Hayden discovered in the early 1940s. After its sonnet-like turn, "In Light" declares that the nightmare horizon—"the anguish of those multitudes"—is contained and borne in the perceiving eyes of Bahá'u'lláh, whose chained imprisonment in a "cold cloacal" prison cell in Tehran must be linked to the chain-hung black man of "Figure." Both are sacrifices of modernity, but while the lynch victim is the symbol of our brutal time, Bahá'u'lláh's is that and something more: his suffering illuminates and transforms the "era's suffering." Hayden accords such value to his Prophet's ordeals because Bahá'u'lláh *himself* asserted that his own torment was a form of redemptive ransom, paid so that humanity might be freed from travail. "In Light" amounts to a declaration of faith, as it gives loyal poetic expression to Bahá'u'lláh's third-person interpretive narration of his own imprisonment:

> The Ancient Beauty hath consented to be bound with chains that mankind may be released from its bondage, and hath accepted to be made a prisoner within this most mighty Stronghold that the whole world may attain unto true liberty. He hath drained to its dregs the cup of sorrow, that all the peoples of the earth may attain unto abiding joy, and be filled with gladness. This is of the mercy of your Lord, the Compassionate, the Most Merciful. We have accepted to be abased, O believers in the Unity of God, that ye may be exalted, and have suffered manifold afflictions, that ye might prosper and flourish. (*Gleanings* 111–12)

Here is the foundation of the soteriology—the doctrine of salvation—to which Hayden would appeal in his later work. Its transactional logic, which presents the suffering of the Holy One—Hayden's "man beatified"—as a sacrificial payment releasing all humanity from its "bondage," is reminiscent of

Christian interpretations of Christ's death as the source of human salvation. However, Bahá'u'lláh's claim differs from the New Testament readings of the crucifixion that would have been significant in Hayden's Baptist upbringing. While well-known Bible verses, such as John 3:16 ("He gave his one and only Son, so that everyone who believes in him will not perish but have eternal life"), cast the redemptive suffering of Christ in "eternal," transhistorical terms, Bahá'u'lláh suggests that he consented to his abuse so as to alter the shape of human history. That is to say, Christ's sacrifice is often figured as the redemption of all, securing the potential salvation of every sinning soul in a heaven *outside of time*. Contrastively, Bahá'í soteriology casts Bahá'u'lláh's suffering and revelation as a quickening of mystical forces that work within a progressivist narrative of material history. As Bahá'u'lláh would write, "In bearing hardships and tribulations and in revealing verses and expounding proofs, it has been the purpose of this oppressed One to extinguish the fire of hate and animosity, that, haply, the horizons of the hearts of mankind be illumined with the light of concord and attain real tranquility" (Bahá'u'lláh and 'Abdu'l-Bahá 206). In this formulation, the Prophet's endurance of hardships and tribulations catalyzes the possibility of a human flourishing in an earthly, rather than a heavenly, future.

After more than a decade of practicing his adopted faith, in *Figure of Time* Hayden intimates his assimilation of a Bahá'í narrative of history founded on the belief that Bahá'u'lláh's sacrifice was meant to yield world-historical dividends. Bahá'u'lláh's promise of worldly salvation in a material, rather than a heavenly, future is a key theological difference between the Christianity of the Negro Church of Hayden's upbringing and the Bahá'í Faith of his adulthood. His assimilation of this new theology allows him to escape the ghostly hauntings of the past; it spiritualizes and reorients his historiography, setting the glimmering "light of concord" promised by Bahá'u'lláh against the darkness of modernity's holocaustal events. Hayden's faith in this Bahá'í hermeneutics of history allows futurity and teleology to reemerge as central components of his later poetics.

The arrangement of the poems in *Figure of Time* foretells the reoriented historiography that Hayden fully deployed in the 1960s and 1970s. *Figure* opens with a recollection of childhood in interwar, Depression-era Detroit and continues its pastward focus in the various poems mentioned in the previous section. But a rapprochement with futurity is indicated in "'Lear Is Gay,'" an homage to brave agedness that closes the collection and enacts a pivot in the book's temporal emphasis—from the past to the future. The poem, by which Hayden muscles his way squarely into a Western tradition, obviously evokes Shakespeare's Lear, but it does so via William Butler Yeats's late 1930s poem "Lapis Lazuli," which contends that, though tragic, "Hamlet and Lear are gay" (153). Written in the European moment defined by the bloody record of Stalin, Hitler, Mussolini, and Franco, "Lapis Lazuli" is Yeats' declaration of faith in the salvation of art, in the beauty of stoicism in the face of tragedy, and in his personal version of history as cycle. Hayden's poem is not as reflexive, craft-obsessed, or metapoetic as Yeats's, and while Yeats confidently alludes to the regenerative gyre of history in which "all things fall and are built again," Hayden is less sanguine. Nevertheless, in the final poem of *Figure of Time* he produces an admiring portrait of Shakespeare's aging king, who can look upon the passage of time without total dread. The final lines of "'Lear Is Gay'" metaphorize time itself as "a scarecrow / whose hobo-shoulders / are a-twitch with crows" (*Figure* 19). Hayden's Lear can countenance this paradoxical symbol of time—comical, yet also gothic and foreboding—and "Can smile and oh / can laugh sometimes," which is to say that by the end of the collection Hayden furnishes an image of a character who is capable of facing a death-promising future. However limited the doddering Lear may be ("has limbs askew /often as not; / has dimmer sight"), he is admired because of his capacity to bear the mortal logic of advancing time.

At the conclusion of his crucial 1955 collection Hayden begins to look to the future once again. And yet, similar to both the religiously inclined older modernists like Eliot, Yeats, and Auden, who were his white oedipal fathers in the early 1940s, and the black cultural nationalists who were his younger sparring partners in 1960s, Hayden gazes into modernity's future by looking to a premodern past. In an untitled prayer-poem tucked into the last page of *Figure of Time*, Hayden waxes mythical, mystical, and nostalgic in an open longing for divinity's presence in a modern world.

> As once in flaring bush, in caves of the hunted,
>   in cloud,
> in guidon flame You did reveal, oh did make known
> Your love, Your keen concern—so now in lab and
>   conference
> room, at diplomat's table, at surgeon's, on freeway,
>   in cockpit,
> on scaffolding, make known, make known Your love.
>   Let now
> Your love oh everywhere oh everywhere be our concern. (20)[2]

The spiritualist, pastward orientation of this antimodern hope for the present and future is productively compared with the materialist political impulse of an emblematic postwar thinker like Arendt. Speaking for a European intellectual elite deeply impacted by the Jewish Holocaust, she responded to the midcentury crisis of modernity with a similar concern for surety, declaring that "human dignity needs a new guarantee," but also with a renunciation of the past: "We no longer hope for restoration of old world order" (vii). Contrastively, Hayden's 1955 supplication seems romantically invested in the restoration of something old, though obviously not of the Old World order of European racism and imperialism condemned by Arendt. For the first time in his writing career Hayden turns with earnest reverence toward the Old Testament symbols that were so central to the imaginative universe of the nineteenth-century Negro spiritual. As Arendt advanced into a materialist future that could be guaranteed only by secular political order, Hayden conjures ancient narratives in which divinity animates the "flaring bush," "caves," "cloud," and "flame." This at first seems the Romantic longing for a mythical past wherein God dwelled in the temple of Nature itself, but Hayden's prayer is anchored in the "now" of twentieth-century modernity—in the technologized, bureaucratic mass society evoked by the prayer's "lab," "conference room," and "diplomat's table." These are the cold symbols of a world seemingly emptied of spiritual meaning. In this world the promises of secular modernity are sought in the accelerated lurch toward a future brought on by "freeway," "cockpit," and "scaffolding." Seeking the reappearance of an ancient spirit in a modernizing world, Hayden sets the premodern past in which faith was organic to life in tension with a post-Enlightenment modernity in which rationalism and technology exile religious belief. The repetitions and interjections of the final lines of the prayer signal both the intensity of the speaker's supplication and the improbability of his wish for a future restoration of lost faith.

Ultimately what Hayden seeks is a reanimated modernity—one where a rationalist intellect coexists with a type of religious faith that the poet associated with the "elders" who looked upon his speaker through "Mosaic eyes" in "'Summertime and the Living . . .'" (*Figure 2*); with the "true believers" humble before "Jehovah's oldtime wrath" in "Electrical Storm" (*Selected Poems* 13); and with the "folks" who long to hear one of their own "sing Jesus down / to help with struggling" in "Mourning Poem for the Queen of Sunday" (*Ballad of Remembrance* 23). In these poems—and others, like "Witch Doctor," "Those Winter Sundays," and "Full Moon"—all originally published between 1955 and 1966, Hayden recalls a childhood in a folk world vivified by the faith system of the Negro Church. As I argue in chapter 2, his frequent return to this past of urban, working-class blackness is an archetypal move for the artist-intellectual negotiating his own *progress* between oral and literary cultures, between folkways and the ways of the academy. In these elegiac remembrances, Hayden often juxtaposes the old-time faith of true believers and the rational skepticism of his "colleged," cosmopolitan poet-speaker, thus creating a tension between premodern religiousness and modern scientism that is an extension of the prayer that closes *Figure of Time*. Just as divine presence was "made known" in the Old Testament bush, cave, and cloud of Hayden's prayer, the spirit of faith animates the recollected ghetto world of his childhood

> when wild street preachers shook their tambourines
> and Bibles in the face
> of tolerant wickedness;
> when Elks parades and big splendiferous
>
> Jack Johnson in his limousine made all
> the arid ghetto bloom
> with fantasies of Ethiopia spreading her gorgeous wings. (*Figure 3*)

If divinity stirred the premodern natural world, it is similarly alive in the sound and color of Hayden's remembered folk world in "'Summertime and the Living . . .'" For the faithful denizens of this territory the opulence and the accomplishment of black boxing champion Jack Johnson is itself a kind of magic that makes "the arid ghetto bloom." Johnson's grandeur is all the more meaningful because it is understood through biblical typology; his being and appearance in the ghetto world are thought of in messianic terms, as fulfillment of the Old Testament promise (cherished by many black believers) that "Ethiopia shall soon stretch out her hands unto God" (Psalms 68:31). Here the ghetto vibrates with a sustaining faith that secular, rationalist modernity would drain from the overdeveloped world. Hayden's speaker is enamored of this faith-animated scene from his past. But he is also all too knowing—the speaker tacitly acknowledges that he, like the believers who read reality through a scriptural lens, must invest in "fantasies." The ghetto is empirically "arid"; it blooms only with ancient mythology that the modern speaker cannot fully embrace. Although desperate and beseeching—"make known Your love"—Hayden is not sustained by what he once described as "the fundamentalism characteristic of the folk milieu in which I grew up" (*Collected Prose* 148).

In 1962 Hayden would publish *A Ballad of Remembrance*. The book was distributed by Paul Breman in England, it was printed in Holland, it would go on to win first prize for poetry at the 1966 Festival of Negro Arts in Dakar, Senegal, and it featured a seven-poem section on Mexico. The artistic material and the material history of the book itself plainly testify to its status as an artifact of the complex circuits of global cosmopolitan modernity. Yet it is "Those Winter Sundays," Hayden's small masterpiece of simple paternal love and black folklife, that has become the collection's (and perhaps Hayden's) most widely recognized poem.

> Sundays too my father got up early
> and put his clothes on in the blueblack cold,
> then with cracked hands that ached
> from labor in the weekday weather made
> banked fires blaze. No one ever thanked him.
>
> I'd wake and hear the cold splintering, breaking.
> and smell the iron and velvet bloom of heat.
> When the rooms were warm, he'd call,
> and slowly I would rise and dress, fearing
>
> the chronic angers of that house, speaking
> indifferently to him, who'd driven out
> the cold and polished my
> good shoes as well. What did I know,
> what did I know of love's austere and lonely offices? (29)

Often hailed for its formal precision and its pathos-stirring articulation of the adult speaker's belated appreciation of his father's imperfect love, the poem is one of many in which Hayden tries to work through his ambivalent feelings about his past and the black folk world that gave it context. Much of the poem's emotion is generated in its contemplation of the experiential gulf that separates the highly literate poet-speaker and the wordless father who knew, but could not name, "love's austere and lonely offices." This paternal figure inhabits a folk world that is alien to modernity's "lab," "conference room," and "diplomat's table." His concerns are elemental and seemingly preindustrial—he is a manual worker "with cracked hands that ached / from labor"; his days begin in the most basic struggle against nature, by bringing heat that breaks the "blueblack cold"; and, fittingly, his worldview is shaped by old-time religious faith.

Whatever else it may be, "Sundays" is also a Sabbath poem. The silent love of the father who not only subdues cold nature but "polished my / good shoes as well" is inseparable from a routinized fidelity to the church. That is to say, the speaker's father "got up early," on what we assume is the only day he might rest, in order to ready his family for worship. This crucial detail sheds light on Hayden's decision to call upon the sonnet form for his remembrance of paternal care that is braided to churchly devotion. The fourteen lines of the poem evoke the sonnet tradition in order to situate and deepen the poem's projections of *love*—from father to the oblivious child who spoke "indifferently to him" and from sensitized adult speaker to the now-absent parent. But by alluding to a sonnet tradition in which emotional expression was controlled and ordered by an exacting formal structure, Hayden also suggests the "austere," self-disciplined character of the loving, religious father. Indeed, the sonnet form was often enough used as "an iconic representation of freely chosen imprisonment, establishing an implicit analogy between the rules of the form and other kinds of moral and social rules" (Phelan 4). And of course, it was the church that established the "moral and social rules" that poets often considered through the sonnet. In alluding to the form with its premodern origins, "Sundays" suggests the father's devoted, disciplined, and religiously organized execution of "love's austere and lonely offices."[3] But in rejecting the formal constraints of the sonnet—its traditional metrical and rhyme structures, its pivoting, problem-solution logic, its single-stanza representation—Hayden asserts a measure of aesthetic independence that is counterpart to the speaker's critique of his father's paternal authority. (Part of what makes the poem so bracing is the texture that is added to the father when it is revealed that the speaker leaves his bed "slowly" not because of lingering cold but because he lives "fearing / the chronic angers of that house.") For Hayden, the father, like the sonnet form, is loved and admired, but not perfect.

Linking the father's ordered, admirable ways to the structured sonnet, Hayden is able to pay homage to both but also to progress past them. "Sundays" performs cathartic, elegiac work, allowing its maker to move on after mourning. And certainly the *sankofa* sense of progression—the effort to reach back in order to move forward—is present in "Sundays" as it reforms the traditional sonnet. This reformation of the most recognizable verse template of the Western tradition is obviously not a bold declaration of poetic freedom. With its precise calibration of poetic narrative and alliterative order, "Sundays" is rather an expression of desire for a new type of regulation resembling the old. Scores of anthologists have recognized that the poem is a master lesson on the emotional energy that can be released when poetic narrative is synergized with formal control—that, like the best sonnets, it is a demonstration of the creative power of discipline. As one critic writes, although the poem is "only loosely a sonnet . . . it has the density and gravity of a sonnet" (Huddle 251). In "Those Winter Sundays," Hayden is not seeking an escape from the weight of poetic order; instead, he converts an old order into a new one—he takes on a "freely chosen imprisonment" that both replaces and recalls the old.

The conservative formal innovation observed in Hayden's most well-known poem is a type of analogy for the religious conversion that significantly impacted his post-1955 poetry. In his adoption and assimilation of Bahá'í philosophies, Hayden seems to reject the order of existing cosmologies, including the belief structures of the Negro Church. But Hayden's adopted spiritualism was also built on a set of "old-time" metanarratives found at the heart of the Negro Church in which Hayden was raised. In fact, the Bahá'í Faith allowed the poet to invest in the ordering beliefs of religion (in a divinely purposed universe, the progression of history and the assurance of future salvation) while also registering a philosophical independence from the folk matrix of his younger years. Hayden's rigorous attachment to his adopted faith can be seen as a "freely chosen imprisonment" within a new cosmological structure that honored old beliefs about divinity, the sacred, and the possibility of absolute knowledge.

But, although the Bahá'í Faith is rooted in an ancient tradition of monotheism, it is not premodern in its origins or orientation. It endorses key tenets of secular modernity by abolishing the authority of the clerical class, embracing the "march of science," and promoting belief in the perfectibility of earthly human society (Effendi, *Advent* 87). The deep progressivist logic of the religion, so compatible with Enlightenment aims, is well expressed in its Prophet-founder's declaration that "all men have been created to carry forward an ever-advancing civilization" (Bahá'u'lláh, *Gleanings* 243). Hayden's Bahá'í beliefs, then, offered mediation between premodern and modern inclinations—they allowed him to sustain what he described as the "God-consciousness" inherited from his religious folk milieu (*Collected Prose* 119), even as they attributed spiritual, existential significance to modernity's "ever-advancing civilization." In this faith system, the "lab," "conference room," and "freeway" that symbolized modernity in Hayden's *Figure of Time* prayer might be animated with divine purpose because they were instruments of a divinely mandated advancement of civilization.

Crucially, the Bahá'í Faith also furnished Hayden with a hermeneutics of history that allowed him to deal with the problem of a radical evil that by the middle of the twentieth century had done much (among intellectuals) to burn away faith in both divinity and in the idea that modernity advanced "civilization." As indicated in my earlier reading of "In Light Half-Nightmare," Bahá'u'lláh cast his own suffering as a ransom that paid the way for the redemption of humanity in an earthly future. But the teachings of the Bahá'í Faith also indicate that the collective suffering of humanity is a travail that will eventually give life to a new world order. This is a historical model that could countenance modernity's holocaustal events while maintaining faith in the belief that human civilization is actually advancing. In this teleology the intense torment brought on by humanity's spiritual heedlessness is the sign and harbinger of a future golden age. As explained in the interwar writings of Shoghi Effendi, the guardian and leader of the Bahá'í Faith at the time of Hayden's conversion, modernity's horrors are preparatory and salutary:

> We stand on the threshold of an age whose convulsions proclaim alike the death-pangs of the old order and the birth-pangs of the new. Through the generating influence of the Faith announced by Bahá'u'lláh this New World Order may be said to have been conceived. We can, at the present moment, experience its stirrings in the womb of a travailing age—an age waiting for the appointed hour at which it can cast its burden and yield its fairest fruit. (*World Order* 169)

Hayden first indicates a faithful adoption of this religious teleology in his *Selected Poems*, published in 1966. The volume opens with a section of ten poems that had not appeared in his previous books. These new works, full of fire and cold, darkness and light, extend imagery motifs that Hayden had employed since the early heritage poems. The opening quartet of the volume—"The Diver," "Electrical Storm," "Full Moon," and "Dawnbreaker"—uses this imagery in assertions of faith against death, in contemplation of the tension between science and religion, and ultimately to offer a vision of humanity's future salvation.

In *Selected Poems*, a sanguine historical narrative emerges as the compliment—and perhaps the impetus—of the difficult but life-affirming climb of the poetic persona that Hayden produces in the opening poem of the collection, "The Diver." "Freefalling" into the "canyon of cold," deep-sea darkness, Hayden's diver explores a "dead ship" and longs to release himself into the suicidal oblivion that he finds in the wreck. But he resists and

> Swam from
> the ship somehow;
> somehow began the
> measured rise. (12)

The poem first appeared in Rosey Pool's 1962 anthology *Beyond the Blues* and was undoubtedly written after the tectonic shifts in religiousness and temporal orientation that register in *Figure of Time*. It seems to announce an ascending move away from Thanatos—from not only the "cancelling arms" of the ghostly dead that invisibly flit through the wreck but also from the ghosts and the harrying dead that crowded Hayden's poetry of the 1940s and 1950s.

"The Diver," which Hayden acknowledged as ambiguous in meaning (*Collected Prose* 161), pivots on the unanswered question posed by the protagonist's decision to return to the surface: Why choose life? Why not "yield to rapturous / whisperings" and "have / done with self and /every dinning / vain complexity" (*Selected Poems* 12)? Conjuring this existential question—which Camus famously described as the "one truly serious philosophical problem" (3)—the symbolist poem presents cipher answers in the form of further questions: "Reflex of life-wish? / Respirator's brittle belling?" Hayden will not spell out the motive behind his diver's rejection of suicide and return to life. However, the will to life and engagement expressly imprinted in "The Diver" braids into the reappearance of a salvific, future-oriented narrative of history in Hayden's oeuvre. That is to say, the "measured" will that the diver displays in his ascent to the surface is of a piece with the purposeful teleology that Hayden faithfully sketches elsewhere in *Selected Poems*.[4]

"The Diver" is immediately followed by "Electrical Storm" and "Full Moon"—poems that extend the tensions of the final prayer of *Figure of Time* as they grapple with the discordancy of "God-consciousness" and modern scientism. But in "Dawnbreaker," the fourth poem of the opening group, Hayden indicates his own acceptance of the redemptive historical narrative offered in the writings of his adopted faith and provides a rationale for optimism despite the violence of modernity. The subject of the poem is the torture and execution of Hájí Sulaymán Khán, a mid-nineteenth-century martyr who submitted to death rather than recant his belief in the upstart movement that would come to be known as the Bahá'í Faith. Here Hayden returns to some of the apparatuses that he used to build his black history poems of the 1940s. In presenting Sulaymán Khán's death, he delves into the archive to interpolate the incident as it was recorded by Nabíl-i-Aʹzam, the seminal historian in the Baháʹí tradition. According to Aʹzam's account, holes were gouged in Sulaymán Khán's flesh and filled with burning candles. As he was lead through the "jeering streets" of Tehran, the martyr is said to have sung out, "You have long lost your sting, O flames, and have been robbed of your power to pain me. Make haste, for from your very tongues of fire I can hear the voice that calls me to my Beloved!" (620). In his rendering of the episode Hayden fixes on the fire imagery and makes the welcomed suffering of the martyr into a metonymic representation of human suffering in the modern moment. The final sentence of the poem is an assurance that rests on a paradoxical interpretation of the painful fires of modernity:

> Flames nested in
> > his flesh
>
> > Fed the
> fires that consume
> us now, the fire that
> > will save. (*Selected Poems* 16)

After a twenty-year hiatus, futurity fully returns to Hayden's poetry through a hermeneutics of history that guarantees salvation even in the face of overwhelming turmoil. The final assertion that it is the violently consuming fire of modernity that will bring on human deliverance is underscored by an assonance pattern that connects *praise* and *Flames* while also fusing the poem's first word, *Ablaze* to its ultimate syllable, *save*. In its assuring movement through material of the past to burning trials of the now and into the salvation of the future, "Dawnbreaker" renews the Janus-faced and linear historical vision of the heritage poems conceived in the early 1940s. However, there are crucial differences in the teleological narrative that Hayden constructs two decades later. While the earlier poems were secular and nationalist—emanations of what James Smethurst has called the "New Red Negro" literary project of the interwar era—"Dawnbreaker" is religious and universalist.

The poem is both an engagement with Baháʹí mythos and an aestheticized articulation of the progressivist theory of history that Hayden gleaned from the central figures of the religion. In its imagery and argument, "Dawnbreaker" seems the poetic reflection of scriptural explanations of modern history offered by Shoghi Effendi, who in 1931 wrote, "Nothing but a fiery ordeal, out of which humanity will emerge, chastened and prepared, can succeed in implanting that sense of responsibility which the leaders of a new-born age must arise to shoulder" (*World Order* 42). Hayden's assimilation of this Bahá'í teleology reorients his angel of history. If his immediate postwar poetry ought to be likened to Walter Benjamin's angel, fixated on the wreckage of the past with its back turned on futurity, "Dawnbreaker" signals Hayden's desire to do what Benjamin's angel could not—that is, "make whole what has been smashed" (Benjamin 257). Casting the "ordeals" of modernity as a bracing conflagration that prepares humanity for future salvation, Hayden uses religious faith to reassemble the teleological framework that had given order to black history in the hopeful, ever-advancing heritage poems of his early maturity.

In the only negative review of *Selected Poems* Hayden's appeal to Bahá'í eschatology comes in for particular criticism. But David Galler's 1967 review in *Poetry* views Hayden's religiousness through a fog of limiting suppositions about black poetic expression. The opening sentence of Galler's assessment indicates the narrow range of subject matter that he would grant the black poet: "If war presents a growing problem for poetry, being an American Negro presents a worse one." Galler's proposal ironically ignores Hayden's deep dive into the horror of war and is prelude to a review that exclusively understands the poetry as a response to the "problem" of being an American Negro. Appearing in the most prominent organ of the American poetry establishment, the review surely frustrated Hayden. His continual efforts to bend modernist aesthetics toward representation of black history and folklife and his struggle to make sense of his particular experience of modernity were implicit assertions that the problem of being an American Negro was nothing more or less than a species of the problem of being human in the twentieth century. The racialist limitations of the reviewer are most apparent in his treatment of the poet's religiousness. Galler writes, "Hayden is capable of high eclecticism when dealing with salvation (on the theological plane); witness his poems concerned with the Bahá'í faith, a prominent nineteenth-century Persian sect whose leader was martyred. Might not the example of Jesus have sufficed? For the white man, probably" (268). It is worth clarifying that Bahá'u'lláh was tortured and imprisoned for a time but not martyred—the factual error indicates that Hayden's convictions were not taken too seriously. But the dismissive superficiality of the review sounds most clearly when Galler packages Hayden's Bahá'í faith as a poetic ploy and, quite inaccurately, as an assertion of racial difference—of categorically black idiosyncrasy. The irony of this misreading shows up when the nationalist teleology of Hayden's 1940s heritage poems is contrasted with the universalist teleology of "Dawnbreaker," which declares that the fire of modernity will eventually save "us" all. While "Middle Passage," "Frederick Douglass," and "Runagate"—written by a younger, less religious poet—anticipate a secular political freedom for an enduring black nation, the rendering of Baháʾí history and eschatology in "Dawnbreaker" anticipates a divinely ordained salvation for *all humanity*. Hayden's turn to the Baháʾí Faith and its universalist theory of history may have been an example of one black artist's response to modernity—a specimen of "black antimodernism"—but it was a response that sought to transcend, not reify, racial categories.

In his stark racialization of Hayden's Baháʾí eschatology, Galler reacts less to the specifics of Hayden's work than to the rising tide of strident Black Arts poetry that by 1967 was flowing into American literary consciousness. For many Black Arts poets, "salvation"—as Galler put it—was in fact a racialized proposition. It was the longed-for utopia in which the grievances of (some of) modernity's victims were redressed in a "last shall be first" script in which redemption was brought to earth through revolutionary black art and life. If black poetry had once looked toward the ideals of democratic citizenship wrapped in the rhetoric of "freedom," after passage of the Civil Rights and Voting Rights Acts of the mid-1960s the dominant voices in black poetry adapted to an emergent political discourse that replaced the telos of freedom with the demand for black power. This adjustment precipitated new conceptualizations of black historiography. Poets invested in an Edenic African past and cast themselves as leaders of a black warrior class that would use rhetorical violence and revolutionary politics to first bring on an Armageddon and then create a new black world. Rather than figuring salvation as full participation in the American democratic project, Black Arts poets usually called for the hastened demolition of an American/Western "Syphilization" conceived as Babylon—and a concomitant destruction of the American part of the double-conscious black psyche first described by Du Bois in the late nineteenth century. Following the psychoanalytic decolonization theories of Frantz Fanon, many iterations of this narrative focused on the violence of the required revolution. In Baraka's "Black Art," for example, the violence of modernity was to be met by a responsive poetic force—by "poems that kill" and help black people to recognize that they are "warriors and sons / of warriors" (*Baraka Reader* 219). Nikki Giovanni's well-known "The True Import of Present Dialogue, Black vs. Negro," similarly spurs a responsive rhetorical slaughter: "Can you kill / Can you piss on a blond head / Can you cut it off / Can you kill" (19). The violence of these poems was multipurposed: it was the poetic translation of Fanon's belief that violence "rids the colonized of their inferiority complex, of their passive and despairing attitude" (51); it was the reflection of the domestic and international turmoil of the 1960s; and in its grotesque hyperbole it was a defiance of white arbiters of aesthetic order like Galler, who assessed the merits of black poetry—often with dismissive, cavalier confidence. But these violent poems were also depictions and enactments of the ritual cleansing that was needed to move history toward utopia. As Baraka put it in "Black Art," the violence was meant to "clean out the world for virtue and love" (*Baraka Reader* 220) and to make possible a pristine "Black World"—a place, according to Haki Madhubuti, "where people can love and create" (Lee, "Toward" 22).

Black Arts advocates like Larry Neal claimed that the era called for art that "posits for us the Vision of a Liberated Future" ("Any Day" 56), but in the revolutionary poetics, futurity made only fleeting appearances. Utopian images shone through from time to time, as in the harmonized space worlds of Sun Ra's poetry or the whimsical pastoral scenes of Welton Smith's "Interlude" to his "Malcolm" poem in the *Black Fire* anthology, or Giovanni's "Walking Down Park"—"the parrot parroting black is beautiful black is beautiful / owls sending out whooooo's making love . . . / and me and you just sitting in the sun" (107). But, for the most part, black love and communalism were ends that provided less poetic material than revolutionary means. Or, to think of it in different terms, poets held to the Fanonian logic that violence "unifies the people" (51). Thus black love and community were thought to be axiomatic products of the revolutionary violence that Black Arts poetry sought to depict and conjure. For example, Marvin Jackmon's "Burn, Baby, Burn" is an homage to mid-1960s black revolution that takes its title from the communal and vernacular chant that was sometimes a mantra of urban rebellion. Jackmon represents violence and riot fire as a renewal of community and hope for black people "LOST IN / THE WILDERNESS OF WHITE AMERICA":

TO THE STREETS, TO THE
KILLLLLLLLLLLL . . . . . .
BOOOMMMMM . . . . . .
   2 honkeys gone . .
MOTHERFUCK THE POLICE
. . .
BURN, BABY, BURN* * * * * * * (Baraka and Neal 269)

Intent on helping to displace the nonviolent leadership and ideology of the Negro Church, Black Arts poetics abided by a historiographical logic that rejected divinely directed Christian teleology and replaced it with a revolutionary historical model that emphasized the catalytic agency of the urban black man. As Gil Scott-Heron famously put it, "You will not be able to stay home, brother . . . / The revolution will put you in the driver's seat" (Gates and McKay 80, 82). In many poems like Scott-Heron's "The Revolution Will Not Be Televised" and Jackmon's "Burn, Baby, Burn," the black brother was urged to assume his rightful position as driver of the revolution and of history itself. Thus the masculine and often muscularly violent rhetoric of Black Arts poetry approximated a struggle for control over the movement of history. This was a poetics that wrested power from the white man, from white America, from a white God, and from Negro compradors. In the Black Arts imagination, these powerful conspirators—shapers of modern history—deserved fiery ruin.

But for Hayden, the gritty call for destruction was the poetic equivalent of throwing bodies onto modernity's long-burning pyre. He rejected Black Arts aggression on aesthetic grounds, arguing that "this kind of verse is, more often than not, informed by a crass naturalism and linguistic violence which delude those responsible for it into believing they are 'telling like it is'" (*Collected Prose* 70). Hayden's aesthetic evaluation was inseparable from his misgivings about the political and historiographic ideals that undergirded many Black Arts poems. The kindling of revolutionary violence in both poetry and politics was, for Hayden, an operation hopelessly mired in the fire of the present. It was reflective of contemporary struggle but it lacked transformative possibility—to his mind it did not actually give life to a reimagined future. Writing in 1975, in his capacity as poetry editor of the Bahá'í publication *World Order*, Hayden would assert that "the truly revolutionary poets are always those who are committed to some integrative vision of art and life. Theirs is an essentially spiritual vision which leads to the creation of new forms and techniques, to a new awareness" (*Collected Prose* 70). Here Hayden underestimates the enduring and generative power of the Black Arts ethos and "techniques" that would come to vivify spoken word poetry, rap, and some schools of literary poetry. Arguably, he would not grant true "spiritual vision" to Black Arts poetics because it grew from conceptions of history that radically diverged from Hayden's Bahá'í teleology, which offered a narrative of history similar to that of the Negro Church—one that put divinity in the driver's seat. Hayden would close his 1975 essay by looking to the Old Testament: "Without vision the people perish" (70).

The future-oriented spiritual vision that guided Hayden through the 1960s and 1970s was first intimated in "Dawnbreaker," but it is given full poetic articulation in *Words in the Mourning Time*. Hayden's 1970 volume takes its title from a ten-poem sequence in which his Bahá'í teleology is both asserted and tested in relation to the violent upheavals that defined the televised 1960s—the many political assassinations, the Vietnam War, and the smoldering urban space that was staging ground for the revolutionary rites celebrated in Jackmon's "Burn, Baby, Burn." The anthemic chant that gives title to Jackmon's poem also appears in the "Words in the Mourning Time" sequence. But in Hayden's rendering it is sung by the misguided followers of a totemic god, described as

> Lord Riot
>   naked
>   in flaming clothes
> cannibal ruler
>   of anger's
>   carousal (*Words* 46)

For Hayden, the Dionysian, communal violence encouraged and reflected in Black Arts poems like Jackmon's was false hope, a "vengeful," reactionary ritual that would cannibalize its purveyors.[5] If Jackmon and others characterized white America as a wilderness that black people might escape by following the beckoning fire of collective violence, the seventh section of Hayden's "Words in the Mourning Time" sequence—titled "*voice in the wilderness*"—designates the agape preached by Martin Luther King as the more difficult but surer route to salvation. The poem offers no direct reference to King, but Hayden identified it (*Collected Prose* 124) as an elegy for the leader who narrates:

> Oh, master now love's instruments—
> complex and not for the fearful,
> simple and not for the foolish.
> Master now love's instruments. (*Words* 47)

In four exhortative stanzas, each rendered emphatic and ordered by line repetition, the poem implicitly contrasts the discipline of King's program of love with the bacchanal of violence suggested by the seemingly haphazard, staggered lineation of the "Lord Riot" poem. Encased in strictly calibrated hexameter quatrains, "love's instruments" are less musical than they are navigational. It is by the rigorously tuned compass of love that humanity finds its way out of the fiery modernity described in the earlier poems of the "Words in the Mourning Time" sequence. In these earlier poems Hayden questions and laments the logic of productive violence advocated by Fanon, some Black Arts poets, and the American military alike—"Killing people to save them, to free them? / With napalm lighting routes to the future?" (*Words* 42). He embodies the horrors of the moment in a corpse monster with "flamed-out eyes / their sockets dripping" (43); and he conjures Vietnamese "villages / mistakenly burning the schoolrooms devouring / their children" (44). For Hayden, these fiery horrors represent the continued burning of the conflagration of "Dawnbreaker"—"the fires that consume / us now" (*Selected Poems* 16). But according to the hermeneutic of history that he took from the writings of the Bahá'í Faith, the flashpoints of the 1960s were also salvific—flames of "the fire that / will save." The logical conflicts of this historical vision would weave into the central elements of Hayden's art during the last decade of his life— during a period in which his poetry would repeatedly return to the question, "how thrive but by the light / of paradox?" (*Angle* 12).

It is in the first poem of the "Mourning Time" sequence that Hayden offers his clearest delineation of the paradoxical teleology that he struggled to believe in during the final stage of his career. The first of three quatrains establishes the national parameters of the elegy:

> For King, for Robert Kennedy,
> destroyed by those they could not save,
> for King for Kennedy I mourn.
> And for America, self-destructive, self-betrayed. (*Words* 41)

The opening gesture toward King is notable. Because African American literary production of the era was so allied to Black Power ideology and the charismatic example of Malcolm X, literary remembrances of King are remarkably scant. (There is certainly no literary equivalent to Nina Simone's epic mourning in "Why?" [1968]—parenthetically titled "The King of Love Is Dead.") In 1972, even Gwendolyn Brooks had little use for the pacifist leader, whom she referred to as "some beaming early saint" possessed by a "dainty spinning dream [that] has wound down to farce" (*Report* 45). While Black Arts tributes to Malcolm are legion, King was most cited as a negative example, as in Clarence Franklin's "Two Dreams (for m.l.k.'s one)," which displaces King's message of interracial agape with one of black diasporic unity and productive violence: "I dreamed a million black hands / linked like a chain, surrounding the world." Franklin's speaker dreams that this seem-ingly international force will hasten "the destruction of" things like "poverty," "hypocrisy," "idolatry" and also "kennedy" (Baraka and Neal 364). Contrasted with Franklin's paradigmatic Black Arts poem, Hayden's effort to establish an interracial and specifically American elegy appears pronounced. As Black Arts poetics explored transnational conceptual geographies and moved to-ward rhetorics of productive destruction modeled after the thinking of Fanon and Malcolm, Hayden anchors the "Mourning Time" sequence in elegiac praise of King and Robert Kennedy, American icons of interracial collabora-tion whose efforts to "save" the nation earned assassination. The memorializa-tion of these twin figures is significant not only because one is black and the other white but also because they similarly held faith in avowedly American ideals of liberal democracy. Hayden's mourning for King, Kennedy, and a "self-destructive" nation is tacitly a declaration of black Americanism at a literary-historical juncture when many black poets sacrificed America at the altar of pan-Africanism or Third Worldism.

Of course, Hayden was not alone in his black Americanism. His invest-ment in America was similar to that of significant artist-intellectuals like James Baldwin, Ralph Ellison, Albert Murray, and King, each of whom held to an Americanism while also offering forceful critiques of the nation's mili-tarism, materialism, and racism. The wary "patriotism" of these intellectuals was mostly the function of pragmatic politics and historical assessment—a belief that black life could never be disentangled from American moder-nity because, as Ellison put it, the black "experience is that of America and the West . . . intertwined, diffused in its very texture" (*Collected Essays* 214). Hayden's Americanism was rooted in similar ideas, but it was also galvanized by the future-oriented hermeneutic of history that he inherited from the Bahá'í Faith. On the occasion of the nation's bicentennial, Hayden explained his belief in the American project through frank appeal to the faith-based narrative of history that structures the "Mourning Time" sequence: "I believe what the Bahá'í teachings tell us about the destiny of America. *All I can do is have faith.* From the Bahá'í Writings we learn that America is to become the spiritual leader of the world" (*Collected Prose* 84, emphasis added). In the last decade of his life, Hayden thought of America not as modernity's dubious experiment requiring proper management or total dissolution but rather as nothing less than the engine of historical progress for all of humanity. In res-onance with his religious beliefs, he saw the nation as a coalescence of global cultures, the germ of an internationalist society of the future.[6] Hayden would go on to acknowledge that his beliefs resonated with American mythologies of Manifest Destiny, but he would add a caveat about the chastening fires that would purge America of its "old-world sickness" and prepare the nation for what the guardian of the Baháʾí Faith, Shoghi Effendi, described as the "unspeakably glorious destiny ordained for it by the Almighty" (*World Order* 36).

Although the "Mourning Time" sequence can be read as an assertion of Hayden's faith in the Baháʾí teleology that gave special importance to America, it should also be understood as the poetic reflection of the struggle that roiled beneath Hayden's understatement, "All I can do is have faith." The challenge of maintaining faith in a purpose-driven narrative of history emerges in the tensions of the second and third quatrains of the opening poem. After bereavement for King, Kennedy, and the nation writ-large, complications creep in:

> I grieve. Yet know the vanity
> of grief—through power of
> The Blessed Exile's
> transilluminating word
>
> aware of how these deaths, how all
> the agonies of our deathbed childbed age
> are process, major means whereby,
> oh dreadfully, our humanness must be achieved. (*Words* 41)

Hayden's speaker begins in conventional elegiac grief but immediately problematizes his mourning by acknowledging its vanity—a sentiment that might suggest artistic self-awareness and a desire to ward off the narcissism inherent in poetic self-consolation. But here grieving is vain because it is the product of what the speaker regards as an indulgent myopia that causes him to focus on the dire events of the era without placing them in the larger arc of history revealed through "The Blessed Exile's / transilluminating word." The metamorphic power that Hayden attributed to Baháʾuʾlláh in his *Figure of Time* poem "In Light Half-Nightmare" is again evoked using the self-same syntax. In the earlier poem the Prophet's "suffering transilluminates / an era's suffering" (*Figure* 13), but fifteen years on it is Baháʾuʾlláh's *word* that alchemizes the speaker's understanding of encompassing death. The title of Hayden's volume and poem may appear self-referential—implying that the (vain) poet calls attention to his own verse as "Words in the Mourning Time."[7] But Hayden's accentuation of the "power" of Baháʾuʾlláh's word suggests that what is needed in the mourning time following the 1960s is not necessarily the word of the poet himself but rather those of the Prophet— the explanatory framework that makes history into theodicy and assures the poet-speaker that the age is something more than the "deathbed" it would seem to be. However, the difficulty of accepting Bahá'u'lláh's word and theodicy is indicated by the speaker's initial inclination to turn toward grief, by the interjectional *oh* that inserts emotional instability into the final stanza's summation of Bahá'í teleology, and most palpably by the grief-stricken poems that ironically follow an opening that indicates grief itself is the sign of vanity.

The "Mourning Time" sequence is much like Hayden's longest poem, "Middle Passage," in that it moves through an extensive, dark tableau before finding sanguine illumination in its conclusion. While "flame-night" anguish burns throughout most of the cycle, as it concludes Hayden guides the work toward hope—first through a set of prescriptive demands that suggest that the poet's teleological view of history does not preclude the individual's participation in it, and finally through a return to the Blessed Exile evoked at the poem's outset.

Like Harriet Tubman of "Runagate Runagate," who levels her pistol at wavering charges and demands that they "keep on going *now* or die," and like the voice of King that earlier in the sequence admonishes, "master *now* love's instruments," in the ninth "Mourning Time" poem Hayden employs an exhortative voice to emphasize the "*now*"—this time doubling the urgency of the present moment while looking toward an idealized future:

> Reclaim now, now renew the vision of
> A human world where godliness
> is possible and man
> is neither gook nigger honkey wop nor kike
>
> but man
>
> permitted to be man. (*Words* 49)

As if demonstrating his own capacity for the millennial vision he prescribes, in the tenth and final poem of the sequence Hayden's narrator significantly alters his tone to speak as an awed suppliant, reverently addressing "Bahá'u'lláh: / Logos, poet, cosmic hero, surgeon, architect / of our hope of peace" (50). This poem is paced by the declarative refrain "I bear Him witness now." Repeated three times, the avowal of faith is an approximation of a Bahá'í "obligatory prayer" meant to be recited once each day by the believer wishing to pronounce his devotion to the Divine.[8] The poet-narrator directs his prayer toward Bahá'u'lláh, performing piety not only by pledging his consecration to the Prophet but also by allowing the words of the Prophet to take over the poem. The narrator's voice gives way to an unaltered transcription of Bahá'u'lláh's own account of the moment in which he claimed to receive the first intimations of his divine revelation:

> "I was but a man
> like others, asleep upon
>   My couch, when, lo, the breezes of the All-Glorious
>   were wafted over Me . . ." (51)[9]

By allowing these words, taken directly from Bahá'u'lláh's *Epistle to the Son of the Wolf*, to displace the mourning-time words of his narrator, Hayden performs an act of self-effacing reverence equal to the declarations of faith that fill the final poem of the sequence.

Understandably, some critics have harshly judged the drastic shift in tone that takes place in the concluding movement of the poem. And indeed, the piety of the finale may seem at odds with the horror and dismay that so powerfully control earlier sections. But the poem's resolution is not unanticipated; its opening sequence characterizes focus upon the "agonies" of the age as "vanity," which must finally be transcended through acceptance of the theory of history offered by Bahá'u'lláh. By ultimately turning to him, the poem achieves the ideal proposed at its outset. And in doing so, the structure of the "Mourning Time" sequence also reflects the theory of history that it advocates. There are lines of hope and light following the verses of darkness; the fires of modernity are painfully chastening and lead toward ultimate salvation. This hermeneutic, crucial to the structure of "Mourning Time" is ultimately fleshed out in the last sentences of the sequence's final poem. They complete the paean to Bahá'u'lláh, arguing that it is not just the poem itself that moves inevitably in his direction:

> Called, as in dead of night
> a dreamer is roused to help the helpless flee
>   a burning house.
>   I bear him witness now:
> toward Him our history in its disastrous quest
>   for meaning is impelled. (51)

In the penultimate stanza Hayden pictures his Prophet as "cosmic hero" raised from human ranks to the station of millennial savior in order to lead humanity out of the conflagration of modernity. But this metaphor is modified in the poem's final assertion, such that Bahá'u'lláh stands—godlike—beyond humanity, giving shape and meaning to its history.

Hatcher's thoroughgoing interpretation of Hayden's work finds precepts of the Bahá'í Faith devoutly expressed in every stage of the poet's mature career. So it comes as no surprise when Hatcher contends that, in the final movement of "Mourning Time," Hayden's poetic persona is "consoled by the certitude of his belief in Bahá'u'lláh" (163). But it is hard to attribute "certitude" to a consciousness that is so bedeviled by the problem of evil. Hayden himself was quick to point out that his faith flowed with uneven turbulence. His assertions of belief were always textured by the perfectionist's attachment to self-doubt: "Indeed, I still struggle with my faith; it harrows up my soul, as I guess it is supposed to do" (*Collected Prose* 27). Despite his spiritual commitment, Hayden's personal faith was tinged by a dark guesswork that limited the consolations of religion. The first lines of "October," which appears in *Words in the Mourning Time* only a few pages after the declarations of faith that conclude the title poem, subtly suggest "the poet's" distance from piety:

October—
its plangency, its glow

as of words
in the poet's mind,

as of God
in the saint's. (57)

Where Hatcher finds virtue in Hayden's capacity for faith, readers like Wilburn Williams, W. Scott Howard, and Ed Pavlić see the poet's lack of certitude as a kind of saving grace. Insinuating that a saint cannot be a good poet, Williams argues that "it is precisely Hayden's faith in the ultimate redemptiveness of the universal and timeless order of spirit that threaten to kill the life of his art" (70). This point is well taken; more often than not, Hayden's later poetry succeeds because it is vivified not by certainty but by a crisis of faith. The work emerges from what Yeats—who was an exemplar for Hayden—designated as the ideal source of all poetry: from the "quarrel" within the poet who is *not* unified in his consciousness. For Yeats, "the other self, the anti-self or the antithetical self, as one may choose to name it, comes but to those who are no longer deceived, whose passion is reality" (286). In this formulation the intense appraisal of "reality" seems to create a desirable fracturing in which the poet's consciousness divides into antiselves, each the Socratic heckler of the other. In the poetry of Hayden's final decades, the animating argument was between the "old-time" (Bahá'í) believer and the "colleged" skeptic in the poet, between one self that could read history as an ordered and ascending narrative and another that is overcome by a chaotic accumulation of holocaustal events. The former looks upon twentieth-century modernity and imagines it a "childbed"; the later recognizes only a "deathbed" where the nightmare of history is dreamed. Hayden's art was always marked by this tension, described by W. Scott Howard as "the juxtaposition of an expressed desire for spiritual release together with a persistent, compassionate return to the world of interminable conflict" (146). However, it was in the later stages of his career, when he was fully committed to both a religious theodicy and an unflinching appraisal of human suffering, that this "juxtaposition" became most apparent and sheering.

Few have drawn adequate attention to the intensity of Hayden's internal torments—what he called "my too-frequently recurring 'dark night(s) of the soul'" (Hayden and Harper 980, 982)—even though they are plainly dramatized in 1970s poems like "'As My Blood Was Drawn'" and "Ice Storm," in which the speaker cannot "sleep, or pray" (*American Journal* 39). Certitude is a far-off goal for the poet of *The Night-Blooming Cereus* (1972), which begins with this epigraphic stanza:

> But I can see none of it clearly, for
> it all takes place in semi-dark.
> A scene one might recall
> falling asleep. (4)

As the quatrain narrows on the page, it is certainty that retreats. And it is the agony of ambiguity and the divided self that advances shrilly in the volume's first poem, "Richard Hunt's 'Arachne.'" Here the poet-speaker projects into Hunt's welded steel sculpture of Arachne, caught midway in her punishing metamorphosis from woman to spider. The transformation of the mythic weaver woman was penalty for doubting the power of the gods—in Hayden's interpretation of the sculpture and myth she is writhing, "Dazed crazed / by godly vivisection husking her / gutting her" (5). This image, seizing on the suffering of the divinely punished and internally riven artist, suggests

Hayden's own predicament as poet-believer torn by doubt. He surely knew that in Ovid's rendering of the Arachne story in *Metamorphosis*, the artist kills herself in shame. There is congruence between Arachne, Hayden's diver, who longed to be "done with self and /every dinning / vain complexity" (*Selected Poems* 12), and the poet himself. Indeed, in a 1975 letter to his confidant, Michael Harper, Hayden admits that he has seen a psychiatrist in the hopes of dealing with a mortal weariness: "I got up one morning, not too long ago, and I felt I could not go on with my life" (Hayden and Harper 997, qtd. in Pavlić 252).

Hayden described visits with a therapist as "an admission of almost complete defeat" brought on by "days of sheer spiritual horror." But his letters show that the turn to psychiatry, to secular modernity's science-based answer to the ancient consolations of religious belief, was not an abandoning of faith. It was an additional strategy that combined with religion and art as bulwark against the deathbed reality that Hayden saw in unfolding modernity. Despite the worldly successes that came in the last decade of his life—when he secured a position at the University of Michigan, was appointed consultant to the Library of Congress, and received frequent accolades and invitations to read throughout the United States—the poet's sense of turmoil intensified to the point of his "near breakdown" (Hayden and Harper 997). Yet it is important to note that Hayden did not, in fact, break down, surrender to the "cancelling arms" that drew the diver into the abyss, or go the way of god-defiant Arachne. Instead, he managed a vacillating course into futurity, never relinquishing faith and never absolutely faithful. In "'As My Blood Was Drawn,'" a terminally ill Hayden evokes the "People of Baha," even as he renews feelings of ambivalence about the "world" and prays to a divinity that is at once "irradiant" and "terrible," like the God of Deuteronomy and Joshua:

> World that I have loved
> and loving hated,
> is it your sickness
> luxuriating
> in my body's world?
>
> In dreams of death
> I call upon
> the irradiant veiled
> terrible One. (*American Journal* 40)

These final stanzas of the deathbed poem blur the distinction between subject and object, between the speaker and his worldly condition of possibility. The metastasizing sickness of the abstract "world," like the "spreading oilslicks" that "burned the seas" in an earlier stanza, breach the speaker's body-boundary. This image of the porous, compromised body comes to Hayden as cancer breaks down his physical frame and the prospect of death promises the dissolution of his own subjectivity. The poem's speaker is darkly ambivalent about this dissolution and union with a world that is regarded with a sentiment that tangles love and hate: he moves toward a God radiating light, a light that was one of the consistent symbols of historical hope throughout Hayden's oeuvre. But that God remains unseen, fearfully sublime behind its veil—and eternally silent. The poem ends in the ongoing present with its speaker forever calling to a "terrible One" that does not respond.

A Lifetime of History

Memory, futurity, and the black past were significant tropes in Hayden's earliest volume, *Heart-Shape in the Dust*. The poems glint with the ideas and the language that he would work within for almost four decades—these motifs and concerns remained with Hayden, even in his final publications. Yet the poems in which they make their first appearances were disclaimed by the stickling craftsman, who up until his last days was in search of a register that was all his "own," as he repeatedly explained in his letters to Harper.[10] But, as I've mentioned, scholars like Keith Leonard and James Smethurst have challenged Hayden's critical judgment of a younger self. Smethurst persuasively reads the volume as a unique contribution to an Old Left literary scene in which black folklife and language were represented in ways that would echo through the twentieth century. He argues that Hayden's poems admirably vie with the work of New Negro luminaries like Countee Cullen and Langston Hughes and accurately points out that these "early poems are fascinating in that the separate (and often apparently contradictory) parts that make up Hayden's mature style are clearly displayed in an unsynthesized form" (*New Red Negro* 189). While Smethurst is mostly interested in the political-aesthetic implications of black vernacular life and language in the early, prefiguring work, Hayden's obsession with history and temporality is also evident but inchoate and "unsynthesized" in *Heart-Shape*.

His career-long misgivings about advancing technological modernity are first felt in *Heart-Shape*'s suspicious response to the world's fair phenomenon and its diorama fantasies of technological promise:

In sliding plush-chairs behold
The glassed-in body of the future.
(The mechanical voice at your shoulder
Falters in its prophecies. . . .) (47)

Here, in one of the volume's less derivative poems, skepticism is the watch-word. But Hayden seems to put aside doubts about plush-chair prophecies of technological tomorrowland as he waxes optimistic in engagements with African American history. Poems like "'What Is Precious Is Never to Forget'" and "'We Have Not Forgotten'" evoke perseverant ancestors whose example inspires a hopeful march toward future freedom. Mystical power arises from the determined will discovered in the slave's "cabin-gloom," and this will becomes "the soil / From which our souls' strict meaning came—where grew / The roots of all our dreams of freedom's wide / And legendary spring" (10). *Heart-Shape* poems like this, derived from New Negro templates, look into the past in order to offer sanguine guarantees about an African American future. But these promises seem to logically clash with doubts about the optimism of modernity's "mechanical voice" futurism.

Thus, in his earliest volume, Hayden's antiselves begin their quarrel—one produces the inert, cadaver-like "glassed-in body of the future"; another looks into an earthy, organic black past and finds the romance of "legendary spring." In Hayden's art these historiographical visions would vie for forty years. In the well-known history poems of the 1940s, Hayden favored the chronicle of hope, discovering "deathless primaveral" (*Collected Poems* 54) strength shining through the dark archive of slavery. At midcentury, looking through the lens of holocaustal horror, a less sanguine poet blurred that same archival material into surreal puncturing images of a "spiked bellcollar" (27) history that occluded futurity. Faith in Bahá'u'lláh—history-impelling "cosmic hero" (99)—restored telos and order to Hayden's later historiography. However, the surety of earlier salvific narratives was never resurrected. Ironically, it was in Hayden's younger years, when he was less devoted to religious belief, that his poems sang in the tones of the Negro spirituals—with a historical vision informed by what Du Bois describes as the spiritual's "faith in the ultimate justice of things" (*Souls* 251). But as the terrible weight of the twentieth century settled onto Hayden and he earnestly buoyed himself with religion, he began to sing of history in an elegiac blues mode in which belief in an ultimate justice is never relinquished, although it seems almost impossible to sustain amid the painful fires of modernity. In full maturity, Hayden's histories come to do the work that Ralph Ellison famously attributed to the blues—"to keep the painful details and episodes of a brutal experience alive in one's aching consciousness, to finger its jagged grain" (*Collected Essays* 129). In his 1975 poem "Crispus Attucks" Hayden distills history itself as violent paradox on the one hand and ground for ideological competition on the other. His elegy for the black man thought to be the first casualty of the American Revolution does not offer the past as nourishing milk to fuel an ascendant journey into the future. Instead history is an opaque, bloody text requiring continual and quarrelling interpretation. Attucks is "moot hero shrouded in Betsy Ross / and Garvey flags—propped up / by bayonets, forever falling" (*Angle* 20).

Sinda, a principal character in "The Dream (1863)"—one of Hayden's lesser-known history poems—falls at precisely the moment when official and redemptive narratives of history would have her rise. The poem, first collected in *Words in the Mourning Time*, is innovative in a number of ways but has garnered little notice from anthologists—perhaps because it registers the complex ambivalence characteristic of Hayden's final decade and offers no easily consumable narrative of history. It approaches the nodal historical occasion of the emancipation through two character-focused sequences. In one, Hayden's erudite narrator describes the experience of Sinda, an aging slave, on freedom day. In its partner sequence, the black soldier Cal is presented through an epistolary vernacular narrative dispatched from the front lines of the Civil War. Sinda's story is told in three ten-line stanzas, each of which is followed by a stanzaic fragment from Cal's letters. Part of the poem's indeterminacy is felt in the slippery relation between the two character sequences. Each might stand on its own, but the two are linked through allusion, imagery, and theme. As James Hall points out, it is impossible to definitively name the relation between Sinda and Cal, whether they are siblings, mother and son, or some other familial pair (247n55). However, in a poem vested with ambivalence and doubt, the undefined relation between the characters is essential apparatus.

Hayden uses Sinda to return to the slave quarters that gave birth to faith and guarantees of future freedom in *Heart-Shape*. But in this return, Hayden revises the historiography that organized his early interpretations of the slave past. Sinda is a "fevered, gasping" woman near the end of her life who struggles to come to terms with the distance between her millennial visions of freedom and the reality that history has furnished. She imagines the fabled Jubilee as restoration—the resurrection and return of heroic loved ones:

> How many times that dream had come to her—
> more vision than dream—

the great big soldiers marching out of gunburst,
their faces those of Cal and Joe
and Charlie sold to the ricefields oh sold away
a-many and a-many a long year ago. (*Angle* 36)

In a poem without rhyme pattern, the presentation of Sinda's dream is marked by repetitions and perfect rhyme, suggesting its simplicity and even its naiveté in the context of unpredictable history. Sinda must confront an almost sordid anticlimax: emancipating "Buckras with their ornery / funning, cussed commands"—not "the hosts the dream had promised her" (36).

Hayden saddles his Sinda with a version of the idealistic and rather unsophisticated vision of history that he had sometimes invested in as a younger poet. Like his character, the older Hayden deals with a history that is more chaotic and less assuring than he had once imagined. In his later career Hayden no longer bandied the abstraction of "freedom" and could hardly believe that history moved organically toward "legendary spring," as he had insisted in early poems. In "The Dream" Hayden ironizes springtide, divorcing it from connotations of easy hope and reassurance. As she hobbles her way across the "wavering yard," Sinda reaches "a redbud tree in bloom, could go no farther, clung / to the bole and clinging fell / to her knees" (37). The blossoming tree is ironically indifferent to Sinda's struggle, as are the droning "whippoorwills / in tenuous moonlight." Hayden reemphasizes the natural world's ominous indifference to human travail in Cal's narrative. The black soldier whom Sinda has evoked writes from the "Dixieland" front lines of the war, describing how "the judas trees is blossomed out / so pretty same as if this hurt and truble wasnt going on" (37). Here again, spring imagery provides only ironic contrast to suffering and offers no promise of a future human flourishing. Indeed, the blooming is particularly dubious because it appears on the *Judas* trees. As in Sinda's dream, simple tropes and scripts of hope seem likely to betray.

By inserting revisionist skepticism into that hallowed moment of American history when slavery was abolished, Hayden's historiography seems aligned with the recent work of historians like Eric Foner, who have used seeming paradox to characterize the emancipation as conferring "nothing but freedom" (which is the title of one of Foner's books about the Reconstruction era). Perhaps more pointedly, Hayden's decision to make the Jubilee itself into a moment of crisis rather than jubilation appears to be in resonance with the thinking of African American cultural theorists like Saidiya Hartman, who have been called "Afro-pessimists." These early twenty-first-century

scholars note the persistence of racialized abjection in America and, look-
ing at moments like "the nonevent of emancipation"—as Hartman describes
it—argue against narratives of progression. In this view, granting freedom to
the enslaved simply gave birth to the "refiguration of subjection" (116), and
the historical milestone of the emancipation is regarded not as a moment
of substantive liberation but as an opportunity for the restructuring of racial
oppression in America.

Although Hayden's religiously grounded belief in the socially ameliora-
tive inclination of the American state would seem to put him at odds with to-
day's Afro-pessimists, in "The Dream" he concentrates on a nodal point in the
American and African American narrative because—like the pessimists—he
seeks a revisionist position that complicates (and undermines) official and
redemptive chronicles of history. But late in life Hayden's intervention is
less an act of scholarly political protest than it is an existential contempla-
tion about the merit and danger of hope in the face of historical uncertainty.
With its various situational ironies, Hayden's more pessimistic aspect seems
to produce the "The Dream," but here again, Hayden's primary quarrel is with
himself and with the sanguine narratives of history that he had offered in his
past. The poet who revised "endlessly" (*Collected Prose* 117)—as he put it—was
continually at work on the adjustment of his historiographical expression,
using palinodic poems written late in life to revise conceptual infelicities that
he felt were etched into frequently anthologized poems produced earlier in
his career.

Among the several tropes that Hayden rejects in "The Dream" is that of
the history-shaping *Übermensch* that towered in his heritage poems about
Douglass, Tubman, and Cinquez. In Cal's vernacular narration, Hayden hu-
manizes the poem's would-be hero—presumably an absconding slave who
has found his way into a Union regiment and "seen some akshun." Cal's first-
person folk voice is not augmented or interpreted through situating narration
(as was Hayden's usual practice when employing vernacular speech). Instead,
it hovers alone and reflects a nuanced, self-effacingly droll figure who seems
only vaguely aware of his own bravery and makes no claims to special righ-
teousness. If Hayden once focused on black champions, memorializing them
as lodestars guiding a people through history, here he shifts honor to the folk
man in the mass whose individual impact on history is negligible but who is
also noble and representative. Cal repeatedly alludes to his own frailty, and he
understands the mission of the war not through grand philosophical narra-
tives but through popular folk knowledge: "I am tired some but it is war you
/ know and ole Jeff Davis muss be ketch an hung to a sour / apple tree like it

says in the song" (36). Cal stands stoically at the heart of American violence, cognizant of all its "hurt and truble" and knowing that there may be a "Bullit with my name rote in it." But rather than feeling dismay at the spring trees that blossom indifferently in the midst of the fighting, Cal takes "it for a sign The Lord remembers Us." Hayden cannot fully endorse this faith, but neither will he fully diminish it. Although he subtly likens the image of the budding tree to Sinda's unrealizable dream (Cal describes the blooming as "Almos like something you mite dream about"), the mature poet will not definitively indicate that Cal has misinterpreted the meaning of the blooming Judas trees. Hayden closes the poem with Cal imagining that he might marry one of the "ficety gals" he has seen in the Deep South. Which is to say, he leaves his black soldier in medias res—fate unknown, yet planning a future. While Hayden identifies with Sinda, who, similar to his diver, "struggled to rise" through the disenchantments of lived history, he admires Cal, whose folk faith gives him the strength to both countenance war killing and also maintain belief in divinity and the promise of futurity. Through these characters, each a facet of the poet's internally quarreling self, Hayden confronts the unforeseeable trajectory of history, suggesting that it both crushes and necessitates idealism. With the meaning of history indecipherable, like the ambiguous Judas trees that bloom amid bloodshed, Sinda and Cal replace the giants who once led the way through history. These folk characters are not exemplars—they are fallible figures who struggle, much like the poet himself, to survive in the maelstrom of history.

"I am tired today / of history" declares the speaker of "The Islands," published in *American Journal* (47). It is an understandable admission appearing in the final volume of Hayden's career. By the late 1970s, he had come to regard history and "its patina'd clichés / of endless evil" as a type of affliction, a layered conundrum impenetrable after decades of engagement. But while the long quarrel with self and history had become a Sisyphean burden for the poet, recent literary history indicates that the poems he produced in that quarrel were Promethean. As we will see in the next chapters, Hayden has shown the way to a host of significant descendants, indebted and responsive to his untiring effort to bring light and humanity to history and to the vocation of poetry.

PART IV

Hayden's Legacies

Chapter 8

Professors and MCs

———

Institutionalizing Black Poetries
in the Post-Movement Era

———

Written in the late 1970s, "The Islands" expresses the emotional exhaustion that Hayden frequently experienced near the end of a career-long effort to make sense of history through poetry. Like the white-collar laborer who cannot disentangle himself from work even while on holiday, the speaker of "The Islands" is "tired of history," which encroaches on his Caribbean vacation. He acknowledges the "waking dream of palmtrees, / magic flowers—of sensuous joys," but the poem hollows out advertised promises of tropical escape and renewal as it lingers on "the tidy ruins / of a sugar mill" where "more than cane / was crushed" (*American Journal* 183). Much like "On Lookout Mountain," published some twenty years earlier, in "The Islands" a trip to a tourist destination provides occasion for a journey toward historical violence. But if both poems are partly about the way that the insistent burden of history thwarts the comforts sought in leisure, the latter is also documentation of the paradoxes of African American economic success and social mobility in the years after the civil rights and Black Power movements (the post-movement era).[1] The poet-professor, having secured coveted upper-middle-class stability in an American era rid of de jure racial discrimination, discovers himself nonetheless discomfited in his new, relatively privileged existence. Rather than finding easy common cause with the black West Indians whom he encounters while vacationing, Hayden's speaker notes their "scorn" for his advantaged position in hemispheric economies. In "The Islands," lush with the repetition of long-vowel internal rhymes and a curated fragment of black (West

Indian) vernacular, Hayden works with his signature Apollonian, genteel, and erudite aesthetic while combining black historical remembrance and a subtle reflection on the newfound affluence of the black artist-intellectual. Its writerly aesthetics, its fixation on history, and its attention to the particular alienations of the salaried black intellectual of the post-movement era make "The Islands" an exemplary model of the poetic temperament that Hayden has bequeathed to recent generations of poets.

Almost four decades have passed since Hayden published "The Islands" in his final volume of poetry, *American Journal* (1980). During that time African American poetics has enjoyed an unprecedented prospering, particularly if the category of poetry admits not only high-status literary verse but also more popular, readily performed and commodified forms like rap and spoken word. In the contemporary cultural context, arguably awash in the influence of black poetics, our fullest understanding of Hayden's poetry and its political-aesthetic comportment emerges from a consideration of his ongoing presence in this fecund moment of poetic production. That is to say, at this historical juncture, full assessment of Hayden begs for an analysis of the *legacy* of poems like the "The Islands." In this concluding section of *Robert Hayden in Verse* I analyze that legacy by following an Ariadne's thread that winds its way from Hayden and the Black Arts era through the proliferation of black poetic production in the late twentieth century and into the work of a number of celebrated poet-professors who have thrived under the patronage of twenty-first-century American universities that now institutionalize high-status literary poetics. My primary contention is similar to that of Charles Rowell, who has argued that Hayden's political aesthetic—honed in the 1960s and 1970s, in tension with the BAM—exerts a powerful, shaping (and perhaps singular) influence on a robust segment of African American poetry. However, my reading of Hayden's contemporary influence makes visible the fragmentation of black poetics in the 1970s and 1980s, arguing that Hayden is a chief progenitor of the Apollonian black poetic mode that is now almost totally subsidized by the American university system, while the Dionysian, preacherly method of the BAM is felt in the poetics of spoken word and hip-hop. The argument first leads me into a rough sketching of the recent emergence of academic and hip-hop poetries as distinguishable modes of class-marked black expression. This schema offers a foundation for comprehension of Hayden's influence on the work of contemporary poet-professors devoted to the sustenance of historical memory and ruminations on black class difference in a cultural era shaped by neoliberal political economy. With particular focus on the archival research poetry of Rita Dove, Natasha

Trethewey, Elizabeth Alexander, and Nikky Finney, I place Hayden's kin-
dling influence at the heart of a veritable explosion of twenty-first-century
poetic historiography—an explosion that I figure as a blackademic response
to post-movement neoliberal phenomena like the intensification of historical
amnesia and the erosion of interclass connections in "black community." And
with concentration on the work of Terrance Hayes and evocation of Douglas
Kearney's poetic innovations, this section finds Hayden's legacy productively
circulating in two of the most important high-status male poets of the early
twenty-first century. Hayes's contemplative craft, careful handling of black
vernacular language, and commitment to aesthetic distancing are signposts
that lead back to the poetic model that Hayden perfected in the 1960s and
1970s. And Kearney's comingling of Hayden's legacy with BAM aesthetic
ideas, and hip-hop-generation sensibility and familiarity, suggests Hayden's
ongoing significance in American poetics.

Programming Hayden

With his permanent appointment at the University of Michigan in 1969,
Hayden had achieved the improbable: on little more than the strength of his
poetry, he had traveled from the ghetto poverty of Detroit's Paradise Valley
to the seeming security of a lifestyle that could afford him the Caribbean
vacation chronicled in "The Islands." This late-life professional and mate-
rial success can be rendered as a narrative of individual accomplishment, a
deserved reward for a toiling artist who worked his way to recognition in a
cultural meritocracy. Hatcher tends toward that narrative in his description
of Hayden's precipitous individual ascent in the late 1960s. Hatcher writes
that, in 1963, Hayden was "unknown, discouraged by his career, financially
poor, and stuck in an institution that did not seem to appreciate his talents."
But by the end of the sixties, the poet "had achieved almost every goal he had
set for himself" (40). This story of personal achievement is both appropriate
and compelling; Hayden himself seemed wonderstruck when—adopting the
third-person voice—he considered his own rise to the position of consultant
in poetry to the Library of Congress: "Was it luck that had enabled him to
make the long and surprising journey from Paradise Valley to the Library of
Congress?" (*Collected Prose* 21). But his success was not only the result of hard
work and good luck; it must also be understood as a function of structural
change in American higher education partly catalyzed by the civil rights,
Black Power, and student movements of the 1960s—change that one histo-
rian of modern black studies calls a "bureaucratic response to a social move-

ment" (Rojas 19). To be sure, Hayden's appointment as a full professor in an English department and his lecture notes focused on the Anglo-American canon make it impossible to confuse him with the cadre of more Afrocentric scholars who established black studies programs in the late 1960s and after. However, Hayden's professional success, as it is indexed by his transfer from resource-poor and historically black Fisk University to the resource-rich and predominantly white University of Michigan, represents one episode in accord with a larger story about how social movements of the 1960s gave rise to multiculturalism in academia and the diversification of the professoriate. In turn, this story about the evolving demography of American universities takes place within the still larger socioeconomic narrative about black class mobility in the post–civil rights era.

When considered within these frames, the professional and economic stability that Hayden enjoyed during the last decade of his life can be understood in terms of a major, but severely underappreciated, development in the history of the African American poetic tradition—that is, the institutionalization of black poets as securely middle-class intellectual/cultural workers in the relatively well-heeled context of an American university system that, up until the late 1960s, retained an almost all-white faculty. Hayden's transfer from Fisk to Michigan is symptomatic of a shift in the patronage system that gave material support to African American poetry. If almost all the important poets of Hayden's generation, like Margaret Walker, Melvin Tolson, Owen Dodson, and Sterling Brown, were fixtures in the mid-twentieth-century ecology of black educational institutions, almost all black poets rising to prominence after 1969 have been professionally situated in predominantly white colleges and universities (PWIs).

This shift in the institutional patronage of black poetry has myriad political and aesthetic implications, most of which are beyond the scope of my analysis. But to assess Hayden's legacy in the contemporary moment, some basic acknowledgements are necessary: When the federal government responded to 1960s social movements by using institutions of higher education to "increase equality of opportunity" (Kerr 129), the demand for black poets and poetry on campuses expanded greatly. The influx (relatively speaking) of black poets at PWIs was also part of the process that Mark McGurl has charted in *The Program Era: Postwar Fiction and the Rise of Creative Writing* (2009), an essential study of the rise of creative writing as a college discipline in the postwar period. McGurl's work shows that the "watermark" of the university system and its creative writing workshop have been ubiquitous in U.S. modernism since the end of World War II, when literary production became institutionalized "as another form of original research sponsored by the booming, science-oriented universities" (4). McGurl's focus is on the impact of MFA programs on American fiction, but his argument that ideological and aesthetic assessment of postwar literature must account for the shaping power of the university-based writing workshop is even more pertinent to American poetry, "which (as a paying profession at least) has been all but entirely absorbed by institutions of higher education" (29). The fact that poetry, tethered to the university system, has become a (good-) paying profession is part of what makes Robert Hayden, rather than the poets of the BAM, a key influence for contemporary black poets. As I argue in part 2, while artist-intellectuals of the BAM often sought to eliminate the distance between themselves and the black folk masses, Hayden's Black Arts–era poetics actively acknowledged and explored experiential differences that separated his erudite poet-speakers and the vernacular world of the folk. In the post-movement era, characterized by both the relative *securitization* of the middle-class black professor-poet and the intensification of cultural and economic separation between the black middle and lower classes, it was implausible for black academic poets to follow the lead of BAM poets, who cloaked themselves in the vernacular styles of the urban poor. These more contemporary poets learned much more from Hayden's writerly efforts to describe, measure, and reach across the divides that distance the literary artist-intellectual from the vernacular folk world.

Spurred on by the social movements of the 1960s, the absorption of black poets into predominantly white institutions of higher education in the 1970s immediately redounded to the financial and professional benefit of a select group, including Hayden and "stars" of the BAM such as Nikki Giovanni, Sonia Sanchez, Larry Neal, and Amiri Baraka, all of whom assumed posts at major universities. It also secured the prospects of a coterie of poets younger than Hayden but less often affiliated with the BAM and its vernacular-heavy and performance-oriented aesthetic. In the 1970s significant poets like Lucille Clifton, Primus St. John, Audre Lorde, Clarence Major, Ed Roberson, and Al Young were afforded some sense of middle-class security by early career employment in well-monetized PWIs.

Charles Rowell has determined that these poets, born in the 1930s, were "outside the Black Arts Movement" and that, after Hayden, they have been the most consequential figures in the developmental arc of African American poetry since the Black Arts era. Several items merit noting here. Some of the influential poets whom Rowell places outside the movement—particularly Clifton, Lorde, and Major—are quite often affiliated with the BAM and cannot be easily unlinked from it; as I've implicitly argued throughout, strict policing of the boundary that lassoes the BAM may be unproductive in new histories of African American poetry. Placing poets inside or outside of categories is, more than anything else, a critical convenience, a provisional move that fades as the scholarship thickens, as we recognize ways in which poets often ignore borders, and as we develop readings that intentionally problematize existing categories. That said, when Rowell attempts to give order to the field of recent African American poetics by selecting, grouping, and periodizing texts and authors, he is doing the thankless work of the anthologist. And it should be noted that in his important role as an editor at *Callaloo* and as an anthologist, Rowell has done much to amplify Hayden's legacy.

In Rowell's account of recent poetic history, offered in his introduction to *Angles of Ascent: A Norton Anthology of Contemporary African American Poetry* (2013), "the poets of the next generations, who have ascended to great heights on the North American literary scene, are not direct aesthetic and ideational descendants of the poets of the Black Arts Movement; they are more akin to Robert Hayden and the poets contemporary to the Movement who wrote outside the Black Aesthetic" (xl). As mentioned in previous chapters, Rowell's remarks on the trajectory of the black poetic tradition came under withering attack from Amiri Baraka; nevertheless, Rowell's general claim is accurate. Undoubtedly, it is the example of Hayden's 1960s and 1970s production, rather than that of poets traditionally affiliated with the BAM, that is sensed in the work of celebrated figures like Yusef Komunyakaa, Rita Dove, Toi Derricotte, and the poet-professors I will examine below. However, a more extensive quotation of Rowell's anthology introduction reveals some of the limitations of a critical perspective that does not fully investigate the implications of the institutionalization of black poetry in PWIs in the 1970s and that fails to register the emergence of spoken word and hip-hop poetics in the same decade. Commenting on poets of the late twentieth and early twenty-first century, Rowell writes,

> As artists coming in the aftermath of the Black Arts Movement, this younger generation of poets had aesthetic and ideational interests of their own that did not include the prescriptive agenda of the Black Aesthetic. Unlike the African American writers who preceded them, this younger generation had the privilege of deciding to write poetry that reflected their individual lives, their own families, and the communities they know. As a result of the progressive achievements of both the Black Power Movement and the Civil Rights Movement,

these new writers are the first African Americans to be free of out-
side political and social dicta from blacks and whites commanding
them on what and how to write. They are the first generation of black
writers who, en masses and by example, asserted the right to commit
themselves to their art, rather than commit their art to Black Ameri-
ca's political, social, and economic struggles. (xl)

This thumbnail sketching does not make much of the fact that all black po-
ets who are prominent "on the North American literary scene" are (or have
been) faculty in elite institutions of American academia. Rowell notes the
"privilege" enjoyed by these successful poets but does not directly link that
privilege to university employment, nor does he call attention to the *deter-
mining* role that MFA programs and academic professionalization play in the
work of recently ascendant black poets. This approach potentially mystifies
and overstates the "literary freedom" (liii) that Rowell finds in contemporary
African American poetry. That is to say, the claim that these poets are "free of
outside political and social dicta from blacks and whites commanding them
on what and how to write" pivots on the assumption that in the contempo-
rary patronage system there are few constraints on poetic production. Yet the
reality is that there is no shortage of unspoken dicta that solemnly govern the
university-based MFA programs and writing workshops that have produced
those black poets esteemed by Rowell. In the great majority of creative writ-
ing programs of the 1970s, 1980s, and 1990s, which were the preparatory acad-
emies of today's poet-professors, BAM-style poetics—preacherly, stridently
political, readily accessible, and saturated in black vernacular language—were
all but verboten.

  "Literary" black poets of recent decades are in the thrall of a highly com-
petitive academic market in which the prized product is the "well-crafted"
poem. In 2012 Marjorie Perloff described this poetic product and its prov-
enance, writing that "the national (or even transnational) demand for a cer-
tain kind of prize-winning, 'well-crafted' poem—a poem that the *New Yorker*
would see fit to print and that would help its author get one of the 'good
jobs' advertised by the Association of Writers & Writing Programs—has pro-
duced an extraordinary uniformity" (60). If, as Rowell argues, contemporary
black poets are no longer coerced to "commit their art to Black America's
struggles," those who seek the good academic jobs mentioned by Perloff
would seem to be under tremendous pressure to commit themselves to the
production of well-crafted poems, very narrowly defined. While it would be
an oversimplifying disservice to suggest that Hayden's poetics is of a piece

with the well-crafted poems that Perloff takes aim at, it is certainly true that the "*New Yorker* poem" of recent decades recalls Hayden more than it does the Black Arts–era work of figures like Larry Neal, Calvin Hernton, Sonia Sanchez, or Haki Madhubuti. Frank appraisal of the contemporary African American poetry scene and its contextualization within American poetry culture suggests that blackademic poets do not simply write what and how they like; instead, like vessels on seemingly open poetic waters, they have been guided away from BAM poetics by strong industry trade winds leading toward "well-crafted" poems.

Disdaining these poems, Perloff contends that they deploy a standardized formula of "irregular lines of free verse," "prose syntax," "graphic imagery," "extravagant metaphor," and the expression of personalized political sensitivity manifest in "a profound thought or small epiphany, usually based on a particular memory, designating the lyric speaker as a particularly sensitive person who really *feels* the pain" of some social or emotional victim (60–61, emphasis in original). Although the vast majority of these well-crafted poems have been published by poets who are not black, Perloff manages to find the quintessential example of this formulaic art in the work of Natasha Trethewey and argues that Rita Dove's editorial selections for the *Penguin Anthology of Twentieth-Century American Poetry* has perpetuated what the critic calls the "dominant poetry culture of our time—the culture of prizes, professorships, and political correctness" (64). While Perloff's irritated characterization of today's poetry industry is in many ways persuasive, in its special targeting of Pulitzer Prize–winners Trethewey and Dove, her frustration with contemporary poetry culture seems to braid into a damnable and resilient strain of racial resentment that has, for almost two and a half centuries, followed African American poetic achievement. Nevertheless, Perloff's ability to place black poets at the heart of her critique of contemporary American poetry *at large* is an indication of the success that a select number of high-profile black poets have had in the era of academically institutionalized poetry. If most of Hayden's career was defined by obscurity, his poetic descendants have grown into widely recognized, richly rewarded faculty-artists occupying the center stage of American poetry culture.

On their way to artistic achievement marked by writerly, history-oriented poetics, both Rita Dove and Natasha Trethewey passed through MFA crucibles. In the middle of the 1970s Dove emerged from the Iowa Writer's Workshop—the cynosure institution of McGurl's Program Era—to embark on an accolade-filled career, which was inaugurated by her volume *The Yellow House on the Corner* (1980). In this first collection, Dove enacts a Freudian

"killing of the father" in a poem that allegorically disavows the BAM, "clear-
ing the way"—as she put it (Pereira 58, 173)—for an artistic vision unen-
cumbered by limitations that apparently constrained black poets in the years
immediately preceding her admission to Iowa. In "Upon Meeting Don L.
Lee, in a Dream," Dove embodies a hectoring black aesthetic in the night-
mare figure of Don L. Lee (Haki Madhubuti), who is—for all intents and
purposes—vanquished when he begins a lecture-sermon only to be inter-
rupted by a narrator who wants no part of his lesson:

> "Seven years ago . . ." he begins; but
> I cut him off: "Those years are gone—
> What is there now?" He starts to cry; his eyeballs
>
> Burst into flame. (*Yellow House* 16)

With the type of ellipticism (literally) and thrift of language that is valued
in the MFA workshop, Dove stunts Lee's speech so that his argument is not
fully articulated; only the historical milieu of the Black Arts era is evoked.
Linguistic economy allows the speaker's victorious confrontation with Lee
to be read in a variety of ways—primarily, it is Dove's assertion that she will
not be, as Rowell put it, an "aesthetic and ideational" descendant of the poets
of the Black Arts Movement. But it is also, then, a refusal of debt and a dec-
laration that literary history moves swiftly; young Dove does not want to be
burdened by the remembrance of a past now a long seven years "gone." In one
sense, the answer to the speaker's question ("What is there now?") is Dove's
poem (and her first book) itself: "now," in the late 1970s, black poetics will
not be an accouterment of the cultural nationalism suggested by the poem's
women singers, who at first "stretch their beaded arms to" Lee but then "float
away" after the speaker asserts herself against the Black Arts leader; instead, it
will flower from MFA workshops in PWIs, and it will be published by major
university presses (as Carnegie Mellon University Press published *The Yel-
low House on the Corner*). Of course, Dove's poetic resistance to the aesthetic
and ideational parameters allegorized in Don L. Lee recalls Hayden's intense
scuffles with the real Lee and his public refusal of Black Arts tenets in the
1960s. Thus, Dove's killing of one paternal bogeyman might be interpreted
as an implicit affiliation to another paternal line that runs through Hayden.
(Although Dove and many of the poets following her—like Alexander,
Trethewey, and a host of successful black women poets—point to Gwendo-
lyn Brooks as their primary ancestral model, Hayden is an equally influential

antecedent, even if he is less acknowledged than Brooks. Hayden's vexed relation to the BAM—in contrast to Brooks's more "reconciled" relation—and his foundational developments of black historical poetics are dimensions of his literary profile that are quite significant for Dove, Alexander, Trethewey, and others.)

Counting Dove as one of his seminal contemporary poets, Charles Rowell keys on "Upon Meeting Don L. Lee" in making his argument that, following maps established by Hayden, Brooks, and Tolson, these new poets "have, in fact, set new directions for African American poetry" that lead away from the BAM (*Angles* xliii). But, by emphasizing that it is the genius of Hayden and the like that has been the guiding light for the poets who populate his Norton anthology, Rowell leaves aside the thick history that *also* produces recent poetics indebted to Hayden. Perhaps more than any other factor, it was the 1970s integration of black poetry into the necessarily conservative rhythms of the American university system that ensured the seeming marginalization of BAM poetics in post-movement "literary" poetry.

Although the academic discipline of black studies is not a perfect analogue for the creative art of black poetry, these enterprises share a similar twentieth- and twenty-first-century history.[2] Black poetry, like black studies, was nurtured in Negro institutions until the movement era of the 1960s, when, propelled by radical politics, it was folded into PWIs and took on a liberal reformist mien. Of particular interest to students of black poetry should be the comparable 1970s processes that assimilated black studies into "white" universities and institutionalized the production of black poetry in PWIs. The former is usefully summarized in a short article that St. Clair Drake wrote and published during the period between Rita Dove's completion of her MFA at Iowa and the appearance of her volume that included "Upon Meeting Don L. Lee." In the essay, entitled "What Happened to Black Studies?," Drake succinctly chronicles the rapid emergence, coalescence, and institutionalization of the discipline in PWIs. Writing in 1979, the eminent black historian could assert,

> Utopian dreams and revolutionary rhetoric lost the appeal they had for college students a decade ago. A "supplementary education" for upwardly-mobile black students that assists them to cope with their own personal problems as well as satisfying their intellectual and aesthetic needs, but without forgetting "those left behind," has become the goal of most black studies programs. (274)

With some minor adjustments, Drake's 1979 appraisal of black studies might very well double as a description of the black poetry that was finding a home in the American university system of the late 1970s.[3] But it should be noted that the radical idealism and revolutionary rhetoric that girded black studies and black poetry of the late 1960s did not spontaneously lose appeal. Rather, as the "upwardly mobile" recognized the opportunities afforded them in the newly multiculturalist PWIs, they carved out niches inside the system. And just as black studies made compromises and consolidated itself in the institutions it once targeted for radical reform, in the late 1970s and 1980s black poetry accommodated itself to the MFA programs housed in those same institutions. To point out this adaptation is not a degradation of university-produced black poetry of recent decades; indeed, as Rowell argues, an important body of art has arisen in this Program Era. However, the best analysis of this poetic mode frankly recognizes that it first answers to the "intellectual and aesthetic needs" of a black cohort educated and employed in the American university system.

Because it is largely the product of a relatively fortunate black middle-class, the strand of post-Black-Arts-era poetics institutionalized in academia is vulnerable to the type of populist, nationalist, and class-based critique exemplified in Amiri Baraka's harsh review of Rowell's anthology. Keying on the individualized and internal focus of the Hayden poem that gives its name to Rowell's collection—"Angle of Ascent"—Baraka sets up a totalizing attack on the anthology by implying that the poetry of Hayden and his literary descendants has "nothing to do with the real world and real people" ("Post-Racial"). For Baraka, the Haydenesque poetry generated in MFA program culture is reducible to a struggle for ascension in an ivory tower that removes art from the sociopolitical exigencies faced by "the Black majority, who have felt the direct torture and pain of national oppression." His disdain for much of the "dull and academic" poetry (terms he applies to the work of Yusef Komunyakaa) emanates from the conviction that the art of the black intelligentsia should be plied on behalf of the black majority. Positing himself and other BAM poets as ideal models, Baraka submits that "conscious Black intellectuals" should be "soldiers" creating art to "function in the ghetto."

These types of arguments are attractive to any advocate of interclass racial solidarity, and the stark adversarialism of Baraka's criticisms of Rowell, Hayden, and others can be adrenalizing for scholar-observers. But Baraka's critique of Hayden and his literary descendants builds from an outdated model of literary leadership—from belief in a heroic narrative about the black intelligentsia that, as Kenneth Warren contends, was born in the Jim Crow–era "idea that certain African American individuals and cadres by virtue of their achievements, expertise and goodwill could direct and speak on behalf of the nation's black population" (*What Was* 146). As I argue in part 2, this idea was at the heart of the literary politics and clerical aesthetics of the BAM, guided by Baraka and other intellectuals of middle-class background who (contra Hayden) felt that they could both lead the black majority and fully inhabit its vernacular culture. Hayden—who "had no pretensions to leadership," as Afaa Michael Weaver notes—eschewed this BAM modus and established an alternative type of black poetics that was more modest in its political ambition, more judicious in its appropriation of vernacular culture, and less willing to speak on behalf of ghettoized masses. While the leadership model embraced by Baraka and other BAM figures led them into preacherly performance poetics, the contemplative, self-scrutinizing poetry of Hayden remained a writerly art of the page—one suited to the graphocentric forms of admiration, analysis, and emulation traditionally undertaken in academic settings.

In the early twenty-first century much academic ink has been devoted to the historical and theoretical evaluation of the BAM, but the movement's aesthetic templates were all but abandoned by the early Program Era black poets who, like Rita Dove, hewed much closer to Hayden than to Baraka and other black aestheticians. As I have suggested, scholars have yet to fully evaluate the processes by which BAM influence was drained from the work of MFA poets. Rowell interprets the turn away from the BAM as a rejection of ideological strictures; Baraka sees it as a function of the "bougie" sensibilities of the middle-class artist-intellectuals who began making their way through PWIs in the 1970s and after. But a thicker description of the dissipation of BAM stridency, vernacularity, and nationalism in recent "literary" black poetry needs to account not only for the institutionalization of the field in an academic context that is primarily the province of the relatively affluent but also for the synchronous rise of hip-hop and spoken word poetries. These "low-culture" strands of poetic expression coalesced in the 1980s and 1990s at the very same historical moment in which black poetry was being firmly folded into the English departments and creative writing curricula of mainstream American universities. Thus the MFA embrace of erudite, historically focused, Apollonian poetics might very well be analyzed as a flip side of the popular explosion of vernacular-saturated, performance-based, Dionysian poetics of recent decades. If Hayden's legacy is imprinted in the poems of the Program Era, the legacy of the BAM is heard in the mass-culture poetry products of the hip-hop era.

Rap Is Poetry

In a 2000 *Black Issues Book Review* article that made efforts to bring high-brow respectability to hip-hop music, Dara Cook earnestly argues that rappers are poets. If this claim—often made by rappers (MCs) themselves—is taken seriously, scholars of poetry might grapple with a fascinating constellation of issues. For example, given rap's ubiquity, hand-wringing about the "death of poetry" would need to cease, and the racism and classism inherent in this contemporary "worry" would need acknowledgment. What's more, if rap is poetry and MCs are poets, a primary scholarly question would have to be: Has human culture ever been more deeply steeped in verse? And a series of residual questions—several of which have implications for Hayden's legacy—would merit exploration. These include: What is the artistic/aesthetic provenance of this now-ubiquitous form of poetry controlled by the MC? And what relation do the songs of the MC bear to the simultaneously existing writerly poetry institutionalized in contemporary academia?

Recognizing that rappers actually "write poems in these songs," as Kendrick Lamar emphasized in a text accessed on the internet more than eighty-seven million times,[4] a number of scholars have sought the *poetic* origins of hip-hop, tracing them into the BAM; and a much smaller number of scholars have offered glancing assessments of the relation between blackademic poetry and hip-hop texts that enjoy mass popularity. Although, as James Smethurst has argued, the BAM tried to bring together high and low cultures in a "popular avant-garde" art (*Black Arts Movement* 58–76), in post-BAM decades high and low black poetic modes seem to have drifted far apart—with poet-professors generally producing work sustained by university, governmental, and philanthropic economies and with "successful" MCs operating for mass markets. Nevertheless, by thinking of poet-professors and MCs in tandem, as cousins in the diverse and fragmenting family of contemporary black poetics, we understand Hayden's important role as a model for those who have, in recent decades, refined their art in academic contexts distanced from that part of the class structure that churns out the black vernacular language that is at the heart of hip-hop poetics.

To begin with, it is best to clarify the nature of the BAM's bequest to hip-hop by underscoring *formal* connections between the movements, while deemphasizing ideological continuities. As historian Clarence Lang points out, it is almost impossible to attribute stable ideological values to the hip-hop movement; it "has no fixed political character, and it is a grave mistake to categorize it as a successor to the black freedom movements of the 1960s" (4). A similar argument holds true for the political content of rap lyricism, which is extremely heterogeneous. However, if the primary medium of hip-hop expressivity is a kind of "rhymed story-telling"—or narrative poetry—that "prioritizes black voices from the margins of urban America" (Rose 2), its basic aesthetic relation to BAM poetics is unmistakable. The poetries of both movements are bound by their common accentuation, and implicit celebration, of black urban vernacular. However, many examinations of the relation between hip-hop and the BAM stress the political legacy of the BAM as it seems to appear in a select subset of "conscious" rappers. For example, in her essay "From Black Arts to Def Jam: Performing Black 'Spirit Work' across Generations," Lorrie Smith offers one of several scholarly assessments that discover hip-hop's roots in the BAM.[5] Noting "bonds of kinship" that connect BAM poets and "the rap and hip-hop inflected spirit of young performers" (350), Smith follows Cook in using a transitive logic to support the claim that rap is poetry. (If Black Arts–era poets are "firmly established in the cannon of contemporary poetry," as Cook perhaps dubiously asserts (24), then a new generation of hip-hop artists who claim kinship to Black Arts–era figures are also poets.) Smith and Cook primarily key on the political "spirit" of the BAM as they trace its influence into the hip-hop generation. But this emphasis on (quasi-black nationalist) political ideology, rather than the formal and aesthetic relationship between BAM and hip-hop poetics, can actually obscure the massive influence that Black Arts–era innovators bequeathed to the ubiquitous "lowbrow" poetry that is now a major pillar of the American and global culture industry.

This inadvertent obfuscation can be felt as Smith calls attention to a photo spread featuring Sonia Sanchez and rapper Mos Def, which appears in Cook's article. Smith suggests that an intergenerational affinity uniting the BAM and hip-hop generations is represented in a photo that depicts Sanchez "embracing Mos Def like a proud mama." Smith also affirms the truth of text that accompanies the photo, enthusiastically noting that the photo is captioned by "a headline asserting (lest any skeptics are still holding out) that 'Rap IS Poetry!'" (Smith 350; Cook 23). Both Cook and Smith imply that rap is elevated—that it can be afforded cultural honor—if it is recognized as poetry. Accordingly, the exemplary rapper-poets whom they link to the BAM—and thus to "poetry"—are honorable, "conscious" rappers like Mos

Def (Yasiin Bey), whose work usually operates at the margins of mainstream commercial hip-hop and carries in it the socially engaged, nationalist tenor of BAM politics.[6] Notably, Cook's claim that rap is poetry seems significantly hedged when she explains that "*some* rap lyrics, like those of Mos Def, are poetry—very good poetry" (25, emphasis added). This qualification insinuates that much rap does not rise to the level of poetry because it does not have what she calls, "intelligent, conscious" lyrical content (25). By this logic, rap is linked to the BAM and elevated to poetry proper only when it is guided by a particular brand of political ideology.[7]

Intentional or not, arguments that use ideological threads to suture hip-hop and the BAM can portray "conscious" MCs as the true artistic progeny of BAM poetry of the 1960s and 1970s while suggesting that a great many MCs—whose lyrics celebrate hedonism, misogyny, acquisitiveness, and so on—are not the heirs of the BAM. But this formulation, which gives pride of place to political content rather than poetic form, produces a skewed perception of the BAM's legacy, which should be felt not only when an artist proffers politically conscious rhymes but any time an MC grabs the mic to perform poetry calibrated by the vernacular idioms heard in the lower levels of the class structure. Indeed, by effectively disowning hip-hop that does not seem to emit what Smith, channeling Houston Baker, calls "the 'eternally transformative impulse' of black poetic 'spirit work'" (Smith 351), literary scholars undersell the BAM's poetic legacy.[8]

While the roots of hip-hop poetics are found in a variety of aesthetic terrains—from the toasting styles of Jamaican reggae artists to the rhyme games of black urban culture and the promotional barking of 1970s New York City dance party DJs—hip-hop's union of performed verses of urban black vernacular and percussive instrumentation taps into poetic innovations that must be associated with the BAM. In 1969, the year that Hayden made his transfer from Fisk to Michigan, the Last Poets presented their drum-driven poems at historically black Lincoln University.[9] Attending the show was an inspired Gil Scott-Heron, who would never graduate from Lincoln or earn a bachelor's degree but would follow in the aesthetic direction of the Last Poets to create iconic poems of the early 1970s—like "The Revolution Will Not Be Televised"—that hastened the rise of hip-hop poetics. The material trace of these poems is rarely found in the writerly work of black poets who entered MFA programs in the 1970s and 1980s, but the conga drums that sound beneath the spoken word texts of Scott-Heron, the Last Poets, and the Watts Poets are nearly replicated in foundational rap songs of the early 1980s, like the Sugar Hill Gang's "Apache" and Grand Master Flash's "The Adventures of Grand Master Flash on the Wheels of Steel."[10] Baraka, eager to concretize the connection between hip-hop and the BAM, once described the Last Poets as "the prototype Rappers, the transmitters of the mass poetry style of the Black Arts sixties" (qtd. in Oyewole xiv). And, although prominent hip-hop artists rarely assert an explicit connection to BAM poetics,[11] Baraka's assessment is implicitly corroborated by a host of MCs and producers who, through sampling, have frequently invoked the pivotal poetry of the early 1970s. Hip-hop acts as ideologically and aurally disparate as Kanye West, Poor Righteous Teachers, and Boogie Down Productions have curated early examples of drum-accompanied spoken word recorded by Scott-Heron, and culture-shifting hip-hop tracks such as A Tribe Called Quest's "Excursions" and N.W.A.'s "Niggaz 4 Life" sample and consciously signify on poems from the seminal, eponymous album of the Last Poets released in 1970.

Somewhat ironically, one of hip-hop's classic Dionysian anthems, "Party and Bullshit" by The Notorious B.I.G. (Biggie), is built around a sample of the Last Poets' "When the Revolution Comes." The poem, also recorded for the group's 1970 album, is a quintessential example of what Baraka termed the "mass poetry style of the Black Arts sixties"—it is saturated in urban black sensibility and vernacular; it is militantly nationalist in its call for social transformation; and its revolutionary directives are delivered through preacherly performance. In the poem, "party and bullshit" is figured as a cardinal sin of black community; the phrase that Biggie's text would repeatedly sample some twenty years later operates in its original context as part of a common Black Arts pattern of social critique and admonishment that emphasizes the perceived shortfalls of black lifestyle. Indeed, the final lines of the poem suggest the mortal consequence of escapist black revelry that retards revolution:

When the revolution comes
Men will look like men
And women will look like women once again
And pride and respect will be as natural as nature
When the revolution comes
When the revolution comes
But until then
You know and I know and we know
Niggers will party and bullshit
Party and bullshit party and bullshit
And some might even die before the revolution comes. (Oyewole 15)

Biggie's anthem echoes the strict gender-role enforcement of the Black Arts poem but rejects its nationalist brand of respectability politics by turning the poem's condemnation of bacchanalia on its head. Where the Last Poets assert themselves as Baraka's "conscious Black intellectuals," using art to paternally guide the masses toward social transformation, Biggie responds as the heedless thug or recalcitrant child, drawn to the very behavior that the preaching father has denounced. He raps,

> Cuz' all we want to do is
> Party and bullshit, party and bullshit,
> party and bullshit, party and bullshit . . .
> . . .
> Bitches in the back looking righteous
> In a tight dress, I think I might just
> Hit her with a little Biggie 101, How to tote a gun
> And have fun with Jamaican rum
> Conversations, blunts in rotation

While a few "conscious" hip-hop artists have attempted to sustain the progressive, oppositional preachment of the BAM, the commercial giants have not often advanced the apparently ameliorative "spirit work" that some consider an essential aspect of the African American poetic tradition. In fact, like proudly wayward sons and daughters, they often appear to aggressively undermine it. Nevertheless, the BAM legacy must be recognized in the most raucous and bacchanalian work of hip-hop's poet-entrepreneurs. As much as any other poets, these pop culture performers are the aesthetic descendants of BAM artist-intellectuals who pulled poetry down from its rarefied perches in books and universities to make it relevant and consumable for the masses. Although many hip-hop stars of recent decades have wanted to party and bullshit rather than revolt against intractable social formations, all rappers carry forward the BAM's liberationist attack on poetry as a graphocentric and rather elitist art. As Baraka put it in praising the 1960s and 1970s aesthetic innovations of the Last Poets, "We created the word as living music raising it off the still, Apollonian, alabaster page" (foreword xiii). Loosening the connection between poetry and the page, BAM artists did indeed advance a populist, energizing, and Dionysian expressive form built on the vernacular language of the urban folk and the performance art of the preacher. This was a poetry that, in Baraka's words, "could function in the ghetto."

By the early 1990s, many rappers emerging from American ghettos had refined the art of making poetry into "living music," distanced from the page and reflective of a black urban experience. But to the dismay of some—like Abiodun Oyewole, the Last Poet who wrote "When the Revolution Comes"—and the apparent elation of millions, in the hands of poet-rappers like Biggie the new living music had little to say about how to quicken social revolution. Instead, it simply became the cultural form most in tune with the experience and language of the black urban poor. No longer primarily the province of proselytizing "conscious Black intellectuals," during the 1980s and 1990s the hip-hop strand of black poetry expressed, on the one hand, the circumstance of a black subproletariat class enduring the brunt of neoliberal socioeconomic policy and, on the other, the escapist and ecstatic fantasies of that class, featuring hyperbolically empowered gangster-, entrepreneur-, and sex-focused protagonists. After Biggie's success with this formula in "Party and Bullshit," Oyewole felt compelled to write a poem in response. As a nostalgic scold with none of the poetic dynamism that young rappers like Biggie were showcasing, in the mid-1990s Oyewole's speaker solemnly entreats,

Party and bullshit party and bullshit

Let's turn the party into the panthers
And give the bullshit to the planters
To fertilize the soil
And to each other let's be loyal . . . (16)

Although commercial rappers, who are the most noteworthy artistic descendants of the BAM, have not been loyal to the movement's political ethos, those rappers have necessarily stayed true to the movement's key aesthetic innovations. They follow BAM artist-intellectuals like the Last Poets who cultivated a powerful Dionysian poetry by releasing the word from the anchoring page and by emphasizing the vitality of the word in its black vernacular iterations. BAM poets put full faith in Zora Neale Hurston's 1934 claim that "the American Negro has done wonders to the English language" (32) and, in so doing, opened the door to a hip-hop poetics that is a prime force in twenty-first-century cultural production—a force measurable in the profits accumulated by the commercial institutions that since the 1980s have underwritten and organized much of the planet's most popular form of poetry.

In the late 1980s moment when hip-hop began transforming into a major commercial force, Houston Baker made a concerted effort to distance himself from certain elements of the BAM, offering up a harsh and—in his own words—"uncharitable assessment" of the movement's "thuggish will to power" (*Afro-American Poetics* 176). Baker highlighted the callous-hearted, seamier sides of the movement as he attempted to lay bare its political and aesthetic weaknesses; in particular, he focused on Amiri Baraka's enchantment with the most wild of the "Wild guys" who were sometimes celebrated in Black Arts poetry. Based on his reading of various sex-and-violence-themed episodes in Baraka's autobiography, Baker contends not only that Baraka was emotionally drawn to gangster types but also that "in private, Baraka who was a foremost advocate for the black arts is: The Artist as Thug" (174). In calling out Baraka and the thug behavior in Black Arts–era radicalism, Baker aimed to complicate critical nostalgia and renounce a romantic view of the period. But reading the era through a progressivist lens, Baker also attributed political efficacy to "tough guy" thuggery played out in the context of a white supremacist order built on violence. Thus he submits, "It is indisputably the case that had there been no aggressive Black Power offensive during the late sixties and early seventies, whites surely would have felt free to continue to whip black heads and to kill black leaders on prime time television. The entrance of the 'tough guys' changed all of that" (177–78). But, while Baker finds redeeming value in tough-guy tactics deployed in the sociopolitical sphere, he does not grant a similar value to the operations of the thug in the cultural sphere. Instead, he sees "loudspeaking" artists and critics as contributing to aesthetic misapprehension that leads to "a plethora of drum-like, monotonous, and sometimes silly utterances passed off as the 'New Black Poetry'"(175).

Rather than evaluate Baker's seemingly dim view of Black Arts poetry, we might note that in the years following the publication of these remarks in his *Afro-American Poetics: Revisions of Harlem and the Black Aesthetic* (1988), the figure of the "Artist as Thug" would reach a kind of cultural crescendo in a plethora of drum-like, monotonous, and sometimes silly hip-hop texts that came to be known as "gangster rap." If, as Baker contends, a thuggish will to power was woven into the complex political-aesthetic DNA of the BAM, that thuggish genetic material also found its way into late 1980s and early 1990s rappers whose bass-drum-accompanied performances of Dionysian poetry launched late twentieth-century culture industry fiefdoms like Bad Boy Entertainment and Deathrow Records. These subsidiaries of multinational entertainment empires prospered through the employment of

Stagolee-styled thug-artists—most notably Biggie, Tupac Shakur, Dr. Dre, and Snoop Doggy Dog—who produced fun-house/haunted-house-mirror reflections of postindustrial black street life. Although these texts helped produce much handwringing in sociological and popular discourse, peppered by terms like *super-predator, endangered species,* and *black nihilism,* the hardcore gangster raps of this period were simply recapitulations of hoary badman toasts that had long animated the African American vernacular tradition and that palpably influenced the violent posturing of BAM poetics. However, while BAM celebration and occasional emulation of those whom Baraka hailed as "some bad bad bad ass niggers" (Baraka and Abernathy n.p.) were ultimately geared toward the amelioration of black life in postindustrial America, the culture industry of the 1990s was, of course, most interested in using the poetry-based expressive art by and about badman figures to extract profit from black life in postindustrial America.

In this profit-driven, extractive endeavor, the prized commodity was vernacular-language narrative poetry that *seemed* to flourish organically in the dark basements of the black class structure. The art form cultivated by "conscious Black intellectuals" of the BAM era was, by the 1980s and 1990s, circulating widely in texts produced by entrepreneurial artists like Biggie who offered growing audiences the opportunity to voyeuristically gaze on a semblance of marginalized black life in the emergent hyperincarceration era. As young men of white suburbia experienced the advances of feminism and domesticating forms of service-sector and white-collar labor in the postindustrial economy, they found thrilling diversion in the hypermasculine, outlaw poems that were harvested in the neoliberal ghetto. For these suburbanites the consumption of black badman narratives was on some level the expression of "an onanistic envy of the Other's capacity for release," as Gregory Pardlo put it in his prose-poem/course description, "Shades of Green: Envy and Enmity in the American Cultural Imaginary" (Rowell, *Angles* 505). But it would be a mistake to think that it was only envious white fascination with representations of the dark, id-driven Other that led to the commercial institutionalization of rap in the 1980s and 1990s, for at the heart of hip-hop is not narrative but aesthetic form. As Robin D. G. Kelley argued in 1997, rap's appeal is the function of the MC's "verbal facility on the mic, the creative and often hilarious use of puns, metaphors, similes, not to mention the ability to kick some serious slang" (146). Kelley's observations, offered in response to fretful sociological appraisals of hip-hop culture in the 1990s, incisively pointed out that much rap analysis was far too literal in its reading of lyrics and that it mostly attended to the politics of textual narrative while "ignoring aesthetics." By centering on the pleasurable effects of rap poetry and highlighting its revelry in "slang," Kelley underscored the importance of vernacular *jouisance* in these texts and contended that ineffable feeling, created by the stylized performance of black language, gave rap its appeal. Kelley cast the nebulous affect so essential to the appeal of rap as an iteration of the "visceral element" of black texts that, in an earlier era, had been termed *funk* or *soul*. For most critics, the attractive, elusive, and immensely monetizable spirit flowing through funk and soul and into hip-hop defies stable description—but, quoting the novelist Cecil Brown, Kelley approximates: "It is what black (hoodoo) people who never studied art in school mean by art" (148).

While this is a very slippery description of the *soul* substance that makes certain black texts pleasurable, here Kelley suggests that the attractive power of hip-hop emerges from its connection to the sensibilities of economically dispossessed black people who have the most tenuous relation to institutions of education. And, of course, many of hip-hop's most popularly esteemed MCs have only a modicum of formal schooling—Jay-Z, Nas, and Biggie did not complete high school. Their art, diverse in themes and politics, is founded on a poetics that draws its primary power from the performance of language that is calibrated by remoteness from social and economic power. However intelligent or sophisticated it may be, however wealthy its practitioner, rap's vernacular idiom carries in it the sound of estrangement from key power structures of Western modernity—like the School. Indeed, in the hip-hop tradition, the School is often cast as insignificant, as in Fetty Wap's quip, "I ain't really trippin over school," or it is the target of pointed critique, as in the Nas track "What Goes Around," which repeatedly returns to the stark couplet "The schools where I learned / They should be burned." In the (perfectly titled) "They Schools," the politically radical duo Dead Prez mounts one of hip-hop's most thoroughgoing attacks on institutions of education. Contrasting idealized experiential learning with the book learning imposed on black students, M1 raps, "Observation and participation, my favorite teachers / When they beat us in the head with them books, it don't reach us." The School, inherently opposed to Dionysian expressiveness and the deformation of official modes of language, is figured in hip-hop as essentially a site of oppressive authority linked to graphocentric forms of knowledge deemed irrelevant to the life of the black majority. But those texts that explicitly show scorn for the School simply articulate a condition that all hip-hop texts implicitly suggest through their slang-heavy vernacular form—that is, estrangement from official institutions of education.

Class, Language, and Division in Post-Movement Poetry

What, then, does this mean for the relation between the MC and the African American literary poet who operates in the upper echelons of an educational milieu? If these figures are related members of an artistic family, then they are certainly distant cousins, both "born" in the wake of the Black Arts era but oriented toward language and "black community" in very different ways. The MC proffers a popular lowbrow art disseminated by commercial institutions to an audience that expects "verbal facility on the mic . . . the ability to kick some serious slang." On the other hand, the blackademic poet stands aloof from the MC and the crowd she or he moves, while producing "well-crafted" poems that demonstrate highbrow acuity chiefly rewarded by the university system. The vernacular language that is the heart and soul of hip-hop symbolically binds the MC to those lower levels of the black class structure characterized by minimum formal education. But the "well-crafted" language of literary poetry is a marker of the blackademic's years of schooling and an indication of experience in the higher levels of the class structure. The separate institutionalization of these two types of black poets, one in the mass marketplace, the other in academia, is notable for literary and cultural historians because it occurs in the post–civil rights era that, according to Michael Dawson (15–45) and others, also witnessed an intensification of economic polarization within black America. As the gains of the movement era mostly accrued to a black middle-class positioned to take advantage of new juridical and policy regimes—like those that brought black poets into PWIs—millions of black people remained locked in economic dead zones, with little opportunity for social mobility. Rap emerged from these masses and, as Tricia Rose put it in her seminal study of hip-hop, "prioritize[d] black voices from the margins of urban America" (4).

With this rich form of poetics arising from those "left behind" as the black middle-class made social and economic advancements, multiple forces distanced black poets in academia from the vernacular voice. Not only were they steered away from it by the conventions of MFA programs; many of them were the scions of a black middle-class that migrated out of the neighborhoods and institutions that were the wellsprings of restless, creative black language. Moreover, with the emergence of a ubiquitous lowbrow poetry featuring vernacular voices that seemed to issue organically from the black masses, poets ensconced in universities could not easily turn to the vernacular in an effort to present themselves as bearers of an authentic message from the black community. Poet-intellectuals of earlier eras, like Frances Harper, Paul Laurence Dunbar, Langston Hughes, Sterling Brown, and many BAM figures, had somewhat credibly adopted the voice of the most marginalized folk, often to speak on their behalf, but, as hip-hop voices permeated American culture in the 1980s and 1990s, it was abundantly evident that the black masses did not need poetic spokespersons from the intellectual class. This array of conditions compelled black literary poets to develop a nuanced relation to the vernacular language that had been so expertly commandeered by MCs who were self-declared representatives of the street.

By extending the tradition of the "mass poetry style of the Black Arts sixties" (Baraka qtd. in Oyewole xiv), Biggie and the vast, multifarious cohort of rappers of the 1980s and 1990s fully colonized what Stephen Henderson had called the "the living speech of the Black community" (*Understanding* 33)—in fact, the MCs were often creators of the lexicon used in the community. If their rapping was akin to folk poetry that had been mined by "literary" poets of the past, this new folk art of the neoliberal city was simultaneously a commercial art and was rarely tapped by the MCs' professorial cousins. In the early 1970s, Henderson was able to argue that "there are two traditions or levels of Black poetry—the folk and the formal—which must be seen as a totality, since they often intersect and overlap one another, and since the people who create them are one people" ("Saturation" 102). But by the 1980s and 1990s there was little intersection between "folk" and "formal" black poetries; it was as though they emanated from separate worlds. And perhaps they did. With the intensified economic division of black America greatly exacerbated by the implementation of neoliberal policies that hollowed out the welfare state while metastasizing the punishing state, it became increasingly difficult to abide by Henderson's confident assertion that black America was composed of "one people." In the decades after the civil rights era, stratifications and fragmentation within the "black community" had become so pronounced that, following the intraracial battles of the Clarence Thomas confirmation hearings in 1991, Toni Morrison would declare, "It is clear to the most reductionist intellect that black people think differently from one another; it is also clear that the time for undiscriminating racial unity has passed" ("Introduction" xxx). And in a 1992 opinion piece published in *Forbes* and titled "Two Nations . . . Both Black," Henry Louis Gates wrote of a "rift within black America"(138). He also deployed a stigmatizing rhetoric prevalent in sociological writing of the era, declaring that "we members of the black upper middle class, the heirs of the Talented Tenth . . . are isolated from the black *underclass*" (135, emphasis added).

Some poet-professors opening careers in the 1980s and 1990s might not have considered themselves heirs of the black elite that W. E. B. Du Bois esteemed in his early career, and they may not have been comfortable with Gates's appeal to rhetoric that was often used in pathology narratives about the black people who bore the brunt of the backlash against movement-era policy shifts. But as stably employed academics, they were (at least somewhat) isolated and insulated from the day-to-day experience of the unemployed, the working poor, and those who labored in shadow economies. For the black poet in residence at a PWI, claims to fast-evolving *contemporary* black vernacular were all but relinquished to the MCs, as were attempts at close identification with the so-called black underclass that was featured in hip-hop. If "popular poetry" of the contemporary era prioritized the voices from the margins of urban America, those black poets "active in institutions of higher education" (Rowell, *Angles* xxiv) had to prioritize different voices. Indeed, the voices that come to life in the poetry of the securely employed blackademic workers reflect the experience of a fortunate middle-class not relegated to the socioeconomic margins of America but still haunted by their nearness to it. Gates described the black middle-class of the emergent neoliberal era as "caught in a no-man's land of alienation and fragmentation"— unable to easily identify with their less-capitalized cousins yet still "humiliatingly vulnerable to racism" ("Two Nations" 135). This middle-class experience helped generate the work of a cadre of important poets—like Dove, Komunyakaa, Toi Derricotte, and later Natasha Trethewey, Elizabeth Alexander, and Nikky Finney—who learned much from black poetics modeled by Robert Hayden in the 1950s, 1960s, and 1970s. Just as the speaker of Hayden's "'Summertime and the Living . . .'" moved in a space that was "above the quarrels and shattered glass" (39) of hardscrabble urban life, poet-professors of the late twentieth and early twenty-first century were inevitably distanced from city districts gutted by trickle-down economics and inhabited by those Biggie would call "my triple-beam niggas," who weighed out crack on triple-beam balances during the various and violent drug wars of the 1980s and 1990s. As the rappers produced verses woven in vivid and lyrical vernacular shaped by the neoliberal ghettos, the poet-professors—following Hayden, Tolson, and Brooks—worked in voices of erudition, indicative of the School scorned in hip-hop, and if they represented contemporary black vernacular they were, like Hayden, curatorial in approach. More often than not, the vernacular language that came to voice in the work of the poet-professors was of an earlier era. Estranged from the beauty and menace experienced by their lumpen cousins and artistically rendered by the rappers, many of the poet-professors of the late twentieth century seemed to feel more confident in an engagement with the past. Here, too, they looked to Hayden—and especially toward his early heritage work—as they developed rich poetic explorations of antebellum and Jim Crow America.

Chapter 9

Hayden's Heirs

———

Poetics of History and Aesthetic Distance in the Post-Movement Era

———

In 1993, the year that "Party and Bullshit" moved Biggie to the forefront of popular poetry, Rita Dove took leave from her professorship at the University of Virginia to begin her stint as U.S. poet laureate at the Library of Congress. She was assuming offices that Hayden had occupied in the middle of the 1970s when he served as the library's first black consultant in poetry. During the 1980s—the decade in which rap came to mainstream America and crack cocaine fell upon urban America—Dove had ascended to the very highest strata of literary accomplishment, winning accolades for *The Yellow House on the Corner* (1980), *The Museum* (1983) and her Jim Crow–era odyssey *Thomas and Beulah* (1986), which won a Pulitzer Prize. In these books, seemingly worlds removed from Reagan-era ghettos, Dove makes almost no attempt to draw in the black vernacular or inchoate hip-hop culture of her moment; instead, the voices and music of a distant past come to life in a clutch of poems that redeploy strategies that Hayden seminally applied to the black historical archive. Although she was not the only poet to undertake Haydenesque historical projects in the 1980s—Michael Harper, Lucille Clifton, Gayl Jones, and Shirley Anne Williams were also writing notable history poems—Dove has gone on to become the most highly regarded poet-historian of the 1980s. Her earliest book features a ten-poem section devoted to antebellum materials; *The Museum* is paced by poems like "Banneker" and "Parsley," built around figures and events gleaned from Afro-Diasporic history; and in *Thomas and Beulah*, Dove uses personal family lore to fashion a twentieth-century African American epic with a chronology that concludes in 1969. Although her work with the black past would develop in later volumes, Dove's earliest historical forays are indicative of patterns that have proven paradigmatic in post-movement-era poetry. They form an important link between the history-oriented enterprise that Hayden undertook in the middle of the twentieth century and the pastward preoccupations nursed by post-movement literary poets who ceded the narratives and vernacular of urban America to the rappers of the 1980s and 1990s.

In his extensive studies of the Black Arts period, Smethurst notes a decided *lack* of interest in the historical record among BAM poets; he posits that the logics of black literary nationalism in 1960s and 1970s led artists toward an "escape from history into a mythical counter-history or anti-history" (*Black Arts Movement* 77). Rather than delve into an archive that they perceived as overflowing with accounts of black oppression, BAM artists imagined an Edenic, prelapsarian black community that would be restored through revolution. Further, in assessing poetic output of the BAM moment, Smethurst describes Hayden as "the most powerful African American writer of historical poetry of that era—and perhaps any era" (76). If Hayden was the chief promulgator of historical verse during the BAM years that led into the institutionalization of black poetry in PWIs, then Dove's archival quarrying represents an important, vitalizing extension of Hayden's legacy in the years immediately following his passing.

As noted in the previous chapter, critics like Rowell have effectively interpreted "Upon Meeting Don L. Lee" as a stark announcement of Dove's early ambition to move beyond the orbit of BAM political aesthetics and a kind of bugle call for the literary poets who would follow her in "new directions" (*Angles* xliii). But the extensive antebellum history section of *The Yellow House* is another significant signpost in the development of post-BAM poetry; it is both an affirmative gesture toward Hayden's historical orientation and a harbinger of the poetics of history that have become a key feature in the repertoire of many literary poets who have risen to prominence in the post-movement era. By devoting one section of her book exclusively to poems set in the antebellum era, Dove replicated an organizational model that Hayden had employed in his *Selected Poems*, in which all of his heritage poems are gathered in a single unit. But more importantly, Dove's methods of historical engagement in *The Yellow House* echo Hayden's pioneering work in several important ways: She curates fragments of antebellum oral texts, she animates the past by frequently inhabiting the personae of historical figures "real" and imagined, and she attempts to dredge up and re-present episodes and figures discovered or understood through *study* of the historical record. Thus, in the ten-poem section of her debut volume, Dove becomes a major practitioner of the *archival research* mode of African American poetry that finds its basic origins in Hayden's work.

In Dove's "Cholera," for example, an erudite narrator fashions scenes of an imagined outbreak of the infectious disease among a slave population. The narrator's rendering of events is set in five stanzas, the first four of which are followed by a curated fragment of the plaintive Negro spiritual "I Know Moonrise," which serves as a weighty antiphonal artifact, anchoring Dove's historical poetry in actual lyric produced by antebellum suffering:

> Some dragged themselves off at night
> to die in the swamp, to lie down
> with the voices of mud and silk.
>   I know moonrise, I know starrise (41)

Here, Dove's documentary quotation of nineteenth-century vernacular culture texts follows a design that Hayden pioneered in the more intricate and polyvocal "Runagate Runagate," laced in several folk voices and spirituals. Dove again uses a curatorial method of quotation as she intersperses splinters of David Walker's *Appeal* into her poem about the radical black abolitionist. However, in "David Walker (1785–1830)" the black voice is not marked by vernacular phrasing; instead, it is Walker's own exhortative and formally eloquent prose that shares the poem with Dove's narrator—as in a stanza that samples his fiery *Appeal* and then imagistically editorializes on the distance and tensions between Walker's radicalism and more moderate white abolitionism:

> *We are the most wretched degraded and abject set*
> *of beings that ever lived since the world began.*
> The jeweled canaries in the lecture halls tittered,
> pressed his dark hand between their gloves. (34)

Dove similarly employs the language of highly educated slavery-era speakers in two of the six persona poems that she includes in the black history sequence of *The Yellow House*. "The Abduction"—written from the perspective of Solomon Northrup, author of the narrative *Twelve Years a Slave*—and "Belinda's Petition" exclusively feature first-person narrations in language that is historically plausible.[1] In fact, "Belinda's Petition" seems to mimic the petitions that Phillis Wheatley actually wrote in late eighteenth-century poems like "To the Right Honorable William, Earl of Dartmouth." Echoing Wheatley, Dove begins her poem with the salutation "To the Honorable Senate and House" (32) and continues on with syntax and conceits that strongly resemble those used by the revolutionary-era poet.

These persona poems written in the language of educated black people of the slavery era are approximations of the work that Hayden carried out in "A Letter from Phillis Wheatley," an *American Journal* poem that achieves power through the creation of a convincing voice based on research into Wheatley's biography coupled with a speculative reading of her corpus. In his epistolary poem, Hayden offers a glimpse of Wheatley on her 1771 tour to England by producing an imagined communiqué to her enslaved friend Obour Tanner, who is just one of a half dozen little-known historical figures networked to the poem's narrator. With her hand controlled by Hayden, Wheatley writes a letter that plausibly surfaces anxieties and resentments that are submerged in her published poems and correspondence. ("At supper—I dined apart / like captive Royalty—" [147].) Feeling that "we generally ignore Phillis as a complex human being," Hayden tried to present her as such while also seeking self-effacement. Rather than showing himself as the poet–puppet-master guiding the thoughts of his character, he acts as the unobtrusive spirit medium, displaying probable but undocumented facets of Wheatley's late eighteenth-century consciousness for a late twentieth-century audience. In fact, in describing the provenance of the poem to Michael Harper, Hayden would write, "Phillis appeared on the old mental ouija board and demanded to be dealt with" (Hayden and Harper 1011). Various forms of this type of conjuring have proven attractive to black poets of the post-movement era, beginning with Dove—so much so that Howard Rambsy has argued that the persona poem has become "integral to the tradition of black verse." Giving Hayden a significant place in this subtradition, which has exponentially expanded in recent decades and more often than not features personae from the past, Rambsy details Hayden's use of voices and documents in "Runagate" but concedes that it "is not a persona poem in any strict sense in which a single poet is writing in the voice of someone else" ("Catching Holy Ghosts" 551). However, Hayden's "Phyllis Wheatley" is a conventional persona poem, and it is an example of the vernacular metaphor of "catching the holy ghost," which Rambsy calls upon to describe the artistic process by which poets operate as vessels wherein characters come to life.

One of the most striking persona poems of the late twentieth century is Elizabeth Alexander's "The Venus Hottentot," first published in 1989. The poem is cast in two parts—and features two ghosts, as it were. One presents

Sarah Baartman, the woman from southern Africa whose body was displayed as an oddity of nature in European metropolises of the early nineteenth century; the other is an unholy ghost that gives voice to the naturalist Georges Cuvier, who knew Baartman, dissected her body after her death, and arranged for the display of her genitalia in the Paris Museum of Man. The poem, which has been critically hailed, is frequently anthologized, and Rambsy has argued that Alexander's crafting "constitutes a notable blueprint" for those who have written persona poems in her lee ("The Rise"). In a number of ways "The Venus Hottentot" is also an elaboration of the archival-research persona-poem tradition that flows through Hayden and Dove. It is particularly resonant with Dove's "extraordinary" poem "Parsley" (Vendler, *Given* 71), which was collected in *Museum* and probes the circumstances that led to the 1957 execution of twenty thousand Haitians by the ruler of the Dominican Republic, Rafael Trujillo. Like "The Venus Hottentot," "Parsley" is organized into two parts—one that offers the interior voice of black sufferers and another that indicts Trujillo by presenting a glimpse into his twisted, obsessive psyche. Both of these poems achieve a "feat of sympathetic imagination"—to borrow phrasing from Helen Vendler's assessment of "Parsley" (75)—through the animation of Cuvier and Trujillo, markedly unholy ghosts of Afro-diasporic history.[2] Vendler argues that, by giving voice to Trujillo, Dove demonstrates an "inveterate wish to imagine and understand, if not to forgive, the mind of the victimizer." The same should be said of Alexander's imagining of Cuvier, who begins his monologue and the poem with the tellingly ironical apostrophe "Science, science, science!," thus indicating that Bartmaan's barbarous victimization ought to be understood as the residual product of an Enlightenment quest to advance human civilization. These haunting experiments in psychological projection, which emerge from the comingling of poetic vision and official narratives of history, are certainly indebted to Hayden's seminal use of archival documents in "Middle Passage." As it gives voice to an array of unholy ghosts—the traders, sailors, and ship captains of the transatlantic slave trade—Hayden's poem amounts to an extensive and exemplary exercise in the type of "sympathetic imagination" that is woven into both "The Venus Hottentot" and "Parsley."

In sketching the creative process that brought to life "The Venus Hottentot," Alexander has emphasized her time in the library stacks and her effort to imagine the hidden interiority of figures discovered there:

I came to the Venus Hottentot through scholarly reading and research. . . . I found everything I could about her that was available, which wasn't a whole lot at the time, the late eighties, and what seemed absent, of course, was her voice—her interior, her self, who she actually was, not just things about her and not just the self seen. This is what I've come to believe poetry can bring to history: We can imagine those voices that we might not have on the historical record. ("Elizabeth" 139–40)

Alexander's account of the scholarly work that went into the creation of her most well-known poem is the echo of Hayden's description of the research process that gave life to the voices that appear in his "Middle Passage." (Indeed, Alexander's "Hayden in the Archive" seems to grant him an archetypal station as poet-researcher, "Stoop-shouldered, worrying the pages" [*Crave Radiance* 240].) His comments tinted by his signature fastidiousness and utter commitment to artistic endeavor, Hayden explains the genesis of the poem that itself marks a genesis in the tradition of African American poetics:

> I began to do research on the slave trade, using the reference material at the Schomburg Collection. I made tentative sketches for the first part of the poem but was dissatisfied with them and soon discovered that I hadn't read enough. . . . I continued research on the slave trade at the University of Michigan library. I read all sorts of books. . . . I read histories, journals, notebooks, ships' logs. (*Collected Prose* 168)

Informed by this broad research, Hayden's early histories seemed to actively mutiny against the archive that the poet explored. Celeste-Marie Bernier has described "Middle Passage" as a creative text devoted to "contesting lacunae within white official records." Hayden entered into these lacunae as a revisionist historian, conceiving a kind of counterhistory, purposed for the political age in which it was written. His deep dive into the archive, along with his use of modernist poetic tools, significantly innovated a tradition of African American history poetry that, before him, had primarily involved the celebration of iconic heroes and black contributions to the history of humanity.[3] If African American history poems of the late nineteenth and early twentieth centuries were mainly meant to cultivate racial pride and politically strategic nationalist coherence advocated by race men like Alain Locke and Du Bois, Hayden's early heritage poems vivified and complicated that project by introducing research-informed specificity to the characters and events of black historical poetics and by *imagining* the unseen interiority of victims and victimizers of Afro-diasporic history. "Middle Passage," "Runagate," and the "The Ballad of Nat Turner" showed that narratives of history that shaped public-sphere discourse could be transformed by envisaging what was beneath and within the many lacunae and suppressions of the inert archival record and also by giving due weight to the folk texts that sung beyond the archive. These poems, conceived in the early 1940s, opened creative and intellectual territory that would not be comparably explored by literary artists for another several decades.

Ashraf Rushdy, in his study of the rise of neoslave narratives in post-movement-era fiction (which coincided with the efflorescence of a similar form of poetics, exemplified in abovementioned works by Dove, Alexander, and others), argues that the literary pivot into first-person narratives set in the antebellum era can be attributed to a number of 1960s sociocultural events. In the sixties "historians developed new methodologies and generated new visions of America's antebellum past" (5) that novelists sought to elaborate on, and these visions became viable as historians started to accord more authority to first-person slave testimony and narratives, which often refuted official archival accounts of slavery and eroded the professional consensus that slavery was a relatively benign institution. Rushdy also contends that the first black writers of neoslave narratives wanted to offer artistic responses to William Styron's *The Confessions of Nat Turner* (1967), which used first-person narrative perspective as it controversially invented Turner's inner psyche. But two decades before the New Left historians shifted academic understanding of slavery and Styron wrote his novel, Hayden had acted upon the historiographical and creative impulses that were so consequential in the 1960s. Indeed, Hayden had used those impulses to imagine the ghostly voice in "The Ballad of Nat Turner," which displaces the obviously artificial—yet "official"—voice created for Turner by Thomas Gray, the slave-holding attorney who recorded the insurgent's "confession" in 1831. Hayden's archival research gave him a depth of knowledge comparable to that of the professional historian, transported him to a creative space that anticipated literary developments of the 1960s and 1970s, and allowed him to credibly imagine voices that had been—as he put it—"traduced" in official and literary texts (*Collected Prose* 179).[4]

In Natasha Trethewey's "Southern History," the young poet-speaker is helpless in her confrontation with traducing yet institutionally sanctioned narratives about black life on the antebellum plantation. The fourteen-line faux sonnet begins, "*Before the war they were happy*, he said, /quoting our textbook. (This was senior-year / history class.)" It goes on to describe how the plantation romance *Gone with the Wind* is screened for the class as a "*true account of how things were back then*" (*Native* 38, italics in original). But the speaker is unequipped to contest the narrative of the past presented in the school. The final couplet laments that this history is "a lie / my teacher guarded. Silent, so did I." Included in her Pulitzer Prize–winning volume *Native Guard* (2006), the poem offers an emotional rationale for the continuing project of revisionary-minded historical poetics set in motion decades earlier by Hayden's desire to "correct the misconceptions and to destroy some of the stereotypes and clichés which surrounded Negro history" (*Collected Prose* 162). Like Dove and Alexander before her, Trethewey has written extensively about the past, often catching the holy ghost by disinterring voices hidden deep in the archive. Her interviews frequently involve the recollection of scenes in the library. Discussing the formative spark of *Native Guard*—which takes its title from a little-known regiment of freed ex-slaves who served in the Union army, guarding Confederate prisoners in Mississippi—Trethewey recalls the moment she heard about these soldiers, insisting, "I went right away to the Gulfport Public Library to try to look up something about them. The first thing I found was a small mention in someone's M.A. thesis" (*Conversations* 46). A crown of ten sonnets written in the voice of one of the Native Guards was conjured from the scholarly detective work that Trethewey describes. Early in the persona-sonnet sequence the act of rewriting—of writing over and within—the documents of the archive is dramatized as the soldier-speaker recounts his own discovery of the book in which he writes:

> We take those things we need
> from the Confederates abandoned homes:
> salt, sugar, even this journal, near full
> with someone else's words, overlapped now,
> crosshatched beneath mine. On every page,
> his story intersecting with my own. (25)

With the poet intervening via the summoned ghost, the extant record—"his story"—is written anew, built upon, expanded. And, as the forgotten black soldier of the nineteenth century comes to voice, so too does the silenced lyric speaker of "Southern History," whose story, like the soldier's, is framed in the sonnet form. This formal linkage underscores the way in which Trethewey's animation of the Native Guard aims to destroy the stereotypes and clichés that her "teacher guarded" in the school.

The historical recovery work advanced by Dove, Alexander, and others in the 1980s and 1990s was not exclusively focused on the antebellum period. Dove's family saga of the Jim Crow era, *Thomas and Beulah*, deeply influenced Trethewey during her formative period as an MFA student and showed a way for the younger poet, who would extensively document black life of the early twentieth century in her first two collections, *Domestic Work* (2000) and *Bellocq's Ophelia* (2002), both of which feature a great deal of ekphrastic engagement with archival photography.[5] A tradition of pastward-looking, research-based poetry continues on into the twenty-first century, particularly nurtured in the network of poets affiliated with the Cave Canem workshop, established in 1996. Indeed, Trethewey's literary breakthrough came in 1999, when Rita Dove selected her *Domestic Work* as the winner of the first Cave Canem Poetry Prize. An exhaustive analysis of the post-movement and twenty-first-century tradition of archive-oriented black poetry would need to include an expansive list of prominent poets, including Michael Harper, Shirley Anne Williams, Yusef Komunyakaa, Brenda Marie Osbey, Kevin Young, A. Van Jordan, Frank X. Walker, Thylias Moss, M. NourbeSe Philip, Adrian Matejka, and Quraysh Ali Lansana, to name only a few. Tyehimba Jess, whose poetry also contributes to the archive-oriented project of this cohort, describes the impetus of his work in terms that would resonate with many of his peers—and that recapitulate Hayden's: "When I write, I do so with a desire to tell stories or project images that have been buried, obfuscated, distorted, deracinated, crushed into near oblivion by the workhorses of mass media and public miseducation" (Rowell, *Angles* 461).

Even a poet like Nikky Finney—not reflexively associated with poetics of history—appeals to the methodological ethos of archival research and recovery in some of her most noteworthy work. Take, for example, "Red Velvet," collected in her National Book Award–winning *Head Off & Split*, published in 2011. The poem is a commemoration of defiant black fortitude embodied in Rosa Parks. In the broadest sense, it is a conventional memorialization of an iconic figure, but "Red Velvet" also carries on the sturdy tradition of historical revisionism by recuperating an essential rebelliousness in a personality that has been thoroughly integrated into self-congratulatory official narratives of American history. The long poem, which focuses on Parks's work as a seamstress and is organized by conceits of sewing and stitching, emphasizes the strategic and willful role that Parks played as an "operative" in the civil rights movement. In remarks offered during a public reading, Finney explained that the poem is marked by her desire "to give you something that you don't know about somebody that you think you know." She added, "That's where the beauty of research comes in for a poet" (Poetry Society). For Finney, interpolated research makes possible the creative reconstruction of history offered in this stanza:

> By forty-two, your heart is heavy with slavery, lynching,
> and the lessons of being "good." You have heard
> 7,844 Sunday sermons on how God made every
> woman in his image. You do a lot of thinking with
> a thimble on your thumb. You have hemmed
> 8,230 skirts for nice, well-meaning white women
> in Montgomery. You have let the hem out of
> 18,809 pant legs for growing white boys. You have
> pricked your finger 45,203 times. Held your peace. (9)

Here the poem imagines that the accumulation of historical grievance—"slavery, lynching" and a responsive acquiescence—accretes to the accumulation of pricking personal slights building within Parks up until the time of her famous act of civil disobedience. In its memorialization, Finney's poem projects the burning interiority of a whitewashed character of Black History Month in the effort to challenge easily consumed public school/public sphere narratives of civil rights–era history.

A related form of challenging historical recovery is carried out in "Dancing with Strom," also collected in *Head Off & Split*. Attending her brother's wedding, the poet-speaker contemplates the admixture of forgiveness and forgetting that allows for the fêting of Strom Thurmond at the event. Thurmond, the famously segregationist and long-lived senator from South Carolina, is despised by Finney's speaker, who watches the party from a porch as "His Confederate hands touch every shoulder, finger, back that I love" (67). The submergence of historical grievance that makes possible this touching is opposed by the speaker, who, throughout the poem, dredges up the record of Thurmond's vehement political opposition to racial integration. But this remembering of the well-documented yet suppressed past is coupled with the recollection of a less known history that the speaker has learned from "the new research just out" (64). This architectural research is introduced as "What the Negro gave America / Chapter 9,206" and reveals—as the speaker watches the wedding dancers from the mansion porch—that "*Enslaved Africans gifted porches to North / America*" (65, italics in original). Thus the poem works through a double consternation as it oscillates between two hidden histories: in one it is the reality of aggressive antiblack racism that is occluded; in the other it is black genius and contribution to the structure of American modernity that has been serially and systematically forgotten. "Dancing with Strom" suggests that these racially guided forms of disremembrance produce official narratives of memory, and—for Finney, like Hayden—the poet is called to disrupt and rewrite these histories through hard will and bookish research.

The Class Politics of Pastward-Looking Poetics

Although "Dancing with Strom" testifies to the importance of historical inquiry for the post-movement poet, it is most apparently a contemplation of the discomfiting position of the economically privileged black intellectual, whose upper-middle-class background brings with it dubious connections and benefits. Through reference to the "research just out," Finney's poem draws attention to its speaker's liminal location—"porch bound," neither inside nor outside of the house, neither integrated into or segregated from the lawn party that fêtes and forgives the living embodiment of America's oppressive past. The speaker is part of a black elite that she would rather not identify with: "Uncle-cousins, bosom buddies, convertible cars / of nosy paramours, strolling churlish penny- / pinchers pour onto the mansion estate" (63). Her difference from the wealthy throng registers in the assertion "I refuse to leave the porch." Here the liminal space of the porch is linked to her principled refusal to dance with Thurmond, and also to slave laborers of southern history. She may be part of a bourgeois black family, but she is the "nose-in-book / daughter, born umoored." Her allegiances are not with her well-off peers; instead, she identifies with the forgotten slaves who built the porches and mansions of the plantations.

As I have argued in this chapter, poetic remembrance of—and identification with—sufferers and heroes of the Afro-diasporic past constitutes a major development in post-movement literary poetics. Finney joins a sizable cadre of pastward-looking, nose-in-book poet-researchers who find major precedent for their historical poetics in literary politics and technique exhibited by Robert Hayden. But I am not suggesting that the post-movement explosion of black historical poetics was *catalyzed* by Hayden's work; the point is that Hayden has provided recent poets with an artistic paradigm that guides those compelled into the archive of history by an array of strong socioeconomic and cultural forces. If post-movement poets have emulated Hayden's writerly aesthetic because institutional and class experiences distanced them from late twentieth-century black orality and vernacular culture, these experiences have also induced literary poets to follow Hayden into the archive.

Unable to easily identify with the economic and social precarity of the black masses enduring the brunt of neoliberal policy regimes of the 1980s and 1990s and the early twenty-first century, university-employed postmovement poets largely avoided deep engagement with subjects like the militarization of American law enforcement, the rise of hyperincarceration, the retraction of the welfare system, work scarcity, rapid shifts in social norms, the vibrancy of hip-hop or "street culture," and so on. Simply put, major literary poets of the 1980s and 1990s did not produce canon-shaping mythopoeic texts documenting or dramatizing late twentieth-century urban space and the lower reaches of the class structure. (There is certainly no late twentieth-century analogue to Gwendolyn Brooks's epic *In the Mecca* [1968], set in the housing projects of the black city.) As MCs of the hip-hop movement eagerly used their verse to chronicle the roiling evolution of black life during the Reagan and Clinton eras—"defined by radical shifts in labor demographics, a bottom-to-top redistribution of wealth, and the development of computerized networks of communication, commerce and public discourse" (M. Neal 104)—the university-employed poets most celebrated by the American literary establishment often turned to contemplations of historical instances of black abjection and heroism. An analysis of post-movement African American poetics profits from an acknowledgement of the way in which subject matter was parceled out: with MCs handling black abjection in the present and poet-professors remembering it in the past.

To be sure, this is not at all to suggest that poet-professors of the 1980s and 1990s did not engage with contemporary affairs or that they followed Hayden into the archive only because they all lacked the experiential resources to authentically represent black struggle at the end of the twentieth century. However, we must posit a relationship between the rise of socioeconomic security enjoyed by poet-professors and the synchronous explosion of historical themes in their art—and, particularly, the proliferation of persona poems that allow poets to inhabit black characters from the past. When Gates declared that "we members of the black upper middle class . . . are isolated from the black underclass," he was only articulating what demographic and economic data of the 1990s would express statistically. The experiential gulf opened up between the black upper middle class and the poor made it difficult for literary poets to credibly identify with the most intense forms of abjection and marginalization experienced by black people at the end of twentieth century. To wit, the predicament of black marginalization in the post-movement era was being thoroughly documented and frequently opposed in the vernacular-saturated work of rappers. If academic poets were going to continue a tradition of African American literary resistance, they were best equipped to do so by working against the postmodern propensity to forget the past. Of course, the historical turn in post-movement black poetics—presaged by Hayden and arguably inaugurated in Dove's first volume—responds to an "age that has forgotten how to think historically" (Jameson ix). The various political and ideological threats presented by American amnesia, exacerbated by techno-social acceleration in the postmodern era, gave poet-professors good reason to do the historical recovery work that brought them into the libraries and archives. Moreover, their status as fixtures in the university system allowed them easy access to the efflorescence of scholarship coming out of history and black studies departments in the post-movement era. Ashraf Rushdy notes these as factors contributing to the proliferation of neoslave narrative novels in the post-movement era. However, a full accounting of the pastward turn in recent black poetics (and fiction as well) calls for a consideration of the liminal social-class status of the university employed black artist, eager to identify with the racial collective but increasingly distanced from the black neofolk class and its culture in the post-movement, neoliberal era.[6]

As Kenneth Warren and others have argued, after the dismantling of de jure segregation regimes in the 1950s and 1960s, it was increasingly difficult to abide by the logics of racial solidarity narratives that were important to Jim Crow–era African American literary and political projects built on "linked fate" theories, which held that the fortune of any individual black person was linked to that of the race (Warren, *What Was* 87). Nevertheless, citing widespread de facto and institutionalized forms of antiblack racism, black nationalist artist-intellectuals of the late 1960s and early 1970s felt justified in proclaiming themselves perfectly aligned with the black majority and cloaked themselves in its vernacular culture. These radicals followed logic summed up by Malcolm X: "Whether you're educated or illiterate, whether you live on the boulevard or in the alley, you're going to catch hell just like I am. We're all in the same boat" (X and Breitman 24). But by the late 1970s and after, artist-intellectuals who enjoyed the upper-middle-class stability afforded by employment at elite universities (and who often hailed from middle-class families to begin with) could not credibly declare themselves to be in the same boat as black people who were being locked up in prisons and sequestered in what the sociologist Loïc Wacquant would describe as "neighborhoods of relegation gutted by the neoliberal restructuring of the market and state" (68). Thus, whatever else it may be, the turn to history in the post-movement era reflects the peculiar and discomfiting position of the salaried poet-professor wanting to assert an authentic form of solidarity with neofolk in the lower levels of the black class structure, despite being distanced from these brethren by significant amounts of economic, social, and cultural capital. By foregrounding shared historical trauma (and triumph) black artist-intellectuals proclaimed a form of racial solidarity that did not require them to posture as though they shared precisely the same life chances and socioeconomic circumstances as their neofolk cousins.

As I have argued above, the antebellum history section of Rita Dove's *The Yellow House on the Corner* announces the beginning of the post-movement efflorescence of pastward-looking poetics that takes its cues from Hayden and moves in a direction not anticipated in BAM poetry. While "Upon Meeting Don L. Lee" marks a bright line in political aesthetic sands, separating Dove and MFA poets from their BAM predecessors, the ten slavery-era poems of the book help signal a distinct thematic shift in African American poetics, preparing the way for the post-movement surge in historical poetry. But in a 1996 assessment that helped solidify Dove's status as a major poet of the late twentieth-century American literary-critical establishment, Helen Vendler takes a dim a view of these history-searching poems, calling them "initial difficulties" and lamenting that in many of them "history has given a prefabricated plot" (*Given* 63, 66). Of all the poems in the section, Vendler most appreciates those that offer sympathetic portrayals of black outsiders, like the slave woman whose seemingly ethical actions inadvertently lead to the capture of a band of runagates in "The Transport of Slaves from Maryland to Mississippi." The critic appreciates this poem because it demonstrates that "the many faces of division within the black community are part of Dove's subject" (65). While Vendler's praise for this demonstration seems tied to her unrelenting disdain for BAM-style, unified-front "protest" poetry, her underscoring of the intraracial fissures that show up in what she calls the "slave poems" is astute.[7] However, Vendler does not plumb the meaning of Dove's most telling early persona poem, "The House Slave," through which the poet identifies with a nineteenth-century domestic slave, even as she uses historical allegory to acknowledge intraracial division in the past and the writing present and to redress a derisive narrative about the black middle-class that was popularized in the movement era. Dove's inhabiting of the house slave persona suggests the vexed condition of the post-movement poet-professor who knows she is not in the same proverbial boat as the black majority yet still feels that her fate is linked to that of the race.

The narrator of "The House Slave" occupies the position of relative privilege in the house Negro/field Negro binary memorably propagated by Malcolm X in public appearances and speeches, including his 1963 "Message to the Grassroots." Malcolm's conceit was a rhetorical strategy meant to discredit members of the integrationist black bourgeoisie of the 1960s by likening them to house slaves, imagined as Uncle Tom lackeys to white masters. As a metaphor for the fortunate bourgeoisie, Malcolm's house Negro was obeisant before a white power structure, loyal to the master class, and scornful of less fortunate black folk. Malcolm often returned to this historical referent, thinking it an apt analogy for intraracial politics of his moment. In one appearance he insisted,

> You cannot understand the present-day twentieth century house Negro or twentieth century Uncle Tom until you have a real understanding of the Uncle Tom who lived on the plantation before the Emancipation Proclamation. And that type of Negro never identified himself with the other slaves. He always thought he was above the field Negroes. The field Negroes were the masses. The house Negroes were the minority whereas the field Negroes were in the majority. (*Four Speeches* 88)

In taking on the persona of the house slave, Dove aims to complicate Malcolm's simplified portrayal of slave society.[8] She gives her speaker the "good diction" that is a notable characteristic of Malcolm's house Negro (*Four Speeches* 89; *February 1965* 27) but attributes to the speaker no affinity to the white owners, who are described in their predawn slumber: "mistress sleeps like an ivory toothpick / and Massa dreams of asses, rum and slave-funk." With the sexual vulnerability of the domestic slave evoked, Dove's narrator concentrates on her anguished connection to the field slaves beginning their labor in dawn's twilight:

> I cannot fall asleep again. At the second horn,
> the whip curls across the backs of the laggards—
>
> sometimes my sister's voice, unmistaken, among them.
> "Oh! pray," she cries. "Oh! pray!" Those days
> I lie on my cot, shivering in the early heat,
>
> and as the fields unfold to whiteness,
> and they spill like bees among the fat flowers,
> I weep. It is not yet daylight. (33)

While Malcolm's house Negro effigy was guided by self-interest and contempt for those in the fields, Dove builds a more historically probable scenario by making her speaker vicariously experience the pain of her whipped, field-working sister. But here there is more at stake than historical verisimilitude; the poem necessarily adjusts both the vehicle and the tenor of Malcolm's metaphorical construction. If it suggests that the simple house/field binary was a misrepresentation of slave society, it also implicitly advocates for a nuanced understanding of late twentieth-century black class politics. Catching the holy ghost of a sympathetic domestic slave who is locked in the house yet emotionally connected to her family in the field, Dove attempts to represent her own *distance from and connection to* the working- and lower-class black people with whom BAM poets sought to simply merge. Notably, "The House Slave" is shot through by liminality and paradox, which give ambience to the condition of both the "privileged" slave and the middle-class blackademic. The poem is set in the twilight between night and day, the speaker is awake in her sleeping cot, and she shivers although she is hot. Like her slave speaker, Dove herself exists in a "no-man's land of alienation and fragmentation," betwixt and between the comfort of full acceptance in America and its ivory towers and the full burden of life at the bottom of the black class structure. While MCs would routinely claim the hardened field slave persona, Dove's poem suggests that the poet-professor of the post-movement era writes most authentically from within the complex ghost of the house slave, intimately linked to, yet still distanced from, the black majority.

Of course, the paradox of intimate alienation, of being "remotely near" to kin and community, was one of Robert Hayden's primary subjects. As I have argued in previous chapters, it is important in his midcareer work like "Electrical Storm," "Those Winter Sundays," "The Witch Doctor," and "'Summertime and the Living . . .'" And it grows increasingly prominent in his poems of the late 1970s, as in the persona pieces "The Tattooed Man" and "American Journal." His refusal of the unmediated folk voice, his insistence on aesthetic distance in the representation of black life and vernacular culture, and his acknowledgement of a sense of loving alienation from even the black segment of the human family distinguished him from most BAM-era poets, who imitated the vernacular voice and sought to meld coherently with the black masses. In a public talk given at the Library of Congress in 1977, Hayden would speak of himself in the third person and suggest his paradoxical relation to the black folk world that was often at the distanced center of his poems: "He had escaped the slum life he had hated so vehemently after he went to college. Yet he remained loyal in many respects to what he called the 'folk'" (*Collected Prose* 21). Despite this sense of loyalty, Hayden could never believe that he was in precisely the same boat as those still relegated to the slums that he had "escaped." This was partly due to an inborn and pervasive "sense of alienation [that] nothing could alter" (*Collected Prose* 22), but it was also because Hayden recognized the undeniable power of those "inexorable social processes" (P. Harper, *Are We* 51)—educational, institutional, economic—that attenuated the connection between the artist-intellectual and the unlettered folk class.

In the final decade of his life Hayden's psychic distance from the black folk class was reinforced by professional attainment. As I suggested at the outset of this section, a vexing class awareness is a feature of "The Islands," the late-career autobiographical poem in which the successful poet-professor can find no respite from history, even as he vacations in the Caribbean. In "The Islands," Hayden's speaker is not simply disturbed by the sugar mill ruins that preserve the memory of body-crushing slave labor. He is similarly discomfited by the labor regimes of his own moment and by his own place in the socioeconomic strata positioned to exploit those regimes. His speaker's middle-class excursion into the Afro-diasporic tropics throws him into contact with black people, but the class-based hierarchies of the tourism economy undermine any romantic notions of racial solidarity with the West Indian branch of a diasporic family. Three of the poem's ten stanzas are devoted to the complicated frictions of intraracial encounter in the Caribbean:

> Scorn greets us with promises of rum,
> hostility welcomes us to bargain sales.
> We make friends with Flamboyant trees.
>
> Jamaican Cynthie, called alien by dese lazy
> islanders—wo'k hahd, treated bad,
> oh, mahn, I tellin you. She's full
>
> of raucous anger. Nevertheless brings gifts of
> scarlet hibiscus when she comes to clean,
> white fragrant spider-lilies too sometimes. (*American Journal* 183)

It seems Hayden's speaker desires communion with the jaded island workers but must substitute the comforting presence of tropical flora—like any (white) tourist. The poem's fleshed-out character, Jamaican Cynthie, offers the speaker a flicker of connection, but ambient alienation fills Cynthie as well. She has her own frictional relations to "dese lazy islanders" who are native to the place where she is an immigrant worker; for a moment it seems that the poem's two principal players might bond in commiseration against the locals, who treat Cynthie badly and scorn the speaker. But the speaker is distanced from Cynthie because of her "raucous anger" and a socioeconomic gulf that registers as the fragment of Caribbean vernacular juxtaposes the speaker's writerly voice. The possibility of both connection and estrangement is deepened as Cynthie brings gifts of flora when she cleans—Are these tokens of heartfelt goodwill? Or are they calculated gestures, meant to elicit financial remuneration? Hayden will not allow himself the comfort of easy identification with "hahd"-laboring Cynthie. Thus the middle-class poet-professor finds himself in a newly uncomfortable role as apparent participant-benefactor in an exploitative tourism industry, risen from the remainders of a crushing slave economy.

The dilemmas of identity particularly experienced by African Americans vacationing in the Caribbean are at the heart of a small subgenre of post-movement-era cultural production. Terry McMillan's popular classic *How Stella Got Her Groove Back* (1996) is a very pulpy, neoliberal riff on the theme; Paule Marshall's novel *Praisesong for the Widow* (1983) offers to the subgenre a somewhat romantic narrative of restorative Afro-diasporic communion; and June Jordan's "Report from the Bahamas, 1982" is an essay riven by the same feelings of class-based intraracial disconnection that run through Hayden's "The Islands."⁹ Jordan, comparing her own economic wherewithal to that of the black men and women who service the Caribbean tourism industry, simply acknowledges, "I am a rich woman" (7). And noting that her island vacation bears some relation to the waves of colonization that have swept through the Bahamas for half a millennium, the poet—who was a professor at SUNY Stony Brook at the time of her writing—numbers herself and other African Americans among a new phalanx of privileged invaders: "And so it continues, this weird succession of crude intruders that, *now*, includes me and my brothers and my sisters from the North" (7, emphasis added). As part of a newly capitalized black middle-class that could "now" afford to vacation in the Caribbean, Jordan—like Hayden—struggles with the implications of a class privilege that inevitably alienates her from other black people. As Phillip Brian Harper has argued, some of Jordan's poems of the late 1960s and early 1970s, like "Okay 'Negroes,'" were typical BAM products in which "politically aware, racially conscious black nationalist" speakers *confidently* scolded (middle-class) "negroes" who were apparently alienated from their own blackness (*Are We* 48). But Jordan's "Report from the Bahamas" suggests that by the early 1980s the poet-professor was less interested in questioning the political awareness of other black people and more interested in working through her own gender- and class-determined relation to a variegated Afro-diasporic family. This internal work is similarly at the heart of Dove's poem "The House Slave," published shortly after Hayden's "The Islands" and just before Jordan's "Report from the Bahamas." While Hayden and Jordan personalize their confrontation with this dilemma while outside of American space, Dove displaces her experience of black class fissures into antebellum times.

These texts help mark a pivot point in the artistic ethos of black literary poets—a point after which social examination merely set the stage for self-examination. The new ethos held that "it is not enough to call out what is happening to us, without an equal measure of what is occurring within us," as poet Vievee Francis explains it (Rowell, *Angles* xxix). As much as anything else, this inclination to "map . . . interiors" represents a reflexive response to a sense of distance and alienation brought on as black poets achieved middle-class security while processing through MFA programs and into academic sinecures at a moment when neoliberal policy regimes began to exacerbate already existing divisions in the black class structure. If, as Harper put it, "radical black intellectual activism of the late 1960s was characterized by a drive for nationalistic unity among people of African descent" (*Are We* 40), black literary and intellectual production subsidized by PWIs of the late twentieth and early twenty-first centuries was characterized by recognition of the obstacles and fragmentation that made fraught the drive for nationalistic unity. Unable to abide in the easy belief that black people were "one people," as Stephen Henderson had declared in the 1970s, literary poets of the post-movement era faced the job of creating art that was up to the challenge presented by the emergence of stark intraracial differences. Hayden's importance for post-movement African American poets and for students and scholars of African American literary history is, in part, a function of the fact that he was simply ahead of his time—deeply attuned to intraracial difference at a time when many of his peers sought to banish or quash it. In the heart of the Black Arts era Hayden was anomalously *uninterested* in the cultivation of nationalistic unity among black people; he was, instead, primarily concerned with what he described as "my own quest for my meaning as an individual" (*Collected Prose* 88). This quest to discern individual meaning—to map his own interior through art—necessarily lead Hayden into considerations of his distance from those closest to him. It spurred him to explore the heterogeneity of black experience well before the socioeconomic transformations of the post-movement period made it all but impossible for poet-professors to imagine themselves as constituent parts of any homogenous black monolith.

The figure of the alien—one among the throng, yet still isolated from it—makes its way through all of Hayden's collections, but it is most prominent in his final volume, *American Journal*. Adopting the position of the intimate alien allows Hayden a variety of responses to the intraracial difference that he studies in the *American Journal* poems, like those collected in the sequence "Elegies for Paradise Valley." In the signature work of the "Elegies" sequence the poet-speaker recalls the complex tapestry of the slum life he had "escaped" but returns to in poetry. While deeply enmeshed in the black cultural life he conjures, the artist works from the distance of the survivor remembering the vibrant diversity of a life he no longer lives. Paradoxically, that life is simultaneously immanent and removed, deeply consequential yet long "vanished." In its compressed evocation of no less than two dozen characters representing the many human facets of a single Detroit neighborhood, "Elegies" is a microcosmic reimagining of Margaret Walker's classic "For My People," in which sundry representatives of black America are hailed in a Whitman-esque catalogue. But Hayden's remembrance of Paradise Valley is not one of the "martial songs" that Walker called for in her 1937 poem. ("Let the martial songs / be written, let the dirges disappear. Let a race of men now / rise and take control" [83].) Far from a rallying call to a coherent black collective seeking political self-determination, Hayden's sequence is a prototype for the late twentieth- and early twenty-first-century black literary poets who, in the words of Charles Rowell, "are now writing self against the backdrop of community" (*Angles* xxxix). As much as Hayden's "Elegies" are about the complex character of black community, they are also about the poet's complex interior and his distance from the denizens resurrected in the poems. The fifth elegy in the sequence is rendered in a traditional *ubi sunt* mode that celebrates the irreducible diversity of the summoned characters, even as it mourns the ephemerality of community and places the poet-professor leagues away from an irretrievable black folk world:

> And Belle the classy dresser, where is she,
> who changed her frocks three times a day?
> > Where's Nora, with her laugh, her comic flair,
> > stagestruck Nora waiting for her chance?
> Where's fast Iola, who so loved to dance
> she left her sickbed one last time to whirl
> in silver at The Palace till she fell?

Where's mad Miss Alice, who ate from garbage cans?
Where's snuffdipping Lucy, who played us "chunes"
on her guitar? Where's Hattie? Where's Melissabelle?
Let vanished rooms, let dead streets tell.

Where's Jim, Watusi prince and Good Old Boy,
who with a joke went off to fight in France?
    Where's Tump the defeated artist, for meals or booze
    daubing with quarrelsome reds, disconsolate blues?
Where's Les the huntsman? Tough Kid Chocolate, where
is he? Where's dapper Jess? Where's Stomp the shell-
shocked, clowning for us in parodies of war?
    Where's taunted Christopher, sad queen of night?
    And Ray, who cursing crossed the color line?
Where's gentle Brother Davis? Where's dopefiend Mel?
    Let vanished rooms, let dead streets tell. (*American Journal* 167)

In his comprehensive reading of Hayden's Detroit poems, Frank Rashid notes that in "Elegies" Hayden focuses on the "tensions in the Valley itself" (213). Indeed, just as "The Islands" is a documentation of intraracial fissures, "Elegies" figures black community as a space of competing ideologies, competing strategies of survival. And these vying worldviews are internalized by Hayden's speaker, who is caught between the Sunday-morning disciplines of the church and the Saturday-night hedonism of "Uncle Crip," the Dionysian figure who emerges as the central character of "Elegies." Distanced from the folk world of his childhood by several decades of academic training and economic success, Hayden ends the elegy sequence with his narrator indicating that, despite this separation, the tensions played out in the black community life indelibly marked his fragmented sense of self:

We'd dance there, Uncle
Crip and I,
for though I spoke
my pieces well in Sunday School,

I knew myself (precocious
in the ways of guilt
and secret pain)
the devil's own rag babydoll. (170)

Although "hatred for our kind" (163) is a backdrop to the action of the poems, by centering on the intricacies of intraracial difference, "Elegies" veers away from various black nationalist rhetorics of unity popular in the BAM era. Moreover, by suggesting that conflicts animating the black world of Paradise Valley are replicated in the inner world of the speaker, the poems prefigure the inward turn that has characterized post-movement poetry. But most important here is Hayden's characteristic implementation of distance between his mature speaker and the characters and community he remembers with such intimacy. The poet-professor acknowledges a distance between himself and the black folk world but also tries to bridge that distance through art.

Intrablack Bridges and the Challenging Tributes of Terrance Hayes

Because Hayden was forthright about his "sense of alienation" and because he did not seek a populist poetry in imitation of the vernacular voice, he was able to explore his own experience of intraracial difference more deeply than other poets of the Black Arts era. And thus his work—in contrast to that of most of his BAM peers—anticipates some key exploratory zones of the poet-professors who have risen to prominence in the post-movement era. It is impossible to fully chart the many examples of the post-movement exploration of the space and connections that exist between the contemporary poet-professor and the neofolk in lower strata of the class structure, but poems by Nikky Finney and John Murillo offer two models of twenty-first-century poet-professors representing their *cleaved* connections to the vernacular world of the black majority. I offer readings of Finney's "The Girlfriend's Train" and Murillo's "Practicing Fade-Aways" in order to contextualize work by Terrance Hayes, the poet who may be Hayden's most important twenty-first-century descendant.

Finney's poem is among the more noteworthy and explicit instances of poets grappling with their distance from the abjection of black people rendered marginal, superfluous, and disposable in the neoliberal order of the twenty-first century. In her 2012 collection, *The World Is Round*, Finney's remarkable meditation begins with an epigraph: "You write like a Black woman who's never been hit before." The quotation is attributed to Patience Rage, a figure the poem reveals to be an audience member at one of the speaker's readings in Philadelphia. The character, who bears the scars of multiple stabbings, is amazed by the poet-speaker's "real soft" writing and offers an interrogative declaration that suggests the exceptional status of the relatively secure poet-professor: "We were just wondering / how you made it through / and we didn't?" Finney's poem calls Patience Rage a "Representative" of the many women less fortunate than the poet-speaker—the "trainload" of women in the "Philly cold" who did not make it into the warmth of the poetry reading. Acknowledging the great distance between herself and the representative of forgotten black women, Finney's speaker asserts her solidarity with this mass represented through synecdoche; she brings her body into contact with Patience Rage and declares herself a part of "the trainload / of *us*" (65, emphasis added). But despite her speaker's will to connection, Finney imbues her poem with a sense of the transient and fleeting nature of this interclass bond. Patience Rage and the speaker do not travel the same track; they are not in precisely the same boat—or train, as it were: "The train blew its whistle, / she started to hurry." Although Finney aligns herself with BAM sensibilities more readily than many poet-professors of recent decades, her attention to the distance that looms between the artist-intellectual and the black sufferer in "The Girlfriend's Train" recalls Hayden's approach to intraracial difference more than it does BAM efforts to disappear the distance between the poet and the people. We might note, for example, the way that Finney curates glimpses of the vernacular voice in the words of her neofolk figure ("Guess how many times I been stabbed?"), while the speaker maintains the lexical register of the "colleged" artist. Even for a poet like Finney, very much committed to antiracist political advocacy in her art, the contranymic qualities of the word *cleaved* best describe the relation between the university-employed cultural worker and the black neofolk class.

In "The Girlfriend's Train" the speaker's poetry-reading venue is transformed into a liminal space of temporary feminine connection; in John Murillo's "Practicing Fade-Aways" it is the basketball court that is presented as the *recollected* zone of masculine bonding. The poem places the speaker in isolation, "On a deserted playground," practicing his game and remembering: "Twenty years ago, / I ran this very court with nine other / Wannabe ballers." In the *ubi sunt* fashion of Hayden's "Elegies for Paradise Valley," Murillo's text offers a small gallery of black lives—"ballers" destroyed by cruelties reserved for the dispossessed. There is "a boy we called 'the sandman' / . . . stabbed to death / Outside the Motel 6"; and there is "'Downtown' Ricky Brown" who eventually "drove himself / Crazy with conspiracy theories and liquor / Was last seen roaming the French Quarter, shoeless, babbling" (*Angles of Ascent* 500). These characters, whose male bodies once spoke fluently on the basketball court, are resurrected in Murillo's poem as a declaration of the speaker's social origin, of his connection to the black vernacular social art of streetball.

But, with only a "long shadow" accompanying the speaker in his moment of remembrance, the piece is filled with a sense of the elegiac distance that separates the poet-professor's speaker from those who never "made it through." As in Hayden's "Elegies," the lost folk world can be conjured in the poem but the speaker cannot return to it.

Finney and Murillo make no special claim to Hayden even as they work within political-aesthetic mechanisms that he structured during the Black Arts era; however, Terrance Hayes has been quite clear about his admiration for Hayden. In extrapoetic commentary, subtle artistic declarations, and general aesthetic orientation, Hayes tips his hat toward Hayden.[10] Hayes may be Hayden's most powerful interpreter. But this is not to insist that he takes a baton from Hayden, only that he has rigorously engaged Hayden's legacy in order to chisel his own voice. Perhaps more than any other twenty-first-century poet-professor, Hayes follows Hayden into conceptual space that looms between the artist and all others, while simultaneously registering devotion to black cultural life. Although Hayes might never describe his love of vernacular as "a predilection for the folk idiom," as the ever-professorial Hayden once did (*Collected Prose* 22), the two poets are similar in their management of a high-culture aesthetic that assimilates the life and language of the masses. One of Hayes's chief poetic accomplishments is an expert integration of *contemporary* vernacular into the writerly métier that Hayden advanced through the Black Arts era. Despite—or perhaps because of—this capacity to mingle high- and low-culture language and life, Hayes frequently speaks in the voice of the universal alien, as in an early-career poem wherein his speaker declares "no one knows / what I am" and insists that he is inscrutable even to the black people whom he loves:

> . . . When I stop
> by McDonald's for a cheeseburger, no one
> suspects what I am. I smile at Ronald's poster
> perpetual grin behind the pissed-off, fly girl
> cashier that I love. Where are my goddamn fries?
> Ain't I American? I never say, Niggaz
> in my poems. My ancestors didn't
> emigrate. Why would anyone leave
> their native land? I'm thinking about shooting
> some hoop later on. I'll dunk on everyone
> of those niggaz. They have no idea
> what I am. (*Muscular* 15)

Although Hayes can be playful in his alienation, in each of his five volumes there is often an aching sense of distance between his lyric "I" and the world. It is the dissipation of human connection that haunts a piece like "Derrick Poem (The Lost World)," wherein the passing of time attenuates the relation between the speaker and an old friend, and the title of a film about extinct dinosaurs alludes to faded camaraderie: "& skinny Derrick rolls up in a bor-rowed Pontiac w/ room / for me, my kicks & Ella on his way to see *The Lost World* / alone" (*Muscular* 21). A recurring theme for Hayes is distance from closest kin, like the speaker's parents in "Late" or like his speaker's pimping half-brother in "As Traffic": "Was on the news: 'Columbia man charged / With human sex trafficking,' he will live in a cell / With beautiful solitude chained about his throat" (*How to Be* 13). In "How to Draw a Perfect Circle," Hayes's speaker is cleaved to and from a crazed cousin who attacks a black policeman and is then killed. The poet-professor refracts his response to the violence by couching it within a circular contemplation of circularity itself, and of the difficulty of drawing a perfect circle. At the distanced center of the poem—nested in a welter of philosophical and semiotic thinking—is the speaker's dead cousin, remembered as a child: "When I looked into my past I saw the boy I had not seen in years" (*How to Be* 91).

While the violence and vibrancy of black life in neoliberal America can be hard to find in the work of university-employed poets of the 1980s and 1990s, Hayes has frequently placed hip-hop culture and the tragic beauty of black neofolk life at the heart of his poetry. And, if antebellum history has been a preoccupation of many recent African American literary artists, Hayes—like the MCs—has been more focused on the contemporary mo-ment and those black folk who "don't know if Toni Morrison / is a woman or a man," as he so evocatively phrases it in "What I Am" (*Muscular* 15). Indeed, in Hayes's work the twenty-first-century prison complex is more ominous than the nineteenth-century slave plantation. But like Hayden before him, Hayes does not render himself as one with those locked in American pre-cincts of relegation; he is most attentive to the distance between his speakers and black people who do not know the intellectual and social geography of the cultural elite. In his "Carp Poem" Hayes attempts to measure this distance as he chronicles a visit inside the American carceral system. Intraracial dif-ference and frictions, rather than easy solidarity, are apparent as the poem's long couplets play on the ghazal form and its themes of love but also call to mind the cell bars that separate the black speaker from the black inmates he walks past:[11]

after I have made my way to the New Orleans Parish Jail down the block,
where the black prison guard wearing the same weariness

my prison guard father wears buzzes me in, I follow his pistol and shield
along each corridor trying not to look at the black men

boxed and bunked around me until I reach the tiny classroom
where two dozen black boys are dressed in jumpsuits orange as the carp

I saw in a pond once in Japan, so many fat, snaggletoothed fish
ganged in and lurching for food that a lightweight tourist could have crossed

(*Lighthead* 31)

In Hayes's poem the artist-intellectual is no redemptive hero or moral
leader bringing art to the abject. The speaker is linked not to the black suf-
ferers packed as animals in the jail but rather to the oppressive state's black
representative who reminds the speaker of his "prison guard father." In a
deeply introspective turn, Hayes works the imagery so that his speaker is
likened to a touring voyeur, treading upon the prisoners as a "tourist" might
have walked upon the carp packed into a Japanese pond. Even the evoca-
tion of the speaker's travels to Japan underscores the contrast between his
own freedom of movement and the intense spatial restriction of the incar-
cerated. There are no comfortable alliances here; certainly, shared blackness
is not the grounds for easy celebration, and the possibility of racial solidar-
ity seems far off for a speaker who is painfully aware that he has made it
through, as others have not.

"Carp Poem" is a reprisal and renovation of Hayden's "The Prisoners,"
published—like "The Islands" and "Elegies for Paradise Valley"—in *American
Journal*. As I suggested in my earlier appraisal of "The Prisoners," Hayden
uses the late-1970s poem to offer a sanguine staging of an encounter between
the artist-intellectual and the urban folk figure at a pivotal historical juncture,
on the eve of the vast expansion of a penal system that would play a central
role in the fragmentation and stratification of black American society in the
neoliberal era. In Hayden's poem, the prison's "guillotine gates"—so sugges-
tive of class difference—are transcended as the speaker and a "scarred young
lifer" commune through poetry and prayer. But publishing "Carp Poem" some
thirty years later, Hayes seems much less hopeful about the possibility of
genuine connection between his speaker and "the boy prisoners waiting to

talk poetry with a young black poet" (*Lighthead* 32). Where Hayden evokes his Bahá'í Faith in the prison poem, Hayes emphasizes religious skepticism in his. And while Hayden's speaker is affirmed by the young convict's appreciation of his "true" poetry, in Hayes's poem the inmates are simply silent and "waiting." Read together, "Carp Poem" tempers the optimism of "The Prisoners": Hayes follows his mentor into the gulf that opens between the university-employed artist and the abject, but by refusing to stage a moment of communion between the poet-professor and the prisoners, Hayes suggests the great social distance that separates the black literary poet and black sufferers of the early twenty-first century.

Henry Louis Gates's distinction between "motivated" and "unmotivated" signifying practices in the black literary tradition does not properly describe the interpoetic relation between "Carp Poem" and "The Prisoners"—or between Hayes and Hayden. Gates holds that motivated signifying involves a parodic, "negative critique" of a prior text, while unmotivated signifying involves a celebration, "underscoring the relation" between black texts—as "between black jazz musicians who perform each other's standards on a joint album, not to critique these but to engage in refiguration as an act of homage" (*Signifying* xxvii). But Hayes signifies on Hayden in manner not quite captured in Gates's critical taxonomy or in his old-school musical analogy: Hayes, who was an adolescent during the Golden Age of hip-hop, does not simply pay homage to Hayden, who was an adolescent during the Jazz Age. In his most compelling signifying, Hayes offers a thoroughgoing remix of Hayden that is both tribute and critique, honoring Hayden even as it resists him. "Carp Poem" bears this complicated relation to "The Prisoners."

At first blush, we may read Hayes's poem "Something for Marvin" as a straightforward example of unmotivated signifying. Hayes remembers Marvin Gaye, the murdered prince of Motown, by remixing Hayden's "Mourning Poem for the Queen of Sunday." In his poem, Hayes samples Hayden's opening vernacular line—"Lord's lost Him His mockingbird"—but tries not to become a mockingbird imitation of his poetic antecedent. Hayden's poem about the murder and funeral of a gospel goddess in interwar Detroit is alive in the distinct but distant echo heard in Hayes's poem that crescendos in a glimpse of the 1980s funeral of Gaye, the Motown legend. And at the end of this dexterous renewal of one of Hayden's most vernacular-heavy poems, Hayes reveals his own aspiration for the immortality of the great artist: "I want to live forever / like the singer resurrected / in the record's groove" (*Muscular* 50). While it is Gaye who is brought to life every time the needle touches the record's groove, it is Hayden who is resurrected in every reading of Hayes's poem.

But there is, of course, a hint of envy—or perhaps *anxiety*—in the words of Hayes's speaker who desires the immortality that "Something for Marvin" gives to both Gaye and Hayden. Indeed, as Harold Bloom has argued, artistic influence often manifests itself in a kind of competitive anxiety, a masculine desire to not simply follow in the path of those who have gone before but to assure one's own deathlessness by outstripping, or moving beyond, predecessors. In the shadow of Bloom's ideas about the anxiety of influence, some significance can be read into the fact that Hayes has published two poems for Marvin Gaye. "Something for Marvin" appears in his first volume, *Muscular Music* (1999), and "A Form of Sexual Healing," which is dedicated to Gaye, is included in his 2010 *Lighthead*, which won the National Book Award. The later poem is set in the speaker's present, features scenes of karaoke singing and bad lip-syncing, and emphasizes echo, but it makes no mention of Hayden. Its first line is, "Will you speak to me now bedeviling, sweet muser?" (*Lighthead* 38). A critic like Bloom might read this deliberate return to a poem about Gaye (without Hayden) as Hayes's palinodic effort to move beyond Hayden—as an assertion of his independence from the poet whom he had echoed when he was younger.

Hayes most often works in playful obliquity, allowing his reader to "solve for X" in a variety of ways, as Hayden would admire. In the *Lighthead* poem "The Avocado," he is oblique even as he asserts his will to resist, or thoroughly remix, Hayden along with other powerful influences in the African American cultural tradition. Somewhat similar to Rita Dove's "Upon Meeting Don L. Lee" and Biggie's "Party and Bullshit," Hayes's "The Avocado" can be read as the repudiation of a Black Arts–era ethos, but in the poem Hayes also explicitly signifies on Hayden's "Runagate Runagate," indicating a desire not only to revise Hayden but also to resist and redirect the powerful tributary of black history poetics that runs through Hayden's early heritage poems. Hayes's poem, which places its distracted speaker in a Black History Month lecture, makes conceptual moves that are typical of post-movement artists who are, as Mark Anthony Neal put it, "distanced from the nostalgia that pervades the civil rights generation" (104). As an aging, self-congratulating lecturer recounts his participation in revolutionary action of "1971," the hungry poet-speaker says, "I'm pretending I haven't heard this one before as I eye / black tortillas on a red plate beside a big green bowl / of guacamole" (*Lighthead* 27). Throughout, the symbols and rhetoric of the Black Power and civil rights movements are spoofed—as the pan-Africanist/Garveyite/ Black Power colors of black, red, and green are summoned in the finger foods the speaker craves in the lines excerpted above. Hayes joins a fair number of "postsoul" artists working in both high- and low-culture mediums as he uses his parodic poem to express ennui in the face of recycled narratives about the movement era (see M. Neal 20–22). But he also humorously probes into the antebellum period, with his speaker conjecturing, "If the abolitionists had a flag / it would no doubt feature the avocado." He later takes up the memory of Harriet Tubman, indicating that his speaker is unmoved by the crocodile tears shed by the lecturer as he recalls movement-era efforts to place a statue of Tubman on the National Mall:

> Brother man is weeping now and walking wet tissue to the trash can
> and saying, "Harriet Tubman was a walking shadow," or, "Harriet Tubman
> walked in shadows," or "To many, Harriet Tubman was a shadow
> to walk in," and the meaning is pureed flesh with lime juice
> (*Lighthead* 27)

By bringing shades of comic satire into his representation of the lecturer's tearful representation of the slavery era, Hayes moves into rarely explored poetic territory. A few works (like Ishmael Reed's "A Flight to Canada") notwithstanding, American poetry about slavery has primarily been an exercise in solemnity. In its satirical portrayal of the aging black radical, "The Avocado" not only suggests that movement-era political rhetoric is now staid and exhausted, it also offers up a critique of formulaic approaches to antebellum history in the post-movement era. Douglas Jones, in his strong interpretation of the poem, argues that Hayes gives three iterations of Tubman's shadow walking in order to show that "no matter which story one tells about Tubman, its most elemental meaning always returns to 'pureed flesh'" (49), which Douglas interprets as the destroyed slave body. That is to say, no matter how many times the dark, grave story of slavery is told, reiteration of the story itself can never restore what was crushed in the past. The various renderings of Tubman's shadow walking also amount to a broad critique of the slave poems that have proliferated in the post-movement era and that usually abide by the solemn conventions of "melancholic historicism." Stephen Best uses this phrasing to describe the work of literary artists and cultural critics following in the path of Toni Morrison and her "paragon literary text" of the late 1980s,

Beloved, which, according to Best, set the stage for appearance of a "Morrisonian poetics" that has dominated recent decades of historiography, cultural criticism, and literary production (459).

As I have argued in this chapter, in post-movement African American poetry, a pastward-focused, archive-oriented, ghost-conjuring "Morrisonian poetics" predates the publication of *Beloved*. Indeed, it is inaugurated in the ten-poem history section of Rita Dove's *The Yellow House on the Corner*, which is itself the extension of an African American tradition of archival research poetics pioneered by Robert Hayden in the middle decades of the twentieth century. Moreover, I have suggested that the historical turn in African American poetics of the 1980s and 1990s must be understood in relation to the intense bifurcation of the black class structure during those decades and the simultaneous emergence of hip-hop poetry. With MCs deeply ensconced in the vernacular and the narratives of post-movement-era neofolk life, university-employed poets turned to explorations of history—and the slave past in particular. In their search for guiding models, the poet-professors inevitably looked to Hayden and his early heritage poems, such as "Runagate Runagate"—the poem that Terrance Hayes samples and remixes in his resistant response to the post-movement tradition of historical poetics. In the final lines of "The Avocado," Hayes evokes Hayden's paradigmatic poem as his speaker resents the posturing of the Black History Month lecturer:

> and I'm thinking every time I hear this story it's the one telling the
>   story
> that's the hero. "Hush now," Harriet Tubman probably said
> near dawn, pointing a finger black enough to be her pistol barrel
> toward the future or pointing a pistol barrel black enough
> to be her finger at the mouth of some starved, stammering slave
> and then lifting her head to listen for something no one but her
>   could hear. (*Lighthead* 28)

Here, as in "Carp Poem," Hayes rejects the idea that the artist-intellectual is a moral hero; rather than aligning himself with Tubman, his speaker—whose hunger has been emphasized throughout the poem—is projected into the "starved, stammering slave" that Tubman admonishes to silence. By imagining himself into the ghost of the silenced slave Hayes suggests that what Tubman would want from him—and other poets—is less poetry that imagines the slave past and the interiority of the enslaved. To make this intervention in the tradition, Hayes returns to its veritable source, resurrecting Hayden once again, so that he—and other poets—might move beyond the powerful predecessor. Here is the fragment of "Runagate" that Hayes remixes:

> And fear starts a-murbling, Never make it,
> we'll never make it. *Hush that now,*
> and she's turned upon us, leveled pistol
> glinting in the moonlight:
> Dead folks can't jaybird-talk, she says;
> you keep on going now or die, she says. (60)

This fragment of the polyvocal, heteroglossic "Runagate" captures the sense of forward movement that is so essential to the poem that Hayden conceived in the 1940s—and to Hayes's twenty-first-century remix. Here, Hayden's Tubman uses her pistol to silence the "murbling" slave so that the band of runaways might "keep on going" toward freedom. But in Hayes's poem Tubman's pistol brandishing is refracted and doubled so that she points toward "the future" in one iteration and toward the "starved, stammering" slave in the next. Through this doubling Hayes's poem suggests the way to "keep on going" into the future is to cease stammering on about the slave past. Jones persuasively argues that "The Avocado" can be read as a brief against post-movement-era critical and cultural projects that address contemporary exigencies through reference to the past. He writes, "The poem tells a history of discontinuity and difference: now is not then. It offers advice to those of us who turn too readily and assuredly to the history of slavery to describe and thus respond to the social and political realities of the present: 'Hush, now'" (D. Jones 50). In order to make the interventionist argument that "now is not then" Hayes must return to the slave past, imagining Tubman anew, and he must return to the African American poetic tradition, charting a path into the future that honors Hayden even as it amends the model of historical poetics he advanced early in his career.

Hayes's resistance to the "melancholic historicism" and archive animation that has been one of the dominant modes of post-movement literary poetry may be read as an effort to bring about what Houston Baker describes as a "generational shift," defined as "an ideologically motivated movement overseen by young or newly emergent intellectuals dedicated to refuting the work of their intellectual predecessors and to establishing a framework for intellectual inquiry" (*Blues, Ideology* 67). It is unlikely that Hayes would describe his project as a *refutation* of forebears—he has described himself as inhabiting the "space between" Robert Hayden and Amiri Baraka (HoCoPolitso)—but he is certainly modifying the work of antecedents, Hayden chief among them. But while he attempts to move beyond his ancestors, he takes Hayden with him. As I have suggested, the "framework for intellectual inquiry" that Hayes builds in his poetry pays close attention to the distance between the university-employed cultural worker and the world of the black neofolk. Unlike poet-professors who rose to prominence in the 1980s and 1990s, eschewing hip-hop culture and its vernacular, Hayes is among a new generation of university-employed poets who wed the rich, Dionysian elements of contemporary black language and culture and the Apollonian virtues of writerly poetics. Like Hayes, many of these poets cleave to the vernacular and life exigencies of the black neofolk, even as they acknowledge the socioeconomic forces that cleave them from those at the bottom of the black class structure. The paradoxical task taken up by these twenty-first-century poet-professors—to intimately love the people while acknowledging distance from them—was modeled by Hayden before, during, and after the Black Arts era, and it remains an enduring element of his legacy.

Hayden's Future

Insightful critics, like Charles Rowell and Phillip Richards, have assessed Hayden's legacy in the decades following his passing and determined that he is our "most influential black poet" (Richards 178). In this final section of *Robert Hayden in Verse* I have tried to make a somewhat different argument. African American poetry has undergone profound developments and massive proliferation in the past thirty to forty years. In the expansive, variegated territory of contemporary African American poetry Hayden haunts a special, cosmopolitan, open-border province. I imagine him gliding in a lush terrain, observing its upas trees and cereuses, maybe tasting its sunflowers, but also deciphering the plangent echo of bass thumping out of far-off poetic kingdoms and queendoms. All pilgrims who find their way to Hayden's region are welcomed and quieted as he floats about his garden; they see him as Margaret Walker did, "Drinking from fountains of / wisdom, truth and beauty / Teaching us Divinity" (*This Is My Century* 117). Those poet-pilgrims who have spent time with Hayden, reading his verse, considering his teaching, have been influenced in a variety of ways. As I have argued, many have followed his lead into the archive, some have tracked him into the recesses of the psyche, attempting to match his "vivid retelling of that inner zone" (Harper, "Meta-physics"), and others have used his model to consider the peculiar station of the black literary poet in relation to the denizens of the "black majority."

Some underplay their debt to Hayden, but many others have paid homage to him in poetry that warrants acknowledgement. In the years shortly after Hayden's passing, Michael Harper would offer poetic remembrances of his friend and mentor as he knew him in the final decade of his life, performing "the sacred / work of race and nation, and the word singing / everywhere" (*Healing Song* 6). Walker's and Harper's personal recollections—"I think of you, sitting there in your bow / tie . . . / your pipe-stem easing of gauze" (Harper, *Healing Song* 5)—have been followed by a steady stream of explicit tributes to Hayden's artistry. Often these tributes are felt in a sampled image, as in Rita Dove's "Upon Meeting Don L. Lee," when the "rustling" wings of the dispersing singers recall the "silken rustling in the air" that is heard when Hayden's winged angel/freak achieves his "angle of ascent" in "For a Young Artist" (Dove, *Yellow House* 16; Hayden, *Collected Poems* 133). Sometimes the poet is honored through a dedicated piece, as in Crystal Williams's consolation poem "Night Bloom."

Among the most exalting of these tributes is a cento poem by Amaud Jamaul Johnson that collages Hayden's own phrasings to create a monument in language:

> Then you arrived, meditative, ironic
> My head gripped in bony vice
>
> Mouth of agony shaping a cry it cannot utter
> What did I know, what did I know. (53)

Abdul Ali's "On Meeting Robert Hayden in a Dream" evokes Dove's "Upon Meeting Don L. Lee, In a Dream," but rather than rejecting a forefather, Ali's speaker draws close to Hayden. He remembers the poet's "wavy comb over," his compassionate alienation, and his insistent connection to urban American space. In the speaker's dream

> border crossing is quintessentially american universal
> crowds gather in squalid ghettoes where every country is a city
> every city is a verse & every verse echoes "Those Winter
>   Sundays."

In reality, the echo of "Those Winter Sundays" can be heard in brilliant lyrics about fathers and fathering, like Yusef Komunyakaa's "My Father's Love Letters" and Kevin Young's "The Crowning," and in Terrance Hayes's remembrance "For Robert Hayden." For at least one poet—Eduardo Corral, who identifies as a gay Chicano—Hayden has served as a powerful but perplexing muse. In "To the Angelbeast," Corral engages specifically with Hayden's *American Journal* poem "Bone-Flower Elegy." And in "To Robert Hayden" he imagines himself as Hayden's lover. Even as Corral's poems celebrate him, they wrestle with the encrypted themes of sexuality that periodically pulse in Hayden's corpus.

The prolific Carl Phillips, another poet whose work often meditates on sexuality, takes as his "motto" lines from Hayden's "The Tattooed Man": "all art is pain / suffered and outlived" (*Collected Poems* 161, see Hennessy 202). Like Phillips, many of the poets who have offered tribute to Hayden would affirm the truth of this definition. But, if all art is ultimately the afterlight of pain, only Apollo insists on pointing this out. Dionysus puts off this thought until later—even when he sings about pain. Which is to say, the poets who have carried on Hayden's legacy are some of the most Apollonian to be found in the expansive territory of contemporary African American poetry. In this final section of *Robert Hayden in Verse* I have argued that a full accounting of Hayden's legacy after the Black Arts era requires sincere acknowledgement of the more Dionysian regions of recent poetry wherein Hayden is not so influential. To that end, I distinguish two tracks, or zones of development, in post-movement African American poetry—one dominated by MCs carrying on the performative, Dionysian aesthetic project of the BAM while negotiating the commercial institutions of the culture industry, and the other led by poet-professors extending the writerly Apollonian aesthetic of Robert Hayden while negotiating institutions of academia. The schemata I offer, with hip-hop and academic poetries figured as flip sides of one black poetic coin, or two domains of one poetic territory, is just that—a schemata. By design, my sketching is not exhaustive; it does not adequately account for the various registers of print poetry—some quite popular—that now flourish outside of the academy, nor does it describe the emergence of semi-institutionalized spoken word poetry in post-movement decades, and I do not attempt to grab hold of the slippery space between the stage and the page, which attracts many contemporary poets.

But in order to think of Hayden's future, I close by calling attention to that liminal place between the streets of the MC and the towers of the academics, which in recent years has been increasingly legitimized in the MFA programs of American universities. Some of the poetic production coming out of that creative zone is gathered in the 2015 anthology *The BreakBeat Poets: New American Poetry in the Age of Hip-Hop*. In his introductory essay, Kevin Coval contends that the anthology collects the work of a new breed of poets who "blow up bullshit distinctions between high and low, academic and popular, rap and poetry, page and stage" (xvii). And, with the work included in the *BreakBeat* anthology representing some of the most recent developments in African American poetry, it seems that the lines between hip-hop and academic verse are fading.[12] Because of generational and institutional evolution in academia, the study and expression of hip-hop culture is becoming increasingly admissible in university settings. It would seem that this might negatively impact Hayden's legacy, which has been primarily sustained by the Apollonian poet-professors of the academy. Indeed, Coval says nothing about Hayden and casts BreakBeat poetics as an "extension of the Black Arts" (xvi); moreover, there is little sign of Hayden in the *BreakBeat* anthology itself. But, underscoring the omnivorous inclusivity of hip-hop culture, Coval also notes that the new breed of poetry emanates from the "radically democratic cultural space where hip-hop lives" (xxii). And, while Hayden does not figure prominently in the *BreakBeat* anthology, several of the poets it features draw from him in their work. These poets find their way back to both Hayden and Black Arts sources as they impel American poetry into the future.

The self-consciously advancing and insurgent character of BreakBeat poetics is captured in the anthologized poem "Slang," by tenured poet-professor Kyle Dargan. Celebrating black vernacular language of the Golden Age of hip-hop and implying that the use of this language is a kind of revolutionary act, Dargan's poem adapts aesthetic politics of the BAM to a more contemporary moment:

> . . . Our diction
> scares our parents. They think
> we speak in knotted tongues.
> "Dog." "What up,
> Kid?" "Son, I told you." We
> lift mutiny against word
> rulers and the world
> bequeathed to us. (Coval et al. 170)

For Dargan, whose poetry chronicles his coming of age in hip-hop's egalitarian culture, attraction to aesthetic values at the heart of the BAM does not preclude a concomitant devotion to Hayden's example. This double affiliation is indicated by Dargan's inclusion in both the *BreakBeat* anthology and Rowell's *Angles of Ascent*.[13] "Microphone Fiend," one of the poems he contributes to the latter, is an ode to childhood in the hip-hop era; it is controlled by rap cadences and incorporates the bars (lines) of a youngster who "freestyles" in the shower, anticipating "emceedom like a growth spurt" (436). But Dargan also supplies *Angles of Ascent* with one of the most stirring commemorations of the poet whose aesthetic spirit presides over the anthology. The title of Dargan's tribute, "Search for Robert Hayden," is both a directive to all who encounter the poem and a description of its speaker's activity as he makes his way through a musty garage full of books: "We are looking for 'The Middle Passage,' first we must clear a walking path." The effort to find Hayden amid so much literary detritus is imagined as a collective endeavor, involving not only the speaker but also an undefined, and thus unlimited, cohort who will search widely and will be humbled in their quest:

> we'll be standing knee deep in
> the unselected poems of black literature.
> This is how we will find him:
> on our hands and knees,
> combing over flailed books—seashells
> beneath a forgotten tide.
> Occasionally we'll wrench something up,
> not what we are looking for, and read it anyway. (435)

Like Terrance Hayes, Dargan demonstrates immersion in BAM-derived hip-hop aesthetics, even as he looks to Hayden as a primary guiding light. This openness to what may be considered disparate influences reflects the "radically democratic" aspect of hip-hop culture—which rarely rejects but relentlessly advances through the innovative repurposing and remixing of cultural material. It is not surprising to see a synthesis of Hayden and Black Arts influences in the currently emergent poet-professors who are most attuned to hip-hop.

Those poets committed to synthesizing the Apollonian page and the Dionysian stage bring Hayden into a new space and offer thoroughly innovative interpretations of his legacy. For example, in a recorded performance of "Frederick Douglass," *BreakBeat* poet DJ Renegade (Joel Dias-Porter) conceives Hayden's sonnet in the ecstatic style of a black exhorter-preacher. Riding the poem's meter into the growling peaks and valleys of a sanctified sermon, Renegade extracts fresh meaning from Hayden's often-anthologized standard by seamlessly fusing its writerly language with black performative orality.[14]

But some of the most inventive engagement with Hayden's legacy is found in the work of Douglas Kearney, also included in the *BreakBeat* anthology. Kearney's poetry is soaked in hip-hop vernacularism but is deeply cognizant of literary origins; it is performance based but also aggressively graphocentric. On stage, Kearney is an event of unrestrained drama, and on the page he often employs "performative typography" that borrows from graffiti aesthetics as it splays, curls, and blurs words against white space (Kearney 309). In praising Kearney's work, Terrance Hayes writes, "I have never encountered poetry like this before" (*Black Automaton* n.p.). But, in the midst of Kearney's innovation, the poet and the reader encounter Hayden. In "Swimchant of Nigger Mer-Folk (An Aquaboogie Set in Lapis)," Kearney braids together source fibers drawn from the music of Parliament Funkadelic, the Disney film *The Little Mermaid*, and T.S. Eliot's "The Love Song of J. Alfred Prufrock" to produce a powerful response to the call of Hayden's "Middle Passage." Kearney's poem is a compressed riot of references and discourses that represents a postmodern acceleration of the fragment-gathering method that Hayden used in creating his enduring modernist poem. While many have offered approximations of "Middle Passage," "Swimchant" takes Hayden into a new orbit wherein "melancholic historicism" is exchanged for imaginative tragicomedy and—as Evie Shockley suggests in her deft reading of Kearney's poem—we are bid "to laugh outrageously in the face of outrageous events" ("Going Overboard" 804).

Tragicomedy is also the mode of Kearney's "Afrofuturism (Blanch says, 'Meh')," which condenses the slave past and the space future in a meditation on the black freedom dreams that have been nurtured in the African American cultural imagination since the era of the transatlantic slave trade. First published in *Poetry* in 2014, "Afrofuturism" is the twenty-first-century remix of the antebellum folk material at the heart of Hayden's "O Daedalus, Fly Away Home," published in *Poetry* in 1943. In "Fly Away Home" Hayden renders the legend of the flying slaves who leapt off New World plantations in search of Old World origins:

> *O fly away home, fly away.*
> Do you remember Africa?

O cleave the air, fly away home.
I knew all the stars of Africa. (192)

Some seventy years later Kearney plays in a technologized crypto-vernacular that follows Hayden only to create a fresh poem, which parodies recognizable images of the black past and the black future:

> o great getting up launchin!
> spacesuited Q.U.E.E.N.S. in foil to fly.
> flight suited kings sky around shinin.
> zip zip zip off the planetation
> beyond the stairs to nigga heaven.

In another key fragment of Kearney's "Afrofuturism," the poem forms an intertextual bond with "Runagate Runagate" in order to imagine a space-age Harriet Tubman using her futurized pistol to hush doubts from the wavering runaways that she leads off the "planetation." Identifying Tubman by one of her aliases listed in Hayden's poem, Kearney remixes the segment of "Runagate" that also attracted Hayes in "The Avocado":

> Moses tote her
> raygun saying
> moonwalk or git
> disinigrated!

With raucous, postmodernizing wit Kearney reanimates Hayden's art in the context of a Janus-faced poetics that reconditions a past and envisions a future, that is meant to be both read and performed, that is highly literate yet saturated in vivid vernacular, and that is simultaneously Apollonian and Dionysian. Kearney ingenuously obliterates many of the boundaries that have organized African American poetry in post-movement decades and brings the territory of the poet-professors closer to that of the MCs. In the work of Kearney and like-minded artists, Robert Hayden is teleported into the living borderlands of contemporary poetics, where he is both honored and challenged as his legacy and that of the Black Arts Movement entwine in discordant concord.

Notes

Introduction

1. Here, and throughout most of the book, when excerpting from Hayden's poetry I quote from *The Collected Poems of Robert Hayden* (1985). (Page numbers remain the same in the 2013 edition of Hayden's *Collected Poems*.) When excerpts from Hayden's poetry are not taken from *Collected Poems*, that is indicated in the text or parenthetically.

Chapter 1

1. Hall notes this inclusive gesture in Henderson's seminal work on Black Arts poetry (75).

2. Aldon Nielsen's important study *Black Chant: Languages of African-American Postmodernism* (1999) suggests that Hayden had not been given the critical attention he merits (23). Nielsen himself simply gives Hayden an "assimilationist position" (7) and elsewhere mentions the poet in lists (40, 75). Fahamisha Patricia Brown admiringly notices Hayden several times in *Performing the Word: African American Poetry as Vernacular Culture* (1999), but she does little to situate him in her examination of the vernacular in African American poetry (73).

3. In 2004 Gabbin and others mounted a similar gathering—"Furious Flower: Regenerating the Black Poetic Tradition"—which again brought together many important voices in the field of contemporary African American poetry. Hayden received little attention during the proceedings—none of the conference papers directly engaged his work.

4. The only substantial treatment of Hayden's work in *The Furious Flowering* appears in Jon Woodson's article, "Consciousness, Myth, and Transcendence: Symbolic Action in Three Poems on the Slave Trade." Woodson's essay is in large part a very unsympathetic reading of Hayden's "Middle Passage" that labels the poet's discourse "ideologically conservative" and "absolutist" (157). This essay may represent the only *negative* appraisal of "Middle Passage" yet published. It is helpful to read Brian Conniff's "Answering 'The Waste Land': Robert Hayden and the Rise of the

African-American Poetic Sequence" as an implicit rejoinder that problematizes many of the striking assertions in Woodson's essay.

5. In her keynote address to the Furious Flower Conference Gabbin drew comparisons between the event she organized and the "historic Fisk Conference in 1967."

6. As I pointed out in the introduction, Brian Conniff contends that at the 1966 Fisk conference Hayden "was being attacked as the scapegoat of choice for a new generation of African American poets" (487).

7. Further evidence of the complicated relation between Hayden and principal figures of the BAM is available in the Hayden Papers archived in the Library of Congress. In 1977, during his period of residence in Washington, DC, while serving as a consultant in poetry at the library, Hayden was invited to a conference at Howard University. Stephen Henderson, who at the time was director of Howard's Institute for the Arts and the Humanities, planned to honor Hayden with a special award (Henderson, "Letter to Hayden"). Haki Madhubuti was slated to moderate the event. Major BAM figures like Larry Neal, Carolyn Rodgers, John Killens, Tom Dent, and Ted Joans were scheduled to appear at the conference, titled "Black Writers and Their People: Craft and Consciousness." In this mix of black aesthetic advocates, Hayden was to be the honored artist. But it seems that he was committed to appear elsewhere. He sent a telegram with apologies and well wishes to conference attendees.

8. Howard Rambsy's work on publishing practices in African American poetry offers strong resistance to simplifying versions of Black Arts era discourse. He notes Hayden's inclusion in the *For Malcolm* anthology and asks, "What about writers such as Al Young, Robert Hayden, and Lucille Clifton, who are not typically identified as black arts poets? Their appearance in so many African American anthologies associated with the cultural movement reveals that they were indeed contributors to black arts discourse" (*Black Arts Enterprise* 53).

Chapter 2

1. This claim could be disputed if the poet's ubiquitous references to God are considered. However, though God may seem to possess a human-like will in some of Hayden's poems, divinity remains a force that is never truly personified. There is certainly no Miltonic God character in Hayden's poetry. If God is ever personified, "It" is manifest through the character of Bahá'u'lláh. Christ is also evoked in several poems, but for the most part the Christian prophet is a function of rhetoric rather than a character.

2. In one such declaration Bahá'u'lláh writes, "The world's equilibrium hath been upset through the vibrating influence of this most great, this new World Order" (*Gleanings* 137). In his poem "Words in the Mourning Time"—which I will come to in part 3—Hayden follows the lead of Shoghi Effendi and more straightforwardly suggests that the travails of his day can be directly associated with the advent of the revelation or "World Order" of Bahá'u'lláh.

3. As in many religious traditions, slumber is a frequent symbol of spiritual heedlessness in Bahá'í writings. Bahá'u'lláh declares, "The peoples of the world are fast asleep. Were they to wake from their slumber, they would hasten with eagerness unto God, the All-Knowing, the All-Wise" (*Gleanings* 137). Elsewhere he states, "Many a dawn hath the breeze of My loving-kindness wafted over thee and found thee upon the bed of heedlessness fast asleep" (*Hidden Words* 20).

4. These last lines are yet another gesture toward the writings of Bahá'u'lláh, who often employed a similar trope in the effort to dramatize the significance of the appearance of the Prophet of God. Referring to himself in the second person in his mystical "Tablet of Carmel," Bahá'u'lláh takes up the very "Prophet's hour" theme that Hayden's poem engages: "And when the hour at which Thy resistless Faith was to be manifest did strike, . . . the entire creation shook to its very foundations" (*Gleanings* 15). In the same exposition he includes this self-referential salutation: "Sanctified be the Lord of all Mankind, at the mention of Whose name all the atoms of the earth have been made to vibrate" (16).

Chapter 3

1. It is worth noting that in his deathbed piece, "And My Blood Was Drawn," the wrathful Jehovah of Hayden's childhood returns as "the irradiant veiled / terrible One" (177).

2. In chapter 5 I offer a more extensive reading of the relation between religion and the quasi-sonnet form of "Those Winter Sundays," arguing that it ought to be recognized as a Sabbath poem that expresses admiration for the father figure's routinized religiousness but that it also suggests a desire to conservatively reform that religiousness, just as Hayden subtly adjusts the sonnet form for his purposes. For other extensive readings of the poem, see Fetrow (*Robert Hayden* 66–65) and Huddle (251–56).

3. In his reading of masculine discourse and what I am calling the "anxiety of rootedness" in the BAM, Harper keys on the potential estrangement of the black intellectual from the folk, attributing this alienation to "inexorable social processes—specifically, the attenuation of the Black Aestheticians' *organic* connection to the life of the folk (to invoke the Gramscian concept) by virtue of their increasing engagement with the *traditional* (Euro-American) categories of intellectual endeavor" (*Are We* 51).

4. Here it is important to note that, in his review of the *Angles of Ascent* anthology, Baraka fabricates an encounter between himself and Hayden at the 1966 Fisk writers' conference. Baraka writes,

Back in 1966 I was invited to Fisk University, where Hayden and Rowell taught. I had been invited by Nikki Giovanni who was still a student at Fisk. Gwen Brooks was there. Hayden and I got into it when he said he was first an artist and then he was Black. I challenged that with the newly-emerging ideas that we had raised at the Black Arts Repertory Theatre School in Harlem in 1965, just after

Malcolm X's assassination. We said the art we wanted to create should be identifiably, culturally Black—like Duke Ellington's or Billie Holiday's. We wanted it to be a mass art, not hidden away on university campuses. We wanted an art that could function in the ghettos where we lived. And we wanted an art that would help liberate Black people. I remember that was really a hot debate, and probably helped put an ideological chip on Rowell's shoulder. ("Post-Racial")

As is clear from chapter 1, Baraka poorly misremembers the 1966 Fisk writers' conference by placing himself at the center of the confrontation between Hayden, Tolson, and other attendees. All accounts indicate that Baraka did not attend the 1966 conference, although he made an appearance at the 1967 conference (see Llorens, "Writers Converge"; Brooks, *Report* 84). While it is possible to excuse Baraka's suspect memory of events that took place almost fifty years prior to his writing the review, the fact that this misremembrance is faithfully recorded in *Poetry* magazine—an apex publication—neatly illustrates the pliability of (black) literary history. In turn, it reminds us that the polemical dynamics of the Black Arts era demand that scholars of recent African American literature vigilantly assess the efficacy of the competing historical, theoretical, and ideological narratives that give life to our field of study.

5. Enchanted by the communal and inspirational qualities of black music, Larry Neal intimates a key principle of the BAM aesthetic in his straightforward advocacy of a literature modeled after musical ritual. Contrasting a history of "failed" black literature with black musical vitality, Neal writes, "But our music is something else. The best of it has always operated at the core of our lives, forcing itself upon us as in a ritual. It has always, somehow, represented the collective psyche. Black literature must attempt to achieve that same sense of the collective ritual, but ritual directed at the destruction of useless, dead ideas. Further, it can be a ritual that affirms our highest possibilities, but is yet honest with us" ("And Shine" 654–55). In establishing a ritual model for a literature based on black music, the Black Aestheticians evaded a troublesome question: If the ritual work carried out in the black musical arts was so potent and effective, why was there any need for literature? The implications of this unspoken question hang like an albatross on the poetry growing out of Black Aesthetic principles. However, later in the chapter I suggest that, in fact, the musician is not the true model for the Black Arts poet—that the ritual artistic work advocated by Larry Neal and others was exemplified in the heart of the black church.

6. Du Bois's belief that the trauma of American exclusion afforded the Negro "second sight" and special observational powers is seminally captured at the outset of *The Souls of Black Folk*. In "The Criteria of Negro Art" Du Bois is most clear about his belief that "we who are dark can see America in a way that white Americans cannot" (17). Other examples of reasoning that link social exclusion to special, unsolicited aesthetic-cum-moral power abound; for instance, it is crucial to James Baldwin's feeling that black people understood the nation's creed and democratic promise most clearly and would "make America what it must become" (*Price* 336).

Without subscribing to Baldwin's faith in an oncoming moral maturation of the nation, Baraka also finds compensatory benefits in black marginality: "The Negro could not ever become white and that was his strength. . . . He is an American, capable of identifying emotionally with the fantastic cultural ingredients of this society, but he is also, forever, outside that culture, an invisible strength within it, an observer" (*Home* 134).

7. The idea that folklife and folk art were to be elevated and transubstantiated in literary production was almost axiomatic among black writers of the first half of the twentieth century. Houston Baker argues that Ralph Ellison adhered to a similar aesthetic theory that did not "underrate folklife," but insisted that "black folklore—and, indeed, all other aspects of the writer's personal and social experience—must be 'raised' to the level of 'art' before it can achieve its most important meanings" (*Journey Back* 69). However, James Smethurst points to a competing aesthetic ideal that flourished in the 1920s and 1930s. Influenced by the Communist Party of the United States, artists began a valorization of the *raw* culture of the southern black agriculturalist. But even in the "authentic" urban vernacular poetry of Langston Hughes and the rural vernacular of Sterling Brown, it is clear that the poet is taking on a folk character's voice that exists at a certain distance from the poet himself. For one thing, within volumes like *Southern Road*, the vernacular poems stand in contrast to poems written in elevated literary diction. (This is also true for Hayden's *Heart-Shape in the Dust*, which features a few poems written exclusively in Depression-era urban vernacular.) And as Alain Locke wrote of Hughes's volume *Fine Clothes for a Jew* (1927), "These poems are not transcriptions, every now and then one catches sight of the deft poetic touch that unostentatiously transforms them into folk portraits" ("Common Clay" 712). Even in the most celebratory of the Old Left–influenced renderings of the raw vernacular voice, a modicum of aesthetic distance is retained. For his treatment of late nineteenth- and early twentieth-century black debates around the relation between low folk culture and high literary culture, see Smethurst, *New Red Negro* 50; Smethurst, *Black Arts Movement* 59.

8. By 1972 the integrationist hope embodied in King was so disdained among the black literati that Gwendolyn Brooks, in explaining her ideological allegiance with leaders of the BAM, would jab at the "saint" with this barb: "I know that the Black-and-white integration concept, which in the mind of some beaming early saint was a dainty spinning dream, has wound down to farce" (*Report* 45).

9. Brooks's epigraphic use of the poem in both her autobiographical *Report from Part One* (1972) and her edited anthology *A Broadside Treasury* (1971) represents its most prominent evocations.

10. The BAM critique is part and parcel of the wholesale reevaluation of the Negro Church that was seminally incited by Malcolm's public attacks and that eventually included reformist arguments by theologians like James Cone (*Black Theology and Black Power* [1969] and *A Black Theology of Liberation* [1970]), who felt that without significantly altered orientation, "Christianity itself will be discarded as irrelevant in its perverse whiteness" (*Black Theology and Black Power* 117). Cone's Black Liberation Theology was quickly challenged by the skeptical materialism of

William Jones in *Is God a White Racist?* (1973), and a large body of scholarship has emerged subsequently—however, less has been written about the BAM's cultural contribution to Black Power–era debates about the philosophical efficacy and role of the Negro Church.

11. The contrasting symbolism of the "shined shoes" in Jordan's "Okay 'Negroes'" and Hayden's "Those Winter Sundays" is worth noting. While Hayden imbues the Sunday church shoes with the warmth of spiritualized paternal care, for Jordan the gleaming shoes reflect the pathetic pretension and naiveté of the black striver who believes that spiritual and social salvation can be secured through "civilized" manners inculcated by the church.

12. Du Bois's short fiction "Of the Coming of John" is probably the earliest treatment of the significant narrative in African American letters that pits the intellectual against the preacher in a contest for folk leadership. In Du Bois's story about the power and peril of education, the simple country boy leaves his rural Southern home for college in the North. Once introduced to the "Kingdom of Culture," he is transformed into a sober race man determined to uplift the poor black farmers of his hometown; however, among the formidable obstacles facing educated John is his inability to connect with the folk whom he finds upon returning home. A key scene finds him flummoxed before a congregation that can't make heads or tails of the secular social theory he tries to share. The same folk gathering is subsequently stirred to passion by the "awful eloquence" of the country preacher who takes the floor once John's impotence is apparent (*Souls* 231). Du Bois's contest is, I think, the most obvious literary representation of the twentieth-century confrontation between black intellectuals and the preachers. The major figures of the African American literary tradition—Du Bois, Hughes, Johnson, Hurston, Ellison, Baldwin, Baraka, and, as I'll discuss in depth in the next chapter, Hayden—have engaged the black preacher figure in the effort to understand, criticize, and inevitably pay homage to this folk hero.

13. Lorenzo Thomas seems to be the only literary critic to note the tension between aesthetic form and political content in much BAM-era poetry. In elucidating the historical development of black poetry performances, he points out that it "became necessary" for BAM poets to "find ideological rationalizations for employing forms that came from the same black church that the poets were otherwise fond of denouncing" (203). However, Thomas does not provide the "rationalizations" that some BAM poets and theorists may have offered.

14. Howard Rambsy calls attention to the market success of Giovanni's *Truth Is on Its Way* album and notes that it managed to bring her poetry to "broader African American Christian audiences—a group that leading black artists regularly criticized because they felt that traditional African American religious practices were counterproductive to radical forms of liberation" (*Black Arts Enterprise* 91). Here it is important to recognize that Giovanni's gospel-contextualized poetry album—or, perhaps more accurately, poetry-punctuated gospel album—was "a remarkable commercial success" (90). She was harshly criticized by Baraka and others for seeming to commodify the revolutionary message of the BAM, but the

relatively broad appeal of Giovanni's "churchified" poetry explains the causal logic of Black Arts adoption of preacherly styles of performance: it was the surest way to connect with the black masses that the poets wanted to revolutionize.

15. The general attraction of jazz and the "jazz aesthetic" to poets is most thoroughly documented in Meta Jones's *The Muse Is Music: Jazz Poetry from the Harlem Renaissance to Spoken Word* (2011). Also see Sascha Feinstein's *A Bibliographic Guide to Jazz Poetry* (1998). Brent Hayes Edwards and John Szwed have compiled an extensive "Bibliography of Jazz Poetry Criticism" in *Callaloo* 25:1 (2002): 338–46.

16. See Lorenzo Thomas's *Extraordinary Measures: Afrocentric Modernism and Twentieth-Century American Poetry* (154) for specific discussion of Baraka's "yearning" for identification with working-class black folk. For a very unforgiving assessment of Baraka's middle-class insecurity and attraction to the working class, see Jennifer Jordan, "Cultural Nationalism."

17. In the 1940s Dizzy Gillespie's horn-rimmed glasses, goatee, and beret were fresh signs of intellectualism and artistic unconventionality—they were sartorial announcements of a black avant-garde assembling an original, amalgamated aesthetic indicative of what LeRoi Jones described as an urban black "fluency with the socio-cultural symbols of Western thinking" that did not fit in existing American scripts (Baraka, *Blues People* 189–91). Although he would not adopt the Bahá'í Faith until 1969, some time after the peak of his musical-aesthetic influence, Gillespie's conversion is congruent with the narrative of innovation, independence, and unorthodoxy associated with the jazz trumpeter's biography (Gillespie and Fraser 466–76). Like Hayden, he understood the religion to be a comprehensive spiritual system, divine in origins and distinct from ideological models available to him in the heart of the Black Power era. Ten years after adopting the Bahá'í Faith Gillespie would write, "Becoming a Bahá'í changed my life in every way and gave me a new concept of the relationship between God and man—between man and his fellow man—man and his family. It's just all consuming" (474).

Chapter 4

1. The heyday of the BAM had passed by the time Baraka gave his first performances of the poem in the mid-1970s. At that point he had moved into "Thirdworld Marxism" and repudiated all forms of "cultural/religious fiction" (*Autobiography* 461). Baraka's critique had broadened beyond the specific target of Western monotheism to include Jesus's "spooky Brother / allah" (the poet's unwavering of admiration of Malcolm X notwithstanding) *and* the faiths associated with black cultural nationalism. While there was a logical continuity linking his BAM-era spiritualism to his late seventies assertion that "we worship ourselves," Baraka's post-BAM devotion to "science and knowledge / and transformation / of the visible world" was part of a Maoist, broadly internationalist political outlook (*Baraka Reader* 252–53).

2. See the Smithsonian Folkways record *Poets Read Their Contemporary Poetry: Before Columbus Foundation* (1980); and the Penn Sound recording "Reading with Ed Dorn at the Just Buffalo Literary Center," Buffalo, NY, December 8, 1978.

3. In his interview with Dennis Gendron, Hayden attributes this critique of "Witch Doctor" to Jones (Baraka), saying, "LeRoi Jones criticized it way back there because it was full of fancy-pants big words and so on" (21). However, it seems that Hayden is referring to a 1964 piece by Jones in *Poetry* magazine that only mentions Hayden's poems in toto, calling them "self-consciously big-wordy"—but also praising them and wishing Hayden a "fuller audience" ("Dark Bag" 397). In Jones's/Baraka's essay, which was published on the eve of the Black Arts era and took a very dismal view of African American writing in general, this was more than faint praise.

4. Notably, Hayden's poem *does not* participate in the materialist critique of transcendent aspiration that drives "Dope" and that constitutes intellectual modernism's primary quarrel with religious faith. Later I elaborate on Hayden's skeptical view of the clerical class—rather than of religious faith in itself—in relation to modernity, literacy, and the tenets of the Bahá'í Faith.

5. The adamant tone of these notes dramatizes a self-divided struggle between an id desirous of communion and engagement and an ego intent on safety and disciplined production through isolation. Ed Pavlić astutely alludes to this double inclination when he calls Hayden's method a "Solitary Poetics of Communion" (152). This paradoxical (and accurate) description of the poetics, along with Hayden's continual turn to paradox and parataxis of various forms, underwrites my feeling that a productive approach to Hayden involves thinking about his poetry as the expression of a divided consciousness manifestly at odds—quarreling—with itself.

6. In this respect, the poet's dim view of sermonic performance anticipates the recent lamentations of devout black church–based intellectuals like Obery Hendricks and Raphael Warnock—seminarians who fear that the prominence of the "prosperity preaching" of "pulpit performers" signals the church's decline "in to the narrow individualism and spiritualized egocentrism that engulfs a culture that is increasingly self-absorbed" (Warnock).

Chapter 5

1. Charles T. Davis's 1973 essay "Robert Hayden's Use of History"—collected in his *Black Is the Color of the Cosmos* (1989)—provides a good textual history of "Middle Passage" and other Hayden poems. Davis chronicles the conception and development of Hayden's historical poetics from its early glimmerings in his Hopwood Award–winning 1941 manuscript "The Black Spear" through to its figuration in collections of the 1960s like *A Ballad of Remembrance* and *Selected Poems*, in which works such as "O Daedalus Fly Away Home," "Frederick Douglass," "The Ballad of Nat Turner," "Runagate Runagate," and "Middle Passage" appear.

2. This myth of origin is credulously evoked by just about every scholar who takes up "Middle Passage." For examples of this, see Fetrow, "Middle Passage" 35–36; Davis 254; and Hatcher 18.

3. In this chapter all quotations from "Middle Passage" are from the earliest published version of the poem—in 1946, in *Phylon*.

4. For a brief discussion of Hayden's interpolation of these documents in "Middle Passage," see Conniff 493–94.

5. It is worth noting that Hayden was never satisfied with this ending and, late in life, expressed a desire to "make it stronger," even after he had revised it for publication several times (*Collected Prose* 171).

6. Here I offer the version of the poem as it was published in *Atlantic Monthly* in 1947. An earlier iteration of "Frederick Douglass" appeared in 1945, but its syntax bears little relation to subsequent versions. However, the earliest version of the poem, which appeared in "Lewis B. Martin's short lived monthly, *Headlines and Pictures*," is like later versions in that it is a faux sonnet that presents Douglass as an inspiring giant—an "allegory of us all"—who strides toward a historical telos described in the final words of the poem as a moment "of man permitted to be man" (see Chrisman 133). Although Hayden abandoned almost all of the syntax of the 1945 version of "Frederick Douglass," a quarter century later he returned to the phrasing "man permitted to be man," using it again as a description of his social ideal—this time at the close of the ninth section of "Words in the Mourning Time" (*Words* 49).

7. John Hatcher reads these early histories as expressive of a "Bahá'í perspective of history" (154)—a perspective that in some ways resembles the salvific, divinely guided teleology of the Sorrow Songs. However, although these poems were first published soon after Hayden converted to the Bahá'í Faith, they were originally conceived from, and are reflective of, an ideological disposition that predates the poet's assimilation of Bahá'í eschatology and concepts of history. In Hayden's 1960s poems—"Dawnbreaker" and "Words in the Mourning Time" particularly—a Bahá'í template of history is clearly established. But, before the appearance of these rather definitive signs of a Bahá'í historiography, it is only fair to say that the models of history that seem to organize Hayden's poetry *resonate* with Bahá'í understandings of history. Implying that the early heritage poems are *guided* by these understandings may be a kind of anachronistic imposition that conceals more probable influences, which I am trying to uncover. As intimated above, it is quite possible to find the imprint of a Marxist teleology in these poems, just as it is possible to find in them the logic of Negro spirituals and the secular political vision of discourse-shaping figures like Du Bois. Because the heritage poems generally abide by a progressive utopian framework, they are compatible with a great variety of materialist, agnostic, and religious visions of history. This is part of what makes them so popular among readers.

8. All quotations from "The Ballad of Nat Turner" are from the earliest published version of the poem in *A Ballad of Remembrance* (1962).

9. Hayden describes Turner, a subject of his Schomburg research, as "a gothic figure, as a rather frightening kind of vengeful mystic whose faith in the Old Testament God of battles was absolute" (*Collected Prose* 178).

10. Although it was not clustered with the other 1940s heritage poems until its appearance in *Selected Poems* (1966) and again in *Angle of Ascent* (1975), "Runagate" was first published in the 1949 anthology *The Poetry of the Negro* and is reflective of

the political-aesthetic thinking that shaped Hayden's early maturity. After initial publication, the poet regarded "Runagate" as "another of my many failures" and did not return to it for more than a decade. But the poem was redeemed for Hayden after he heard it read in public by Rosey Pool in 1963. Several iterations of the poem were published thereafter. Some versions of the poem rush immediately into the opening strophe; others begin with epigraphic lines that key on the conflation of "Canaan" and America's "mythic North" as the motivating goal of the Underground Railroad (Pool 44). In this chapter I quote from the 1949 "Runagate" as it was published in *Negro Digest* in 1966. Pool, writing the *Negro Digest* essay, hoped to demonstrate how "a poem improves in the hands of a diligent poet," and along with her essay presents both 1949 and 1964 versions of "Runagate" (43).

11. Although he did not participate in the collection of oral slave narratives undertaken by the Federal Writers' Project (FWP) in 1936–38, Hayden's "Runagate" is undoubtedly informed by that unprecedented effort to transfer the oral narratives of former slaves into the written record. As a key figure in the Michigan division of the FWP, researching and writing informational articles on the state's abolition movement and underground railroad, Hayden was certainly aware of the narratives that were mostly being gathered in southern states. For the most detailed account of Hayden's role in the Michigan FWP, see Sporn 276.

Chapter 6

1. I quote from the earliest published version of the poem—in *The Lion and the Archer*, which does not have page numbers. All quotations from "Ballad of Remembrance" and "Eine Kleine Nachtmusik" in this chapter are from the unpaginated *Lion*.

2. "Theme and Variation" was first published in 1950, in *Phylon*. Hayden would alter lineation and phrasing in later iterations of the poem, but in every published version, he retained the language quoted here.

3. Selden Rodman was a white New York intellectual known at midcentury for his particular interest in Latin American and African diaspora art and literature. Ironically, Cedric Dover, the Anglo-Indian author of the *Crisis* review, was somewhat prescient in his association of Hayden and Rodman, who praised *The Lion and the Archer* in the *New York Times Book Review* piece mentioned. In 1947 Dover served a brief stint as a visiting lecturer in anthropology at Fisk, and he had some interaction with Hayden during his period. It is worth noting that the ways in which Dover wields the aesthetic politics of black authenticity anticipate dynamics that would attend Black Arts–era critiques of Hayden. Despite Hayden's destitute ghetto childhood and adolescence, BAM writers with middle-class backgrounds—like Baraka—shored up their own black legitimacy by taking Hayden to task for his failure to organize his work around black lumpen idiom and exigency. Similarly, by mocking Hayden for experimenting with a poetic register not "Negro" enough, Dover is able to legitimatize his own status as a left-leaning analyst of African American culture, despite his Indian and Anglo back-

ground. His maligning of Hayden's apparent desire to escape "the negro caravan" is a reference to the major anthology of the same name edited in 1941 by Sterling Brown, Arthur Davis, and Ulysses Lee.

4. In recent decades black studies scholars attempting to create vivified relations between the black past and present have been particularly attracted to Benjamin's seminal work. In fact, appeal to the theses has been common enough that Kenneth Warren dubiously calls Benjamin's aphoristic offerings "virtually irresistible." He contends that, in black studies, scholars have used the "epigrammatic" chunks to expound self-serving theories of history that perilously ignore the *differences* between the past and the present. Warren believes that theoretical models that readily conflate the exigencies of the early twenty-first century with those of the early nineteenth century, for example, cannot produce a helpful analysis of contemporary culture. As he puts it, "To understand both the past and the present we have to put the past behind us" (*What Was* 84). While Warren is right to question the *political* utility of continually reading the past into the present, Benjamin's "theses" do provide a powerful prism through which to view recent black literary production, particularly the neoslave and Jim Crow narratives. The fact of the matter is that post-civil-rights-era writers have frequently looked to the past to make meaning of the present. Whether or not this pastward perspective gives us a politically enabling sense of the present is another question. Warren is certainly correct to challenge the self-congratulatory disposition of some scholars and artists who cast themselves in "the role of potential hero, or even freedom-fighter," simply because they recover injustices of the past, connect them to contemporary injustices, and posit a seamless continuum of abjection across the centuries. Warren's call to "put the past behind us" is not counsel to forget about the past but rather a summons to accurate historicizing. Reading Hayden's midcentury poetry in the light of Benjamin's essay of the same era is qualitatively different than taking a Benjaminian aphorism as a touchstone for analysis of contemporary culture or political economy.

5. In his only extensive discussion of the poem, Hayden reveals that the New Orleans trip that gave rise to "A Ballad of Remembrance" came about when he was invited to read at a war bond rally at Xavier University. "This was just after World War II," he says (*Collected Prose* 155). As I've implied, I think that the connection between war death and the surrealist ghosts of the New Orleans poem is quite strong. Hayden's contextualizing of "Remembrance" in an interview given almost twenty-five years after its initial publication endorses a reading that situates its theme, imagery, and form in both local and global history.

6. It is profitable to think of Hayden's detached delineation of the lynched body as a poetic approximation of Mamie Till's decision to simply display her son's brutalized remains in an open-casket funeral. In both cases it is the call to observe the black body destroyed by race hatred that articulates protest—perhaps more powerfully than any discursive argument.

7. Until its final stanza, the poem proceeds by way of an emotionless recitation of material detail. This matter-of-fact recording of the hanging gnomon figure suggests the excision of what is vital. Like the lynchers, we see the man's body but

not his humanity. Hayden included "Figure" in his 1962 collection *Ballad of Remembrance*, but the poem does not appear in his later compilational volumes, *Selected Poems* (1966) and *Angle of Ascent* (1975). In these later books, the antilynching genre provides only the vaguest outline for "Night, Death, Mississippi," the poem that seems to replace "Figure." In "Night," black humanity and even the black body are further distanced as the ritual of racist murder is represented only through the colloquial remembrance of an aged lynch-party leader. (This method of indictment, wherein the full horror of racist violence registers not in the protestations of black voices but rather only in the words of those who carry out the violence, is a recapitulation of the technique employed in "Middle Passage.") Hayden's efforts to excise black humanity in "Figure," and his further elision of the black body in "Night," play upon notions of the unrepresentability of the sacred and the secret, as Sarah Wyman points out in her assessment of the latter poem. Wyman argues that, in "Night," "Hayden tears away the rhetorical veil that falls over episodes too terrible to recount" (263). However, as Hayden tears away veils in both "Night" and "Figure," he also affixes them, sacralizing the black humanity that he will not represent in the lynching context.

8. Julius Lester reports Hayden saying, "Maybe I'm not comfortable using the same word 'suffering' to describe what we have gone through and what the Jews have gone through. . . . I'm not saying that Jews have suffered more. How can you measure what a human being suffers? But there is a difference, and we need a word to make that difference clear" (n.p.).

Chapter 7

1. I evoke the formal properties of the sonnet—the volta—because "In Light" is certainly organized using the problem-solution formula associated with that form. When Hayden included the poem in *A Ballad of Remembrance* (1962), its sonnet qualities were amplified by a lineation change that leaves the poem with the fourteen lines of a traditional sonnet, rather than the fifteen that appear in the *Figure of Time* iteration. It is possible that the *Figure of Time* version, which floats the single word *horizons* on its own line, was impacted by printing constraints that produced a fifteen-line, rather than a fourteen-line, poem. In *A Ballad of Remembrance*, the only change to the poem is the suturing of *horizons* to the long line preceding it, producing "From Johannesburg, from Seoul. Their struggles are all horizons, / their deaths encircle me. Through ruins" (42). This issue of line splitting is not just hair splitting if Bahá'u'lláh is the "solution" that Hayden finds in his effort to come to terms with the struggles of modernity. As I argue in chapter 2, Bahá'u'lláh is the single most important figure in Hayden's poetry. As I will argue in the final section of this chapter, the poet's full assimilation of the religious eschatology outlined by Bahá'u'lláh allows him to return to a vision of futurity absent in his postwar work. By introducing this singular figure following the turn in the poem, Hayden calls on the logical conventions of the sonnet form to underscore his tacit argument that this "Godly mystery" represents a solution for humanity's suffering. The version of

the poem published in Hayden's *Selected Poems* (1966) is retitled ("'From the Corpse Woodpiles, from the Ashes'"), marked by several significant syntactical revisions, and is organized into six tercets (see *Selected Poems* 60). By reshaping the poem in this way, eliminating any allusion to the sonnet, Hayden backs away from some of the didacticism produced by the premodern form, but he retains his argument about the salvific station of Bahá'u'lláh, calling "His pain / . . . our anodyne."

2. The vital lines at the end of *Figure of Time* have attracted no critical commentary that I am aware of. The small poem bears no title, and it is not published elsewhere in Hayden's corpus, but it contains one of his most straightforward engagements with the problem of spiritual faith in a technologized, bureaucratized twentieth century.

3. Hayden's adopted father, William Hayden—a "coal wagon driver," is the obvious model for the paternal character in "Sundays." Fred Fetrow, who interviewed the poet on several occasions, writes that "Pa" and Sue Hayden provided Robert with "true parental concern and real love, along with a strong dose of old-fashioned, guilt-inducing, hell-and-damnation religion" (*Robert Hayden* 2). In "Sundays" the quality of the father figure's religiousness is not spelled out. However, "Sundays" is a sweeping revision of "Obituary," a poem published in Hayden's disavowed 1940 collection, *Heart-Shape in the Dust*. This earlier poem captures little of the complicated filial relationship that permeates "Sundays," but it corroborates some of Fetrow's description as it focuses on the encompassing religiousness of the father figure. A litany of biblical references and unimaginative end rhymes follow these opening lines, which offer the conceptual template that Hayden would eventually elaborate in "Sundays":

> My father's hands
> Were gnarled and hard,
> The fruits of their labor
> He shared with the Lord
> His roots sat deep
> In the rock of The Word,
> In Abraham's bosom
> He nestled like a bird. (*Heart-Shape* 28)

In the later poem, Hayden distills much of the meaning of "Obituary" in the connective logic linking the word *Sunday* and the phrase *polished my good shoes*. It should also be noted that the elegiac function of "Sundays" is underscored if it is recognized as the conceptual descendent of a poem titled "Obituary."

4. Edward Pavlić identifies "The Diver" as the "key poem" for understanding "Hayden's Afro-Modernist method and vision," and calls it "the poetic preface" to Hayden's "best work." (145). The critic's strong analysis seizes on repeated use of paradox in "The Diver" to argue that Hayden sought to disturb binaries like life and death, safety and danger, ascent and descent in order to point "toward a level of experience beyond rational compartmentalization" (147). For Pavlić, this method of

disruption jibes with modernist conceptions of subjectivity built on Freud's theories about the irrational unconscious and also helps describe Hayden's effort to continually destabilize essence-seeking ideologies. He reads Hayden as perceptively perched in liminality, somehow equally committed to engagement and detachment, faith and skepticism, and so on. While I agree with much of Pavlić's reading of the later poetry, I think that he underplays the diver's "rise," which is definitive, even if it is "measured." Like John Hatcher, I read the diver's ascent as an affirmation of religious faith, as an expression of spiritual optimism against all odds, that is an especially important element of Hayden's poems of the 1960s and early 1970s. Although Pavlić guides his argumentative thread into the various "intersection[s] of consciousness and experience" (153) that appear in *Selected Poems*, he does not comment on "Dawnbreaker"—a poem that, in its decisive commitment to faith in an ascendant, telos-driven narrative of history, complicates Pavlić's intriguing emphasis on Hayden's "angles of *descent*."

5. In his published poetry, Hayden had offered no explicit response to the 1943 race riots in Detroit, which is sometimes considered the first time in American history that black people adopted an "offensive" posture during urban racial conflict. The World War II–era uprising, sparked by labor tensions and de facto segregation regimes, ravaged the Paradise Valley neighborhood of Hayden's youth; it also foreshadowed the Detroit rebellion of 1967, which was more destructive and lethal than any other domestic occurrence of the American sixties—thirty-three black people died in violence associated with the riot. Although Hayden's "Lord Riot" poem is not grounded in the specifics of a particular event, the poem's evocation of "sniper on tower" suggests the 1967 Detroit riot, in which the specter of sniper killings loomed large. Leaving aside the long-term consequences of the urban unrest of the 1960s, Hayden's characterization of the rioting as cannibalistic has some merit, considering that most of its casualties were poor black people. His response offers stark contrast not only to the poetic call for violent insurrection in the 1960s but also to a tradition of black literary militancy epitomized in Claude McKay's famous reaction to the Red Summer race riots of 1919: "If we must die—let it not be like hogs" (53).

6. In an interview—his only published exchange with a fellow Bahá'í—Hayden would indulge an optimism that was significantly tempered in his poetry but that sheds light on the apparent Americanism of his later work. Asked about the "destiny of America," Hayden explained that "Bahá'í Teachings assure us that America will be an instrument for peace in the future. I think that maybe America is being prepared for that as a result of having all the races, cultures, and nationalities of the world in one way or another in the country" (*Collected Prose* 86).

7. Fritz Oehlschlaeger seems to interpret the title in this way in his article "Robert Hayden's Meditation on Art: The Final Sequence of *Words in the Mourning Time*."

8. The full text of what Bahá'ís call "The Short Obligatory Prayer" is as follows: "I bear witness, O my God, that thou hast created me to know Thee, and to worship Thee. I testify, at this moment, to my powerlessness and to Thy might, to

my poverty and to Thy wealth. There is none other God but Thee, the Help in Peril, the Self-Subsisting" (Bahá'u'lláh et al., *Bahá'í Prayers* 117).

9. Compare with Bahá'u'lláh, *Epistle* 11.

10. Interestingly, Smethurst conjectures that Hayden's efforts to suppress circulation of the *Heart-Shape* poems can be attributed to his desire to "distance himself from the fairly open homoeroticism of some of the early poems" (*New Red* 188). For a number of reasons, I think this speculation is off the mark: The shrouded homoeroticism of *Heart-Shape* is not easily detected; indeed, the expressions of same-sex desire that Smethurst points to in poems like "Southern Moonlight" and "Poem for a Negro Dancer" are quite indirect. Hayden's later work more suggestively alludes to socially transgressive sexual impulses. If he was so intent on disassociating himself from the perceived taint of non-normative sexuality, he would not have allowed sexually charged allusions to color later poems like "Day of the Dead," "Elegies for Paradise Valley," "The Tattooed Man," "Bone-Flower Elegy," and others. Hayden's animus toward the early work that he called "a trial flight" and "'prentice pieces" (*Collected Prose* 138) was primarily a function of the poet's aesthetic conscientiousness. After his move into high-modernist, symbolist, algebraic poetics, Hayden most feared the taint of artistic provincialism and intellectual simplicity that marked some of his early work. In personal letters to Dudley Randall, who wanted to anthologize a *Heart-Shape* poem on Gabriel Prosser, Hayden was at first adamant in his opposition—even though "Gabriel" had no sexual inferences (Letter to Randall).

Chapter 8

1. In this chapter I will frequently appeal to *post-movement* as a periodizing shorthand term, designating an era that extends from about 1975 into the early decades of the twenty-first century. I use the term *only* to suggest what comes after the various "movements" associated with the 1960s and early 1970s—the civil rights movement, the Black Power Movement, the Black Arts Movement.

2. The recent sociohistorical evolution of the former has received more scholarly attention than the latter, and the study of contemporary black poetry is illuminated through reference to important scholarship like that gathered in the tellingly titled volume *Dispatches from the Ebony Tower* (2001), edited by Manning Marable.

3. There are no thorough studies of the events and processes that bound together black studies and black poetry of the late 1960s and early 1970s, and while historians and sociologists have closely analyzed the incorporation of black studies into the American university system, there has been no attempt to trace the processing of Black Arts–era poetry in the multiplying MFA programs of the 1970s and 1980s.

4. See KendrickLamarVevo, YouTube, 22 Feb. 2013.

5. For similar arguments connecting hip-hop to the BAM, see Alim; Hayman; Ongiri, 92–103; introduction to Powell and Baraka; and Rabaka 83–129.

6. Mos Def is among the relatively small cohort of twenty-first-century rap-

pers who have had success working through the complicated aesthetic, political, and commercial calculus required to court mass popularity while consistently offering lyrical content that is "progressive" in its politics. The tension between commercial popularity and various forms of political authenticity and righteousness was explored rather frequently in the early 1990s' "Golden Age" of hip-hop. (Texts like Gang Starr's "Mass Appeal" and EPMD's "Crossover" might be considered iconic examples of this thematic subgenre.) But Mos Def is one of the few veteran artists, along with acts like Lupe Fiasco, Big Boi and Andre 3000 of Outkast, and—perhaps—The Roots, who has been able to regularly foster a counterpublic within and against the mainstream of the acquisitive and escapist neoliberal hip-hop that has flourished commercially since the mid-1990s.

7. Ironically, Mos Def himself took a different view in 1999, asserting, "All hip-hop is poetry" (Alim 133).

8. Cultural studies scholars have also underplayed the connections between the Black Arts and hip-hop movements. Ambitious histories of hip-hop like Jeff Chang's *Can't Stop Won't Stop* (2007) and extensive hip-hop studies readers like *That's the Joint!* (2012), edited by Murray Forman and Mark Anthony Neal, pay almost no attention to Black Arts–era poetry. Some critics have made explicit efforts to separate rap from other forms of poetry and music. For an example of this, see Salaam. Salaam tries to distinguish the rapper's "flow" from "other music with spoken lyrics." While some critics consider Gil Scott-Heron and the Last Poets to be early rappers, Salaam explicitly contends that these artists do not rap. Arguing that "rap lyrics are delivered in rhythmic cadence, not simply recited or melodically half-sung" (305), he makes a rather subjective distinction between the prosody of rap and performed poetry. This inclination to distinguish rap from other forms of poetry might, in fact, be brought on because the categorical boundaries separating rap from other poetic forms are so porous.

9. While Lincoln University was once a veritable production house of black poetics—graduating Larry Neal, Melvin Tolson, and Langston Hughes—in the post-movement Program Era it has cultivated no recognized poets. Like Hayden's move from Fisk to Michigan, Lincoln's dissipated role in the development of post-movement poetry is a reflection of the 1970s processes in which institutional patronage of high-status African American poetry became the purview of well-endowed, predominantly white universities.

10. In his study of rap poetics, Alexs Pate makes the same general claim that I am making here: "Gil Scott-Heron, the Last Poets, and many others, running on the fumes of the fading Black Power movement, created the conditions for what became the Big Bang explosion of rap" (23). This somewhat impressionistic assertion is one that deserves closer scholarly attention from rap genealogists and those interested in Black Arts legacies.

11. William Jelani Cobb makes a similar point when he notes that "critics and writers generally recognized the influence of the Last Poets more than hip-hop artists did themselves" (43). Cobb also contends that the Last Poets were "proto-rappers" (42).

Chapter 9

1. The antebellum history section of *The Yellow House* also includes two persona poems with rather implausible voices: "The Slave's Critique of Practical Reason" and "Kentucky, 1883." In both, the first-person narration is couched in literary flourish and metaphor-heavy language that strains against the dialect of the folk personae that Dove inhabits. By showing her late twentieth-century literary sensibility so obviously within the characters she conjures, in these poems Dove parts ways with Hayden, who was always concerned about the plausibility of his poetic personae. As he put in discussing "A Letter from Phillis Wheatley," "I think of it as an exercise . . . in probability" (Hayden and Harper 1011). The voices that Hayden created always maintained some measure of historical verisimilitude.

2. Patricia Smith accomplishes a similar feat by entering the consciousness of a violently driven anti-black racist in her frequently cited persona poem "Skinhead" ("I sit here and watch niggers take over my TV set"). Smith's unholy ghost differs from those conjured in "Parsley" and "The Venus Hottentot" in that hers is completely imagined, detached from any identifiable figure in the historical record. Indeed, it is somewhat anomalous in post-movement persona poetry because the poet enters a character that is her contemporary. Arguably, Smith's poem is a post-movement-era reprisal of Hayden's "Night, Death, Mississippi," which innovatively takes on the subgenre of the lynching poem by moving in and out of the nostalgic voice of a lynch-party leader who can no longer pursue his desire, "fevered as by groinfire."

> Christ it was better
> than hunting bear
> which don't know why
> you want him dead. (16)

3. Nineteenth-century poets like Paul Laurence Dunbar and James Madison Bell—who dubbed himself the Poet of Hope—were essentially the founders of African America poetics of history. Beyond simply blackening extant poetic modes of historical remembrance and argument, they offered a theory of black historical *ascent* exemplified in the future-oriented assurance of Dunbar's 1890s tribute to Frederick Douglass, which includes the sentimental pledge that "O'er all that holds us we shall triumph yet" (36). In its sociohistorical context, such affirmation was no commonplace. Preparing the way for Harlem Renaissance poets like Langston Hughes, Dunbar and Bell refuted a narrative of black historical declension or retardation assumed by Enlightenment thinkers like G. W. F. Hegel and Thomas Jefferson and confirmed in a brand of racial Darwinism latent in the thinking of an American luminary like Walt Whitman, who—in personal letters—would conjecture that the "nigger, like the Injun, will be eliminated: it is the law of races, history, what-not" (Traubel and Schmidgall 195). As I argue in chapter 5, Hayden's early heritage poems—sanguine, future oriented, and marked by Communist teleology—invest in a very different law of races and history.

4. Discussing the controversy surrounding Styron's *The Confessions of Nat Turner*, Hayden calls attention to the fact that his poem about Turner appeared "long before the revival of interest in this figure" (*Collected Prose* 178). Hayden also defends the novelist's right to imagine characters as he chooses. The poet, sensitized by radical black criticism of his own work, argues that "chauvinistic censorship" is not "the proper remedy" for wounds brought on by the tradition of literary misrepresentation of black life (178). It would seem that, for Hayden, the type of revisionist historical work carried out in his poems was a more potent response to longstanding cultural caricature of the black past. And judging from the post-movement-era upwelling of literary production about black life in the slavery, Reconstruction, and Jim Crow periods, it would seem that many black artists ultimately agreed with Hayden.

5. Trethewey's *Bellocq's Ophelia* (2002) uses the early twentieth-century portrait photographs of E. J. Bellocq to imagine the voice of a New Orleans prostitute whose letters constitute the volume. Poetic animation of historical photography is an important methodological trope throughout Trethewey's oeuvre. She foregrounds these archival items; in contrast, Hayden relied on photography to inspire his pastward-looking poetics, but photographic texts do not frequently appear in his work. Describing the background research that went into his historical poetics, Hayden said, "Looking at pictures helps too. I very often study old prints, illustrations in books, old posters, photographs. I've spent hours and hours going through such books as Mathew Brady's volumes of Civil War Photographs. This kind of research helps me to visualize my characters and their setting, gives me a feeling for the period in which they lived" (*Collected Prose* 179).

6. David Nicholls opens his study of the relation between literary and popular culture in the Harlem Renaissance, *Conjuring the Folk: Forms of Modernity in African America*, by quoting from Langston Hughes's memoir *The Big Sea*: "The ordinary Negroes hadn't heard of the Negro Renaissance. And if they had, it hadn't raised their wages any" (1). Nicholls appeals to this relatively well-known line from Hughes in order to give color to the key term in his book—*the folk*. Through Hughes, Nicholls suggests that the folk are those "ordinary" black people who most desperately desire better wages. But Hughes's quip also underscores the distance between ordinary black urbanites and black literary production. My term *neofolk* refers to a contemporary, post-movement cohort and appeals to both the economic and cultural connotations that have accompanied "the folk" throughout African American intellectual history. I use the prefix *neo-* to suggest that the experience of ordinary, lower-class black people in the post-movement period differs from that of lower-class black people in earlier American eras and to imply that this difference results from neoliberal social and economic policies involving processes like "radical shifts in labor demographics, a bottom-to-top redistribution of wealth, and the development of computerized networks of communication, commerce and public discourse" (M. Neal 104).

7. In her analysis of Dove's "Parsley" Vendler argues that poems that only offer the perspective of the aggrieved often end up in mediocrity—which is appar-

ently characteristic in black literature: "Poems of victimage, told from the point of view of the victim alone, are the stock-in-trade of mediocre protest writing, and they appear regularly in African-American literature" (*Given* 72). Vendler's very low tolerance for "angry outbursts" of black verse was on full display in her 2011 public excoriation of Dove for editorial decisions the poet made in assembling *The Penguin Anthology of Twentieth-Century American Poetry* (2011) ("Are These"). It should be noted that, while attacking Dove for putting together an anthology with too many nonwhite poets, Vendler subtly uses Hayden as a kind of weaponry in her argument. She calls attention to some of his justifiably "famous" poems and implicitly holds him up as an example of the *good black poet*, worthy of critical recognition, capable of standing alongside the (lesser) major figures of twentieth-century American verse. This strategic use of Hayden's legacy is lamentable for a host of reasons. It turns him into both a critical cudgel and the (white) teacher's pet. It potentially perpetuates his critical marginalization by accentuating his uniqueness as a black poet and obscuring his deep connections to various traditions of African American poetry.

8. There is a certain element of unexpected irony in Dove's effort to "correct" folkloric conceptions of the house Negro. While much of African American historical poetry sets out to contest mythologies propagated by "the workhorses of mass media and public miseducation" (Rowell, *Angles* 461), this key text of post-movement historical poetry aims to amend a mythology promulgated by Malcolm X, widely considered one of black America's most ardent opponents of "public miseducation." A testament to the lasting power of Malcolm's binary schema can be found in the many twenty-first-century examples of rappers taking on the field Negro persona—or, most often in hip-hop, the field *nigga* persona. See texts such as "Field Nigga Boogie" by Paris (*Sonic Jihad*, 2003) or "Complexion" by Kendrick Lamar (*To Pimp a Butterfly*, 2015), or lines by Meek Mills on the track "By Any Means" (*MMG Presents: Self Made Vol. 1*, 2011): "I'm a field nigga, you a house nigga / I'm a real nigga and you's a mouse, nigga." For an ironic play on the house Negro/field Negro binary and the way in which black people with light skin color are thought to have enjoyed privileged status in slave society, see Kanye West's "All Day" (2015): "Like a light skinned slave, boy, we in the muthafuckin' house!"

9. Like the post-movement texts mentioned, Louise Meriwether's 1968 short story "A Happening in Barbados" similarly features an upper-middle-class black American woman on vacation in the Caribbean. However, Meriwether uses this narrative template to consider identity dilemmas at the intersection of race and gender, while downplaying class issues.

10. For examples of Hayes's appreciation for Hayden, see Rowell, "Poet"; HoCoPolitso; and Fox.

11. Although "Carp Poem" does not follow the rhyme and repetition patterns associated with the ghazal, the implication of the form is felt not only in the long-line couplets but also in the speaker's turn to third-person self-reference in the final couplet—a common element of the ghazal. This formal gesture is important to my reading of the poem as an example of the *cleaved* relation between the poet and the

people because, through the ghazal, Hayes alludes to his deep love for the imprisoned "black boys," even as his speaker continually suggests that he is distanced from them.

12. The *BreakBeat* anthology does not demonstrate a mutual sharing. MFA poets are now demonstrably influenced by Kanye West; Kanye West is not influenced by MFA poets. However, one prominent MC, Chance the Rapper, offers praise for the anthology in a blurb included in the anthology.

13. Dargan is one of only four poets to appear in both *The BreakBeat Poets* and *Angles of Ascent*. The others are Thomas Sayers Ellis, Major Jackson, and John Murillo.

14. The performance of "Frederick Douglass" is archived at DJ Renegade's website, https://www.reverbnation.com/joeldiasporter/song/1144840-frederick-douglas-by-robert-hayden

Bibliography

Adorno, Theodor. *Prisms*. Cambridge: The MIT Press, 1983.

Alexander, Elizabeth. *The Black Interior*. St. Paul, MN: Graywolf Press, 2004.

Alexander, Elizabeth. *Crave Radiance: New and Selected Poems, 1990–2010*. Minneapolis: Graywolf Press, 2012.

Alexander, Elizabeth. "Elizabeth Alexander." *Saving the Race: Conversations on Du Bois from a Collective Memoir of Souls*. Ed. Rebecca Carroll. New York: Broadway Books, 2013. 139–46.

Alexander, Elizabeth. "New Ideas about Black Experimental Poetry." *Michigan Quarterly Review* 50.4 (2011): 598–621.

Ali, Abdul. "On Meeting Robert Hayden in a Dream." *Journal of Bahá'í Studies* 25.3 (2015): 64.

Alim, H. Samy. *Roc the Mic Right: The Language of Hip Hop Culture*. New York: Routledge, 2006.

Allison, Raphael. *Bodies on the Line: Performance and the Sixties Poetry Reading*. Iowa City: University of Iowa Press, 2014.

Anderson, S. E. "For the Children." *Negro Digest* 17.7 (1968): 62.

Arendt, Hannah. *The Origins of Totalitarianism*. New York: Harcourt Brace Jovanovich, 1973.

Assmann, Jan. *Moses the Egyptian: The Memory of Egypt in Western Monotheism*. Cambridge, MA: Harvard University Press, 1997.

Auden, W. H. *Lectures on Shakespeare*. Ed. Arthur C. Kirsch. Princeton: Princeton University Press, 2002.

A'zam, Nabíl. *The Dawn-Breakers: Nabíl's Narrative of the Early Days of the Bahá'í Revelation*. Trans. Shoghi Effendi. Wilmette, IL: Bahá'í Pub. Trust, 1932.

Bahá'u'lláh. *Epistle to the Son of the Wolf*. Trans. Shoghi Effendi. Wilmette, IL: Bahá'í Pub. Trust, 1941.

Bahá'u'lláh. *Gleanings from the Writings of Bahá'u'lláh*. Trans. Shoghi Effendi. Wilmette, IL: Bahá'í Pub. Trust, 2005.

Bahá'u'lláh. *The Hidden Words*. Trans. Shoghi Effendi. Wilmette, IL: Bahá'í Pub. Trust, 2002.

Baháʼuʼlláh. *The Kitáb-I-Iqán: The Book of Certitude*. Trans. Shoghi Effendi. Wilmette, IL: Baháʼí Pub. Trust, 2003.

Baháʼuʼlláh and ʻAbduʼl-Bahá. *Baháʼí World Faith*. Wilmette, IL: Baháʼí Pub. Trust, 1976.

Baháʼuʼlláh, ʻAlí Muḥammad Shírází Báb, and ʻAbduʼl-Bahá. *Baháʼí Prayers: A Selection of Prayers*. Wilmette, IL: Baháʼí Pub. Trust, 2002.

Baker, Houston A. *Afro-American Poetics: Revisions of Harlem and the Black Aesthetic*. Madison: University of Wisconsin Press, 1988.

Baker, Houston A. *Blues, Ideology, and Afro-American Literature: A Vernacular Theory*. Chicago: University of Chicago Press, 1987.

Baker, Houston A. *The Journey Back: Issues in Black Literature and Criticism*. Chicago: University of Chicago Press, 1991.

Baldwin, James. *The Price of the Ticket: Collected Nonfiction, 1948–1985*. New York: St. Martin's/Marek, 1985.

Baraka, Amiri. *The Autobiography of LeRoi Jones*. Chicago: Lawrence Hill Books, 1997.

Baraka, Amiri. *Blues People: Negro Music in White America*. New York: William Morrow, 1963.

Baraka, Amiri. Foreword. *The Last Poets on a Mission: Selected Poems and a History of the Last Poets*. New York: H. Holt, 1996. xiii–xvii.

Baraka, Amiri. *Home: Social Essays*. New York: Akashi Classics, 2009.

Baraka, Amiri. *The Baraka Reader*. Ed. William J. Harris. Berkeley, CA: Thunder's Mouth Press, 2000.

Baraka, Amiri. "A Post-Racial Anthology?" *Poetry* 202.2 (2013): 166–68. https://www.poetryfoundation.org/poetrymagazine/articles/detail/69990

Baraka, Amiri. *Raise, Race, Rays, Raze: Essays since 1965*. New York: Random House, 1971.

Baraka, Imamu Amiri, and Billy Abernathy. *In Our Terribleness: Some Elements and Meaning in Black Style*. New York: Bobbs-Merrill, 1970.

Baraka, Imamu Amiri, and Larry Neal, eds. *Black Fire: An Anthology of Afro-American Writing*. Baltimore: Black Classic Press, 2007.

Barthes, Roland. *Image, Music, Text*. Trans. Stephen Heath. New York: Hill and Wang, 2009.

Baucom, Ian. *Specters of the Atlantic: Finance Capital, Slavery, and the Philosophy of History*. Durham, NC: Duke University Press, 2005.

Bauman, Zygmunt. *Modernity and the Holocaust*. Ithaca, NY: Cornell University Press, 2000.

Bell, Bernard W. *The Folk Roots of Contemporary Afro-American Poetry*. Detroit: Broadside Press, 1974.

Benét, Steven Vincent. *John Brown's Body*. Garden City, NY: Doubleday, 1928.

Benjamin, Walter. *Illuminations*. New York: Schocken Books, 1986.

Benston, Kimberly W. *Baraka: The Renegade and the Mask*. New Haven: Yale University Press, 1976.

Benston, Kimberly W. *Performing Blackness: Enactments of African-American Modernism*. London: Routledge, 2000.

Bernier, Celeste-Marie. *Characters of Blood: Black Heroism in the Transatlantic Imagination.* Charlottesville: University of Virginia Press, 2012.

Best, Stephen. "On Failing to Make the Past Present." *Modern Language Quarterly* 73.3 (2012): 453–74.

Betts, Dwayne. "Remembering Hayden." *Collected Poems of Robert Hayden.* New York: Liveright Publishing, 2013. xv–xvii.

Bloom, Harold. *Poets and Poems.* New York: Chelsea House, 2005.

Bloom, Harold, ed. *Robert Hayden.* New York: Chelsea House, 2005.

Bolden, Tony. *Afro-Blue: Improvisations in African American Poetry and Culture.* Urbana: University of Illinois Press, 2004.

Bolden, Tony. "Cultural Resistance and Avant-Garde Aesthetics: African American Poetry from 1970 to the Present." *The Cambridge History of African American Literature.* Ed. Maryemma Graham and Jerry Washington Ward. Cambridge: Cambridge University Press, 2011. 532–65.

Boyd, Melba. *Wrestling with the Muse: Dudley Randall and the Broadside Press.* New York: Columbia University Press, 2003.

Brooks, Gwendolyn, ed. *A Broadside Treasury.* Detroit: Broadside Press, 1971.

Brooks, Gwendolyn. *In the Mecca.* New York: Harper & Row, 1968.

Brooks, Gwendolyn. "Poets Who Are Negroes." *Phylon* 11.4 (1950): 312.

Brooks, Gwendolyn. *Report from Part One.* Detroit: Broadside Press, 1972.

Brown, Fahamisha Patricia. *Performing the Word: African-American Poetry as Vernacular Culture.* New Brunswick, NJ: Rutgers University Press, 1999.

Brown, Scot. *Fighting for US: Maulana Karenga, the US Organization, and Black Cultural Nationalism.* New York: New York University Press, 2003.

Brown, Sterling Allen. *A Son's Return: Selected Essays of Sterling A. Brown.* Ed. Mark A. Sanders. Boston: Northeastern University Press, 1996.

Bullough, Edward. "'Psychical Distance' as a Factor in Art and as an Aesthetic Principle." *Art and Its Significance: An Anthology of Aesthetic Theory.* Ed. Steven David Ross. Albany, NY: SUNY Press, 1994. 458–68.

Burroughs, Margaret G., and Dudley Randall, eds. *For Malcolm: Poems on the Life and Death of Malcolm X.* Detroit: Broadside Press, 1969.

Camus, Albert. *The Myth of Sisyphus and Other Essays.* New York: Vintage Books, 1991.

Chang, Jeff. *Can't Stop Won't Stop.* New York: Macmillan, 2005.

Chrisman, Robert. "Robert Hayden: The Transition Years, 1946–1948." *Robert Hayden: Essays on the Poetry.* Ed. Laurence Goldstein and Robert Chrisman. Ann Arbor: University of Michigan Press, 2001. 129–54.

Cobb, William Jelani. *To the Break of Dawn: A Freestyle on the Hip Hop Aesthetic.* New York: New York University Press, 2007.

Cone, James H. *Black Theology and Black Power.* Maryknoll, NY: Orbis Books, 1997.

Conniff, Brian. "Answering 'The Waste Land': Robert Hayden and the Rise of the African American Poetic Sequence." *African American Review* 33.3 (1999): 487–506.

Cook, Dara. "The Aesthetics of Rap." *Black Issues Book Review* 2.2 (2000): 22–27.

Coval, Kevin. Introduction. *The BreakBeat Poets: New American Poetry in the Age of*

Hip-Hop. Ed. Kevin Coval, Quraysh Ali Lansana, and Nate Marshall. Chicago: Haymarket Books, 2015. xv–xxii.

Coval, Kevin, Quraysh Ali Lansana, and Nate Marshall, eds. *The BreakBeat Poets: New American Poetry in the Age of Hip-Hop*. Chicago: Haymarket Books, 2015.

Cullen, Countee. *My Soul's High Song: The Collected Writings of Countee Cullen, Voice of the Harlem Renaissance*. Ed. Gerald Lyn Early. New York: Doubleday, 1991.

Dance, Daryl Cumber, ed. *From My People: 400 Years of African American Folklore*. New York: Norton, 2003.

Davis, Charles T. *Black Is the Color of the Cosmos*. Washington, DC: Howard University Press, 1989.

Dawson, Michael C. *Behind the Mule: Race and Class in African-American Politics*. Princeton, NJ: Princeton University Press, 1995.

Dead Prez. "They Schools." *Let's Get Free*. Loud Records, 2000.

Dodson, Owen. *The Confession Stone: Song Cycles*. London: P. Breman, 1970.

Douglass, Frederick. *Autobiographies*. Library of America. New York: Penguin Books, 1994.

Dove, Rita. Introduction. *"Harlem Gallery" and Other Poems of Melvin B. Tolson*. Ed. Raymond Nelson. Charlottesville: University Press of Virginia, 1999. xi–xviii.

Dove, Rita. *The Yellow House on the Corner: Poems*. Pittsburgh: Carnegie Mellon University Press, 1989.

Dover, Cedric. "Review of *The Lion and the Archer*." *Crisis*, 1948, 252.

Drake, St. Clair. "What Happened to Black Studies?" *The African American Studies Reader*. Ed. Nathaniel Norment. Durham, NC: Carolina Academic Press, 2001. 265–74.

Dubey, Madhu. "The Postmodern Moment in Black Literary and Cultural Studies." *Renewing Black Intellectual History: The Ideological and Material Foundations of African American Thought*. Ed. Adolph Reed and Kenneth Warren. Boulder, CO: Paradigm, 2010. 217–51.

Du Bois, W. E. B. "The Criteria of Negro Art." *African American Literary Theory: A Reader*. Ed. Winston Napier. New York: New York University Press, 2000. 17–23.

Du Bois, W. E. B. *Dusk of Dawn: An Essay toward an Autobiography of a Race Concept*. New York: Oxford University Press, 2007.

Du Bois, W. E. B. *The Souls of Black Folk*. New York: Simon & Schuster, 2014.

Dunbar, Paul Laurence. *Selected Poems*. Ed. Herbert Woodward Martin. New York: Penguin Books, 2004.

Effendi, Shoghi. *The Advent of Divine Justice*. Wilmette, IL: Bahá'í Pub. Trust, 1990.

Effendi, Shoghi. *The Promised Day Is Come*. Wilmette, IL: Bahá'í Pub. Trust, 1980.

Effendi, Shoghi. *The World Order of Bahá'u'lláh: Selected Letters*. Wilmette, IL: Bahá'í Pub. Trust, 1991.

Ellison, Ralph. *The Collected Essays of Ralph Ellison*. Ed. John F. Callahan. New York: Modern Library, 1995.

Ellison, Ralph. *Invisible Man*. United States: Paw Prints, 2008.

Emanuel, James. "On *Selected Poems*." *Robert Hayden: Essays on the Poetry*. Ed. Laurence Goldstein and Robert Chrisman. Ann Arbor: University of Michigan Press, 2001. 63–64.

Fanon, Frantz. *The Wretched of the Earth*. Trans. Richard Philcox. New York: Grove Press, 2004.

Fetrow, Fred. "'Middle Passage': Robert Hayden's Anti-epic." *Robert Hayden*. Ed. Harold Bloom. Philadelphia: Chelsea House, 2005. 35–48.

Fetrow, Fred. *Robert Hayden*. Boston: Twayne, 1984.

Fetty Wap. "Wake Up." RGF/300 Entertainment, 2016.

Finney, Nikky. *Head Off & Split: Poems*. Evanston, IL: TriQuarterly Books/Northwestern University Press, 2011.

Finney, Nikky. *The World Is Round: Poems*. Evanston, IL: TriQuarterly Books/Northwestern University Press, 2013.

Forman, Murray, and Mark Anthony Neal, eds. *That's the Joint! The Hip-Hop Studies Reader*. New York: Routledge, 2012.

Foucault, Michel. *Security, Territory, Population: Lectures at the Collège de France, 1977–1978*. Trans. Graham Burchell. New York: Picador, 2009.

Fox, Curtis. "Honor Thy Father's Day." *Poetry Off the Shelf*, Poetry Foundation, 17 June 2009. https://www.poetryfoundation.org/podcasts/75336/honor-thy-fathers-day?id=1648&page=19

Franklin, John Hope. "History—Weapon of War and Peace." *Phylon* 5.3 (1944): 249–59.

Frazier, E. Franklin. *Black Bourgeoisie*. New York: Free Press, 1997.

Frazier, E. Franklin. *The Negro Church in America*. 1964. New York: Shocken Books, 1986.

Gabbin, Joanne V. "Introduction: Essays and Conversations in African American Poetry." *The Furious Flowering of African American Poetry*. Ed. Joanne V. Gabbin. Charlottesville: University Press of Virginia, 1999. 1–14.

Galler, David. "Three Recent Volumes." *Poetry* 110.4 (1967): 267–69.

Gates, Henry Louis. *The Signifying Monkey: A Theory of African American Literary Criticism*. Oxford: Oxford University Press, 2014.

Gates, Henry Louis. "Two Nations . . . Both Black." *Forbes*, 14 Sept. 1992, 132–38.

Gates, Henry Louis, and Nellie Y. McKay, eds. *The Norton Anthology of African American Literature*. 2nd ed. New York: Norton, 2004.

Gayle, Addison. "A Review Essay: Under Western Skies." *Black World*, July 1973, 40–48.

Gikandi, Simon. "Race and the Idea of the Aesthetic." *Michigan Quarterly Review* 40.2 (2001): 318–50.

Gillespie, Dizzy, and Al Fraser. *To Be, or Not—to Bop*. Minneapolis: University of Minnesota Press, 2009.

Gilroy, Paul. *The Black Atlantic: Modernity and Double Consciousness*. London: Verso, 2002.

Giovanni, Nikki. *The Collected Poetry of Nikki Giovanni*. New York: HarperCollins, 2009.

Gladney, Marvin J. "The Black Arts Movement and Hip-Hop." *African American Review* 29.2 (1995): 291.

Glaude, Eddie S. *In a Shade of Blue: Pragmatism and the Politics of Black America.* Chicago: University of Chicago Press, 2007.

Glissant, Édouard. *Poetics of Relation.* Ann Arbor: University of Michigan Press, 1997.

Goines, Donald. *White Man's Justice, Black Man's Grief.* Los Angeles: Holloway House, 2007.

Gramsci, Antonio. *The Gramsci Reader: Selected Writings, 1916–1935.* Ed. David Forgacs. New York: New York University Press, 2000.

Greasley, Philip A., ed. *Dictionary of Midwestern Literature.* Bloomington: Indiana University Press, 2001.

Guyer, Sara Emilie. *Romanticism after Auschwitz.* Stanford: Stanford University Press, 2007.

Hall, James C. *Mercy, Mercy Me: African-American Culture and the American Sixties.* Oxford: Oxford University Press, 2001.

Harper, Michael. "Every Shut Eye Aint Sleep / Every Good-Bye Aint Gone." *Robert Hayden: Essays on the Poetry.* Ed. Laurence Goldstein and Robert Chrisman. Ann Arbor: University of Michigan Press, 2001. 104–11.

Harper, Michael. *Healing Song for the Inner Ear: Poems.* Urbana: University of Illinois Press, 1985.

Harper, Michael. "The Metaphysics of *American Journal.*" Academy of American Poets, 3 Feb. 2006. Poets.org

Harper, Michael S., and Aldon Lynn Nielsen. "Conversation: Michael S. Harper and Aldon Lynn Nielsen." *The Furious Flowering of African American Poetry.* Ed. Joanne V. Gabbin. Charlottesville: University Press of Virginia, 1999. 77–90.

Harper, Phillip Brian. *Are We Not Men?: Masculine Anxiety and the Problem of African-American Identity.* New York: Oxford University Press, 1996.

Harper, Phillip Brian. "Nationalism and Social Division in Black Arts Poetry of the 1960s." *Is It Nation Time? Contemporary Essays on Black Power and Black Nationalism.* Ed. Eddie S. Glaude Jr. Chicago: University of Chicago Press, 2002. 165–88.

Hartman, Saidiya V. *Scenes of Subjection: Terror, Slavery, and Self-Making in Nineteenth-Century America.* New York: Oxford University Press, 1997.

Hatcher, John. *From the Auroral Darkness: The Life and Poetry of Robert Hayden.* Oxford: George Ronald, 1984.

Hayden, Robert. *American Journal: Poems.* New York: Liveright, 1982.

Hayden, Robert. *Angle of Ascent: New and Selected Poems.* New York: Liveright, 1975.

Hayden, Robert. *A Ballad of Remembrance.* London: Paul Breman, 1962.

Hayden, Robert. *Collected Poems.* Ed. Frederick Glaysher. New York: Liveright, 1985.

Hayden, Robert. *Collected Prose.* Ed. Frederick Glaysher. Ann Arbor: University of Michigan Press, 1984.

Hayden, Robert. "Dead Soldiers: Pacific Theater." *Phylon* 12.2 (1951): 171–72.

Hayden, Robert. *Figure of Time.* Nashville: Hemphill, 1955.

Hayden, Robert. *Heart-Shape in the Dust.* Detroit: Falcon Press, 1940.

Hayden, Robert. *How I Write.* New York: Harcourt Brace Jovanovich, 1972.

Hayden, Robert. "An Interview with Dennis Gendron." *Robert Hayden: Essays on the Poetry*. Ed. Laurence Goldstein and Robert Chrisman. Ann Arbor: University of Michigan Press, 2001. 15–29.

Hayden, Robert, ed. *Kaleidoscope: Poems by American Negro Poets*. New York: Harcourt, Brace & World, 1967.

Hayden, Robert. Letter to Dorothy Lee. 5 Oct. 1977. Hayden Papers. Library of Congress.

Hayden, Robert. Letter to Dudley Randall. 7 July 1969. Hayden Papers. Bahá'í House of Worship, Wilmette, IL.

Hayden, Robert. Letter to Jay Wright. 22 Sept. 1976. Hayden Papers. Bahá'í House of Worship, Wilmette, IL.

Hayden, Robert. Letter to Margaret Walker. 2 Dec. 1976. Hayden Papers. Bahá'í House of Worship, Wilmette, IL.

Hayden, Robert. *The Lion and the Archer: Poems*. Nashville: Counterpoise, 1948.

Hayden, Robert. "Middle Passage." *Phylon* 6.3 (1945): 247–53.

Hayden, Robert. *The Night-Blooming Cereus*. London: Paul Breman, 1972.

Hayden, Robert. "O Daedalus, Fly away Home." *Poetry* 62.4 (1943): 192–93.

Hayden, Robert. "Runagate, Runagate." *Negro Digest* 15.8 (1966): 46–47.

Hayden, Robert. "Runagate, Runagate." *The Poetry of the Negro*. Ed. Langston Hughes and Arna Bontemps. New York: Doubleday, 1949. 169–71.

Hayden, Robert. *Selected Poems*. New York: October House, 1966.

Hayden, Robert. "Theme and Variation." *Phylon* 11.4 (1950): 361.

Hayden, Robert. "Tour 5." *Phylon* 19.3 (1958): 296.

Hayden, Robert. Untitled essay. N.d. Hayden Papers. Bahá'í House of Worship, Wilmette, IL.

Hayden, Robert. *Words in the Mourning Time*. New York: October House, 1970.

Hayden, Robert, and Michael Harper. "Robert Hayden and Michael Harper: A Literary Friendship." *Callaloo* 17.4 (1994): 980–1016.

Hayes, Terrance. *How to Be Drawn*. New York: Penguin Books, 2015.

Hayes, Terrance. *Lighthead*. New York: Penguin Books, 2010.

Hayes, Terrance. *Muscular Music*. Pittsburgh: Carnegie Mellon University Press, 2006.

Hayman, Casey. "People's Poetics: Amiri Baraka, Hip-Hop, and the Dialectical Struggle for a Popular Revolutionary Poetics." *Massachusetts Review* 50.1/2 (Spring/Summer 2009): 82–97.

Hejinian, Lyn. *The Language of Inquiry*. Berkeley: University of California Press, 2000.

Henderson, Stephen. Letter to Robert Hayden. 18 Apr. 1977. Hayden Papers. Library of Congress.

Henderson, Stephen. "Saturation: Progress Report on a Theory of Black Poetry." *African American Literary Theory: A Reader*. Ed. Winston Napier. New York: New York University Press, 2000. 102–12.

Henderson, Stephen. *Understanding the New Black Poetry; Black Speech and Black Music as Poetic References*. New York: Morrow, 1973.

Hennessey, Christopher. "About Carl Phillips: A Profile." *Ploughshares* 29.1 (2003): 199–204.

Hernton, Calvin. "Shining." *Robert Hayden: Essays on the Poetry*. Ed. Laurence Goldstein and Robert Chrisman. Ann Arbor: University of Michigan Press, 2001. 322–28.

Hirsch, Edward. *A Poet's Glossary*. Boston: Houghton Mifflin Harcourt: 2014.

HoCoPolitso. "Tara Betts and Terrance Hayes on Poetry." 26 Jan. 2013. Youtube. com. https://www.youtube.com/watch?v=ivMtCEirmj0

Howard, W. Scott. "Resistance, Sacrifice and Historicity in the Elegies of Robert Hayden." *Reading the Middle Generation Anew: Culture, Community, and Form in Twentieth-Century American Poetry*. Ed. Eric L. Haralson. Iowa City: University of Iowa Press, 2006. 133–52.

Huddle, David. "The 'Banked Fire' of Robert Hayden's 'Those Winter Sundays.'" *Robert Hayden: Essays on the Poetry*. Ed. Laurence Goldstein and Robert Chrisman. Ann Arbor: University of Michigan Press, 2001. 251–55.

Hughes, Langston. "Some Practical Observations: A Colloquy." *Phylon* 11.4 (1950): 307–11.

Hurston, Zora Neale. "Characteristics of Negro Expression." *African American Literary Theory*. Ed. Winston Napier. New York: New York University Press, 2000. 31–44.

Huyssen, Andreas. *Twilight Memories: Marking Time in a Culture of Amnesia*. New York: Routledge, 1995.

James, C. L. R. *The Black Jacobins: Toussaint L'Ouverture and the San Domingo Revolution*. New York: Vintage Books, 1989.

Jameson, Frederic. *Postmodernism, Or, The Cultural Logic of Late Capitalism*. Durham: Duke University Press, 1991.

Jemie, Onwuchekwa. *Langston Hughes: An Introduction to the Poetry*. New York: Columbia University Press, 1976.

Johnson, Amaud Jamaul. *Red Summer*. Dorset, VT: Tupelo Press, 2006.

Johnson, James Weldon. *God's Trombones: Seven Negro Sermons in Verse*. New York: Penguin Books, 1990.

Jones, Douglas. "The Fruit of Abolition: Discontinuity and Difference in Terrance Hayes's 'The Avocado.'" *The Psychic Hold of Slavery: Legacies in American Expressive Culture*. Ed. Soyica Diggs Colbert, Robert J. Patterson, and Aida Levy-Hussen. New Brunswick, NJ: Rutgers University Press, 2016. 39–50.

Jones, LeRoi. "A Dark Bag." *Poetry*, Mar. 1964, 394–401.

Jones, Meta. *The Muse Is Music: Jazz Poetry from the Harlem Renaissance to Spoken Word*. Urbana: University of Illinois Press, 2011.

Jordan, Jennifer. "Cultural Nationalism in the 1960s: Politics and Poetry." *Race, Politics, and Culture: Critical Essays on the Radicalism of the 1960's*. Ed. Adolph L. Reed. Westport, CT: Greenwood, 1986. 29–60.

Jordan, June. "Report from the Bahamas, 1982." *Meridians* 3.2 (2003): 6–16.

Joyce, Joyce A. "Bantu, Nkodi, Ndungu, and Nganga: Language, Politics, Music, and Religion in African American Poetry." *The Furious Flowering of African*

American Poetry. Ed. Joanne V. Gabbin. Charlottesville: University Press of Virginia, 1999. 99–117.

Kearney, Douglas. "Artist Statement." *The BreakBeat Poets: New American Poetry in the Age of Hip-Hop*. Ed. Kevin Coval, Quraysh Ali Lansana, and Nate Marshall. Chicago: Haymarket Books, 2015. 309–10.

Kearney, Douglas. *Black Automaton*. Fence Books, 2009.

Keith, Nelson W. *Outline of a New Liberalism: Pragmatism and the Stigmatized Other*. Lanham, MD: Lexington Books, 2015.

Kelley, Robin D. G. "Looking for the 'Real' Nigga: Social Scientists Construct the Ghetto." *That's the Joint: The Hip Hop Studies Reader*. Ed. Murray Forman and Mark Anthony Neal. New York: Routledge, 2012. 134–52.

KendrickLamarVevo. "Kendrick Lamar—Poetic Justice (Explicit) ft. Drake." YouTube, 22 Feb 2013. https://www.youtube.com/watch?v=yyr2gEouEMM

Kerr, Clark. *The Uses of the University*. 5th ed. Cambridge, MA: Harvard University Press, 2001.

King, Martin Luther. *A Testament of Hope: The Essential Writings and Speeches of Martin Luther King, Jr.* Ed. James Melvin Washington. San Francisco: Harper, 1991.

King, Richard H. *Race, Culture, and the Intellectuals: 1940–1970*. Baltimore: Woodrow Wilson Center Press and Johns Hopkins University Press, 2004.

Knight, Etheridge. "A Survey: Black Writers' Views on Literary Lions and Values." *Negro Digest* 17.3 (1968): 10–48.

Komunyakaa, Yusef. "Journey into 'American Journal.'" *Robert Hayden: Essays on the Poetry*. Ed. Laurence Goldstein and Robert Chrisman. Ann Arbor: University of Michigan Press, 2001. 332–34.

Kristeva, Julia. *The Kristeva Reader*. Ed. Toril Moi. New York: Columbia University Press, 1986.

Kutzinski, Vera M. "Changing Permanences: Historical and Literary Revisionism in Robert Hayden's 'Middle Passage.'" *Callaloo* 26 (1986): 171–83.

Lang, Clarence. *Black America in the Shadow of the Sixties: Notes on the Civil Rights Movement, Neoliberalism, and Politics*. Ann Arbor: University of Michigan Press, 2015.

Lee, Don L. "On *Kaleidoscope* and Robert Hayden." *Negro Digest* 17.3 (1968): 51–52, 90–94.

Lee, Don L. "Toward a Black Aesthetic." *Negro Digest* 17.11–12 (1968): 27–32.

Leonard, Keith D. *Fettered Genius: The African American Bardic Poet from Slavery to Civil Rights*. Charlottesville: University of Virginia Press, 2006.

Lester, Julius. *Lovesong: Becoming a Jew*. New York: Skyhorse, 2013.

Lewis, R. W. B. *The American Adam*. Chicago: University of Chicago Press, 1955.

Llorens, David. "Don Lee." *Ebony* 24.5 (March 1969): 72–80.

Llorens, David. "Writers Converge at Fisk University." *Negro Digest* 15.8 (1966): 54–68.

Locke, Alain. "Common Clay and Poetry." *Saturday Review of Literature*, 1927, 712.

Locke, Alain. "Dawn Patrol: A Review of the Literature of the Negro for 1948: Part I." *Phylon* 10.1 (1949): 5–14.

Locke, Alain. "Negro Youth Speaks." *The New Negro*. Ed. Alain Locke. New York: Touchstone, 2014. 47–53.

Locke, Alain. "The New Negro." *The New Negro*. Ed. Alain Locke. New York: Touchstone, 2014. 3–16.

Locke, Alain. "Reason and Race: A Review of the Literature of the Negro for 1946." *Phylon* 8.1 (1947): 17–27.

McGurl, Mark. *The Program Era: Postwar Fiction and the Rise of Creative Writing*. Cambridge, MA: Harvard University Press, 2009.

McKay, Claude. *Harlem Shadows*. New York: Harcourt Brace, 1922.

Meehan, Kevin. *People Get Ready: African American and Caribbean Cultural Exchange*. Jackson: University Press of Mississippi, 2009.

Mills, C. Wright. *The Sociological Imagination*. New York: Oxford University Press, 2000.

Mitrano, G. F. "A Conversation with Yusef Komunyakaa." *Callaloo* 28.3 (2005): 521–30.

Morrison, Toni. "Introduction: Friday on the Potomac." *Race-ing Justice, Engendering Power: Essays on Anita Hill, Clarence Thomas, and the Construction of Social Reality*. Ed. Toni Morrison. New York: Pantheon Books, 1992. vii–xxx.

Mullen, Harryette. *The Cracks between What We Are and What We Are Supposed to Be: Essays and Interviews*. Tuscaloosa: University Alabama Press, 2012.

Mullen, Harryette. Introduction. *Gathering Ground: A Reader Celebrating Cave Canem's First Decade*. Ed. Toi Derricotte, Cornelius Eady, and Camille T. Dungy. Ann Arbor: University of Michigan Press, 2006. 7–10.

Nas. "What Goes Around." *Stillmatic*. Columbia Records, 2011.

Neal, Larry. "And Shine Swam On." *Black Fire: An Anthology of Afro-American Writing*. Ed. Imamu Amiri Baraka and Larry Neal. Baltimore: Black Classic Press, 2007. 637–56.

Neal, Larry. "Any Day Now: Black Art and Black Liberation." *Ebony* 24.10 (August 1969): 54–62.

Neal, Larry. "The Black Arts Movement." *SOS/Calling All Black People: A Black Arts Movement Reader*. Ed. John H. Bracey, Sonia Sanchez, and James Edward Smethurst. Amherst: University of Massachusetts Press, 2014. 55–66.

Neal, Larry. *Black Boogaloo: Notes on Black Liberation*. San Francisco: Journal of Black Poetry Press, 1969.

Neal, Mark Anthony. *Soul Babies: Black Popular Culture and the Post-Soul Aesthetic*. New York: Routledge, 2002.

Neal, Mark Anthony, and Murray Forman, eds. *That's the Joint!: The Hip-Hop Studies Reader*. New York: Routledge, 2004.

Newton, Huey P. *Revolutionary Suicide*. New York: Penguin Books, 2009.

Nicholls, David. *Conjuring the Folk: Forms of Modernity in African America*. Ann Arbor: University of Michigan Press, 2000.

Nielsen, Aldon Lynn. *Black Chant: Languages of African-American Postmodernism*. Cambridge: Cambridge University Press, 1997.

Nielsen, Aldon Lynn. *Writing between the Lines: Race and Intertextuality*. Athens: University of Georgia Press, 1994.

The Notorious B.I.G. "Party and Bullshit." *Who's the Man? Original Motion Picture Soundtrack.* Uptown Records, 1993.

Oehlschlaeger, Fritz. "Robert Hayden's Meditation on Art: The Final Sequence of *Words in the Mourning Time.*" *Black American Literature Forum* 19.3 (1985): 115–19.

Ong, Walter J. *Orality and Literacy: The Technologizing of the Word.* London: Routledge, 2002.

Ongiri, Amy Abugo. *Spectacular Blackness: The Cultural Politics of the Black Power Movement and the Search for a Black Aesthetic.* Charlottesville: University of Virginia Press, 2010.

Oyewole, Abiodun. *Branches of the Tree of Life: The Collected Poems of Abiodun Oyewole, 1969–2013.* New York: 2Leaf Press, 2013.

Oyewole, Abiodun, Umar Bin Hassan, and Kim Green. *The Last Poets on a Mission: Selected Poems and a History of the Last Poets.* New York: H. Holt, 1996.

Pate, Alexs D. *In the Heart of the Beat: The Poetry of Rap.* Lanham, MD: Scarecrow Press, 2010.

Pavlić, Edward M. *Crossroads Modernism: Descent and Emergence in African-American Literary Culture.* Minneapolis: University of Minnesota Press, 2002.

Pereira, Malin. *Rita Dove's Cosmopolitanism.* Urbana.: University of Illinois Press, 2003.

Perloff, Marjorie. "Poetry on the Brink." *Boston Review* June 2012, 60–69.

Phelan, J. P. *The Nineteenth-Century Sonnet.* New York: Palgrave Macmillan, 2005.

Poetry Society of America. "Nikky Finney: Reading at Lillian Vernon Creative Writers House, New York, April 7, 2011." Audio blog post. 5 July 2011. http://www.poetrysociety.org/psa/poetry/audio/?count=3&cstart=20

Pool, Rosey. "An Assessment." *Negro Digest* 15.8 (1966): 42–46.

Post, Constance. "Image and Idea in the Poetry of Robert Hayden." *Robert Hayden: Essays on the Poetry.* Ed. Laurence Goldstein and Robert Chrisman. Ann Arbor: University of Michigan Press, 2001. 194–204.

Powell, Kevin, and Ras Baraka. *In the Tradition: An Anthology of Young Black Writers.* New York: Harlem River Press, 1992.

Rabaka, Reiland. *Hip Hop's Inheritance: From the Harlem Renaissance to the Hip Hop Feminist Movement.* Lanham, MD: Lexington Books, 2011.

Rambsy, Howard. *The Black Arts Enterprise and the Production of African American Poetry.* Ann Arbor: University of Michigan Press, 2011.

Rambsy, Howard. "Catching Holy Ghosts: The Diverse Manifestations of Black Persona Poetry." *African American Review* 42.3/4 (2008): 549–64.

Rambsy, Howard. "The Rise of Rita Dove and Elizabeth Alexander during the Late 1980s." *Cultural Front,* 12 May 2013.

Rampersad, Arnold. "Biography and Afro-American Culture." *Afro-American Literary Study in the 1990s.* Ed. Houston A. Baker and Patricia Redmond. Chicago: University of Chicago Press, 1992. 194–208.

Rampersad, Arnold. Afterword. *Collected Poems of Robert Hayden.* Ed. Frederick Glaysher. New York: Liveright, 2013. 197–212.

Rampersad, Arnold, and Hilary Herbold, eds. *The Oxford Anthology of African-American Poetry*. Oxford: Oxford University Press, 2006.

Randall, Dudley. Letter to Robert Hayden. 13 Apr. 1966. Hayden Papers. Bahá'í House of Worship, Wilmette, IL.

Randall, Dudley. Letter to Robert Hayden. 29 Apr. 1966. Hayden Papers. Bahá'í House of Worship, Wilmette, IL.

Randall, Dudley, and Margaret Burroughs, eds. *For Malcolm: Poems on the Life and the Death of Malcolm X*. Detroit: Broadside Press, 1969.

Rashid, Frank Damian. "Robert Hayden's Detroit Blues Elegies." *Callaloo* 24.1 (2001): 200–226.

Redding, J. Saunders. *To Make a Poet Black*. Ithaca: Cornell University Press, 1988.

Redmond, Eugene. *Drumvoices: The Mission of Afro-American Poetry: A Critical History*. Garden City, NY: Anchor Press, 1976.

Reed, Adolph L. *The Jesse Jackson Phenomenon: The Crisis of Purpose in Afro-American Politics*. New Haven: Yale University Press, 1986.

Richards, Phillip M. *Black Heart: The Moral Life of Recent African American Letters*. New York: Peter Lang, 2006.

Rodgers, Carolyn. "Black Poetry—Where It's At." *Negro Digest* 18.11 (1969): 7–16.

Rodman, Selden. "Negro Poets." *New York Times Book Review*, 10 Oct. 1949, 27.

Rojas, Fabio. *From Black Power to Black Studies: How a Radical Social Movement Became an Academic Discipline*. Baltimore: Johns Hopkins University Press, 2007.

Rose, Tricia. *Black Noise: Rap Music and Black Culture in Contemporary America*. Hanover, NH: University Press of New England, 1994.

Rowell, Charles H., ed. *Angles of Ascent: A Norton Anthology of Contemporary African American Poetry*. New York: W. W. Norton, 2013.

Rowell, Charles H. "The Editors Note." *Callaloo* 27.4 (2004): vii–ix.

Rowell, Charles H. "'The Poet in the Enchanted Shoe Factory': An Interview with Terrance Hayes." *Callaloo* 27.4 (2004): 1068–81.

Rowell, Charles H. "'The Unraveling of the Egg': An Interview with Jay Wright." *Callaloo* 19 (1983): 3–15.

Rushdy, Ashraf H. A. *Neo-slave Narratives: Studies in the Social Logic of a Literary Form*. New York: Oxford University Press, 1999.

Salaam, Mtume Ya. "The Aesthetics of Rap." *African American Review* 29.2 (1995): 303–15.

Salvatore, Nick. *Singing in a Strange Land: C. L. Franklin, the Black Church, and the Transformation of America*. New York: Little, Brown, 2005.

Santayana, George. *The Works of George Santayana*. Vol. 6. New York: Scribners, 1936.

Schneider, Dan. "Robert Hayden: His Day Is Now." 19 July 2003. Cosmoetica.com

Schomburg, Arthur. "The Negro Digs Up His Past." *The New Negro*. Ed. Alain Locke. New York: Touchstone, 2014. 229–49.

Shaw, Robert Burns. *Blank Verse: A Guide to Its History and Use*. Athens: Ohio University Press, 2007.

Shockley, Evie. "Going Overboard: African American Poetic Innovation and the Middle Passage." *Contemporary Literature* 52.4 (2011): 791–817.

Shockley, Evie. *Renegade Poetics: Black Aesthetics and Formal Innovation in African American Poetry*. Iowa City: University of Iowa Press, 2011.

Smethurst, James Edward. *The Black Arts Movement: Literary Nationalism in the 1960s and 1970s*. Chapel Hill: University of North Carolina Press, 2006.

Smethurst, James Edward. *The New Red Negro: The Literary Left and African American Poetry, 1930–1946*. New York: Oxford University Press, 1999.

Smith, Lorrie. "From Black Arts to Def Jam: Performing Black 'Spirit Work' across Generations." *New Thoughts on the Black Arts Movement*. Ed. Lisa Gail Collins and Margo Natalie Crawford. New Brunswick, NJ: Rutgers University Press, 2006. 349–68.

Smith, Patricia. *Big Towns, Big Talk*. Cambridge: Zoland Books, 1992.

Snyder, Timothy. *Bloodlands: Europe between Hitler and Stalin*. New York: Basic Books, 2010.

Sporn, Paul. *Against Itself: The Federal Theater and Writers' Projects in the Midwest*. Detroit: Wayne State University Press, 1995.

Steiner, George. *Nostalgia for the Absolute*. Toronto: Anansi, 1997.

Stewart, James. "The Development of the Black Revolutionary Artist." *Black Fire: An Anthology of Afro-American Writing*. Ed. Imamu Amiri Baraka and Larry Neal. Baltimore: Black Classic Press, 2007. 3–10.

Tate, Claudia, ed. *Black Women Writers at Work*. New York: Continuum, 1983.

Thomas, Lorenzo. *Extraordinary Measures: Afrocentric Modernism and Twentieth-Century American Poetry*. Tuscaloosa: University of Alabama Press, 2000.

Traubel, Horace, and Gary Schmidgall. *Intimate with Walt: Selections from Whitman's Conversations with Horace Traubel, 1888–1892*. Iowa City: University of Iowa Press, 2001.

Trethewey, Natasha D. *Native Guard*. Boston: Houghton Mifflin, 2006.

Trethewey, Natasha, and Joan Wylie Hall. *Conversations with Natasha Trethewey*. Jackson: University Press of Mississippi, 2013.

Turner, Darwin. "Robert Hayden Remembered." *Robert Hayden: Essays on the Poetry*. Ed. Laurence Goldstein and Robert Chrisman. Ann Arbor: University of Michigan Press, 2001. 87–103.

Vendler, Helen. "Are These the Poems to Remember?" *New York Review of Books*, 24 Nov. 2011. 19–22.

Vendler, Helen. *The Given and the Made: Strategies of Poetic Redefinition*. Cambridge, MA: Harvard University Press, 1995.

Wacquant, Loïc. *Punishing the Poor: The Neoliberal Government of Social Insecurity*. Durham, NC: Duke University Press, 2009.

Walker, Margaret. "For My People." *Poetry* 51.2 (1937): 81–83.

Walker, Margaret. "Harriet Tubman." *Phylon* 5.4 (1944): 326–30.

Walker, Margaret. "New Poets." *Phylon* 11.4 (1950): 345–54.

Walker, Margaret. *This Is My Century: New and Collected Poems*. Athens: University of Georgia Press, 1989.

Warnock, Raphael. "To Redeem the Soul of the Black Church." *Huffington Post*, 15 Nov. 2013. TheHuffingtonPost.com

Warren, Kenneth W. *So Black and Blue: Ralph Ellison and the Occasion of Criticism.* Chicago: University of Chicago Press, 2003.

Warren, Kenneth W. *What Was African American Literature?* Cambridge, MA: Harvard University Press, 2011.

Weaver, Afaa Michael. "Masters and Master Works: On Black Male Poetics." Academy of American Poets, 28 July 2005. Poets.org

West, Cornel. "The Paradox of the Afro-American Rebellion." *Social Text* 9/10 (1984): 44–58.

Whitman, Walt. *Song of Myself.* Mineola, NY: Dover, 2001.

Williams, Pontheolla T. *Robert Hayden: A Critical Analysis of His Poetry.* Urbana: University of Illinois Press, 1987.

Williams, Wilburn. "Covenant of Timeless and Time: Symbolism and History in Robert Hayden's *Angle of Ascent.*" *Chant of Saints: A Gathering of Afro-American Literature, Art, and Scholarship.* Ed. Michael S. Harper and Robert B. Stepto. Urbana: University of Illinois Press, 1979. 66–75.

Wintz, Cary D. *Remembering the Harlem Renaissance.* New York: Garland, 1996.

Woodson, Jon. "Consciousness, Myth and Transcendence: Symbolic Action in Three Poems on the Slave Trade." *The Furious Flowering of African American Poetry.* Ed. Joanne V. Gabbin. Charlottesville: University Press of Virginia, 1999. 154–68.

Wright, Jay. *Transfigurations: Collected Poems.* Baton Rouge: Louisiana State University Press, 2000.

Wyman, Sarah. "Beyond the Veil." *Comparatist* 36 (2012): 263–91.

X, Malcolm. *February 1965: The Final Speeches.* New York: Pathfinder, 1992.

X, Malcolm. *The End of White World Supremacy: Four Speeches.* New York: Arcade, 2011.

X, Malcolm, and George Breitman. *Malcolm X Speaks: Selected Speeches and Statements.* New York: Grove Weidenfeld, 1990.

Yeats, William Butler. *The Major Works.* Oxford: Oxford University Press, 2001.

Index

academia. *See* American university system

Adorno, Theodor, 150–51, 152

aesthetic distance, 9, 88, 117, 119, 267n3
  artist-intellectuals and, 88, 244–46
  from black folk and oral culture, 60–66, 117, 119, 249
  circle of blackness and, 60–66
  Hayden and, 5, 15–16, 59, 71–72, 88–90, 92, 102–3, 106, 119
  integrationism and, 66
  in post-movement era, 226–64

aesthetics, 7–8. *See also* preacherly aesthetics; vernacular aesthetic
  Apollonian aesthetic, 98–99, 103, 212, 259, 261–62, 263
  of BAM, 92–111, 212, 227, 260–61, 268n5
  black aesthetic(s), 4, 6–8, 19–20, 27, 41–42, 83, 85–90, 149
  Dionysian aesthetic, 212, 216–22, 259, 261–62, 263
  elliptical aesthetic, 142, 145, 150
  performance and, 66
  print culture aesthetic, 92–93, 98–103, 106, 108–11, 117, 172
  Western, 63–64
  writerly aesthetic, 88–90, 92–93, 98–103, 106, 108–11, 202, 212, 259

Afrocentric cosmology, black nationalism and, 76–78

"Afro-pessimists," 195–96

Alexander, Elizabeth, 4, 7, 13, 15, 22, 28–29, 41, 203, 210, 224
  archival research poetry and, 229–31, 233–34
  The Black Interior, 20
  "Hayden in the Archive," 231
  "The Venus Hottentot," 229–31

Ali, Abdul, "On Meeting Robert Hayden in a Dream," 258–59

alienation, 15, 108, 224, 243–44
  artist-intellectuals and, 88, 89, 241–46
  from blackness, 243–44
  Hayden and, 89, 244–47
  Hayes and, 249–51
  poet-professors and, 244–46

American Renaissance, 37

American Revolution, 194

American university system, 56, 59, 202, 222, 224, 237–39, 244, 259
  black studies in, 210–11
  hip-hop culture in, 260–61
  MFA programs, 203–13, 260–61
  social movements and, 203–7

the *Amistad*, 125–30

Anderson, Charles, "Prayer to the White Man's God," 67

Anderson, S.E., 80